THE KIRGHIZ AND WAKHI
OF AFGHANISTAN

THE KIRGHIZ AND WAKHI OF AFGHANISTAN

ADAPTATION TO CLOSED FRONTIERS AND WAR

M. NAZIF SHAHRANI

WITH A NEW PREFACE AND EPILOGUE BY THE AUTHOR

UNIVERSITY OF WASHINGTON PRESS
SEATTLE AND LONDON

Library of Congress Cataloging-in-Publication Data

Shahrani, M. Nazif Mohib, 1945–
    The Kirghiz and Wakhi of Afghanistan : adaptation to closed fron-
tiers and war / M. Nazif Shahrani ; [with a new preface and epilogue
by the author].
        p.   cm.
    Includes bibliographical references and index.
    ISBN 0–295–98262–4
    1. Kyrgyz.   2. Wakhi (Asian people).   3. Vakhan (Afghanistan :
Region)—Social life and customs.   I. Title.

DS354.6.K57 S5   2002
305.891'59—dc21   2002018095

Contents

In memory of my parents
Haji Gada M. Karim Shahrani
Zeebun-Nesah Naim Shahrani

and

Haji Rahman Qul Kutlu of Pamir
Wakeel M. Ismail Pamiri of Wakhan

 # Acknowledgments

THE IDEA of preparing a new, updated paperback edition of this book was born almost immediately after its first hardcover edition sold out in the mid-1980s. Because of my preoccupation with other projects, however, it did not become a serious proposition for another twenty years. In the fall of 2001, Professor Jere Bacharach, director of the Henry M. Jackson School of International Studies at the University of Washington (my alma mater), invited me to make a presentation at the Open Classroom Lecture Series there. Titling my talk "September 11: Context and Consequences," I spoke on October 18, 2001, to a receptive audience of well over a thousand. Immediately after the lecture, I was approached by Michael Duckworth, executive editor of the University of Washington Press, who asked if I would consider preparing my presentation as a preface to a new paperback edition of *The Kirghiz and Wakhi of Afghanistan.* Despite my misgivings that post–September 11 commitments might not allow me to bring the project to a speedy conclusion, I accepted the proposal, with the understanding that an epilogue detailing the trials and tribulations of the Kirghiz community—and their leader, Haji Rahman Qul Khan—after the 1978 Communist coup in Afghanistan would also be included in the new edition. For their encouragement and support, I am indebted to Michael Duckworth and his colleagues at the Press, and to Mary Ribesky for her thoughtful editing of the new material.

Without the continuing welcome and assistance of the Kirghiz community during their years of exile and resettlement, especially that of the late Khan, I would not have been able to complete the work. I want to express my gratitude to members of the Khan's immediate family, and remember especially Abdul Wakil, Bibi Maryam Haji, and Harun Yeja (all of whom passed away in Turkey), and thank Abdul Wahid, Abdul Malik, Muhammad Ekber, Muhammad Arif, and Menderes for their friendship and hospitality. A number of other Kirghiz elders deserve special mention as well: Mahmood Haji, Hayet Muhammad Haji, Muhammad Amin, Abdul Halim Vatan, Mawlawi Abdul Baaqi, and Juma Taj.

A special thank you is due to Mr. Gultekin Sertkaya, the Ulupamir village school principal, for providing me with useful information about the school and the village, and to my good friend and colleague Professor Ibrahim Erol Kozak for his help in translating some materials from modern Turkish. I am also grateful to Melissa Drain, a graduate student at Indiana University, for help on this new edition. My debts for institutional support of my research among the Kirghiz are many and are acknowledged in the footnotes.

My eldest son, Samad, who is now a college student, spent his second birthday in eastern Turkey doing fieldwork with me. Over the years, he and his mother, Mavis Anderson Shahrani, supported me and my work among the Kirghiz, and they deserve my immense gratitude. Maha Noureldin and our younger sons, Abdurahim and Noorhadi, have suffered the most from my post–September 11 absences from home because of frequent travels and responsibilities that kept me in my office often late into the night. I am deeply grateful to them for allowing me to get this work done. *Shukran jazilan ya Maha!*

M.N.S.
SEPTEMBER 2002

 # Preface to the 2002 Edition: Afghanistan, the Taliban, and Global Terror, Inc.

AS A NATIVE AFGHAN and a naturalized citizen of the United States, in the very tough days following September 11, 2001, I found myself in a very serious predicament. My adopted country, the United States, is at war with my homeland, where my natal family, my siblings and their children, are living. As many of my other compatriots from Afghanistan have been, I'm torn. Should I support America, my adopted country, or Afghanistan, my homeland?

All of us have been challenged by the events of September 11th to try to make sense out of this senseless crime. Crimes of this magnitude challenge us simply because they pose fundamental problems of meaning. Why could such a thing happen? And why in a place like New York? Some people who call themselves Muslims are implicated in this crime, and this puts an additional burden on the 1.2 billion Muslims around the world, including myself. How could members of the religious community I belong to commit such a crime?

Suicide bombings have happened in other places, but they were far away from our shores. This time it has happened in the safe haven of the United States. After September 11th, some newspapers reported that the churches were filled. When we are faced with problems of this magnitude, when we are called to make sense out of an apparently senseless event, we often turn to religion. Within a religious context, such problems are sometimes resolved for us, and people can somehow come to grips with such a disturbing reality. But in a secular society such as this one, we also rely on certain metaphors to explain events that may not have an easy explanation.

Indeed, there has been considerable reference in the media to a particular metaphor or model to explain why these senseless events happened in New York, Washington, and Pennsylvania. That model has been one of a "clash of civilizations": it happened because the alleged perpetrators are not like us, but are some kind of beasts belonging to another and radically different civilization! They don't value freedom, don't share our values, and are something other than human beings. They are not civilized. Of course they hate us, and that's why they committed this crime against us.

Unfortunately, this clear-cut construction of the problem as "we're in the right, they are in the wrong" because of differences in religion and civilization has led us to a policy where our president has enunciated a very clear partition of the world as we know it. Those who are with us are our friends, and those who are not with us are with our enemies, the terrorists.

I don't think of myself as either an Afghan or American nationalist. In that, I don't have a choice. If I pronounce myself an Afghan nationalist, I cannot be an American nationalist, and if I pronounce myself an American nationalist, I cannot be an Afghan one. The definition of nationalist to me is someone who supports his country and government, right or wrong.

But I hope that I am a good Afghan and American patriot at the same time. The distinction is that I am willing to support the U.S. government when it does the right thing, and I'm willing to criticize my government when it does the wrong thing. I would like to speak the same way about Afghanistan. That country hasn't had a government to speak of for many years, but if Afghanistan's new government is in the right, I will be a patriotic Afghan in supporting their policies, and when they do the wrong thing, I won't be with them.

Unfortunately, after September 11th many people in the United States used the word "patriotism" in ways that made a joke of the concept. Many were acting like nationalist Americans, but wrongly calling themselves patriots. They acted and are continuing to act like nationalists, and nationalism ultimately becomes fascism. There is nothing that nationalism could lead to other than fascism.

EXPLAINING TERRORISM

President Bush is not alone in using the clash of civilizations model to explain the problem. Those who watched Osama bin

Laden's videotapes, released after the United States began bombing Afghanistan on October 7, 2001, could see that bin Laden views the world in the same manner as President Bush. The difference is that he does not talk about languages, cultures, civilizations, and so forth. Bin Laden's distinction is that those with him are true Muslims, and those who are not with him, even if Muslims, are unbelievers. Thus he wages war against unbelievers as well as the Western world led by America, which he claims is against Muslims and Islam. He wages war against his mind's picture of his enemy. Clearly, we do the same.

Can this new war on terrorism accomplish the goals it has set out to accomplish? Can the war on global terrorism get rid of terrorists lodged in Afghanistan without many innocent civilians losing their lives due to high-altitude bombings, which is sometimes referred to as "collateral damage"? Even if this war could eradicate all the existing terrorist networks in Afghanistan and beyond anytime soon, could we be sure that a new and more violent breed of terrorists and terrorism will not arise to take their place in a few years, especially since this war does not seem to address the root causes giving rise to terrorism? More importantly, is terrorism simply a security problem that can be solved by waging war and by exercising greater military vigilance?

The above questions have yet to be answered. But insisting on a division of the world as the civilized versus the uncivilized, our war against theirs, will not help us solve the fundamental problem of our lost sense of national security.

Indeed, there is something terribly wrong in how our national leaders initially constructed this problem, and with the kinds of questions raised and the answers offered in the American media after September 11th. Important questions remain unexamined. Who produces terrorism? What countries contribute to the production of terrorism, and why? Who traffics in violence, and for what reasons? If we pose these questions to ourselves, we will see that Americans have had their own part in this mess.

Working within a successful capitalistic society, Americans often employ an economic metaphor to explain national events. But few observers have applied the economic metaphor to explain the security problems that have come to light since the September 11th terrorist attacks. Yet terrorism today is a commodity in the global market, a product of a globalizing economy. Terrorism has its producers and consumers, and those who profit from violence as a commodity.

Another very common explanatory model in use in the United

States is the medical, pathogenic model. What if we focused like a good doctor on trying to diagnose this particular societal disease? What if we looked for the real causes of terrorism and for real cures from this societal malady? Will the medicine being administered now, the war on terrorism, cure the epidemic of global terrorism? If not, what will? Unfortunately, this popular explanatory model is also not employed in furthering our understanding of the symptoms of this social cancer.

There is yet another model that is important for Americans and the U.S. government to focus on: the political model. Although we're rarely willing to use this model, terrorism is fundamentally a political problem intimately connected with the institution of the modern nation-state. Historically, terrorism in its most egregious form occurred only after the introduction of the nation-state system, which is at the very bottom of the problems of terrorism, war, and violence. As we have witnessed for the last three hundred years, since the rise of nation-states, which occurred at the expense of traditional imperial states based on a system of indirect rule which tolerates various forms of community self-governance, wars and terrorism have become a prominent part of modern world history.

Why did Afghanistan become a safe haven for Terrorism, Inc.? Given the kinds of models I've suggested, how can we explain what is happening to Afghanistan? Is the Taliban movement unique to Afghanistan? Is Afghanistan unique in bearing no resemblance to other similar Third World nations in its development processes? Why has a prolonged war of twenty-three years cost this poor country at least two million lives and the devastation of virtually its entire infrastructure? Why has it created half a million orphans and widows?

One way to answer these questions would be to label the Taliban as Islamic fundamentalists, and fundamentalism as the responsible ideology for the kind of misery Afghans are experiencing. This is a very simplistic way of explaining the problem. The term "fundamentalism" doesn't explain events, but merely labels them. We can label those who perpetrated the acts in New York as fundamentalists who are against liberty, civilization, and a host of other Western values. But within this approach, we rarely confront the question of whether these terrorists actually have a cause. Political problems generally arise from some fundamental causes, and violence may become the last resort for people who have tried every other means of resolving their problems. Such people resort to extreme acts because they cannot get their voices heard or their concerns addressed. Yet how could these individual hijackers be so motivated to sacrifice their own, precious lives to destroy other people's lives?

Soviet invasion (1979) and the subsequent two decades of "low intensity wars" in Afghanistan, which were waged, financed, and directed by foreign proxies—the United States, Pakistan, Iran, Saudi Arabia, India, and China, among others—not only resulted in the collapse of the Afghan state but made it impossible for the Afghans to reverse the course of endless conflicts and wars. The devastations which began with the Soviet-inspired Communist coup of April 1978 and evolved into bloody inter-ethnic and mul-tifactional fighting gave rise after the Soviet withdrawal (1989) to the Taliban militia rule, and turned Afghanistan into an ideal safe haven for international terrorist groups. Since 1995, the Taliban and their foreign terrorist allies, including bin Laden's Al Qaeda organization, have killed tens of thousands of Muslims during their six-year reign of terror in Afghanistan. Where is the clash of civilizations in that? Muslims are killing Muslims. Even in New York, there were hundreds of Muslims killed. What if the deeds committed by the Taliban and their terrorist allies in Afghanistan had been condemned by Muslim scholars and leaders long before September 11th? Unfortunately, this lack of condemnation is a major shortcoming of Muslim leadership.

Suicide bombings, airplane hijackings, and other terrorist acts in the Middle East began more than thirty years ago. For the first fifteen to twenty years, however, those who committed such acts never did so in the name of Islam. Most of the terrorists sprang from political causes and groups, such as leftist organizations, Marxist revolutionaries of the Al Fatah variety, members of the PLO, etc. The phenomenon of Islamist groups committing terrorist acts in the name of Islam is very recent. In the late 1980s, HAMAS (Harakat Al-Muqawama Al-Islamia or Islamic Resistance Movement), a resistance wing of the Palestinian branch of the Muslim Brotherhood, was formed (December 1987) in the Israeli-occupied Gaza Strip to rival the PLO and Al Fatah. Before the outbreak of *intifada* (anti-Israeli uprising), the Palestinian Muslim Brotherhood's objectives were focused on supporting Muslim education and social purification as the basis for Palestinian social and spiritual renewal. Strongly hostile to secular nationalist groups within the PLO, the Brotherhood did not advocate overt acts of anti-Israeli resistance. Hoping to divide the Palestinian community, Israel consciously, but quietly, assisted Hamas to flourish as an alternative to Arafat and the PLO—Israel's most ardent enemies of that period. Later, members of Hamas began the *intifada* in the West Bank and Gaza. Indeed, it is members of Hamas who've been strapping bombs onto themselves and committing acts of terror against Israelis in response to Israel's policies of Jewish settlement expansion in the occupied territories, complemented by acts of collective punishment against the Palestinians. Even then in the late 1980s, if the Muslim community had spoken out against these acts of terror as unacceptable to Islam, as they undoubtedly are, we might not be where we are today.

Some have suggested that the hijackers and suicide bombers have acted in extreme ways because in most Muslim countries where dictators rule, Muslim scholars could not voice their true thoughts and speak out. In Saudi Arabia you can't do it; in Egypt you can't do it; and in Turkey, of course, you never could do it. Muslim dissidents faced and are still facing punishments ranging from restriction of their civil rights to long-term incarceration, torture, and even death or forced exile in these and other Muslim countries.

But what about the millions of Muslims here in America? Current estimates claim that some five to seven million Muslims now reside in the United States, and in Europe there are perhaps as many or more. They certainly have the freedom to speak up. Yet they haven't. In the mosques that I have attended in many parts of the United States, including those in the Washington, D.C., area, I have never heard anybody talk about this. At the convention of the Islamic Society of North America (ISNA) that I attended at the beginning of September 2001, Afghanistan as a topic was not even on the program. Every other trouble spot in the world was, however, covered: there were sessions on Chechnya, sessions on Kashmir, etc. Why was Afghanistan missing from the agenda? Because these scholars don't want to face the reality that Muslims are killing, oppressing, and torturing other Muslims. They don't want to show their dirty laundry in public. Even for that there is an excuse of sorts: Muslims are basically under siege. They're being attacked from all directions. Given how often their misdeeds are exposed, why should Muslim scholars and critics contribute any more to such attacks?

But that's no justification. Muslim leadership in the United States and in Europe has a great responsibility to speak up. When individuals do things in the name of Islam that are wrong and unacceptable, their acts should be condemned. It was not just four planes that were hijacked in the attack on September 11th. The perpetrators hijacked 1.2 billion Muslims along with them. The blot that they left on this religion is going to be with the Muslim community for a long time.

Muslim leaders should have spoken earlier, but it's not too late. Muslims can still speak out against deeds that are committed in the name of their religion by any fringe element today.

LEGACIES OF A MODERN "NATION-STATE"

At first glance, the problem in Afghanistan might seem to have begun with the Communist coup in 1978, which ignited a war that has continued for twenty-three years. The problem, however, extends back to the creation of the first modern state under the name Afghanistan more than a century ago.

Afghanistan's foundation for a troubled history was established when Britain invaded Afghanistan from the Indian subcontinent in 1879, for the second time in forty years. They could not control the country by 1880, as there was a prolonged bloody civil war underway over succession. Britain had already lost a lot of people during its wars of conquest, and it was now faced with the opposition of many warring groups headed by competing princelings of the Muhammadzai clan of the Pashtun, who had been fighting each other for the Kabul throne for some time. The British picked one of the princelings, Abdur Rahman, and pronounced him emir or king of the Afghans. They gave him weapons and money, and asked him to create a buffer state between czarist Russia and British India. Every inch of the boundaries of this new buffer state was put on the map by British India and czarist Russia. Not a single inch of the country's frontiers was ever defined by any Afghan. The impact of these borders on the ethnic composition of Afghanistan and its neighboring states has been enormous.

The borders of Afghanistan, drawn during the onset of the "Great Game" in Central Asia in the closing decades of the nineteenth century, were gerrymandered to split members of every ethnic group that lived among or between different neighboring states. Along the northern frontiers, those seriously affected were the peoples of Turkistan, the territory inhabited by Turkic- and Tajik-speaking Muslims such as the Uzbek, Turkmen, Kazak, Kirghiz, and Tajiks. A large area of southern Turkistan between the Hindu Kush mountains and the Amu Darya (Oxus River) was included within the borders of the new buffer state of Afghanistan. In fact, a large province of Turkistan in northwestern Afghanistan continued to exist until the 1960s. In 1967, the government in Kabul eliminated the province of Turkistan by means of an administrative "reform" and replaced it with the newly named smaller provinces of Balkh, Jawzjan, Samangan, and Faryab. This politically motivated administrative fiat by the Pashtun-dominated Afghan government in the 1960s paralleled Stalin's National Delimitation of 1924, when the Soviets eliminated the name of Western (Russian) Turkistan by creating the five language-based Central Asian Soviet Socialist Repub-

lics of Uzbekistan, Turkmenistan, Kazakstan, Kirghizstan, and
Tajikistan across Afghanistan's northern borders. Further east in
western China, a large territory occupied by Turkic-speaking
Muslim Uyghur, Kazak, and Kirghiz peoples called Sharqi Turkistan, or Eastern (Chinese) Turkistan, became officially known in
China as Xinjiang province. Thus, as a result of the creation and
recreation of national borders that began with the frontiers of
Afghanistan in the 1880s, the larger identity and territorial reality
of Turkistan was wiped clean from the face of the world map.

A little further to the west, the Farsiwan, who speak the same
dialect of Persian as eastern Iran, were also divided on both sides
of the Iran-Afghanistan borders. The area to the south and southeast populated by the Baluch was divided among three countries:
Afghanistan, Iran, and British India (now Pakistan). And the
Pashtun/Pathans (Afghans) were also divided by the Durand Line
on the eastern borders, leaving most of the Pashtun/Pathans on the
British India side. If you look at the Durand Line, which marks
Afghanistan's eastern frontiers with Pakistan, you can see that it
was drawn by the British to effectively divide the Pashtuns between
two separate states.

These borders were all drawn purposefully by the British during the reign of Amir Abdur Rahman (1880–1901). The foundation for the creation of the modern nation-state of Afghanistan was
also firmly laid with these boundaries. How this was accomplished
is worth noting. Abdur Rahman was not only given weapons and
money by Britain, he was also given free rein to terrorize the people
within his freshly marked borders. Amir Abdur Rahman and his
Muhammadzai Pashtun clan hailed from Kandahar, the current
spiritual headquarters of the Taliban. The Pashtun in this southwestern area of Afghanistan belong to different tribes from those
living farther east along the borders with Pakistan. Abdur Rahman
first decimated the leadership of the eastern Ghilzai Pashtun tribes,
whom he did not trust. He then moved against the Hazaras in the
center of the country. The Hazaras are Persian-speaking Shia Muslims with Mongol features. They resisted Abdur Rahman's conquest
of their territory and were subjected to harsh punishments. He decimated the Hazara community leaders and committed many atroc-
ities against the Hazaras: massacring entire villages, skinning people
alive, and enslaving their women and children. A particularly grue-
some form of torture perpetrated against the Hazara people was to
form a rim of dough around the shaven heads of men so that boiling oil could be poured on them to fry their brains. These stories
form a permanent part of the public memories that still circulate

a century after the death of the founder of the modern Afghan nation-state.

Abdur Rahman Khan widely employed violence and torture in his rampages, conquests, and subjugation of all the peoples within his designated domain. In the eastern part of the country in Kafiristan, where the inhabitants were not Muslims, he forcibly converted the inhabitants and renamed the area Nooristan (Land of Light). The same brutalities were used in subjugating the Uzbek, Turkmen, Tajik, and other ethnic communities in the northern region. Throughout the entire country during his reign, people were terrorized into submission, and he created a relatively strong centralized state with the help of foreign money and weapons. Indeed, Amir Abdur Rahman—nicknamed the "Iron Amir" by his British colonial masters for his cruel, two-decade-long rule—laid the foundation for an ill-suited centralized state structure that lasted for most of the twentieth century.

The Iron Amir was intensely suspicious of his subjects, especially those Pashtun who did not belong to his own clan or tribe and the non-Pashtun groups in the center and northern regions of the country. In order to ensure domination of those non-Pashtun peoples, Emir Abdur Rahman mobilized large groups of Durrani Pashtun nomads from the south to move and occupy large areas of pastureland in central Afghanistan belonging to Hazaras. He also resettled tens of thousands of Pashtun tribesmen from the south in strategic parts of Afghan Turkistan, along the borders with central Asian Khanates under czarist Russian control. By doing so, he established the enforcement of century-long policies of forced resettlement that were nothing but crude forms of internal colonialism run by the ruling clique in Afghanistan. These policies resulted in much distrust and resentment against the internal Pashtun colonizers who abused and micro-managed the affairs of the local communities from the center.

Needless to say, the centralized administration of the country was based on corruption and nepotism. A first-hand experience from my youth serves as a brief example. In the village in Badakhshan province where I grew up and attended elementary school in the 1950s, a man was appointed from Kabul to be the principal of our elementary school. He was a Pashtun from the eastern province of Nengarhar. He brought his elderly uncle with him to be our school's custodian instead of finding a more deserving person from the local community to be custodian.

This system of governance continued until the 1960s, when a very small window of opportunity for democratic experimentation opened up as a result of constitutional changes that occurred from 1964 to 1973. It was during this brief period that some freedom of the press and rudimentary forms of political activities were permitted. Under pressure from the former USSR, the government did not object to the formation of an Afghan Communist party (Khalq, in 1965), although it strongly opposed Islamist youth movements. By 1973 King Muhammad Zahir Shah was overthrown by his own cousin and brother-in-law, Prince Muhammad Daoud, with help from leftist military officers belonging to the Parcham faction of the Communist party. Five years later, the Communists killed Muhammad Daoud, massacred his entire family, and installed a Communist regime. In 1979, faced with overwhelming popular resistance, they "invited" the Soviets to invade the country, and Afghanistan's long war of twenty-three years began.

A country that had been under a strict dictatorship run at the center by one clan and one family, with foreign arms and financial backing, was about to enter a new era of proxy wars imposed on its people, again by outsiders. From the Soviet-inspired Communist coup of 1978 to the beginning of 1981, popular resistance against the Communist regime and against the Russians was completely indigenous. People across the country fought with sticks and stones against the Soviet Red Army and Afghan Communists, and only gradually captured weapons. During the first year and a half of conflict, the United States and Europe basically gave up on Afghanistan. Western leadership believed that Afghanistan would become a permanent part of the Soviet domain and that nothing could be done to stop it.

FROM JIHAD TO PROXY WARS

After initially ignoring the Afghan resistance, people in U.S. government circles realized that these Afghans were willing to fight. Why not give them weapons to fight the Soviets, the U.S. enemy? This decision was the beginning of the end for the Afghan resistance as an independent national movement. Once money and weapons from the United States began to be sent to Afghanistan through the proxy of the Pakistan Inter-Services Intelligence (ISI), disaster was in the making. The people of Afghanistan lost control of their own struggle and the ability to speak for themselves. Others began to speak for them. Others began to organize their lives. Others began to organize their wars.

In the early 1980s, Pakistan's ISI orchestrated the formation of not one, but seven Afghan political parties among the Afghan refugees living in and around the city of Peshawar, Pakistan. These seven Mujahideen parties were used as a means for the delivery of arms and ammunition to fight the war against Soviet occupation forces. Six of these Mujahideen parties were either led by or were made up of Pashtun from the southern border area of Afghanistan. Only one of the seven was headed by non-Pashtuns: Burhanuddin Rabbani and his well-known commander Ahmed Shah Massoud. (Commander Massoud fell victim to Al Qaeda suicide bombers on September 9th, just two days before the attacks in New York.) This was done because Pakistan did not want Afghanistan to have a united opposition; it was deemed too threatening to Pakistan's national interests. The ISI, by creating multiple parties and favoring certain groups over others, created intergroup and inter-ethnic tension while manipulating the situation to their own national advantage.

By the mid-1980s, Pakistan was hosting some 3.2 million Afghan refugees in dozens of camps all across the Northwest Frontier Province (NWFP) and in the Baluchistan area. In addition, an estimated two million Afghan refugees had entered Iran. Over 85 percent of those Afghans who came to Pakistan were Pashtun. Only 15 percent were non-Pashtun. It was here in the refugee camps that traditional Muslim seminaries (madrassas) were built. At the madrassas, Afghan refugee children received training (i.e., became Taliban) in rudimentary Islam. The Afghan refugees in Iran didn't do any better: the Iranians only allowed and encouraged Afghan Shia communities from central Afghanistan to organize politically, and they did. Ten to fifteen contentious Shia parties were funded, equipped, and sent to central Afghanistan to fight.

During this anti-Soviet, anti-Communist struggle, communities everywhere across Afghanistan organized militarily and created civilian structures at the local level to provide basic health and educational services with the help of international nongovernmental organizations (NGOs). By 1989, with financial and military help from the United States and other nations, Afghans serving as the expendable foot soldiers of this proxy war managed to defeat the Red Army. The Soviets were forced to withdraw their troops from Afghanistan in April 1989.

But the Communist regime left behind in Kabul lingered on until 1992. In the meantime, Pakistan encouraged their homegrown Afghan political parties to fight against not only the Communist regime and the Soviets, but also amongst themselves. The ethnic dimension of the Afghan conflict was thus purposefully highlighted and manipulated by both Pakistan and Iran.

The United States reportedly invested some three billion dol-

lars in the anti-Soviet war in Afghanistan. Then, after the Soviet
defeat and troop withdrawal in 1989, the United States simply abandoned Afghanistan by walking away. Our common enemy, the
Soviet Union, was defeated, and the Cold War was won. The U.S.
objectives had been realized. Who cared about the foot soldiers that
had done the United States a favor? Or perhaps the United States
had done Afghanistan a favor by its willingness to help fight the
Soviets, even to the last Afghan! The critical fact is that America
abandoned the situation and left behind a country that was shat-
tered economically, politically, and in every conceivable sense. The
devastated country was left to the mercy of two neighboring vul-
tures: Pakistan to the east, and Iran to the west. The Russian Federation, an even greater vulture to the north, was also trying to get
its hand on the future of Afghanistan.

PROXY WARS AND COMMUNAL STRIFE

In 1992, when the Communist regime in Kabul finally fell,
Pakistan quickly cobbled together a so-called broad-based government of the Mujahideen in which the only party Pakistan did not
favor, the one headed by non-Pashtun Burhanuddin Rabbani,
managed to take control of Kabul. After the interim presidency of
Sebghatullah Mujadidi, which lasted about two months, Rabbani
became president of the Mujahideen government. Pakistan's favorite
Pashtun, Gulbuddin Hekmatyar, who was head of Hizbi Islami
(Islamic Party), became the prime minister. But Hekmatyar was not
happy being prime minister and refused to take up his post in
Kabul. Feeling slighted by the usurpation of power by the non-
Pashtun groups from the rightful Pashtun rulers, Pakistan urged
Hekmatyar to fight for control of the capital from the Tajiks.
Hekmatyar thus began to bombard Kabul for two years. The worst
imaginable crimes happened in and around Kabul from 1992 to
1994. The resistance against Hekmatyar's onslaught in Kabul was
fierce, as the Shia Hazaras had a powerful presence in major areas
of the city. Also, the Uzbek forces of Abdul Rashid Dostam, which
had played a critical role in the collapse of the Communist regime
and in the Mujahideen takeover of Kabul by the Tajik forces of
Ahmad Shah Massoud, all fought together initially to resist Hekmatyar. In time, however, the alliances of forces shifted repeatedly,
and inter-ethnic factional fighting in and around Kabul grew
worse. The prize was the control of the city of Kabul. The Pashtun
wanted to reclaim control of the capital city from the hands of, in
their view, non-Pashtun usurpers.

Hence, Kabul, which had remained more or less intact up until the fall of Najibullah's (the last of the Communist quislings) regime, was utterly destroyed by the inter-ethnic wars of succession from 1992 to 1994. During a visit to Kabul in the summer of 1996, I cried time and again. I couldn't believe what the Afghans, my own compatriots, had done to themselves, to their country, and to their own capital at the behest of Pakistan and Iran. The destruction of the city's business districts and neighborhoods was worse than the pictures of Dresden after World War II. Three quarters of the city was in utter ruins. There was not a single wall standing in the two boarding schools that I had attended. Entire neighborhoods, entire avenues, marketplaces—everything, except for parts in the northern sector—were leveled to the ground in Kabul.

And for what? For the prize of running a central governmental authority in the name of one ethnic group over any other. This was the attempt to reimpose the same old system of government dating back to Abdur Rahman, a centralized state where officials could send their cousins and nephews and daughters and sons to rule the rest of the country for them.

Yet two years of warfare by Gulbuddin Hekmatyar against Kabul could not win the prize that Pakistan wanted him to win. At that point Afghanistan had more or less been divided into five or six different semi-independent regions. There was the western region of Persian-speaking Farsiwan communities, which had created an alliance under Ismail Khan, with the city of Herat as its center. Ismail Khan had actually disarmed his own population and had universities, a legal system, and schools operating. General Abdul Rashid Dostam, who has been vilified as a Northern Alliance warlord by his Pakistani detractors in the media after September 11th, in fact had managed to unify several provinces in the northwestern region, where he had also brought peace and order. The area under his control, centered around the city of Mazar-i-Sharif, was predominantly inhabited by Uzbeks, and the conditions were ideal for the local population at that time. They had local autonomy and thriving commercial ties with the newly independent Central Asian republics. Schools and universities were functioning, and radio, television, and print media enjoyed considerable freedom and support. The northeastern parts of the country, along with mountain valleys just north of Kabul such as Kohistan, Kohdaman, Panjsher, and Tagaw wa Nijraw, were populated largely by Tajiks. These areas were ruled by the Shura-i Nazzar (Northern Council) under the command of Ahmed Shah Massoud and were also more or less peaceful. In the center, the Hazara Shias controlled their own territory and sectarian community with virtual autonomy. In the east, the Pashtun had created a coalition of several provinces under Shura-i Mashreqi (Eastern Council), and they, too, were peacefully running their own affairs. The real mess of factional fighting was mostly limited to the national capital, Kabul, and to Kandahar, a predominantly Pashtun tribal belt. In the city of Kandahar there was no order: many partisan groups and tribes fought among themselves, and this area formed the real heart of Afghanistan's chaos.

THE RISE OF TALIBAN

Not surprisingly, it was the city of Kandahar from which, in 1994, Mullah Mohammed Omar emerged, along with a group of ex-Mujahideen fighters. Mullah Omar challenged some of the most notorious of the local warlords. Initially he succeeded in attracting considerable popular support in and around Kandahar, and was able to bring a semblance of order to that unruly city.

By 1995, a plan by a consortium of oil companies, including UNOCAL and Delta Oil of Saudi Arabia, was underway to build a natural gas pipeline from Turkmenistan to Pakistani seaports through Afghanistan. Immediately Pakistan saw the potential usefulness of the newly rising Pashtun force in Kandahar, and it adopted Mullah Omar's small movement, naming it Harakati Taliban (Muslim Seminary Students' Movement). Pakistan offered the Harakati Taliban money, weapons, and logistical support in securing a corridor for Pakistan so that UNOCAL and its partners could build the Turkmenistan-Pakistan oil pipeline across western parts of Afghanistan. Early in 1995, the Taliban secured the allegiance of local Pashtun commanders, mostly through bribes, all across the southern and southeastern Pashtun belt approaching the capital, Kabul. Then in the autumn of 1995, they attacked the forces of Ismail Khan in western Afghanistan. Since the population of Herat had been disarmed by its own leaders, the area quickly fell to the Taliban, and Ismail Khan took refuge in Iran.

The capture of Herat by the Taliban did not end the war. Emboldened by their easy victory, the Taliban and their Pakistani masters now wanted to take the rest of the country by force, and thus pursued a policy of total war against the rest of the country. During this hideous period of Taliban rampages of conquest, there were large-scale massacres of non-Pashtun civilians of northern and central Afghanistan as they defended their territories against the Taliban and their Pakistani allies. When the war against the Soviet

Union was fought, no Pashtun came from any other part of Afghanistan to help liberate these territories, inhabited by the Uzbeks, Tajiks, and Hazaras. They were instead defended and liberated by local inhabitants. Indeed, these inhabitants claimed it was the non-Pashtun Afghans who had joined their Pashtun compatriots in southern Afghanistan and had fought to liberate the Pashtun areas. The non-Pashtun peoples of Afghanistan were therefore shocked to find themselves fighting a Pashtun army led by the Taliban and supported by the government of Pakistan. They felt they were being subjugated once again to a form of internal colonialism. In light of this and the fact that they had just recently liberated their own territories from the Soviet-Russian invaders, these non-Pashtun ethnic communities put up a stiff resistance.

TALIBAN ALLIANCE WITH OSAMA BIN LADEN

Another significant event of 1995 was the return of Osama bin Laden to Afghanistan. Osama bin Laden had initially come to Afghanistan in 1981 to fight in the jihad against the Soviet invaders. At that time, he was reportedly urged by CIA and Pakistani ISI operatives to recruit Arabs for the Afghan jihad, not only from the Arab lands, but also from Europe and the United States. Bin Laden is said to have had offices here in the United States that recruited willing volunteers to go and fight in Afghanistan.

After the Soviet defeat and withdrawal, bin Laden had returned to Saudi Arabia. He was not opposed to America at that time. But when the Gulf War broke out, bin Laden became a vocal opponent of the U.S.-led coalition. He apparently organized anti-war demonstrations in Saudi Arabia. It was then that the Saudi government stripped him of citizenship and threw him out of the country. Osama bin Laden then went to Sudan, where he remained for a couple of years until Sudan was pressured to get rid of him. In 1995, the Pakistani ISI brokered a deal to move bin Laden and his entourage from Sudan to Pakistan and into Afghanistan. In doing so, the Pakistani ISI also brokered a marriage between the new forces of terror they had created in Afghanistan: the Taliban and bin Laden.

From then on, bin Laden not only financed the Taliban war against non-Pashtun opponents, but his Al Qaeda militants fought alongside the Taliban forces. He also began to support the training of other disgruntled Muslim militant groups from Chechnya, Kashmir, Uzbekistan, China, Algeria, and around the world. He accepted virtually anyone who was willing to come to Afghanistan and fight with them.

Ultimately, bin Laden came to rule Afghanistan. He and his Al Qaeda organization became the financial and even the ideological brain behind the Taliban terror in the country. Today, the majority of those fighting the war against the non-Pashtuns in the north are not even Afghan Pashtuns. They are Pakistani radicals and extremists as well as elements from western China (Xinjiang), Chechnya, the Arab countries of the Middle East and North Africa, and Uzbekistan, among others—radicals and extremists who came to Afghanistan to get the necessary training. Afghanistan as a failed state became a safe haven for global terrorism. And the militant radicals hoped that if they could take complete control of one state, Afghanistan, this could provide them with a base to direct their jihad against presumed enemies in the region and beyond.

THE ROOT CAUSES OF TERRORISM MUST BE ADDRESSED

This, then, is the reality confronting us: if we divide the world into our friends, the dictators and the colonial occupation forces on the one hand, and our enemies, the terrorists and the rogue states which offer them safe haven and support on the other hand, we avoid addressing the fundamental question of who produced these terrorists. Afghanistan did not produce them; these terrorists are produced elsewhere. They are produced in Chechnya, by Russia, because of Russian policies of oppression directed against the Chechen nation. They are produced by India in its occupation of Kashmir. They are produced in Palestine by the Israeli occupation forces. They are produced by the regimes in Egypt, Iraq, and Saudi Arabia (fifteen of the nineteen hijackers of September 11th were Saudi citizens).

How can we solve this problem by cozying up with the very states that produce these terrorists? They're part of the problem and thus cannot be part of the solution. Pakistan is part of the problem; it cannot be part of the solution. If we are thinking politically, many of those with whom we're now in alliance to fight global terrorism are themselves responsible for the production of terrorism. When we support these regimes, we therefore become part of the production process.

Perhaps we're also consumers of it as well. We have to face the fact that, today, terrorism is a commodity and part of the globalization process. Until we face this fact squarely, we're not going to be able to solve the problem. We cannot continue to embrace only those aspects of globalization that benefit us while ignoring the forces of globalization which harm us. If we are serious about this, we have to abandon the regimes that are producing these terrorists.

If instead we continue to support the regimes that produce terrorists, we will deal with the symptoms only: today, tomorrow, a month from now, a year from now, every terrorist network on earth may be eliminated—and it may be possible to do this. But if we don't deal with the root causes that produce terrorism, in five years we will have a fresh crop of terrorists who are more virile and hateful than they are today.

GOVERNING AFGHANISTAN AFTER TALIBAN

Now that the coalition war has dislodged the Taliban and their Al Qaeda allies from power, who should govern Afghanistan? The old monarch, Mohamed Zahir Shah, who is partly responsible for bringing this misery on his people in the first place? Or the dominant Pashtun ethnic group, which has most recently given us the Taliban? Or the constantly quarreling and unruly Northern Alliance? Or even a "broad-based" interim government made up of a few of these groups headed by Hamid Karzai, which was cobbled together by the Bonn agreement? The truth is that none of them, including the interim regime of Karzai or the transitional government formed after the Loya Jirga (Grand Assembly) on June 22, 2002, will ever be able to solve the problem of misrule in Afghanistan. We must not ask who should rule Afghanistan, but how should a multiethnic society such as Afghanistan be governed, so that we will not again face problems of internal colonialism, ethnic tensions, and communal violence. Post-Taliban political developments, so far, appear to be concerned solely with the reimposition of direct central government authority in all parts of the country.

The first step, however, towards responding positively to Afghanistan's future governance would be to support those people who have managed to liberate their own territories from the clutches of the Taliban and their global terrorist allies. This can be accomplished by accepting the principle of self-governance at the local level. The majority of ethnic groups in Afghanistan live in relatively compact communities in rural Afghanistan. At the rural local level and even in some urban environments, communities are ethnically fairly homogeneous. A system of governance or an administrative structure that takes into account the make-up of the local communities and gives them the right to govern themselves locally must therefore be devised. At the village level, the district level, and the provincial level, people should have the right to either elect or to hire their own community administrators. Wherever feasible, adjacent provinces should be encouraged to create a common regional administrative unit. This kind of governance structure radically differs from the old centralized system of misrule that has characterized the history of Afghanistan since 1880. Afghanistan must create a loosely structured federal government that is decentralized. This structure can be akin to the U.S. model of governance, but adapted to the local and national conditions in post-Taliban Afghanistan. The U.S. system of governance offers an important model for managing the political problems of multiethnic states the world over. In the United States, the principle of community governance is primarily territorial. In other countries, including Afghanistan, the organizing principle can be the combination of territoriality and other pertinent communal identities: sect, religion, language, etc.

The governance system with which much of the world has been living has not been the U.S. model, but a far less appropriate model that dates back to late-nineteenth-century colonial France and England. For more than a hundred and fifty years Europeans fought with each other, not only to establish their own national boundaries but also to draw the national boundaries of most of the rest of the world. In the last thirty years, however, the Europeans have been busily deconstructing their national boundaries in favor of one united European community. But the European colonial powers also drew national maps and delineated boundaries, which people are still fighting over and dying to protect. We must therefore think of alternatives to the legacies of the old centralized state systems left behind by the colonial regimes. These systems have led to nothing but internal colonialism. These colonial systems have been kept in power and supported by the same old colonial regimes and, in some cases, by the United States of America.

The United States must help Afghanistan in a number of significant ways. First, it must continue to help rid the country of the Taliban and their international terrorist allies, who have turned that suffering nation into the virtual center of Global Terrorism, Inc. Second, it should assist in the establishment of an appropriate national governance structure that not only avoids returning to the past history of centralized misrule, but can also be instrumental in the national reconstruction of that battered society. Finally, the United States should take the lead in mobilizing sustained and long-term international reconstruction assistance for Afghanistan.

It is by means of these integrated and coordinated international efforts in Afghanistan that we may be able to accomplish the goals we've set out to accomplish. It's obvious to me that our strategy of waging war against global terrorism, no matter how militarily effective, will not solve Afghanistan's problems and will not solve our own national security concerns. We must be willing to change course in the conduct of our foreign policy and do things differently for once. Our current involvement in Afghanistan offers a very important test case to do it right.

COPING WITH THE MODERN NATION-STATE AND ITS FAILURE: THE KIRGHIZ AND WAKHI CASE

Research for this book began exactly thirty years ago, in the summer of 1972, when I returned to Afghanistan after five years of studying anthropology in the United States. My research goals were to explore the cultural ecological adaptation of the Kirghiz, a small pastoral nomadic community, and their agriculturalist neighbors, the Wakhi, to high altitudes and cold climatic conditions. These two ethnically distinct groups lived in one of the remotest corners of northeastern Afghanistan—the Wakhan Corridor and the Afghan Pamirs. Once in the area, I quickly realized that what demanded understanding was not only *how* the Kirghiz and Wakhi communities had adapted to the harsh environmental constraints of Wakhan and the Pamirs, but also *why* they came to inhabit this extremely marginal environment in the first place.

In my attempt to address these closely related ethnographic and historical questions, I embarked on an ambitious project to uncover the dynamics of Kirghiz and Wakhi cultural ecological adaptations to the physical environment. But I also wished to recount these communities' troubled social, economic, and political relationships with each other and with their other neighbors in the area within the context of closed borders imposed by more powerful and expansive modern states—the former Soviet Union, China, and British-India (now Pakistan).

Although extremely stratified in terms of herd ownership, the Kirghiz community was led, however, by a benevolent and highly effective leader or Khan, Haji Rahman Qul. Through innovative herd management techniques, the Khan had been able to ensure that most households enjoyed access to herds and the necessary livestock products for a relatively prosperous pastoral nomadic lifestyle.[1]

1. For further details, see M. Nazif Shahrani, "The Kirghiz Khans: Styles and Substance of Traditional Local Leadership in Central Asia," Central Asian Survey 5, no. 3/4 (1986): 255–71.

Indeed, by the mid-1970s, the Afghan Kirghiz, a distant and strategically located frontier community, had created a relatively comfortable economic and political niche for themselves within the framework of the Afghan nation-state. This was unlike many other small ethnic minorities in Afghanistan—including the neighbors of the Kirghiz, the Wakhi Ismaili Shia community. The Khan had established direct ties to Kabul via his annual or semi-annual homage to the royal court and various ministers. Clinging to the safety of the mountain ramparts of the Pamirs, the Kirghiz leader used his cordial relations with the center to full advantage, and his tiny community was able to fend off avaricious local and provincial officials.

Repeatedly victimized during the twentieth century by their two giant neighboring Communist states—the former USSR and China (PRC)—the Kirghiz of Afghanistan were highly suspicious of all governments and state officials. Although they had managed to cope rather successfully with the difficulties of living in a harsh and erratic climate, they were, however, constantly worried about the intentions of the surrounding states, including Afghanistan, towards them and their freedom and liberty.

Their chronic fear about the intentions of distant states turned into a full-fledged nightmare following the Soviet-inspired Communist coup of April 1978 in Kabul. The Kirghiz were among the first refugees to cross over to northern Pakistan, where they spent four difficult years (1978–82) before resettling in the Van province of eastern Turkey. Their neighbors, the sedentary Wakhi villagers, were unwilling or unable to vote with their feet.

Both of these relatively isolated frontier communities, like the rest of Afghan society and culture, have undergone considerable changes and transformations because of the prolonged war and state failure in Afghanistan as well as the unanticipated implosion of the former Soviet Union (1991) and the birth of the five new independent Muslim states of Central Asia. It is hoped that by offering an ethnographic account of their experiences within a multiethnic, twentieth-century nation-state, this updated second edition of *The Kirghiz and Wakhi of Afghanistan* will shed some light on our understanding of the dynamics of state and society relations in general and those of war-ravaged Afghanistan in particular.

 Preface to the Original Edition

THIS BOOK IS based on twenty months of anthropological field research, from July 1972 to February 1974, in the Wakhan Corridor and the Pamirs of Afghanistan. My primary research focus was on the Kirghiz pastoralists of the Afghan Pamirs, with only a secondary interest in their agriculturalist neighbors, the Wakhi. A return to the area in July and August of 1975 gave me the opportunity to check and augment data.

My initial reasons for choosing to study the Kirghiz and Wakhi of Afghanistan were twofold: first, the almost total absence of serious anthropological studies of high-altitude adaptations in Central and Southwestern Asia in general, and of the Kirghiz and Wakhi in particular; and second, although there are larger Kirghiz and Wakhi populations in the region, the small segments in Afghanistan are the only ones outside Soviet or Chinese control, and the only ones who still practice their traditional ways of life. What was disclosed in the field was the significance of the closing of the frontiers by the Soviet Union and Communist China upon the adaptation strategies of the Kirghiz and Wakhi communities in Afghanistan, in addition to those internal constraints and incentives imposed by an emerging, relatively powerful, centralized Afghan nation state.

Other factors, less academic but equally significant, also influenced my decision to study the Kirghiz and Wakhi. The Wakhan Corridor and the Pamirs are restricted frontier areas and as such are closed to foreign researchers, but my Afghan citizenship and formal affiliation with Kabul University at that time offered me relatively easy access. Furthermore, my Turkic background and native language, Uzbek, facilitated communication with the Kirghiz, the principal subjects of this research. Finally, although somewhat apprehensive about the physical hazards of not only traveling to, but living in, the high altitudes of the Pamirs, I was intrigued by the area and the peoples.

My native Uzbek village, Shahran, is about six hours by horseback from Faizabad, the capital of Badakhshan province in northeastern Afghanistan. After primary school in Shahran, I spent nine months of each year in government-run boarding schools in Kabul. From about twelve, unlike most of my age mates in the villages of Badakhshan, I traveled through Faizabad and several other major towns in northern Afghanistan to school in Kabul, tracing the same route each spring and fall.

It was during one of these long truck rides in the fall of 1959 that I first met a number of Kirghiz who told us they were on a pilgrimage to Mecca. After that, I saw small numbers of Kirghiz either on the road or in Faizabad each fall. They were distinctive in their black fur hats, padded black corduroy pantaloons tucked into high leather boots, and their padded jackets and overcoats. Most of them wore long, though sparse, moustaches. In their looks, darker skin color, facial features, and style of dress, they were unlike any other group of people I had known.

A few old traders in our village who had traveled through the Pamirs before the Chinese Communist revolution spoke of the Kirghiz with both admiration and fear. The Kirghiz were reputed to be very fierce, warlike, independent, and free of any outside government control, yet also friendly, cooperative, and generous to those who became their friends. I had also heard dramatic tales of the wealth of some of the Kirghiz khans, of their hospitality, generosity, courage, and fame.

I had heard other "facts" about the Pamirs. There were stories of the richness and power of the soil in the Pamirs, where the cream from the milk of Kirghiz animals fed on the highland vegetation was abundant and of a thickness unknown elsewhere. The soil was so rich that people cut pieces of the earth and burned it as fuel (in Badakhshan the use of peat is unknown). Furthermore, the power of the Pamir land was so great that it was unsafe to lie on one's back or side. Anyone who did lie down and go to sleep never woke up! People in the Pamirs were said, therefore, to sleep by leaning against high piles of bedding in an almost upright position from the waist up. People from outside the area who went there were allegedly unable to sleep.

I had a little acquaintance with the Wakhi, however, since poor Wakhi came to our village seeking seasonal work. My own and the neighboring villages were traditionally good poppy-growing areas so many Wakhi came to work to support their habit of opium use. I was well accustomed to their impoverished looks and to the almost universal dislike of them expressed in numerous ways by the local Sunni majority because of their Shi'a Ismaili beliefs.

Nevertheless, my knowledge of the Wakhi, although based on more frequent contact with them than with the Kirghiz, was limited to those who came to Badakhshan, and was tainted by ethnic biases. Indeed, my knowledge of the Kirghiz and Wakhi at that time varied but little from what I knew of many other ethnic, linguistic, sectarian, and regional populations in Afghanistan.

My interest in anthropology developed during my first year at Kabul University, but since there was no anthropology program at the University at the time, it was not until my third year, when I was offered an East-West Center Scholarship from the University of Hawaii at Honolulu, that the possibility of studying anthropology became a reality. The thought of working among the Kirghiz did not occur to me until my last year in graduate school, and I returned to Afghanistan after five years in the United States for the sole purpose of conducting anthropological research among the Kirghiz and Wakhi.

After a brief visit to my family in the village and a few weeks of preparation in Kabul, I set out on the first of three trips to the field in Wakhan and the Afghan Pamirs. These three journeys from Kabul to Wakhan and the Pamirs took an average of about twenty days of travel each way by bus, truck or jeep, and horseback, including time on the road waiting for transportation.

I spent most of the initial two and one-half months of field work in Khandud, the capital of the district of Wakhan. There I was given a room by a long-time Uzbek trader in the Wakhan and Pamirs, originally from a village near my own in central Badakhshan. I met many Kirghiz who came each fall to buy grain and market goods from the shopkeeper/itinerant traders who are based in Khandud bazaar, the only one in Wakhan. While in Khandud I was able to study Kirghiz trading activities and social relations with the Wakhi, the traders, and the local government officials.

In mid-October 1972 I went to the Great Pamir for a brief exploratory trip and spent about a week with the Kirghiz. It was then that I asked them about the sleeping posture in the Pamirs. Much amused, they assured me there was no truth to what I had heard, that if I stayed long enough in the Pamirs I was more likely to feel sleepy all the time than to suffer from lack of sleep. Despite these assurances I spent a couple of nights wide awake in my sleeping bag until sheer exhaustion took over.

This visit to the Pamirs also demonstrated that my native Uzbek was indeed very similar to Kirghiz and I had little difficulty understanding most of what was discussed. After a few months I had virtually no problem communicating in Kirghiz.

Following a quick survey of the Great Pamir, where I gathered some general information as to number of people, households, livestock, and so on, I returned to Khandud, hoping to make a similar tour of the Little Pamir. There I learned that the Kirghiz khan was due in Khandud soon, on his way to Kabul to sell a herd of sheep and goats, so I was advised to wait for him in Khandud rather than make the long trip to the Little Pamir.

When the khan arrived with his party of about fifteen other Kirghiz, including three women (the khan's sister, one of his two wives, and a daughter-in-law, all of whom needed medical attention) and two of his younger sons, I traveled with them to Kabul. During the next two months I spent a great deal of time with the khan and his party while they sold their animals, made official visits, and carried on general business.

Early in February 1973 I joined the khan's party to return with them to the Pamirs. After more than a week of bus and truck rides we reached Khandud, where a caravan of horses and camels was waiting. The next nine days of horseback from Khandud to the khan's camp in the Little Pamir was like a royal journey. In the company of the khan and a caravan of fifteen Bactrian camels, nearly thirty horses, and about as many people, we threaded our way through narrow, frozen gorges, stopping in tiny Wakhi hamlets and small, isolated Kirghiz camps. On the way the khan conferred with frontier officials, the Wakhi theocratic leader, the Shah of Qala-i-Panja, and many other influential Wakhi. The talks ranged from pasture conditions and agricultural harvests to discussions of national and local politics and interpersonal conflicts. Debts were also collected, land and goods bought and sold, and new arrangements made.

Upon our arrival at the khan's camp, Kirghiz from all over the Little Pamir, rich, poor, old, and young, came to visit the khan over the next few days to pay their respects, to receive small gifts of sweets, tea, cloth, and so on, and to hear the news from Kabul and other towns. I was introduced to the visitors as a friend and the purpose of my visit was explained by the khan and his sons. For the next four and one-half months the khan's guest house became my permanent base of operations, and I met, and talked to, his many visitors, some of whom came from different areas, with different interests and different knowledge of Kirghiz life.

After about a month I began to move slowly from camp to camp, conducting a household economic and demographic survey, sometimes spending several days in a camp before moving to the next. Before my return to Kabul toward the end of June I was able to complete a survey of more than two-thirds of the 246 households in the Little Pamir.

During my third and last trip in late August 1973, I was fortunate enough to travel in the company of Wakeel M. Ismail Pamiri of Khandud, then the Wakhan deputy to the Afghan parliament, who was making a tour of the upper section of Wakhan and the Little Pamir. Having traveled through the same area in another season with the Kirghiz khan, I found it both interesting and fruitful to observe a local politician among his constituents.

We arrived in the Little Pamir when several weddings were in progress and preparatory work for the long winter was at its height. Once again I was based in the khan's guest house at his summer camp, but I traveled to every summer encampment throughout the entire length of the Little Pamir to complete my household survey.

After about a month and a half I took the summer route from the Little Pamir to the Great Pamir, crossing three glacier-covered passes 5,000 to 5,300 meters high. Here my main task was to complete my household census among the Kirghiz of the Great Pamir. I found them in the midst of moving camp from their summer to fall camping grounds and was able to visit all but two camps, composed of three households, in the area. The demographic and economic information I needed for these three households was supplied by others in the community, so in one month I was able to complete my acquisition of data on the Kirghiz of the Great Pamir.

I again returned to Khandud, where I continued to collect further data about the Wakhi and the traders until early in December. In Kabul once again I was with a group of nearly twenty Kirghiz including the khan, his younger brother, and at least three other Kirghiz elders for most of December 1973 and January 1974. During this period I also searched for archival and printed information in the libraries in Kabul before returning to the United States in February.

It is obvious that because my research was focused on the Kirghiz, the quantity and quality of data obtained about the Kirghiz and Wakhi are uneven. Furthermore, because I am primarily concerned with the significant aspects of Kirghiz and Wakhi adaptations to a number of dominant environmental constraints, this book does not pretend to be a comprehensive ethnography of either the Kirghiz or the Wakhi of Afghanistan.

I would like to express my gratitude to the several organizations and the many people who have given me assistance and encouragement in the making of this book. A fellowship grant from the Foreign Area Fellowship Program of the joint committee of the Social Sciences Research Council and the American Council of Learned Societies, together with supplementary funds from the Grant-in-Aid program of the Wenner-Gren Foundation for Anthropological Research, made the eighteen months of field research in Afghanistan possible. In Afghanistan the staff of the Office of Cultural Relations, Ministry of Foreign Affairs of the Government of Afghanistan, and the Office of Cultural Relations of Kabul University provided me with letters of introduction on several occasions, which gave me access to documents, and also facilitated my return to the United States after completion of my field work.

Many friends, colleagues, government officials, and former teachers in Kabul, Badakhshan, and Wakhan were helpful to me. In particular I would like to thank Dr. A. G. Rawan-Farhadi, a distinguished scholar, Mr. Gulam Ali Ayin, my former teacher at Kabul University who, at the time of this research, was Governor of Badakhshan, and Mr. Gulnoor Khybaryar, then the Woluswal of Wakhan.

Numerous Kirghiz and Wakhi individuals and families gave generously of their time and resources, material and intellectual. Without their help, advice, and most of all, their wealth of information, this book and my other writings would not have been possible. I have benefited from them enormously with, regrettably, little possibility of being able to reciprocate except to say *biy nihayat tashakur.* I want to specially mention and thank Juma Gul, Baz Mohammad, M. Yar, Jamshid, and Wakeel M. Ismail Pamiri of Wakhan; Mowlana M. Murad, Osman Haji, A. Samad, A. Jalil of the Great Pamir; and Mahmood Haji, Afghan Bek Haji, Bai Haji, Hait Be, M. Ayoub, Telow Aldi, A. Wakeel, A. Wahid, A. Malik, M. Akbar, M. Arif, Maryam Haji, and Bibi Harun Yeja of the Little Pamir. These people called me *bir toghan* (born of one parent, or brother) treated me as one of their own, and always made me feel welcome in their midst.

Haji Rahman Qul spent long hours explaining Kirghiz history

and the intricacies of their way of life to me. Several of his young sons, who became my close friends and companions, also encouraged and instructed me, and then tested my progress! The outcome of my research could not have been the same without the help of Haji Rahman Qul and his family.

My parents and extensive extended family in Badakhshan did not quite understand my reasons for spending all my time away from them in Wakhan and the Pamirs, but they accepted it gracefully and aided me in many ways during my field work. My young cousin, Shamsudin, was permitted by his family to accompany me on all three of my journeys to the Pamirs. He was of tremendous assistance to me on the road and in residence in Wakhan and the Pamirs, doing most of the housekeeping chores. I thank him and his family for their generous help.

Professor Charles F. Keyes of the University of Washington has, over many years, provided me with unceasing encouragement and intellectual stimulation. This work has benefited greatly from his critical comments in both the earlier drafts and the final revision of the manuscript for publication. I owe him much gratitude for his genuine interest in my work, gracious help, confidence, and friendship.

Several others were of great assistance: At the University of Washington, Professors Edgar Winans and Paul Hiebert, who read and commented on an earlier draft of this work, and Simon Ottenberg, Harold Amoss, and Jere Bacharach; at the Center for Middle Eastern Studies at Harvard, Professors Michael Fischer, who read the entire manuscript and commented in some detail, and Nur Yalman; and Dr. Richard King, who introduced me to anthropology more than a decade ago and has remained a continuing inspiration.

The works of such scholars as Owen Lattimore, the late Sir Aurel Stein, and the late Ole Olufsen have been of inestimable value to me. The Royal Geographical Society of Great Britain kindly granted permission to use an adaptation of a map of the Silk Road prepared by Sir Aurel Stein and published in the *Geographical Journal* 65 (1925): 557. Enayatullah Shahrani adapted the map for use in this book, and has my gratitude.

The publication of this book is made possible through the assistance of the Comparative Studies in Ethnicity and Nationality Program of the School of International Studies, University of Washington. I am indebted to Professor Paul Brass, chairman of the Committee on CSEN, and the committee members for their interest, as well as to Professor John Reshetar, chairman of the Publications Committee of the School of International Studies, for his enthusiasm and support.

Mrs. Jane Keyes read an entire draft of the manuscript and made many constructive comments and numerous stylistic and grammatical corrections. I offer her my sincere thanks for her kindness.

Mrs. Margery Lang, the editor of the Publications Program of the School of International Studies, used her keen eye and light hand to add much needed clarity to the text. She raised many pertinent questions and demanded speedy answers, yet made the entire editorial experience, at least for me, instructive and enjoyable. This book has benefited enormously from her personal interest, enthusiasm, and gentle insistence on accuracy and consistency. Her able assistant, Ms. Jean Chatfield, made the proofreading simple and her interest in the book was encouraging and appreciated. Ms. Elizabeth Smith of the program staff skillfully adapted a Kirghiz motif to use on the chapter headings.

My good friends Lorraine and Tom Sakata and Maureen Davis helped in innumerable ways. Tom Sakata willingly prepared all but one of the maps and he deserves very special thanks.

Finally, I thank my wife Mavis for her patience, understanding, confidence, and immeasurable contributions, the least of which has been correcting my English and typing many drafts of the manuscript.

The responsibility for any shortcomings in analysis or presentation rests only with me.

A note about the transliteration of native terms and names: the problem of transliterating any of the Middle Eastern languages into English is enormous. In this instance the difficulty is compounded because the native terms appearing in this book come from at least three different languages—Kirghiz, Wakhi, and Tajik or Dari Persian spoken in Afghanistan. For the sake of lightening the burden on the general reader all native terminology in the text is transliterated as closely as possible to the local pronunciation in common English spelling, without the use of any diacritical marks. For example, long vowels are represented by double vowels. The spelling of names of peoples and places is retained where possible in their Anglicized form, even if such spelling does not in fact coincide with the way these names are pronounced by the people of the region—e.g., Kirghiz is used instead of Qirghiz and Kazakh instead of Qazaq.

However, for the benefit of area specialists all native terms are listed in the glossary and where necessary alternative transliterations are given using the transliteration system for Persian and Turkish followed by the *International Journal of Middle Eastern Studies.* In the glossary every effort is made to identify the native terms by their linguistic origin and usage. It is hoped that this will be of some consolation to the professional.

# Introduction

THIS BOOK IS primarily concerned with the cultural ecological adaptation of a small group of Kirghiz pastoralists and Wakhi agro-pastoralists to the sociopolitical conditions of closed frontiers, and to the constraints of the marginal high-altitude environment they inhabit. The Wakhan Corridor, where they live, which for many centuries served as part of the Silk Road and as a major path of communication and trade between China and central and south-western Asia, the Near East, and Europe, was until recently the main gateway of economic and cultural exchange between the peoples of Russian and Afghan Turkistan to the west of the Pamirs and the peoples of Chinese Turkistan to the east. At the present time, however, because of the recently closed borders, it is one of the most isolated and remote frontier areas of Afghanistan.

The Kirghiz of Afghanistan, a group of Turkic-speaking people, consisting in 1972-74 of some 330 households numbering a little over 1,800 persons, occupy the extreme northern and southern tip of the Wakhan Corridor—the high-altitude mountain valley areas of the Pamirs of Afghanistan. The banks of the upper Amu Darya and its major tributary in the Wakhan Corridor, the Sarhad River, are inhabited by a group of about 6,000 Wakhi peasants.[1] The Wakhi

1. Some clarification of the population figures is necessary. The figures cited for the Kirghiz are based on my own household demographic survey con-

are mostly confined to cultivated areas with the exception of a few families who use the high pasturage for a short period during the summer months.

Despite the existence of anthropological literature depicting the many forms of pastoral nomadism in the desert and low steppe regions of Asia and Africa, there are, with minor exceptions (Ekvall 1968), no systematic studies of high-altitude pastoral nomadism in continental Asia—Tibet, the Himalayas, and the Pamirs. Studies of rural, agricultural adaptations to high-altitude environments, particularly in the Near East and western and central Asia, are practically non-existent. Therefore, one of the main objectives of this study is to provide such a systematic description, and to explore and explain the dynamic processes of cultural ecological change, continuity, and viability of the Kirghiz and Wakhi communities in their environmental context.

A cultural ecological approach in anthropology addresses itself to the description and analysis of the relationships among at least four referential components of human environments: the cultural, social, biotic, and physical (cf. Helm 1962). In this approach the emphasis is put, as Clifford Geertz has stated, on the organization of the "pervasive properties of system *qua* system (system structure, system equilibrium, system change) rather than on point-to-point relationships between paired variables of the 'culture' and 'nature' variety" (1963, p. 10). All the elements in the ecological system are treated as interdependent variables in a dynamic process of change and adaptation through time, each acting as a constraint on the others, af-

---

ducted during field work. The figures cited for the Wakhi however are not based on any kind of systematic census by me or anyone else. The figure of 6,000 is my own estimate at the time of the research, based on observations and discussions in the field. Published population estimates by the government of Afghanistan cited in *A Provisional Gazetteer of Afghanistan*, 1975, 2: 717-19, based on the 1965 estimates of the Afghan ministeries of Agriculture and Interior (each with separate and independent estimates for different purposes), are as follows:

Ministry of Interior	
Kirghiz population estimate	801
Wakhi population estimate	3,492
Ministry of Agriculture	
Kirghiz	5,600
Wakhi	4,650

For a discussion of earlier estimates of Wakhi and Kirghiz population size and demographic processes in the area see chapter 2 of this book.

fecting their mode of organization and being affected by them in return. Furthermore, in this view of cultural ecological adaptation the role of blind selection processes characteristic of Darwinian evolution (what Boehm calls "teleonomic" adaptation), as well as "rational preselection" (characteristics of adaptation systems among some higher primates, including man) as mechanisms of adaptation are considered of equal significance (see Boehm 1978, pp. 265-96). Both teleonomic and purposive preselection processes are assumed to occur alongside one another in human adaptations.[2] Also, there is no question of any one factor in the ecosystem always determining or limiting the others. Instead, the aim is to explore how, given certain environmental conditions and modes of subsistence, the various components of an ecosystem are organized, how the system operates, how stable the system is, and through what processes such an order has been created and maintained (see Geertz 1963; Parsons 1960; Berrien 1968; and Boehm 1978).

No ecological process is fully comprehensible in a time vacuum. Arnold Schultz, a plant and animal ecologist, asserts that "in an ecosystem the elements are space-time units in that they [the components of an ecological system] occupy some volume in space for a certain length of time" (1969, p. 78). Therefore, for the purpose of this study, an historical perspective is adopted along with a cultural ecological framework, based on a belief that it is not possible to fully comprehend the nature, direction, and magnitude of the adaptive success or failure of any kind of systemic change unless the dynamic relationship among the parts within a system, as well as its relations within the larger complex, are assessed under different conditions at different times.

Within recent history, European colonial expansion brought changes that have had significant territorial, social, economic, and cultural consequences for many small communities (ethnic minorities

2. Christopher Boehm's critical essay "Rational Preselection from Hamadryas to *Homo Sapiens:* The Place of Decisions in Adaptive Process" (*American Anthropologist* 80, no. 2 [June 1978], 265-96) appeared at a time when most of this book was already in press. I find his argument on the role of purposive ("rational") preselection on the part of human communities both in instances of micro-decisions as well as long range adaptational and evolutionary processes very persuasive. I am certain the analysis of data in this work would have benefited greatly from it. However, I believe the material presented here lends support to Boehm's argument, although at times it may not be as explicitly stated as one would wish. I personally believe that rational purposive decisions or what Boehm calls "preselection concept" provides a clearer direction and precision to our understanding of the mechanisms of cultural ecological adaptation.

in particular) and for many larger national groups. This is primarily because *the new frontiers are no longer free and open zones* allowing socioeconomic and cultural exchanges between the communities straddled along them. Instead, they are marked by boundaries that are in most instances absolute, both in theory and in practice. This attribute of modern frontiers is taken for granted by frontier historians and political scientists and as a result their studies have been concerned largely with the foreign policies and the military and strategic defenses of the closed frontiers, and the conflicts and confrontations over territorial claims between nation-states (see, for example, Razvi 1971).

Little attention has been paid by either historians or social scientists to the sociological effects of territorial loss and/or confinement that result from arbitrarily drawn and closed borders upon the human communities concerned. Anthropologists have rarely studied the impact of the frontier phenomenon, either as an expanding and open geographical zone or as an area marked by a boundary that separates adjacent societies. Most anthropological studies done during the colonial period deal with cultural contact—diffusion and acculturation processes. The frontier in such studies has been viewed as having only a cultural dimension, and only rarely have its geographical, spatial, historic, and socioeconomic aspects been considered.

There is, consequently, much anthropological literature, both recent and old, on the social change rising from the contacts of cultures. What is still lacking are studies of the processes of change and adaptation where cultural contact has been severed, resulting in the dislocation of communities.

This study of the Kirghiz and Wakhi of Afghanistan is, therefore, an attempt to demonstrate that the effects of severance of sociocultural contact is as important as the establishment of new cultural contact. The argument in favor of examining the impact of closed frontiers is quite simple: that it too creates different ecological conditions and imposes constraints to which communities must adapt. It is hoped that exploration of sociological and adaptational processes of both small communities and larger national groups who live in cultural and economically strategic areas under new and changed frontier situations will draw some attention from anthropologists, as well as other social scientists.

One of the aims of this study, therefore, is to assess the impact of the external constraints that have influenced the *direction of change* in the processes of Kirghiz and Wakhi adaptation during the past several decades.

Leach has suggested that changes resulting from demographic, ecological, economic, and external political situations could be usefully categorized under two general types: (a) changes "which are consistent with the continuity of the existing formal order," and (b) changes reflecting "alterations in the formal structure" (1954, p. 5). The second type is also called "disjunctive change" and may take two general forms: disjunctive social structural change with or without accompanying cultural change; and disjunctive cultural change with or without social structural change (see Geertz 1957; Wallace 1956; Barth 1967; Keyes 1972). The time referent in this type of social and cultural change is always historical or irreversible and the nature of change is accumulative, not cyclical. One particular type of structural change without accompanying cultural change that is of theoretical significance for the purposes of this study is what is termed by Clifford Geertz (1963) *involution* (also Goldenweiser 1936).

The data indicates that the change the Kirghiz of Afghanistan have experienced in their adaptation efforts under the new conditions represents this involutionary social structural change. The direction is one in which a greater development and specialization within the existing adaptive pattern is pursued without radical transformation to a new form of subsistence system or accompanying cultural change. It is in this respect that I am tempted to call the present trend in the Kirghiz ecological adaptive processes a *pastoral nomadic involution*.

The use of a broad historical perspective and a multidimensional cultural ecological approach has made it possible to focus equally on a discussion of two interdependent processes: first, the changing processes of the temporal properties of the environmental constraints that the Kirghiz and the Wakhi have experienced; secondly, the organization of the temporal order of the Kirghiz and Wakhi adaptive responses to changing circumstances, and the cumulative consequences of such responses upon their systems of adaptation.

The Kirghiz social and cultural systems have shown a remarkable resilience in their response to the problems of territorial loss and confinement to high altitudes and to the severance of social, economic, and cultural ties. They have been able to retain a viable pastoral nomadic economy in the face of tremendous odds over the past several decades. The Kirghiz case further demonstrates that in the context of political developments in modern nation-states the direction of social change in a pastoral society need not be always toward an agricultural or urban way of life; the possibility of change within a pastoral regime exists and can provide a practical and successful alternative.

PART I.

SPACE, TIME, AND HUMAN COMMUNITIES

Above, crossing a pass on the trail to the Little Pamir; *below*, camel caravan on the winter route to the Pamirs; *preceding page*, fall camp in the Little Pamir.

1. The Ecological Setting

THE WAKHAN CORRIDOR and the Afghan Pamirs form the narrow finger of land extending eastward from Afghanistan. It touches the People's Republic of China (Sinkiang Province) in the east and is sandwiched between the Soviet Union (Tajik S.S.R.) in the north and Pakistan in the south. This stretch of Afghan territory lies within the confines of 71° 50' to 74° 50' degrees east longitude and 36° 35' to 37°30' degrees north latitude.

Some of the loftiest mountain ranges in the world meet in this area (Kunlun, Tien Shan, Karakoram, and Hindu Kush), creating the three important Asian watersheds—the Tarim basin in the east, the Amu Darya (Oxus) drainage in the west, and the Indus channel in the south. All of these watersheds have nourished important centers of civilization in the course of history.

The headwaters of one of these three major Asian drainage systems, that of the Amu Darya, lie within the area of the Afghan Pamirs and Wakhan. The Amu Darya is formed near the village of Gaz Khan where the Pamir River and the Sarhad (Wakhan) River join. These two rivers, the Pamir and the Sarhad, spring from the high plateau land that the inhabitants of this area refer to as *Bam-i-Dunya*—the "Roof of the World." The specific area with which we are concerned includes the territory to the south of the upper Amu Darya valley (also locally known as Darya-i-Panj), and the watershed areas of the two rivers that form the Amu Darya—the Sarhad and the Pamir (see map on end paper).

The Pamir River originates from the Zor Kol (Lake Victoria) in the Zor Pamir (Great Pamir). It was traced by John Wood of the British-Indian Army in 1838 to the Zor Kol, which he assumed to be the source of the Oxus River.[1] The Pamir River begins as an overflow of the Zor Kol from its western shores at an altitude of 4,130 meters (13,600 feet) above sea level. It runs a southwesterly course for about 100 kilometers, collecting a considerable amount of water from tributaries and developing swift currents in its descent of over 1,100 meters to its junction with the Sarhad River. The Pamir River marks the international boundary between the Soviet Union and Afghanistan from the point of its origin along its entire length. The Amu Darya continues to delineate the Afghan and Russian frontiers for some 1,100 kilometers along a west-southwest course before changing direction to the northwest, entering Russia to complete its run of 2,500 kilometers and discharging into the landlocked Aral Sea. The Zor Kol and the Pamir River serve as the principal drainage system for the Afghan as well as the Russian side of the Great Pamir plateau and the adjacent Nicholas II and Wakhan Massif (Selsela Koh-i-Wakhan).

The Sarhad River, which lies to the south of the Pamir River, is the longer and more voluminous of the two. It rises from the glacier melt streams west of the small Lake Chaqmaqtin Kol (also known as the Lake of the Little Pamir), which lies at an elevation of 4,020 meters above sea level in the Kechek Pamir (Little Pamir) plateau. The Sarhad River carries the discharge from many tributaries within the southwestern portion of the Little Pamir before its long passage through the narrow Darra gorge. Its bed becomes wide and meandering in certain places, such as near the Wakhi village of Sarhad, but generally it remains narrow, deep, and turbulent to the end of its 180-kilometer run.

The ecological significance of the upper Amu Darya and the two rivers that feed it within the Wakhan Corridor ecosystem differs from that of rivers elsewhere. Generally, the primary functions of rivers are provision of irrigation waters, fishing, and transportation, but these are not the functions of the three rivers in this area. Because of the mountain folds dominating this region, rivers mark the only low-altitude tracts suitable for cultivation and human habitation, and they and their numerous tributaries offer the easiest, and often the only, passage to both the resources available in the high pasturage and to the towns and cities of the plains beyond.

The altitude determines the different ecological conditions in the Wakhan Corridor and the Afghan Pamirs. Thus, on the basis of alti-

---

1. Later expeditions in the area proved, however, that Zor Kol was not *the* source of the river Oxus (or Amu Darya) but *a* source of it. For the account of Wood's journey to this area, which contains some very interesting information about the region at that time, see Wood (1841, 1872).

tude variations and the apparent differences in the type and nature of flora and fauna found in this region, two different ecological zones are identifiable: the lower altitude Wakhan[2] ecological zone and the high-altitude Pamir ecological zone.

THE WAKHAN ECOLOGICAL ZONE

Topography

The Wakhan ecological zone includes all the areas within the Afghan Wakhan where cultivation of crops is possible. It comprises the strip along the southern banks of the upper Amu Darya, between the hamlets of Putur in the west and Gaz Khan in the east where the Pamir and the Sarhad rivers join the Amu Darya. It also includes the territory within the confines of the Sarhad River valley from its mouth up to the village of Sarhad-i-Broghil. This stretch of land from west to east is about 160 kilometers long, and the elevation between the two points ranges from 2,770 meters at Putur to about 3,400 meters at Sarhad. Because sheer canyon walls along the Pamir River gorge offer little arable land, there are no Wakhi settlements along the Pamir River course beyond Gaz Khan.

The arable land on the southern banks of the upper Amu Darya valley is very limited. The width of the valley floor varies from a few meters to about two kilometers. From the south the Amu Darya valley is bounded by an impressive branch of the Hindu Kush range with peaks over 6,850 meters that separate the Afghan corridor from Pakistan. The mountain slopes facing the Amu Darya valley are incised by numerous narrow tributary ravines and dry washes, some of which lead into large glacier fields. The mountainsides are barren except for very sparse, hardy, mountain-desert plants dotting the rough terrain above the valley floor.

The valley floor along the Sarhad River is narrower than that of the Amu with the exception of the Sarhad-i-Broghil basin, where it opens up for some distance to a width of about two to three kilometers. The Hindu Kush range continues to the south, permitting no passage except for Broghil Pass at 3,804 meters, which is located directly to the south of Sarhad and leads to the area of Chitral and the upper Indus valley in Pakistan. The range to the north is the

2. The area of the upper Amu Darya and Transoxiana to the north are all referred to as Pamir as well as Wakhan in Soviet literature or Soviet-influenced writing about this region (see Luknitsky 1954, and the *New Encyclopaedia Britannica* 1974, 13:938-40). For the purposes of this study, however, the two areas are not the same and they refer to geographically and ecologically distinct areas.

Wakhan Massif (Selsela Koh-i-Wakhan), which separates the Wakhan proper from the Pamirs, as well as dividing the two Afghan Pamirs.

A Typology of Microenvironments

The Wakhan ecological zone, despite the variation of over 650 meters between the high and low elevation points, is ecologically uniform, which is reflected in the native categories of the significant microenvironments in this zone. This typology of the local environment by the inhabitants is expressed in terms each of which convey a particular bundle of ecologically significant features associated with a specific kind of area or a niche that is generally recognizable by all members of the society. The vocabulary of microenvironmental typology is a cultural way of organizing the physical setting to enable interpersonal communication as well as elucidating the interdependent relations of the people and the various environmental resources and constraints. Therefore, to understand the environmental conditions it is important to define the native terminology.

Jangal: This term (literally, *jungle* or *forest*) refers to the dense growths of stunted red willow (Salix), sea buckthorn, birch, wild rose, and hawthorn, which are found along the riverbanks. Such vegetation grows on the sand banks that intersperse the river bed when the river becomes sluggish. Dense undergrowth also grows along the banks of the numerous tributaries, especially near the delta if the gradient is gentle. The wood from these thickets is used mainly for fuel and building. Where the *jangal* is extensive and dense, it provides a likely sanctuary for hares, foxes, wolves, and numerous wildfowl. In areas where the underbrush is not so thick the *jangal* provides a favorable pasturage for domestic animals.

Dargaw and *sail:* *Dargaw* is the term used for a tributary, while *sail* refers to the numerous alluvial fans or cones formed at the mouth of each tributary ravine. Many of these alluvial fans are composed of boulders and large rocks transported by the streams during the annual summer floodings brought about by melting glacial ice and snow. These layers of alluvium are deepest at the mouth of steep tributary ravines. The size of the fan depends upon the volume and the velocity of the stream and the nature of the transported materials. The *sail* cover a great deal of the piedmonts and valley floor, claiming more land each year. These flood deposits, as well as being unproductive, hinder all forms of traffic and cause much inconvenience for the villagers, particularly during the summer. It is the silt-loaded turbid waters from the glacier-fed permanent tributary streams that are used for irrigation by the Wakhi cultivators, since the rivers are much lower than the fields and therefore not suitable as a source of irrigation.

Raig: The large tracts of sand found in several places on the valley floor. Great masses of sand are also found at the fringes of the alluvial fans as well as on the dried-up river bed, particularly where the river loses speed and becomes sluggish. Sandstorms are caused by these sand fields when caught by the devastating westerly wind, the *bad-i-Wakhan*, which prevails in the Wakhan Corridor most of the year. The severity of the combination of the *raig* and *bad-i-Wakhan* has been noted by most travelers. Olufsen stated that it "causes such blinding sand-storms that one can with difficulty see one's hand before one's face" (1969, p. 11, also see Wood 1872, p. 199; Montgomerie 1871, p. 157; Stein 1964, p. 271).

Maghzar: Marshy land covered with fine grass. *Maghzar* consists of soggy, poorly drained ground near ponds. It is created by seepage from the high mountain slopes and covered with a mat of fine grass. Such areas are found along the riverbanks, particularly where the water has overflowed natural levees and left the nearby flats as marshy land. Small patches of *maghzar* are also common near the delta of sluggish tributaries. It provides a portion of winter fodder and is the prized pasturage of cattle and horses.

Kesht gah: Land under cultivation. Agricultural fields are generally located within close proximity to permanent tributary streams. Such arable tracts are usually found on the narrow mountain terraces that fringe the sides of the valley, and on the sides of the alluvial fans that often extend to the outlying *maghzar* patches. The fields consist of cleared and terraced plots or paddies of varying sizes, irrigated by an elaborate network of ditches.

Irrigation water is diverted for as much as three or four kilometers from permanent streams high above arable land and sluiced into the fields along the mountain spurs above the alluvial fans. Dry farming at this altitude is not possible, therefore building and maintaining the irrigation networks is absolutely necessary and requires a great deal of time and labor annually to keep the channels in good repair. The porous nature of the thin, sandy topsoil requires adequate moisture during the brief growing season, which also necessitates irrigation. It should also be pointed out that sediment from the snow- and glacier-melt floodwaters used for irrigation is quite rich in minerals, and is very beneficial to the crops. No record of total acreage under

cultivation is available. I would estimate, however, that the *keśht
gah* accounts for less than 10 percent of the area of the valley floors
and a very nominal amount of the total land surface of the Wakhi
territory.

Dasht: Desert, referring to areas within the valley that are potentially
arable but are barren because of distance from streams or insufficient available water. These areas are thinly covered with various
types of hardy desert shrubs upon which the livestock feed and
which are also collected for kindling and fuel by the villagers. These
waste lands are generally located on the sides of alluvial fans.

Koh: Literally, mountain. The ecological significance of the mountains that dominate the area lies in the snow- and glacier-covered
peaks that feed the tributary streams. Otherwise, the mountains
have very sparse vegetation that changes with increasing elevation
from mountain-desert flora to mountain drought-resistant plants,
then to mountain-steppe vegetation. These mountain pastures are
little used for grazing domestic livestock by the Wakhi of this zone.
However, they provide sufficient grazing ground for native ruminants
such as alpine ibex and the Marco Polo sheep *(Ovis poli)*, the world's
most prized trophy.

Among the various microenvironmental types discussed, the area
offering essential resources for human society accounts for less than
15 percent of the valley floors (approximately 300 square
kilometers), and a much smaller fraction of the total land surface
(approximately 4,000 square kilometers) in this ecological zone.
The type and nature of resources are influenced by the rugged topography, high elevation, and the severe climate.

Climate, Domestic Plants, and Animals

The climate of Wakhan is arid and continental, marked by great
differences in seasonal and diurnal temperatures. There is no systematic meteorological information available, but precipitation
is generally low, and rarely in the form of rain. The higher mountain slopes receive a greater amount of snowfall than does the valley
floor.

Because of the general east-west orientation of the main valleys
of the Amu Darya and Sarhad, both sides of the valleys are exposed
to direct sunlight during most of the daylight hours. In the numerous
deep and narrow north-south oriented side ravines, however, the
sunlight cannot penetrate except for a short period of about one

hour each day. This uneven exposure of the land surface to the only source of heat, the sun, has a tremendous influence upon the atmospheric conditions within the confined valley environment. One of the common results is the mountain winds that sweep with sudden gusts down the valleys. In the afternoons whirlwinds fill the air with dust and sand, particularly during the summer and fall.

Most areas of the two valleys are also continually afflicted by the dreadful *bad-i-Wakhan*. During the summer and fall this wind causes great sand and dust storms, while during the winter it adds to the severity of the blizzards.

Change in the weather conditions is abrupt. Sudden marked changes of temperature between day and night and light and shade cause rocks to crack, and the loose deposits of slate to crumble into dust. This, together with other erosive elements such as melting snow and ice, avalanches, rock falls, and turbulent mountain streams, are the principal forces shaping the microenvironmental features in the area that are described earlier.

Spring and summer are short in the Wakhan. Snow melts during April and May and by early June and July the valley oases are dotted with green fields. The vegetation in the area lasts for about four months—May through August. Daytime summer temperatures of 30° to 40°C. during July and August are not uncommon. During these months the land and air are dry and warm with a very high solar radiation effect. In the shade and in the evenings it is cool and comfortable.

Fall begins in September, when thick clouds and snowstorms appear in the high mountain peaks and occasional rain falls in the valley. By November the storms descend into the valleys and the long winter sets in. Thick clouds swirl around the mountains for most of the winter, with light snow accompanied by gusty, westerly winds in the valleys, and only occasional clear, frosty weather. Whatever snow falls on the valley floor is usually quickly blown away by the wind. This cold, desolate condition sometimes lasts until the end of May. The winter temperatures during the night fall as low as 25° C. to 30° C. below zero, while the daytime temperatures generally remain at about 15° C. below zero (see Olufsen 1969, pp. 50-55).

The domesticated plants that can be raised under these conditions are limited. They include a local variety of wheat, *gandem-i-safedak*, *kaljow* (or gymnospermous barley), *patuk* (lupine), *mojuk* (lentil), *baqla* (horsebeans or *Faba sutiva*), *arzen* (millet), *zaghir* (flax), yellow tobacco, and some alfalfa and clover for hay. The Wakhi do not grow any vegetables, although recently some non-Wakhi settlers from out-

side the corridor have found potatoes to thrive in the area; the only
fruit-bearing tree is apricot. There are a number of poplars and willows
along the streams and irrigation ditches that provide wood for building
and, to some extent, fuel. The domestic beasts herded here are goats,
a small native dwarf sheep called *gadek*, donkeys, horses, yak, common cattle, Bactrian camels, and a few dromedaries.

Communication

The Wakhan Corridor is connected to the provincial city of
Faizabad in Badakhshan and to the rest of the country by a dirt
motor-vehicle road that terminates at the village of Qala-i-Panja
near the eastern extremity of the upper Amu Darya. There is no
regularly scheduled truck service into the area, and the use of this
road is sporadic, limited to vehicles hauling supplies for traders and
government agencies. Hamlets beyond Qala-i-Panja are connected by
narrow trails, suitable only for pack animals and foot traffic. The
trail system, although very old and regularly used, remains dangerous
and hard to navigate. A single telephone line connects the government
border patrol posts along the Amu Darya as far as Gaz Khan. Work
was underway as of September 1975 to extend this line to link the
last government post in Sarhad-i-Broghil, which is also the last Wakhi
settlement in the corridor.

Social services are either very poor or nonexistent. There is only
one coeducational primary school (first through sixth grade) at the
District Center (Khandud) and six village schools (first through third
grade) in the entire District of Wakhan. There is no permanent medical
or health-related service of any kind. The nearest medical center,
which is poorly staffed and supplied, located in Ishkashim in the
adjacent district, is not easy for most people in the area to reach.

THE PAMIR ECOLOGICAL ZONE

Geography

This ecological zone consists of the Afghan Pamirs located to the
north and northeast of the Sarhad River valley, well above the altitudes of agricultural production. The Afghan Pamirs are a very
small portion of the high, flat-surfaced areas created by a combination
of east-west and north-south ranges that dominate this region. This
series of high valleys is known among the Kirghiz as *onder,* and
thirteen inhabited *onderlar* (plural form) are recognized in the area,
each referred to by a specific name. The Afghan Pamirs consist of

only about half of the area of two *onderlar* known as Pamir Onderi and Aqsu Onderi. The rest of the named Pamirs lie in Soviet Tajikistan and in Sinkiang in the People's Republic of China.[3]

Pamir Onderi is also referred to as Chung or Zor Pamir (the Great Pamir) signifying its relatively higher altitude in relation to other *onderlar*. The Great Pamir has a general east-west orientation, with the southern Alchur Range (Yuzhno-ali-Chursky Khrebet) and the Wakhan Massif forming the north and south rim respectively of this high valley. Both of these ranges draw close together in the west, forming a passage to the Pamir River (the only drainage system of this *onder*) through a deep, narrow defile, which also connects it with the upper Amu Darya valley and beyond. The eastern outline of the Great Pamir is defined by the small spurs from both the northern and southern ranges, which form a low saddle. This low saddle separates the Great Pamir from Qezyl Rabat and the north-south extension of the Aqsu Onderi. It should be pointed out that only the area to the south of Lake Zor Kol and the Pamir River is part of the Afghan Great Pamir, that to the north belongs to Soviet Russia.

Aqsu Onderi consists of two sections with different orientations. The small east-west oriented portion of it belongs to Afghanistan and is commonly called Kechek Pamir (Little Pamir). It is delineated in the north and west by the Wakhan mountain range, which also separates it from the Great Pamir. To the south it is hemmed in by the parallel Hindu Kush range, which forms the borders between Afghanistan and Pakistan and also China. This section of Aqsu Onderi runs into a huge barrier, the Sarikol range in the east, behind which lie the Chinese Pamirs. This north-south mountain range, which forms the international boundary between Afghanistan and China as well as China and Russia, dictates the orientation of the second and greater part of the Aqsu Onderi, which lies in Soviet territory.

Topography and Microenvironmental Features

The distinguishing feature of the Pamir ecological zone is the ele-

3. Pamirs, although often referred to as plateau or tableland, are not in fact so in the true sense of the word. They are more high intermountain plateaulike valleys hemmed in by parallel mountain ranges, to which the Kirghiz assign the appellation *onder*. Aside from the Pamir and Aqsu *onderi* there are other named high valleys such as Alchur, Aratesh, Qosh Aghel, Qara Choqor, Taghdumbash, Tagharma, Qara-Kol, Su-Bashi, Bolan Kol, Choqor-Aghel Kon-Teybus, Moujo Qeyaq Bashi, and Tashkurghan. These are the names remembered and recognized for all the Pamirs in the area. Colonel Etherton mentions the existence of eight Pamirs, but only names a few (see Etherton 1925, pp. 25-26; Younghusband 1896, pp. 291-305).

vation. Although the mountain ranges average about 5,450 meters above sea level, the peaks surrounding the valleys often do not exceed 1,000 to 1,500 meters above the valley floor. The mountain ranges forming the Afghan Pamirs generally have rounded contours, while the peaks of the Hindu Kush range, which forms the southern outline, are sharp and serrated, enclosing many amphitheatrelike depressions with steeply rising faces, created by glacial plucking. Glaciers also lie in the mountain slopes and ravine depressions of this range at altitudes of above 5,000 meters.

The Afghan Great Pamir *onderi* is some sixty kilometers long and topographically it is the more rugged of the two Afghan Pamirs. It is comprised of a series of both large and small *jelga* (narrow tributary valleys) interspersed by *sert* (high flat or low gradient ground between two tributary streams). These *jelgalar* are generally long and the difference in elevation at the inhabitable upper areas and the confluence may vary from 300 to 700 meters, ending with a brief flat basin near the Pamir River and the branches of the Zor Kol. On the other hand, Aqsu Onderi, which consists of both sides of the approximately one hundred-kilometer long valley, has a rather wide (up to ten kilometers) and relatively flat basin and shorter *jelgalar*, with the exception of Wakhjir *jelga*. Wakhjir *jelga* was known to early travelers and merchants traveling with the long caravans into China because of its accessible pass (elevation 4,922 meters) of the same name. The U-shaped valley floor is dotted with a large number of glacier-fed lakes, Chaqmaqtin Kol being the largest of them, nine by two kilometers at its widest. Chaqmaqtin Kol is also located at the crest of the Little Pamir valley bottom and its overflow drains into the Aqtash stream to the east. It delineates the two sides of the Aqsu Onderi. The northern section of the valley (i.e., the sunny face) is referred to as *kongey* and the southern portion of it (the shady face) as *terskey*. The watershed areas are known to the occupants as *suni boyi*. Each of the three, *kongey*, *terskey*, and *suni boyi*, signifies a specific type of microenvironmental system that is used respectively as the winter, summer, and spring/fall camping grounds by the inhabitants of the Pamirs.

The surface of the Pamirs' valley floor is covered with various formations of alluvial and glacial deposits. Of these, the most conspicuous are the morainal ridges and numerous small, rounded hills and irregularly shaped and sized mounds of glacial drift with their adjacent depressions, which are distributed throughout much of the area of these high plains. This kind of gently graded but rough surface is further scarred by ravines and dry channels created by the tributary streams, which also produce narrow alluvial terraces and flats along their courses. Some of these flats are salt fields while others are covered with fine alpine meadows. Both are significant to the ecology of the Kirghiz, since one provides prized pasturage while the other satisfies the needs of animals and some poorer human inhabitants for the otherwise scarce salt.

Climate

Climatically, the Pamirs are arid and continental. Cold air is retained within the confined basins, while the high mountain barriers intercept the moist air currents. This is particularly true in the Little Pamir because of its higher and more completely encircling mountain range, and its annual precipitation is lower than that of the Great Pamir area. Annual precipitation is estimated between six and twelve centimeters, and the depth of the snow blanket reaches five to twelve centimeters. The air circulation is mixed, with more persistent northwesterly cyclonic and less frequent southern monsoonal air currents roaming this area. During the winter months the continuous northwesterly wind blows the snow from *kongey*, transporting it to the *terskey* side of the valley. The winter pastures are thus left clear of snow, but the continuous wind adds to the extreme harshness of the winter.

T. G. Montgomerie, an officer with the Great Trigonometrical Survey of India, gives a very graphic account of winter conditions in the Little Pamir in his "Report of the Mirza . . . ". This report is based on the account of the Mirza, who was one of Montgomerie's "native" agents who crossed the area on his way to Chinese Turkistan in the winter of 1869:

Though the Mirza and his men were all well supplied with warm clothing—their bodies being encased in woollen chogas, and sheepskin posteen or coats, their heads in fur caps, and their feet in two pairs of long woollen stockings, and their boots filled with wool—they nevertheless felt the cold very much . . . the intenseness of the cold was extreme whenever the wind blew, and they then felt as if they were going to lose their extremities, the glare from the snow was very trying to the eyes, all suffering from snow blindness; their breath froze on their moustaches, and every one moreover had to walk in order to keep some warmth in the body. . . . [1871, p. 160]

In the Pamirs only two seasons are distinguishable, winter and spring *cum* summer. Winters are cold, severe, and very long (mid-September to late June). The temperatures are as low as -50° C. and below zero for most of the year. Summers are short (late June to early September) with temperatures reaching 30° C., but the possibility of early morning frost is always present throughout these months. Thus, with the high solar radiation, the diurnal temperatures alternate between burning and freezing, ranging on the average from around 20° to 40° C., depending upon the season, cloud cover, and the presence or absence of wind.[4] The total vegetation growing period is 100 to 120 days.

Flora, Fauna, Hypoxia

Vegetation in the Pamirs is generally poor. Much of the land surface is covered with rocks or loose debris and rubble. Within the inhabited altitudes (4,400 to about 5,000 meters) no woody vegetation exists. There are, however, some copses of dwarf willow, birch, sea buckthorn and hawthorn found along the river gorges up to altitudes of 4,000 meters. There is also some juniper *(archa)* scattered over a small area of the steep northern slope of the Darra gorge along the Sarhad River. Vegetation in the Pamir plateaus proper is restricted to low-growing plants that are adapted to severe conditions. These include the various forms of native and Central Asian drought- and cold-resistant mountain steppe vegetation. In the dry mountain slopes of the *kongey* grow low shrubs of sagebrush (locally known as *shewagh* and *tersken*). Apart from supplying good feed for sheep and goats, these plants when uprooted make the only brush fuel found in this area. The vegetation on the valley floor, especially the *terskey* side of the valley, includes the Pamir tansy, a local species of wormwood, the bulbous iris, low-lying cushion plants, and alpine meadow grasses. Areas that are sufficiently moist, for example those near lakes, ponds, streams, or with irrigation, are covered with a thick, tall growth of sedges and cobresia. There are also large, thick peat bogs, particularly in the *terskey* and watershed of the Little Pamir plateau. These peat bogs usually form behind crescent-shaped morain ridges, the convex of which faces downstream, serving as a dam for shallow reservoirs filled by sediment and accumulated decaying vegetation. When these bogs are not too soggy they provide good pasturage, particularly for horses, and when the peat is cut and dried it is one of the main sources of fuel.

The Afghan Pamirs' fauna is not abundant. The wild animals include Marco Polo sheep *(Ovis poli)*, mountain goat, the large-eared Tibetan wolf, brown bear, the long-tailed marmot, and hare. The few birds are the Tibetan mountain turkey, snow vulture, eagle, and a few migratory waterfowl that inhabit the lakes during the summer months. The number of domesticated beasts is also limited,

---

4. Luknitsky notes a temperature fluctuation recorded in the Bash Gumbaz Pass in the Soviet Pamirs on 9 July 1934 as follows: 1:00 p.m. 33°C., 4:00 p.m. -6.4° C. The lowest temperature recorded was -51.2° C. (see 1954, p. 233).

because of the marginal ecological conditions. The flocks and herds of the pastoralist inhabitants comprise Central Asian fat-tailed sheep, long-haired goats, yak, and Bactrian double-humped camels. Horses are kept, but they cannot be bred in the Pamirs. About ten donkeys and perhaps a dozen chickens are in the area; their number is limited because they are also unable to breed at that altitude.

The main reason given by the inhabitants for their inability to breed horses, the mount and pack animals required in the pursuit of their normal livelihood activities, is the effects of "thin air." This phenomenon is referred to by the natives as *tutak* or mountain sickness and its effects may be clearly felt by the traveler in the Pamirs. The symptoms of high altitude sickness (hypoxia), are severe headaches, high pulse rate, nausea, short-windedness and sometimes insomnia. These symptoms may be suffered by anyone, even the ac-climatized inhabitant who engages in any activity that demands even a small amount of physical exertion.

The two major environmental constraints prevailing in both the Wakhan and the Pamir ecological zones are the cold and the effects of high altitude—hypoxia. "According to Humlum (1959, p. 17) 82.9 percent of the Wakhan-Pamir area is above 10,000 feet (3,000 meters), and 17.1 percent between 6,000 and 10,000 feet (1,800 to 3,000 meters)" (quoted in Dupree 1973, p. 6). These factors limit the type and nature of biotic resources in the area that are essen-tial for the sustenance of human society. Human groups inhabiting the two ecological zones exhibit adaptive responses to the stresses of cold, hypoxia, and the varying degrees of isolation, both culturally and physiologically. Although I recognize the importance of the human physiological responses to these physical environmental con-straints, I am not able to discuss them in any detail.[5]

Communication

Distance and accessibility into and out of the Afghan Pamirs at the present time is significant in the ecological adaptation of the peoples of the Afghan Pamirs. The area is linked by a system of dangerous trails. The tracks always follow the frequently circuitous courses of rivers and usually involve traveling on the edge of precipi-tous mountain ridges and trails built into the side of hanging cliffs

5. Although research on hypoxia in continental Asia is nil, the Andean high-altitude adaptation studies provide a great deal of information on physiological adaptation of humans and animals to high altitudes. See the following Andean studies: Baker and Weiner 1966; Baker et al. 1965, 1968; Monge 1948; Monge and Monge 1966; Van Liere and Stickney 1963; Weihe 1962; and McClung 1969.

more than a hundred feet above the swollen rivers. When, at several points, the riverbanks are impassable, it becomes necessary to make a steep zig-zag ascent and descent of high passes over 550 to 900 meters above the valley floor. Although there are several suspension bridges it is also necessary at times to ford icy streams.

The road to the Great Pamir, although not easy, is not as dangerous as the route to the Little Pamir. It is possible to travel to the Great Pamir year round without serious threat of being stranded along the trails. It takes five to seven days to complete the journey, a distance of little over 100 kilometers, involving a gradual ascent of over 1,500 meters from Khandud in the upper Amu Darya area to the Great Pamir.

The trails to the Little Pamir are always harder to cover. The best time to travel is during the winter months when the smooth, frozen Sarhad River bed can be used as the highway. This is not possible, however, for more than three to four months and then there is always the danger of thin ice, ice bridges giving way, or the threat of avalanches. Movement is also restricted in late fall and early spring, when the passes are closed because of heavy snow. In spring it is not possible to ford the river because it is swollen by melting ice, while in fall the ice sheet on the river is not thick enough to support passage (see Stein 1964, pp. 41-42, and Montgomerie 1871, pp. 157-60).

The summer trip to the Little Pamir involves the negotiation of a series of high passes (Dahliz, Toquz Bash, and Marpech). A journey from Khandud to the Little Pamir takes eight to twelve days, covering a distance of less than 200 kilometers and an ascent of over 1,500 meters.[6]

The physical environmental stresses and limitations have had a remarkable influence upon the social, demographic, and political-historical processes in the area, and consequently upon the cultural ecological adaptive responses of the human communities to the total environmental constraints.

6. The possibility of extending a telephone line and constructing a small air strip in the Little Pamir was being considered by the Afghan government authorities at the time of this research. However, no positive plan of action has as yet been taken toward these goals. The only air traffic in the area has been an occasional rescue mission for an injured foreign hunter in the state-run Marco Polo sheep reserve in the Great Pamir. Establishment of air services to the Pamirs is feasible but the effects of hypoxia upon the air travelers and the unpredictable weather have to be given thorough consideration.

Left, bridge over tributary of Sarhad river; *right*, descent to Sarhad via Dahliz Pass.

Elderly Wakhi

Kirghiz portrait

2. History and Demographic Process

THE SOCIOPOLITICAL HISTORY and demographic processes in the Wakhan Corridor and the Afghan Pamirs are dominated by two significant and interconnected factors—the geographical location and imposing topography of the Pamirs and the use of the corridor as a highway of trade and communication. The Pamirs were described by Sir Aurel Stein half a century ago as follows:

It [the mountain barrier formed by the Pamirs] joins the Tien Shan on the north to the ice-clad Hindu Kush on the south, and was known already to the Ancients by the name of *Imaos*. Ptolemy in the Geography quite correctly describes it as the range dividing the two Scythias, *intra* and *extra Imaon*. These terms closely correspond to the Inner and Outer Tartary of our grandfathers' geography and to the more appropriate one of Russian Turkistan and Chinese Turkistan of our own . [1925, p. 380]

The Pamirs not only divided western and eastern Turkistan, but for many centuries also kept apart several ancient, thriving cultural centers in India, Southwest Asia, the Near East, and Europe, denying them contact with the ever-flourishing Chinese cultural centers to the east. Yet, the geographical and historical significance of the Pamirs and their primary drainage channel, the Amu Darya valley, exists because they could be crossed, allowing the exchange of cultural influences between these distant regions of the world for more than a millennium.

This area was a highway for traders, political emissaries, invading armies, refugees, pilgrims, explorers, adventurers, missionaries, and travelers long before the Christian era, and served as such until a few decades ago. These wayfarers, with many diverse goals, have included individuals and groups from China as well as from the West. In this long and arduous historic process the Wakhan Corridor and the Afghan Pamirs have served as a means of achieving many ends, but rarely has the area been the end in itself. The historic process in this region has involved the discovery of an ancient strategic passageway, its establishment, expansion over many centuries, and its recent abrupt closure.

HISTORY

From Early Times to 1800

During the pre-Christian era the existence of a Chinese civilization was unknown to the centers of Western culture. However, there is evidence that journeys were made across the massive mountain plateau barriers from both the east and the west during that period. From the west, for example, the army of Alexander the Great is believed to have approached Kashgar in the Tarim River Basin to the east of the Pamirs, and controlled it for a short time (see Dabbs 1963, p. 11).

The Chinese *Annals* show that in 1000 B.C. or thereabouts a member of the Chou dynasty made a journey to visit the eastern watershed areas of the Pamirs, in the region of Khotan (see Sykes 1933, p. 20). It was not until about the third century B.C., following the unification of the Chinese Empire and the construction of the Great Wall that the Chinese Empire pushed westward, thereby diverting the westward migration of various northern tribes to Central Asia. To cite an example of this:

. . . in the second century B.C., . . . the Huns attacked and drove out the Yue-chi [Yüeh-chih], an Iranian tribe which inhabited the Kansu province . . . thereby setting in motion a series of human avalanches. The Yue-chi crossed the Gobi to Kucha, and in their turn drove the Sakae from Kashgar [a town in Chinese Turkistan] in 163 B.C. and settled in their place, while the Sakae occupied Bactria [Balkh and Badakhshan in northern Afghanistan], driving its Greek dynasty across the Hindu Kush. [Ibid., pp. 20-21]

The Chinese emperors remained preoccupied with protecting the empire from the neighboring Huns. It was the reign of

the Great Han Emperor Wuti [Wu Ti] (140-87 B.C.) [that led] to the Chinese conquest of the northern slopes of the Nan Shan. The almost inevitable sequel of this again was the policy of Central-Asian expansion which more than two thousand years ago first opened the route along Sulo Ho to Loulan and thus into the Tarim basin . [Stein 1925, p. 396]

Distrust of the Huns led Emperor Wu Ti to dispatch a young

Chinese officer, Chang Ch'ien, on a Central Asian mission in about 138 B.C. (see Lattimore 1968, pp. 22-35; and Mirsky 1964, pp. 13-25). Chang Ch'ien was instructed to seek military and political help from the Yüeh-chih[1] kingdom on the Amu Darya in a fight against their common enemy, the Huns. After an absence of thirteen years Chang Ch'ien returned to the Tarim Basin, but had failed to secure military help. Nevertheless, his mission opened a new era in Chinese relations with the rest of the world to the west. He returned with ample information about the Central Asian countries he had passed through, telling of "the rich territories corresponding to the present Farghana, Samarqand, Bukhara and Balk, as well as about the still more distant regions of Persia and India" (Stein 1925, p. 398).

The potential for trade and military aid was soon realized by Emperor Wu Ti, who strongly favored expansion towards Central Asia. By 115 B.C., as a result of several military campaigns against the Huns, the Chinese emperor had secured, in Sir Aurel Stein's words, "nature's true highway towards the Tarim basin and the Oxus region" (ibid.). This military advance was soon followed by the organization and dispatch of Chinese political emissaries to the various states in the Tarim Basin, and as far west as Bactria and Persia. Based on Chinese historical records preserved from this period, Sir Aurel Stein has concluded that

the great westward move initiated by the Emperor Wu Ti was directed quite as much by political aims as by economic considerations connected with trade. No doubt the development of China's internal resources which the Han dynasty had from its foundation taken care to foster, made it very important that the route which Chang Ch'ien's pluck and persistence had opened should be used to secure direct access to fresh markets for China's industrial products, and in particular the most valuable among them, its silk textiles. [Ibid., p. 399]

This combination of military, political, and economic effort on the part of the Chinese Empire in its Central Asian expansion policies led to the opening and establishment of a remarkable network of land routes connecting China to many distant centers of civilization in the West. The ancient network of caravan routes

ran around the rim of the Taklamakan [desert] like a loop of string, on which the oases hung like beads. Historically, the first line of communication is that known as the Silk Road. It ran from the western point of Kansu toward Lob Nor and then along the foot of K'unlun all the way to Khotan, Yarkand, and Kashgar. Later the Chinese began to open up communication with the oases north of the Taklamakan. . . .

1. The Yüeh-chih, also known as Indo-Scythians, were a tribal group living on the northern slopes of the Nan Shan until about 160 B.C., when they were driven out by the Huns. The Yüeh-chih moved west and established a new kingdom in the Amu Darya region (for further details see Stein 1925; also cf. Grousset 1970, pp. 26-29).

[The road] . . . north of the Taklamakan ran east and west the whole
length of the southern foot of the Tien Shan, from Hami [Qomul] to Kashgar,
and was accordingly known to the Chinese as the Tien Shan Nan Lu, the Road
South of the Tien Shan. At Kashgar it converged with the Silk Road, thus closing
the loop around the Taklamakan. From Kashgar a pass traversed the mountains westward [i.e., the Pamirs] to the oasis region of Ferghana, Khokand, and Samarkand,
in the south of Russian Turkistan of today, and thence in turn roads led to Persia
and the whole Near East. [Lattimore 1951, pp. 172-73. See map on p. 23]

After the convergence of the Tien Shan Nan Lu and the Silk
Road[2] at Kashgar, there were at least two alternative routes in use
across the Pamirs to the Amu Darya region and beyond. The first
route was directly due west from Kashgar across the Pamirs to the
Karategin, Fergana, and Kokand oases in Russian Turkistan mentioned by Lattimore. The second route was due south and west
from Kashgar and west southwest of Yarkand. The road from both
of these two cities converged at Tashkurghan, the nearest town
to the Afghan Pamirs and the Wakhan in Chinese Turkistan. Speaking
of roads passing through Tashkurghan, over a century ago T. G.
Montgomerie wrote, "Tashkurghan commands the roads from Badakhshan and Chitral to Kokhan [Kokand], Yarkand and Kashgar, and
is still considered a place of importance" (1871, p. 163). Therefore,
it is the southwestern branch of the Silk Road passing through Tashkurghan that is of significance for our purposes.

The strategic trade roads referred to by Montgomerie passed
through the Little Pamir and the Great Pamir area and the Sarhad
and upper Amu Darya valleys of Wakhan. The specific routes taken
by travelers depended upon their destination—that is, Chitral, Badakhshan, or other parts of Afghanistan, as well as on the season.[3] The
stretch of the Silk Road that lies within the Wakhan and the Afghan
Pamirs has been described as " 'the most direct thoroughfare' [which]

2. For extensive information concerning the Silk Road route, the geographic
factors affecting its course, establishment, and control in ancient times, see Stein
1912, 1925, 1928, 1964; Sven Hedin 1938; Grousset 1970.

3. From my own discussion with several merchants who had traveled this
stretch of the Silk Road from Badakhshan to Chinese Turkistan, I learned that the
travelers who took the road across Wakhjir Pass to enter the Little Pamir did not
always continue down the Sarhad River valley on their way to Chitral. The road
between Langar and Sarhad through the Darra gorge is especially difficult and
during most of the year it is dangerous. Therefore, after crossing the Wakhjir Pass
valley travelers turned northeast into the main portion of the Aqsu Onderi and
crossed the Andamin Pass (5,000 meters) into the Great Pamir area and followed
the Pamir River to the upper Amu Darya. People who entered the Little Pamir
across the Sarikol Range near Aktash proceeded directly to the Great Pamir over
what Lord Dunmore (1893a, p. 392) called the "Fox Pass."

It should be pointed out, however, that this easy march from the Little Pamir
to the Great Pamir is no longer possible since the passage between the Andamin
Pass and the Great Pamir area of Afghanistan lies in Soviet territory.

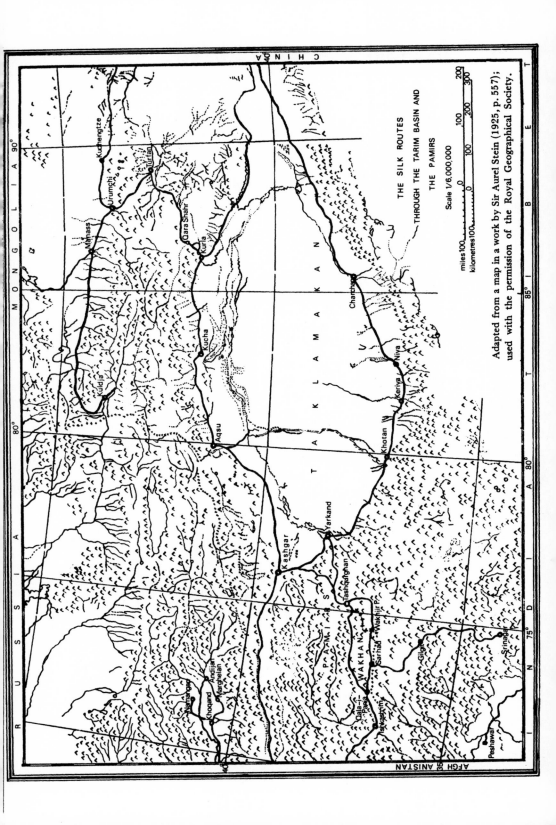

THE SILK ROUTES

THROUGH THE TARIM BASIN AND

THE PAMIRS

Scale 1/6,000,000

Adapted from a map in a work by Sir Aurel Stein (1925, p. 557);
used with the permission of the Royal Geographical Society.

has been used from very early times for communication between
settled areas of northern Afghanistan (Balkh) and those of the modern Chinese Turkistan" (Minorsky, 1929, p. 1103).

There is no doubt that for centuries this direct route was used
frequently, particularly during the immediate period following its
discovery and establishment by the Chinese.[4] However, early travelers
left little or no information about the people they met and the areas
they passed through. The earliest available information about the
area of Wakhan and the Pamirs was recorded by the famous Chinese
Buddhist pilgrim, Hsüan Tsang, who after fifteen years of travel
and study in India and Afghanistan returned to China in 644 A.D.
"with 657 sacred Buddhist books and 150 holy relics" (Dabbs 1963,
p. 13).[5] This famous Buddhist master passed through Takharistan
and Badakhshan and the Po-mi-lo (or the Pamir) and left us with the
earliest recorded description of the Pamirs.

The valley of Pamir is about a thousand *li*[6] from east to west, and a hundred
li from south to north. It is situated between two snowy mountains. The cold is
glacial, and the wind furious. Snow falls even in spring and summer, day and
night the wind rages. Grain and fruit cannot grow there, and trees are few and
far between. In the middle of the valley is a large lake, situated in the center
of the world on a plateau of prodigious height.[7] [Quoted in Sykes 1933, p. 29]

During this same period the Nestorian and Manichaean missions,
and later representatives of Mazdaism, reached Turkistan and even
China. These Iranian based religions were widely accepted in the
area and continued to be upheld until the establishment of Islam
(see Barthold 1956, p. 9; Dabbs 1963, p. 14).

The Chinese Empire, prior to Hsüan Tsang's journey to India,
had adopted a policy of exclusion towards Central Asia. However,
by 660 A.D. they had begun westward expansion. This new policy
resulted in the subjugation of Western Turks and the colonization of

4. For further information on the history of early explorations using the ancient
overland Silk Road, see Sykes 1933; Cary and Warmington 1929; works by Skrine
and Ross, 1899, on Russian Central Asia; and Dabbs 1963 on Chinese Turkistan
(contains extensive bibliography), all of which are particularly useful.

5. For more complete information on Hsüan Tsang's travels see Stein 1919,
pp. 265-77; Grousset 1970, pp. 118-20.

6. According to Sykes there are three *li* to a mile (1933, p. 29), but Stein reckons
about five *li* to a mile (1922, p. 120). *Webster's New International Dictionary* (Un-
abridged, 2nd ed.) defines *li* as a Chinese measure of distance equal to about 1,900
feet, that is, about three *li* per mile.

7. On the basis of a number of marches Hsüan Tsang had made to reach the
Pamirs from the upper Oxus valley, and his general description of the part of the
Pamirs he had passed through, it is clear that he had taken up the route along the
Pamir River to Zor Kol in the Great Pamir, and crossed the Sarikol Range to
Kashgar and Khotan in the Tarim Basin.

their vast domain from the Altai mountains to areas south of the Hindu Kush mountains.

For a number of reasons this expansion of Chinese power in Central Asia soon caused problems for the empire. First, the Turkic people in the newly acquired territories continually disrupted the peaceful use of the trade routes. Second, Muslim armies were advancing rapidly from the west. Finally, the Tibetans from the south had become a fresh and strong threat to Chinese domination. Sir Aurel Stein wrote that toward the middle of the eighth century

The Tibetans were endeavoring to join hands with the Arabs as common foes of China's Central-Asian supremacy. By pushing down the Indus valley and thence across the Hindu Kush territories corresponding to the present Gilgit and Yasin they actually reached the uppermost Oxus valley. This junction threatened the Chinese position in the Tarim basin with being outflanked simultaneously both in the east and west. . . . [Stein 1925, p. 493]

In the year 747 A.D., in order to put an end to the Tibetan challenge, a Chinese force of ten thousand men, led by General Kao Hsien-chih, engaged in an ambitious and unprecedented campaign that took the Chinese force from Kashgar through Taghdumbash Pamir across the Wakhjir Pass and the Little Pamir to the Hu-mi, or Wakhan, in the uppermost Amu Darya. Sir Aurel Stein has noted the accomplishments of this military expedition:

After effecting a successful concentration at Sarhad, the highest habitable point in Wakhan, Kao Hsienchih completely defeated the Tibetan force which was guarding the Broghil, the only pass across the Hindu Kush practicable for military purposes in this region. [Ibid.][8]

This impressive victory by the Chinese did not give them permanent Chinese control of the region, for only two years later at the city of Tashkent they faced a complete defeat at the hands of the Muslim invading armies and their allies, the rebellious Turkic tribes.

Chinese influence in the Tarim Basin soon gave way to Tibetan rule for almost a century, and thereafter the Turkic tribes in the area took charge of the region. From the ninth to the twelfth century the weakening Chinese Empire maintained a policy of passive defense towards Central Asia. The passageway of the Silk Road through Turkic Central Asia was not interfered with during this time.

Until the middle of the tenth century the spread of Islam remained confined to the area of Samarkand, Fergana, and northern Afghanistan. During this period, according to a Muslim geographer, ibn-Khurdahbih, the Wakhan was politically subject to Muslim rulers and paid a tribute of 20,000 dirhams (see Barthold 1958, p. 65).

8. For full details of Kao Hsien-chih's expedition to Wakhan and Shighnan in Badakhshan see Stein 1922, pp. 112-31.

By the second half of the tenth century A.D. Islam reached the states to the east of the Pamirs. In 999 the Karakhanids, an Islamized Turkic group, moved westward from Kashgaria and established themselves in Samarkand and Bukhara, and were in control of the entire Transoxiana until the twelfth century (see Wheeler 1964, p. 23; Chen 1977, pp. 92-96; Grousset 1970, pp. 141-48).

During the tenth to the thirteenth century various Turkic peoples established themselves in Samarkand and controlled much of the Amu Darya region, while new waves of Mongolian groups (Karakhitai) ruled eastern Turkistan (see Wheeler 1964, p. 23; also see Grousset 1970, pp. 148-70). The area was conquered and brought under the rule of Jengiz Khan during the early part of the thirteenth century.[9]

The Mongols revived the diminishing trade and communications between China and the West and for more than a century an undisturbed flow of traffic continued along the Silk Road.

Marco Polo passed through Badakhshan, Wakhan, and across the Pamirs during the latter part of the thirteenth century on his way to the court of Kublai Khan, and left us a brief description of his observations in the area. He wrote of Wakhan as

a country . . . of no great size, for it is three days journey across every way. The people, who worship Mahomet [Mohammed] and speak a language of their own, are doughty warriors. They have no ruler except one whom they call *nona*, that is to say in our language "count," and are subject to the lord of Badakhshan. They have wild beast in plenty and game of all sorts for the chase. [Latham 1958, p. 79]

Continuing his trip for three days towards the northeast (i.e., to the Great Pamir) he observed they traveled

. . . through mountains all the time, climbing so high that this is said to be the highest place in the world. And when he [a traveler] is in this high place, he finds a plain between two mountains, with a lake from which flows a very fine river. Here is the best pasturage in the world, for a lean beast grows fat here in ten days. Wild game of every sort abounds. There are great quantities of wild sheep of huge size [*Ovis poli*]. Their horns grow to as much as six palms in length. . . . From these horns the shepherds make big bowls from which they feed, and also fences to keep in their flocks. There are also innumerable wolves, which devour many of the wild rams. The horns and bones of the sheep are found in such numbers that men build cairns of them beside the tracks to serve as land marks to travellers in the snowy season.

This plain, whose name is Pamir, extends fully twelve days' journey. In all these twelve days there is no habitation or shelter, but travellers must take their

---

9. For information on the history of the expansion of Islam in Turkic Central Asia and the history of the Mongol invasions see Barthold 1956, vol. 1, 1958; Skrine and Ross 1899; Gibb 1923; Bretschneider 1888; Wheeler 1964, 1966; and Grousset 1970.

provisions with them. No birds fly here because of the height and the cold. And I assure you that, because of this great cold, fire is not so bright here nor of the same color as elsewhere, and food does not cook well.[Ibid., pp. 79-80]

A century after Marco Polo's journey to China the Mongol Empire faced internal problems that divided the empire into many independent states. In China the Ming dynasty came to power and a new phase of Chinese isolation began. Benedict de Goëz, a Jesuit priest in search of Cathay (China), made his way across the Wakhan and the Pamirs between 1602 and 1606 and was detained by the extremely cautious Chinese on his arrival at Suchow. He later died in Chinese custody (see Chu 1966; Stein 1925).

The significance of the Silk Road as a trade route had been dwindling for some time before Benedict de Goëz's search for Cathay, particularly for the Western world. "The rapidly developing use of the sea route to China, following upon the first Portuguese voyages to India had . . . deprived that ancient Central-Asian highway of its former importance for Western trade" (Stein 1925, p. 497; also Spuler 1970, p. 483).

After the fall of the great Mongol Empire of Jengiz Khan and later those of Timur and Babur, the peoples of Turkic Central Asia faced a long period of cultural and political decay and decline. The area was divided into small states without any type of supraregional importance. In Spuler's words "From the threshold of modern time Central Asian history becomes provincial history . . . " (1970, p. 470).

These small Central Asian khanates were periodically plundered by pastoral nomadic peoples roaming the steppes and mountain areas. A small but persistent flow of trade continued across the Pamirs from Chinese Turkistan and across the Hindu Kush to Chitral and Tibet. This period of provinciality and seclusion for the khanates of Central Asia soon faced fresh threats, political and military, from all sides—tsarist Russia, British India, and China.[10]

Nineteenth Century: The Creation of a Buffer Zone

The 1800s brought not only a new wave of travelers from the West into the Wakhan and the Pamirs, but also people with new and varied interests. Nineteenth-century travelers represented three general categories: explorers, particularly those concerned with geographical discoveries and the gathering of topographic data to make new and

10. For a review of the history of Central Asia from the sixteenth century to the time of the Russian conquest see Holt et al. 1970, vol. 1; also consult Skrine and Ross 1899; Chu 1966; Grousset 1970.

accurate maps of the area; military, political, and commercial recon-
naisance personnel; and finally, true adventurers and hunters. Some
of these travelers, during the course of their journeys, revealed their
true identity and intent while others traveled in disguise as merchants and traders accompanied by Central Asian native traders. One
major difference between these travelers and the early adventurers
who had made passage through this area was that the Western sojourners during the 1800s were usually well educated and they almost
always made written reports of their findings and observations at
the conclusion of their journeys. Therefore, we have a much better
view of the nature of the local conditions during this period than in
earlier times.

The first Westerner since Benedict de Goëz to travel in this region
was John Wood of the East India Company's navy in the years
1836-38. Initially he had come to Kabul as a member of the British
East India Company mission headed by Sir Alexander Burnes, to
the court of Amir Dost Mohammed Khan of Kabul. The stated purpose of this mission was trade negotiation, but it had as a secondary
purpose the collecting of material to construct "an entirely new
map of Afghanistan" (Wood 1841, p. 173). Wood had been sent
by the Amir of Kabul, with a medical officer, Dr. B. P. Lord, to
pay a visit to the court of the Uzbek ruler of northern Afghanistan,
Murad Beg, in Kunduz. From Murad Beg, Wood received permission
and support to trace the river Oxus (Amu Darya). On his way to the
Oxus Wood reported seeing two Kirghiz slaves from the Pamirs in
the city of Taliqan (the provincial center of present-day Takhar
province). He described the Kirghiz as follows:

Although their features were Chinese, their complexions were fair, and even rosy.
One, a good looking young woman, had a child at her breast, and cried bitterly
when detailing the circumstances attending her capture. The other was more ad-
vanced in years, and did not seem to feel the loss of liberty so acutely. [Ibid.,
p. 242]

He did not, however, give the details surrounding the capture of the
enslaved Kirghiz. He mentioned a war being waged by Murad Beg
against the ruler of Badakhshan in 1823 that had resulted in the
subjugation of Badakhshan. He also noted the complete or partial
depopulation of the towns and villages throughout much of Badakhshan. The people had fled the invading armies of Kunduz or after
the conquest were forcibly moved to areas closer to the new center
of power. Wood contends that at the time of his journey, "Already
has the country been twice bereft of its inhabitants; first by Kokan
Beg of Kundus about forty years back and again by Murad Beg, in
1829" (ibid., p. 250).

He found the city of Faizabad "once so celebrated throughout the east" left in ruins. The capital of Badakhshan had been moved east to Jurm, the next largest town, and Wood spent some time there since the roads to Wakhan were not passable at the time. While in Jurm Wood learned of the venture of a local trader who had started from Jurm:

With forty iron pots . . . loaded [on] five yobus [pack horses], and made his way to Chitral. Here he readily disposed of them, and after investing part of the proceeds in honey, started for the Chinese frontier. . . . On reaching Pamir he lost a mule by the cold of that elevated region. . . he pressed on for Yarkand, where he safely arrived and sold his Chitral investment to such advantage that he cleared fourteen times the value of his original venture—the forty cast-iron pots.[Ibid., pp. 290-91]

Wood also noted the widespread slave trading and trafficking through this area. The slaves were brought from Chitral and taken to the markets of Russian Turkistan and also to the towns of northern Afghanistan. He particularly mentions one man in Jurm who at the time of his visit had thirty slaves and could have "received from Chitral as many as a hundred in a single investment" (ibid., p. 302).

From Jurm Wood continued his journey through the Wardooj valley and across the Ishkashim saddle into the upper Amu Darya valley, where he traced the northern headwater of the Oxus, the Pamir River, to Lake Zor Kol, which he called "the source of Oxus."

In Wakhan he stayed in the village of Khandud (the present district center of Wakhan), which consisted of only fifteen families. He noted the extreme poverty of the Wakhi and their beehivelike abodes, the use of which persists to the present time. Perhaps the most important event noted in his report is the encounter with a large Kirghiz camp not very far to the east of Khandud, which he described as follows:

The horde consisted of 100 families and possessed about 2,000 yaks, 4,000 sheep, and 1,000 camels; not the ugly-looking camels of Arabia, but the species known as Bactrian . . . . This was the first year of their abode in Wakhan, and the only instance of the Kirghiz having made this district their winter quarters. They had been solicited to do so by the Uzbeks of Kunduz, with whom the Kirghiz profess to be connected by blood . [Ibid., p. 325] [11]

His next stop was the Wakhan stronghold of Qala-i-Panja, the seat of the Wakhan chieftain, Mohamed Rahim Khan, of whom Wood wrote:

. . . the chief of Wakhan, Mohamed Rahim Khan, had suffered greatly from the

11. From all available accounts, this first Kirghiz winter camp in the upper Amu Darya among the Wakhi might well have been also the last. The Kirghiz, Wood reports, were those of the Great Pamir plateau.

exactions of the Badakhshi ruler Kokan Beg, and at length rendered desperate
refused to pay tribute. Immediately Kokan Beg carried fire and sword into his
territories. The Wakhanis [Wakhi] were eventually worsted, and took refuge
in Chitral; but their chief threw himself into Kila Panj [Qala-i-Panja], and defended it until an amicable arrangement was agreed to by the two leaders, on
which Kokan Beg, confiding in the honor of his opponent, entered his castle,
and was immediately slain. The Badakhshis, disheartened at the loss of their
leader, withdrew, and the exiled Wakhanis returned to their homes. Mohamed
Rahim Khan . . . though nominally tributary to Kunduz, . . . was virtually
independent. Sometimes . . . to ward off a threatened visit from Murad Beg
[the ruler of Kunduz] he would send him an inconsiderable tribute. Distance
and poverty had hitherto been his security. [Ibid., pp. 329-30]

In speaking of the chieftain's revenue Wood stated that

In former times, when a considerable trade passed through Wakhan, the Mir
drew a small revenue by taxing in kind the Yarkand Kafilas [or caravans] for
which he escorted them from the southern limits of his territories to the east
end of lake Sir-i-Kol, where the Chinese frontier begins. This was an exaction
on the part of Mohamed Rahim, since, for this very protection, the chief of
Kunduz previously levied fifteen rupees on each camel-load. . . .
    Another source of income to the ruler of Wakhan is from his slaves. [Ibid.,
pp. 369-70]

The Mir of Wakhan, according to Wood, enslaved the natives of Shakh-
darah, an area to the northwest of Wakhan. The slaves were "bartered
with the Uzbeks of Kunduz for horses, and . . . sold by them
to Shah Kittor, the Chitral ruler at an advance of fifty per cent"
(ibid.).[12]

The Anglo-Russian rivalries over control of the court of the Amir
of Kabul resulted in the first Anglo-Afghan War (November 1838
to 1842). At the end of this war the British were faced with their
first political and military setback in the area, which also gave incentive to their rival, the Russian imperial forces, to advance upon Central Asia.

This state of animosity hindered British trade interests not only
in Afghanistan but also in the rest of western Turkistan. In addition,
it was impossible for the British India Company to use the ancient
Silk Road through Afghanistan to reach another vast area of political
and economic interest, that of eastern Turkistan. Therefore the
British sought an alternative route through Kashmir, Ladakh, and
over the Karakoram mountains (over 5,500 meters) to reach Chinese

---

12. Wood's narrative of his journey was initially published in 1841 and re-
vised by his son in 1872. It is the only source of much of the history of Wakhan
and the Pamirs of that period. It should, however, be read with caution since
at times it sounds not only purely conjectural but expresses strong feelings of
contempt towards certain groups in the area and their way of life.

Turkistan. The important task of surveying this possible alternate route was given to the Great Trigonometrical Survey of India. The most active explorer of Central Asia in this group was T. G. Montgomerie, who was in charge of training native surveyors to assist the GTSI in their efforts.[13]

Trans-Karakoram expeditions to Chinese Turkistan started early in the 1860s, but no attempt was made to visit the upper Amu Darya region until the latter part of that decade. This period was marked by intensive competition between the Royal Geographical Society of Great Britain and the Imperial Geographical Society of Russia in Central Asian explorations. The Russians, without doubt, had much easier access to the area than did the British, and each was watching closely the activities of the other.

Sir Roderick Murchison, in his presidential address to the Anniversary Meeting of the Royal Geographical Society in 1866, aired his feelings on the subject.

Among the numerous desiderata which remain to be worked out by geographers . . . the great table-land of Pamir, as well as vast adjacent tracts of wild countries, still remain to be surveyed by topographers. For although Lieutenant Wood visited the source of the Oxus, and several others of our countrymen have explored adjacent tracts, still the old map in the possession of the Russians as described by M. M. Khanikof and Veniukof, must be viewed as a curious document. . . . [14] The valleys and upland of Badakhshan and Pamir, lying to the north of the lofty Hindoo Kush, will therefore I trust remain for ages to come the neutral ground between British India and Russia, and in which geographers of both countries may meet to promote the science which they cultivate. [1866, 37:clxx-clxxi]

Two years later, in 1868, Montgomerie sent off one of his native explorers, known as "the Mirza," who, disguised as an Indian trader, traveled through Kabul, Badakhshan, Wakhan, took the Sarhad River valley, and crossed the Little Pamir to Tashkurghan in Chinese Turkistan. In his report of the Mirza's exploration, Montgomerie (1871) gave a very interesting account of the conditions in Badakhshan, Wakhan, and the adjacent areas.

The Mirza had found the area between Kabul and Wakhan in a very "lawless state" where slavery was as rife as had been reported some thirty years earlier by John Wood. In particular he noted a close relationship between the Mirs of Badakhshan and those of Hunza

13. For details of these early explorations across Karakoram see Montgomerie 1866, 36:157-72; Hayward 1870, 40:33-166; and Shaw 1870, 14:124-37, and 1871.

14. See Veniukof 1866, 37:248-63; Morgan 1869, 14:229-34; 1887, 9: 423-37; 1893, pp. 55-63.

and Chitral, who were said to pay tribute to the ruler of Badakhshan. In Qala-i-Panja, Wakhan, he found Mir Fatteh Ali-Shah, its hereditary chief, in command of a garrison some two hundred strong, and who also held allegiance to the ruler of Badakhshan. His income was "derived partly from land tax and customs duties, but mostly from a tax on the slave trade, and on actual slave dealing on his own account" (1871, p. 156).

Like Wood, the Mirza reported the Wakhi to be Shi'a Muslims looking to the (then) Aga Khan of Bombay as their spiritual guide. The Mirza secured himself a caravan of horses and a *kafila bashi* (caravan leader) from Faizabad and proceeded to Wakhan in January of 1869. He found the Sarhad River frozen and quite suitable for travel, which, he pointed out, was the main reason for merchants choosing the winter to travel from Badakhshan to Kashgar and vice versa. Another reason he cited was that "snow and cold induced the Kirghiz hordes to remove their cattle and sheep to a lower ground and there is, consequently, less chance of a Kafila being plundered" (ibid., p. 155).

He further noted that "The Kirghiz hordes seem to be numerous, and still adhere to a nomadic way of life. . . . The men take temporary service with the Kashgar, Kokhan [Ququand or Kokand] and Badakhshan chiefs, but they are not willing to submit to much discipline, and change from one party to another without the least hesitation. The Kirghiz have large herds of horses, camels, cattle, yaks, and sheep" (ibid., p. 149).

While Montgomerie's report of the Mirza's account stated that the Kirghiz and their southern neighbors the Kunjuti were said to plunder and rob caravans, the Kunjuti were reportedly doing this as a full-time occupation. It is also reported that the Kunjuti during that time had the better of the Kirghiz since they had taken possession of Kirghiz huts and killed many of them during a recent raid at a camp in Buzai Gumbaz.

The Mirza had crossed the Little Pamir and described the Little Pamir in his report as "the most desolate he ever saw," lacking a sign of man, beast, or bird. On his arrival in Tashkurghan to the east of the Sarikol range, he was met by Kirghiz soldiers of the Muslim rebellious force of Yakub Beg, known as the Atalik Ghazi (1862-78), then the ruler of Chinese Turkistan.[15] In Qala-i-Panja he met the ex-chief of Tashkurghan, Alif Beg, and some fifty of his slaves and

15. For details of the Muslim rebellion headed by Yakub Beg, known as the Atalik Ghazi, see Chu 1966; Chen 1977, pp. 148-61; Kuropatkin 1882; and Shaw 1871.

servants who had fled from Atalik Ghazi. The Mirza had discovered from Alif Beg that "the Atalik Ghazi had directed all who were attached to Alif Beg's rule to be removed to Kashgar and Yarkand, and this included nearly every inhabitant; their place had been sup-plied by Kirghiz, who seemed to like the change . . ." (ibid., p. 163).

It is apparent that the Mirza's report confirms the accounts left by Robert Shaw (1870 and 1871) and Captain Hayward (1870) that the Kirghiz enjoyed considerable liberty and power, particularly in the area to the east of the Sarikol range—in the Chinese Pamirs and Turkistan—during the rule of Atalik Ghazi. It is not clear from the Mirza's report, however, if there were any Kirghiz living in the Little Pamir.

Five years later, in 1874, the Wakhan Mission was dispatched by Sir Douglas Forsyth from Yarkand.[16] This mission was carried out by Captain Gordon and Captain Trotter. Their party reported that "both of the Pamir were thickly inhabited by Kirghiz in former years, subject to Wakhan, but they are now unoccupied, the constant feuds between the Shighnis, Wakhis, the Kirghiz from the Alai, and the Kunjudis, having rendered the country quite unsafe" (Trotter 1878, 48:210).

Captain Trotter also noted that Alif Beg, ex-ruler of Tashkur-ghan, was still in residence at Qala-i-Panja, near the fort of the Wakhan ruler, and that the Mir of Wakhan, along with the neighboring petty feudal states such as Ishkashim and Zebak, were tributaries of the ruler of Badakhshan. Their report contained a very thorough geo-graphical description of the topography of the two Pamirs and the Wakhan, including the strategic passes and distance between various points of interest in the Amu Darya valley and as far west as Qalai Wamar in Shighnan. This mission, the last of its kind of the British Indian Empire, seems to have laid the solid groundwork for the delineation of the frontiers between Russia and British India some twenty years later.[17]

Not long after the Wakhan Mission, during the height of Anglo-Russian rivalry in Turkistan,[18] the second Anglo-Afghan War (1878-81) was fought and as a result the Afghan government reaffirmed

16. Sir Douglas Forsyth was head of a mission dispatched by the Viceroy of India to sign a treaty of friendship and commerce with the ruler of Eastern Turkistan, Yakub Beg, the Atalik Ghazi of Yarkand, who was known as the Amir of Kashgar.

17. For additional information on the reports of the Wakhan Mission of 1873-74 also see T. E. Gordon 1876 and E. C. Gordon 1876.

18. See Vambry 1874; Frechtling 1939; Becker 1968; Rodenbough 1885.

its policy of denying permission to Westerners to travel through Afghanistan on their journeys to Chinese Turkistan. Explorers were obliged to make their way through Russian Central Asia over the Karakoram passes from India.

One group of French explorers, however, traveled through Russian Turkistan, the Afghan Pamirs, and across the Hindu Kush to India during 1886-87. They crossed the Little Pamir in April of 1887 but failed in their attempt to reach Kunjut over the Tash Kupruk Pass, so they were forced to go to Sarhad in Wakhan and over the Broghil Pass to Chitral and British India. The French group found the Kirghiz in small groups, having spent the winter of that year in the Little Pamir, keeping their distance from the Chinese forces who, after Atalik Ghazi's death (1877) had reoccupied Chinese Turkistan and were in control of the Little Pamir. The explorers also heard from the Kirghiz that the British had established themselves in Kunjut while Amir Abdur Rahman of Afghanistan had a firm grip on the Wakhan for some distance beyond Sarhad.

The French found the Kirghiz in economic despair, for they had lost most of their herds from extreme cold and heavy snow. They told the French that they would not spend another winter in the Pamirs because of the climate. The explorers also met some stranded traders who had come from Chinese Turkistan and who had lost most of their goods and pack animals on their way. The Kirghiz and Wakhi were reported to have had a close economic relationship at this time since the recent political tension around them had denied both groups access to their traditional centers of trade, and the small number of traders passing through their territory had drastically decreased their revenues. From their own experience of the Pamir winter and the losses suffered by the Kirghiz inhabitants, the French observed

One need really have committed some great crime to be compelled to remain upon the Pamir, while, as a matter of fact, many of those who inhabit it have committed a murder or some other misdeed in the neighboring countries. Compelled to fly, they come straight to the Pamir, where no one is very particular, and they spend the winter in the remote corners of the valley of Ak-Su [Little Pamir]. When the summer arrives, bringing with it the Chinese agents upon one side, and the Kunjuti upon the other . . . the Kirghiz belonging to the powerful tribes of the valley . . . make for the heights of the Alitchur [Pamir], or the center of the 'roof of the world' . . . out of fear of gunners. . . . [Bonvalot 1889, pp. 179-80]

The group spent a few days in detention at Sarhad in the hands of the newly established Afghan government authorities, and were later escorted by the Afghans over the Broghil Saddle to Chitral.

In 1890, Francis Younghusband of the British India Staff Corps was commissioned to explore the Pamirs further. In his book *The Heart of a Continent* he speaks of drastic changes in the Pamirs since the time of the Forsyth Mission to Wakhan (1873-74) and adds that the Wakhan Mission had been carried out

in the time of Yakoob Beg [Atalik Ghazi], before the Chinese had re-established themselves in Eastern Turkistan, and since then the state of affairs had very materially altered. The Pamirs form a sort of no-man's land between the British dependencies on the south, the Russian on the north, the Chinese on the east, and the Afghan on the west. The waves of conquest which surged all round had not yet thoroughly immersed them, and the state of this meeting-place of the three great empires of Asia was, therefore, of interest and importance. [1896, p. 291]

During his trip of 1890, Younghusband found a small number of Kirghiz camps in the Pamirs and noted that despite the severity of the climate the Kirghiz and a few refugees from Wakhan remained in the Pamirs the whole year around. In Aktash, the eastern extremity of the Little Pamir, he found "three or four tents and a 'beg' *[be]* or headman appointed by the Chinese. He . . . made no difficulties whatever about our proceeding round the Pamirs, which at that time were considered Chinese territory" (ibid., p. 297).

Younghusband traversed the entire Pamir area and reported that Russian military parties had also by then repeatedly made their way through the region. He collected some topographic and climatic information and returned to Kashgar in the autumn of 1890. In the summer of 1891 Francis Younghusband, on his way back to India, traveled through Taghdumbash Pamir and across the Wakhjir Pass to the Little Pamir in order to make his way to Chitral. While in Taghdumbash Pamir he had heard that a small Russian military detachment had entered the Pamirs and "proclaimed them Russian territory." He had met several Kirghiz families in Taghdumbash who had fled the Little Pamir ahead of the Russians.

In Buzai Gumbaz, across the mouth of the Wakhjir valley, Younghusband found a party of ten Cossacks guarding stores left there by the main body of Russians who at the time were headed in the direction of the Broghil Pass. He later met Colonel Yonoff of the Russian party and inquired as to whether the Russians had claimed the Pamirs as their territory. The answer was affirmative and he was shown a map by the Russians marking their newly claimed boundary, which "included the whole of the Pamirs except the Tagh-dum-bash, and extended as far down as the watershed of the Hindu-Kush by the Khorat Bhort Pass" [or Bai Qara and Tashkopruk Pass] (ibid., p. 327).

Younghusband rested in Buzai Gumbaz for a few days after the Russian party had left. But three days later Yonoff and thirty of his mounted Cossacks returned to inform Younghusband that they were ordered by the Russian government to escort him back to Chinese territory. Under protest he was forced to retrace his footsteps over the Wakhjir Pass and back into Taghdumbash. His report of the incident triggered further exchanges of protests and apologies between London and St. Petersburg and affected the Pamir Agreement, which was signed four years later and in which Buzai Gumbaz and much of the Great and Little Pamirs remained within the Russian sphere of influence.

In the meantime Amir Abdur Rahman had conquered Badakhshan and its Amu Darya dependencies of Shighnan and Darwaz and had also taken control of Wakhan, whose ruler Ali Mardan Shah had fled to Chitral. The Amir had taken possession of the Pamirs as far as the neighborhood of Yashil Kul (Olufsen 1969, pp. 212-13).

The Russians, who had claimed the Pamirs, were busy militarily during 1891-92 trying to bring the region under the control of their empire (Luknitsky 1954; Krader 1971). Lord Dunmore, who made his hunting and adventure excursion through the Pamirs in 1892, reported the ouster of the Chinese from Aktash by the Russians, and he found the Aktash post in complete ruins. He traveled through the Little and Great Pamirs on his way to the Alchur Pamir. He also visited Surmatash (or Somatash) in the Alchur near Yashil Kul, where on June 22, 1892, Colonel Yonoff and his party had staged a raid upon a small Afghan frontier post that the Russians annihilated in furtherance of their claim to the territory (Dunmore 1893a, 2: 385-402, 1893b, vol. 2).

These new Anglo-Russian and Russo-Afghan frontier rivalries in the Pamirs triggered a series of negotiations between various parties that led to the demarcation of permanent boundaries. The first of these negotiations began when a British mission, headed by Colonel A. Durand, was sent to the court of Amir Abdur Rahman in Kabul in 1893. At this meeting the Amir threatened to withdraw entirely from Wakhan, saying, "he had a hand cut off at Somatash the other day, and *he is not going to stretch out a long arm along the Hindu Kush to have that shorn off also*" [emphasis added] (quoted in Sykes 1940, 2:175).

Further negotiations were carried out by the British and the Russians during 1893 and 1894. By the end of 1894 the two parties had reached an agreement that dictated the existing Russo-Afghan frontiers in the area. However, at the time, their agreement was "contingent upon the evacuation by the Amir of Afghanistan of all the territories occupied by him on the right bank of the Panja [Amu River], and by the Amir of Bukhara of the portion of Darwaz, which lay to the south of the Oxus [or Amu Darya]" (ibid., p. 180). Further, the implementation of this agreement included a special annual subsidy of 50,000 rupees from the British government to the government of Amir Abdur Rahman of Afghanistan to retain the administration of the valley of Wakhan, which he was initially unwilling to do (ibid., p. 181).

The Anglo-Russian official commissions and the unofficial representatives of the Afghan government met in July 1895 at Lake Zor Kol in the Great Pamir, and the demarcation of the boundaries between Russia, Afghanistan, the British Indian Empire, and China was completed. Although the Chinese government did not participate in the negotiation, they did not raise any objections.[19] Finally, the Wakhan Corridor and the Afghan Pamirs were established, as Murchison had hoped, as a "neutral ground" or buffer zone between three of the world's strongest powers—though the British felt that the decision favored Russia.[20] As for the British, "the delimitation of a definite boundary was of great importance, a boundary which . . . did not touch the Indian Empire at any point, thanks to the Amir's [of Afghanistan] acceptance of the narrow district of Wakhan" (ibid., p. 183. Also see Lattimore 1950, pp. 259-68).

Buffer Zone to Barricade: 1896 to 1950

After the Anglo-Russian Pamir treaty, a new era of exploration by Westerners and Russians began in the Pamirs and the Wakhan region, the beginning of scientific expeditions. None of these expeditions was allowed access to the Afghan Wakhan or the Pamirs by the Afghan government, with very few exceptions.

These scientific missions began with the first and second Danish Pamir Expeditions during 1896-97 and 1898-99. These expeditions were comprehensive in their goals and multidisciplinary in their composition. They collected a wide range of data including meteorological, geological, geographical, general ethnographic, and linguistic (see Olufsen 1969). Although their research dealt strictly with the peoples and areas to the north of the Amu Darya, it is, however,

19. The Afghan and Chinese borders were not officially established by either side until 1964 when a boundary commission of both countries met in the Pamirs during the summer of that year and, after a survey and demarcation, recognized the border (see Dupree 1973, p. 424).

20. For the Russian side of the Pamir Treaty see Wheeler 1964, p. 244.

equally revealing of the conditions on its southern banks during that period. We will have occasion to turn to the results of their work later.

On his second mission of archaeological and geographical exploration in Chinese Turkistan in May 1906, Sir Aurel Stein was granted permission by the Afghan government to enter Sarhad via the Broghil Saddle from Chitral on his way to the Tarim Basin. He was met by the Afghan authorities who escorted him and his party to the Little Pamir and across the Wakhjir Pass into Taghdumbash Pamir in Chinese territory.

During his brief passage through the Little Pamir Sir Aurel Stein learned from a Kirghiz headman, Mohammed Isa, that after the visit of the Pamir Boundary Commission to the area in 1895, a "hundred odd Kirghiz families which crossed from the Russian side to the Afghan Pamirs . . . have continued to graze there. The official tax annually gathered for the governor of Wakhan, [being] one sheep in every 10" (Stein 1912, 1:79).[21] He further stated that

The ancient trade route up the Oxus from Badakshan to Sarikol and to Yarkand is still frequented during the summer months by enterprising Bajauri [northwest frontier area] traders . . . the total amount of merchandise carried was represented by only about one hundred pony loads each way in the year [which] scarcely surprised me, seeing how trade between Afghanistan and Chinese Turkistan is handicapped by present economic conditions in both regions and powerful competition from the Russian and Indian sides. [Ibid., p. 80]

However, he was told by the Wakhan Hakim (district officer), Mansur Khan, that Amir Habibullah Khan, then the King of Afghanistan, intended to build *sarais* (caravan halting places) at regular intervals along the Amu Darya and Sarhad River up to Wakhjir, to help revive the trade to China and Chinese Turkistan. This plan was never realized.

During his third journey to Central Asia in 1915, Sir Aurel Stein made his way through the Great Pamir and the upper Amu Darya region. On this trip he made an extensive archaeological survey of the Amu Darya valley and collected a considerable amount of anthropometric and linguistic data. However, he was denied access to the southern banks of the Amu to continue his work in Afghan territory (see Stein 1912, 1928). The Afghan Pamirs and Wakhan on the

21. The new group of Kirghiz immigrants to the Afghan Pamirs had probably left Russian soil after the suppression of the Andijan rebellion of 1898 (in which the Kirghiz took a very active part), and not only as a result of the demarcation of the frontiers. For additional details of Turkic movements against the Russians see Krader 1971 and Wheeler 1964, pp. 89-92.

southern bank of the Amu remained closed to any kind of research or even casual outside travelers until quite recently.

In 1916 a general revolt broke out throughout much of Turkic Central Asia in opposition to some repressive wartime changes in the tsarist colonial policies towards the peoples of this region (Wheeler 1964, p. 92). In fact, "The 1916 revolt was the first of a series of movements and actions of a revolutionary nature which reached their peak in the following years, 1917-1920. Their overt expression did not die down until 1930" (Krader 1971, p. 108).

One of these movements known as the Basmachi (or Basma-ji) movement, started in defense of the Kokand Autonomous Government in Fergana district, immediately to the north of the Wakhan Corridor and Afghan Pamirs. After the liquidation of the Kokand government by the Soviet forces this movement continued resistance to the Soviet government for many years to come (see Chokaev 1928, pp. 273-88). This and other armed uprisings were followed by the Soviet's "bloody suppressions and judiciary repressions," the result of which "was that over 300,000 Kazakhz and Kirghiz fled to Kashgaria and Kulja in Chinese Turkistan" (Krader 1971, p. 108).

Not all the Kirghiz who fled from Soviet control went to Chinese Turkistan; some came to the Afghan Pamirs. The present khan, or leader, of the Afghan Pamirs in a conversation with me, said,

My father was the Meng Bashi [Turkic title for district officer or subgovernor] of Murghab for fourteen years during the Nikalay [Nicholas] period. But at the start of the Communist takeover, when I was only one year old, my father, together with many of his kinsmen and administrative officers, came here to the Little Pamir in Afghan territory. At that time, the Beks' Revolt[22] [or Basmachi Movement] against the Communists had also started in many parts of Turkistan. . . . Before the arrival of my father to this Pamir only about fifty Kirghiz households had been living here. About two hundred fifty households had come to this place with my father, many of whom later either returned to the Soviet Union or went to the Chinese Pamirs.

In 1921 General Mohammed Nadir Khan, in his official capacity as the minister of defense for the government of Amir Amanullah Khan of Afghanistan, visited Wakhan and the Little Pamir. His secretary, Burhanuddin Khan Kushkaki, who accompanied him on his journey and who wrote the official report of the tour, estimated

---

22. *Beklar din Qozghaleshi*, which literally means "the headmens' uprising," or the Beks' Revolt, was a name used by the peoples of Central Asia to refer to the armed struggle against the Bolsheviks. *Basmachi*, a Turkic work that means "robber, " "plunderer," or "bandit" was the name given to the revolutionaries by the Soviets (see Chokaev 1928, p. 273).

the population of the Afghan Pamirs at two thousand persons, with about one hundred families living in the Little Pamir and about thirty households in the Great Pamir (see Kushkaki 1923, pp. 285-309). The khan believes that this estimate of the number of households was conservative. In the report it was stated that the Kirghiz were buying the wooden lattice frames used in their yurts from Kashgar, and that sixty of the one hundred Kirghiz households resident in the Little Pamir seemed to have been among the well-to-do, while only forty families were considered poor herders and servants. The father of the present khan is mentioned as being particularly knowledgeable, wealthy, and powerful, and reportedly possessed over a dozen British-, German-, and Russian-made rifles. The present khan also told me that his father was unofficially entrusted with the duties of frontier commissioner of the Pamirs by General Nadir Khan.

The Kirghiz khan and other elders recall that for a number of years after the Soviet suppression of the peoples of Turkistan (until the early 1930s), movement from the Afghan Pamirs to the Russian Pamirs was not wholly restricted. During the winter the Afghan Kirghiz were allowed to enter Soviet territory with their herds and spend up to four months in the relatively milder climate of their traditional winter camping grounds in what had become the Russian Pamirs. But the Afghan Kirghiz had to pay *izbor* or *wot poli* (a pasturage fee) of one animal for every ten of the same type (or the equivalent thereof) to Soviet authorities for the use of pasturage. Some Tajik from the neighboring Sarikol area of the Chinese Pamirs also went to the Russian territory during the winter under the same *izbor* arrangements. The Afghan Kirghiz did not use the Chinese Pamirs for temporary seasonal pasturage because the accessible Chinese Pamirs were very small and more densely populated than the Soviet Pamirs.

During the early 1930s the Soviet government closed the border to the Kirghiz of Afghanistan. As a result, the Kirghiz lost many of their former privileges, including a large portion of their pasturage and camping territory in the Soviet Union. The Kirghiz, however, maintain that the Soviets not only sealed their frontiers against them but also staged a series of military raids, as well as other forms of harassment, against the Afghan Kirghiz camps inside the Afghan Pamirs. An elderly *haji* (one who has made the pilgrimage to Mecca) gave me the following account of the first Soviet raid, which took place in 1935.

The Russian soldiers raided the present khan's father's *qeshtow* [winter camp] at Gonju Bai [a place near Aq Tash at the Afghan and Russian borders]. The

Soviets took most of their belongings including some important documents, among which was their *shajara* [genealogical tree chart]. The soldiers took the present khan, his elder brother and another important man from their lineage to Murghab as prisoners. The khan was released and he returned after about six months, but his elder brother and the other person were taken to Dushambi [then Stalinabad, the capital of Tajik S.S.R.] and were set free a year later. After their return they moved their camp from Gonju Bai to their present *qeshtow* at Mulk-i-Ali away from the Russian frontier lines.

In a later discussion on the same subject, the khan told me that the Soviet soldiers had actually wanted to capture his father, who was very much against communism and actively sought to influence the Kirghiz to oppose the Soviet regime in the area. Since his father had been aware of the possibility of the Russian raids he had gone to stay temporarily with some Kirghiz living in the Chinese Pamirs. Being unable to find the father, the Russians took his sons and another relative as hostages, and robbed them of almost everything they owned, including a few rifles. His father, the khan said, returned to the Little Pamir and died there about five years later. His elder brother died a few months after his father, leaving him as the head of their influential family.

Another major Soviet attack on the Afghan Kirghiz took place in the fall of 1941. These raids were carried out in both the Great and Little Pamirs, during which about forty Kirghiz in the Great Pamir and three in the Little Pamir were murdered and many were taken prisoner, some of whom never returned. Just as in the past, the Soviet soldiers looted the Kirghiz livestock and other belongings.

This tight control of the Russian frontier put an end to the use of that portion of the ancient Silk Road that went through the Great Pamir along the banks of the Pamir River, since part of the ancient track was in Soviet territory. However, trade between northern Afghanistan and Chinese Turkistan through Wakhjir and other passes leading through the Little Pamir continued. The traders from Badakhshan and other parts of northern Afghanistan were taking such things as pistachio nuts, furs, and pelts (fox, tiger, wolf, and lamb), spices such as cumin seed, and later opium, to Kashgar. They brought back from Chinese Turkistan carpets, chinaware, a large selection of silk and cotton material, raw silk, copper utensils, *jambu* (Chinese silver ingots), and gold coins. These early traders did not trade with either the Wakhi or the Kirghiz, but both the Kirghiz and the Wakhi benefited, since they were hired by the merchants during their passage through the territory.

Scores of Muslim pilgrims from Chinese Turkistan also passed through this area annually on their long journey to Mecca, and they also provided an important source of revenue in return for services rendered to them by the Kirghiz and the Wakhi. The payment for services was generally in market goods, or in gold and silver.

The Kirghiz, when hired to serve traders who made the ten- to twelve-day-long trip from the Pamirs to the city of Kashgar and its satellite villages, took the opportunity to buy goods for their own consumption. However, the Sinkiang Uyghur (a Turkic group) traders brought virtually all that the Kirghiz required—cloth, *chapan* (quilted long robes), tea, flour, dried fruits, rice, wheat, chinaware, cast-iron caldrons, cast-iron dutch ovens, copper teapots, carpets, the wooden lattice frames used in building yurts, horses, camels, *jambu*, and gold. Since the Russian traders from Andijan and Murghab who used to frequent these Pamirs could not now participate directly, the Russian commodities were brought to the Afghan Pamirs by the Uyghur traders. The traders exchanged their market commodities for sheep, goats, yak, wool, sheepskin, yak hides, *mai* (clarified butter), dried curd, furs (fox, wolf, and *dala khafak* [mink?]), horse covers, and other Kirghiz products. The Kirghiz themselves did not take their livestock to Chinese Turkistan markets at all.

The Kirghiz state that the people of Wakhan did not come to the Pamirs for trade or work then, except for a number of rich families from Sarhad who, during the summer, camped with their herds as far as Langar and Mirza Murad (areas now claimed and used by the Kirghiz). The Wakhi did not engage in any trade themselves, and as Badakhshi traders showed no interest in trading with them, they had very little cloth, salt, or other market goods. The Kirghiz, who were coming to the Wakhan in the service of traders, would exchange with the Wakhi. Rather than trading their animals and livestock products, which had little or no exchange value with the Wakhi and the traders, they traded market goods from Kashgar and salt from the Pamir salt fields with the Wakhi for grain.

The last Soviet raid was in the summer of 1946,[23] and was aimed at capturing or killing the present khan. The khan, who had been forewarned, put his men on guard and resisted the small group of Russian soldiers, forcing them to pull out of Afghan territory. He then reported the incident to the Afghan authorities in Wakhan, but received no support from them. Fearing for their safety, the khan and his relatives marched out of the Little Pamir to the Qara Chuqor

23. The reason for this raid as well as previous raids by the Soviet forces, although not officially stated, has been to retaliate against the real or imagined Afghan Kirghiz staging of similar raids on Russian posts across the border. The Kirghiz deny these charges and say the Russians wanted to frighten them off and take over their land, just as they had taken the rest of their territory.

area of Taghdumbash in Chinese Turkistan. He and his group lived there in relative peace and quiet, tending their herds, and engaging in some agricultural activities. This venture for him and his people lasted only two years before the Chinese Communist revolution caught up with them. Faced by this new threat he and his men fought a Chinese frontier detachment to re-enter the Afghan Pamirs. But by this time Shah Mahmood Khan, the prime minister of Afghanistan, had dispatched an envoy to invite the khan and his people to return to their former territory, promising that they would be protected against outside harassment. This was obviously welcome news for the Kirghiz.

The khan recalled that only ten days after their return to the Little Pamir from Taghdumbash Pamir an American couple, Franc and Jean Shor, arrived with a few Afghan government officials. The Shors were planning to retrace the steps of Marco Polo to China but, as they have documented in their travelogue, they were not able to proceed to Sinkiang and instead were guided by the khan's men to Hunza in Pakistani territory (see J. and F. Shor 1950; J. Shor 1955).

This new political development in China closed the ancient route that had been founded by the Chinese. The route had served as an important means of trade, communication, and cultural relations between the East and West and the societies of Chinese Turkistan and those of northern Afghanistan, Russian Turkistan, and the Kirghiz of the Afghan Pamirs.

1950 to the Present: The Closed Frontiers

The post-1950 era brought about the consolidation of the Pamirs and the gradual inclusion of the Kirghiz within the Afghan nation-state. The Kirghiz paid taxes on their livestock to the national government and became an integrated part of the administrative district of Wakhan within the province of Badakhshan. But for some years they stood aloof, only frequenting the Wakhan Corridor as far as Ishkashim to secure their needed cereals.

During the last part of the 1950s the khan made his first journey through Badakhshan to Kabul with a great deal of trepidation. However, he found himself well received by various high officials of the government, and was granted a royal audience.

In the early 1960s the famous Marco Polo sheep were rediscovered in the Pamirs and trophy hunters from Kabul, including the king and the princes, came to the Pamirs. This involved the Kirghiz in some hospitality and service that resulted in better relations between the elders of the small group of Kirghiz and courtiers of Kabul.

In the latter part of the 1960s the Afghan Tourist Organization set up a Marco Polo sheep-hunting reserve in the Great Pamir that operates during the summer months to serve less than two dozen international trophy hunters a year, most of whom come from the United States (see Abercrombie 1968). Some of the high, glacier-clad mountain peaks of the Hindu Kush range along the corridor have been open for mountain-climbing expeditions from Europe in recent years. The Kirghiz have also seen some "celebrity" visitors during the 1970s, such as a former British ambassador to Afghanistan and his entourage, a German zoological expedition, a National Geographic magazine writer (see Michaud 1972), and a mixed Afghan and Russian mining survey group. During my own research an Italian expedition attempting to retrace the footsteps of Marco Polo visited the area. In the summer of 1975 the Afghan government granted Granada Television Limited of Britain permission to make a documentary film about the Kirghiz. The author participated as the consultant anthropologist in the making of the film entitled *The Kirghiz of Afghanistan* that was screened in Britain in December 1975.

The most significant period for the purpose of this study is the last twenty-five years, during which time the Kirghiz of the Afghan Pamirs, under the closed frontier conditions, have experienced, and are still experiencing, an important ecological and sociocultural adaptation to their new environment. However, before discussing the new closed frontier conditions and the various aspects of their adaptation, I would like to recapitulate the demographic processes to which I have alluded during this review of the history of this region.

POPULATION COMPOSITION AND DYNAMICS

The Wakhi

The terms *Wakhi* or *Wakhani* are generally used to refer to the indigenous population of Wakhan living on both sides of the upper Amu Darya and Sarhad River valleys as far up as the hamlet of Sarhad. The Wakhi are frequently lumped together with many other neighboring groups, such as the Shighni, Ishkashimi, and so on, and collectively referred to as the Mountain Tajiks or Pamir Tajiks. Two other appellations, *kheek* and *sart*, are also in use. *Kheek*, a term with two meanings in the Wakhi language, is used by the inhabitants to differentiate themselves (the Wakhi) from all "others," and to identify the sixth and largest layer within their social stratification, the Wakhi commoners (see chapter 3). The term *sart* had a much broader connotation in its earlier usage among the Kirghiz and Kazakhs of Central Asia. At present, however, it is applied by the Kirghiz with unconcealed contempt to their neighbors the Wakhi.[24]

There is no information available as to how long the Wakhan has been inhabited by the Wakhi or some other primordial stock, but it is believed to have been populated before the time of Zoroaster (see Olufsen 1969, p. 208). The earliest available account of the people is a remark by Hsüan Tsang regarding the "greenish eyes of the people of Ta-mo-si-t'iet-ti . . . and its capital Hun-t'o-to [Khandud] with its great Buddhist vihara" (Minorsky 1929, p. 1103; also see Mirsky 1964, pp. 108-9).

There are the remains of several forts in different parts of the upper Amu Darya and in the Sarhad River valley, particularly in Sarhad, that are attributed by the Wakhi to the *atash-parast* (fire-worshipper, i.e., Zoroastrians) or *kafir* (infidels) and/or *seahpoosh kafir* (the black-robed infidels). Some differences of opinion as to the identity of the builders of these early strongholds exist between Sir Aurel Stein (1928) and Olufsen (1969), both of whom made an archaeological survey of the sites on the right banks of the upper Amu. They do agree, however, that the construction of fortresses indicates that Wakhan enjoyed a larger population at that time compared to that existing at the turn of this century.

As I have remarked earlier, the small Wakhi population might have resulted from the continuing state of war between the neighboring feudal states in attempts to exact taxes and control the trade route to Chinese Turkistan as well as from the slave trade. Oppression by the local rulers, including some of the earlier Afghan officials, also caused the flight of many families and individuals south of the Hindu Kush to Chitral, Gilgit, and the mountain ramparts to the west of the Tarim Basin (see Kushkaki 1923, pp. 309-14).

John Wood reported that the total number of souls living between Ishkashim (at the entrance to the corridor) and Sarhad did "not exceed one thousand" in 1838 (Wood 1841, p. 369). In 1899 the Danish Pamir Expedition reported 17 Wakhi hamlets containing 180 households on the Russian side alone. Assuming an average population of 5 persons per household (a very low estimate for Wakhan), the Wakhi living in Russian Wakhan would be 900 persons (Olufsen 1969). Later (1916) Sir Aurel Stein puts the Wakhi population in

24. The general explanation for *sart* given by the Kirghiz and Kazakh has been an etymology of the word itself, *sari et* or yellow dog. For a full description of its use see Barthold 1934, pp. 175-76, and Alizadeh 1927, pp. 50-52.

Russian territory at 190 households and about 2,000 persons, re-
marking that the Afghan side had more than that number (1928,
pp. 869-70). Minorsky (1929) supported the figure of 2,000 persons
(in 27 hamlets) on the Russian side. He also estimated the Afghan
Wakhan to have contained about 64 villages with about 3,500 inhabitants (cf. Kushkaki 1923). There is no Afghan census available
on Wakhan or other parts of the country to date. In my own discussions with various district officials at Khandud, I found that at
present there are some 65 hamlets, each consisting of from 2 to about
35 dispersed households, with the exception of Khandud (about
50 households), with an estimated population of over 6,000 Wakhi
living in about 700 household units within the District of Wakhan
(i.e., from the hamlet of Putur to Sarhad).

The Wakhi are of ancient Iranian stock from the Turkistan region.
On the basis of anthropometric data collected earlier in the area,
they are said to have *Homo alpinus* features (Stein 1928, p. 862).[25]
They speak Wakhi, an old Indo-Iranian dialect, also referred to in
the literature as *Ghalcha* (Minorsky 1929, p. 1103; Grierson 1921,
pp. 457-65). The Wakhi adhere to an Ismailia sect of Islam,[26] which
is also practiced by their neighbors in Shighnan, Zebak, and those
of Hunza and Chitral in the southern folds of the Hindu Kush
range. It is not known when this particular sect of Islam, which
developed during the ninth century A.D. in Iraq, reached this part
of the world.

In the past this small colony of Shi'a in the Wakhan Corridor
and its adjacent valleys was regarded with unconcealed contempt
by the orthodox Sunni adherents of Badakhshan and Turkic Central
Asia and attempts were made to convert them. The Ismailite Wakhi
and other Shi'a groups in the country are subject to a Sunni-based
legal and judicial system and a Sunni-dominated administrative bureaucracy that has been, and remains, a continuing source of frustration for the Shi'a population.

The Kirghiz

The origin of the Kirghiz people is still subject to speculation.
The suggestions include Mongol, Uralic, or independent northern
origin. There is general agreement among authorities, however, that

25. For details of Wakhi physical characteristics see Joyce in Stein 1928,
pp. 996-1012 and Hansen in Olufsen 1969, pp. 217-29.
26. For details concerning the history and doctrine of Ismailism and Shi'aism
see Rahman 1968 and *The Shorter Encyclopedia of Islam*. For the distribution
of Shi'a groups in Afghanistan see Canfield 1973.

whatever their origin they were not originally Turks but were Turkicized very early (see Barthold 1924; Menges 1968; Grousset 1970;
Krader 1971). Their language belongs to the northwestern group
of Turkic languages.

The Kirghiz are first mentioned as a Turkic group in the Chinese
Annals of the second century A.D. under the name *Kien-ku.* Their
habitat at that time is not identified but is believed to have been
in the steppes north of the Altai mountains. The Kirghiz are mentioned in the Orkhon (a Turkic language) inscriptions of the eighth
century as then inhabiting the Upper Yenisei to the north of the
Sayan mountain range. They were not a significant political force
until 840 A.D. when they conquered the Uyghur territory in Mongolia
(Barthold 1924, p. 1025; Grousset 1970, pp. 106-9). In the tenth
century the Kirghiz were either driven out of Mongolia during the
rise of the Karakhanid state or migrated southward to the area of
Aqsu in Chinese Turkistan, where some of them pursued agriculture
while the rest tended their herds (Barthold 1930). The Kirghiz are
not mentioned again in relation to this region until the sixteenth
century. During that period they were at some point subject to
the Mongols and at other times to the Kalmuck (Qalmaq) who drove
the Kirghiz from their earlier habitat into the area of Fergana and
Karategin.

By the sixteenth century the Kirghiz had embraced Islam and
were engaged in several long religious wars against the Terma Qalmaq,
which are vividly described in the Kirghiz *er* (epics) called *Manac
(Manas)* (see Tel Jana Adabeyat Institute 1958). After the defeat
of the Kalmucks by the Chinese (1758-59), the Kirghiz came under
Chinese domination. It was during this period that some Kirghiz
returned to their former territories in Chinese Turkistan.

During the nineteenth century much of the Kirghiz territory
came under the political sovereignty of the Fergana Uzbeks until
the Russian conquest of the region in 1864. The Kirghiz of Tien
Shan and the Pamirs, however, enjoyed considerable political power
for a brief period during the reign of the Atalik Ghazi (1862-78)
in Chinese Turkistan.

There is ample archaeological evidence in the Pamirs at the present
time that, if excavated and studied, could provide information about
its habitations and the early inhabitants of the high intermountain
valleys. For example, there are a great number of petroglyphs in
various parts of the Little Pamir, the most interesting of which is
at an occasional caravan bivouac site off the main trail at Zankuk
near Langar. The impressions left on the rocks are mostly those of
mounted horsemen with bow and arrow, hunting wild yak. Not

far from Zankuk on top of a rather inaccessible spur well above
the tracks there is also a small tower of a regular geometric shape
called Karwan-Balasi.[27]

Another archaeologically significant site is the *gumbaz* or mausoleum, the only early permanent structures in the Pamirs, which
were built in honor of rich and famous Kirghiz. These structures,
of which there are many, are built of stone and mud with a rectangular base surmounted by a sun-dried mud-brick domed roof. They
are found in a number of places such as Buzai Gumbaz, Chelap,
Andamin, Sari Tash, and Orta Bail. In addition to these there is
also an extensive floor plan of an early residential site with permanent
stone foundations at Andamin where, I was told, there had stood
a very high, arched gateway that had been visible for miles. It col-
lapsed not more than two decades ago.

It is almost certain that the area was uninhabited during the
passage of Marco Polo when he remarked that the " . . . Pamir,
extends fully twelve days' . . . there is no habitation or shelter,
but travelers must take their provisions with them" (Latham 1958,
p. 80). From all we know, he apparently crossed the Pamirs during
the summer. Furthermore, given the severity of the climate, I am
confident that in earlier periods the Pamirs were frequented only
during the warmer seasons, and that although a short-term, year-
round habitation of the Pamirs by small groups seeking sanctuary
from their enemies during the earlier period might have occurred,
permanent habitation came about only during this century. The present Kirghiz inhabitants of the Afghan Pamirs believe that some one
hundred years ago, possibly after the death of Atalik Ghazi in Chinese
Turkistan, a small number of households (approximately thirty)
used the area of the Little Pamir on a regular basis for summer pasturage.

We know from Wood's report (1841) that some hundred Kirghiz
households, whom he saw during the winter of 1838 in Wakhan,
were spending their summers in the Great Pamir. The first report
of a small group of Kirghiz spending the winter in the Little Pamir
came from the French explorers in 1887 (Bonvalot 1889). This group
of Kirghiz had reportedly suffered heavy losses during that winter
and so in all probability they did not remain another winter. The
next report of a group of Kirghiz inhabiting the Little Pamir was

27. It is believed that this small tower was built by a merchant as a monument to his young son who had died near there. The name, Karwan-Balasi, in
Kirghiz means the son or child of the caravan man. The tomb near Buzai Gumbaz
is also marked by a small stella built of flat slabs similar to the Kirghiz mud and
brick coned structures built to honor their dead (see Stein 1912, 1:76).

made by Sir Aurel Stein who noted the presence of about one hundred families in 1905 (Stein 1912). This group, I believe, fled the Russian Pamirs following the suppression of the Andijan (Fergana) rebellion of 1898 and took sanctuary in the Afghan Pamirs (cf. Wheeler 1964, pp. 89-96).

I was told by the present Kirghiz khan that a large group of Kirghiz (close to 250 families) emigrated to the Afghan Pamirs during the major Kirghiz-Kazakh exodus from the Soviet Union to Chinese Turkistan. This particular emigration followed the 1916 armed struggle against the tsarist regime and the consequent unsuccessful liberation movements of the Turkic people of Central Asia against the Soviets.

The total number of Kirghiz in both of the Afghan Pamirs in 1921 was estimated at about two thousand persons (Kushkaki 1923). This figure was reduced by a number of Soviet raids that forced some Kirghiz to leave. In 1946 about twenty-five or thirty families from the Great Pamir migrated to Badakhshan and northern Afghanistan (see Shahrani 1978). At the same time a much larger number fled to the Chinese Taghdumbash Pamir, but returned to the Little Pamir in 1949 after the success of the Communist revolution in China. The area has been quite peaceful since 1950 and the population in the Pamirs has remained relatively stable during the past quarter of a century.

My own census during this research showed the present population of the Afghan Pamirs to be about 1,825 persons, living in some 333 *oey* (family, household) units. Of the 1,825, 1,380 persons, members of 246 *oey* units, lived in the Little Pamir while the Great Pamir held 445 persons in 87 *oey* units.[28]

The etymology of the ethnonym Kirghiz is not clear. But Turkologists and the Kirghiz themselves believe it is a compound of *kirgh* or *qirgh* (forty) and *qiz* (girl, daughter). Another compound *qirgh* and *yuz* (one hundred) is offered (see Krader 1971, p. 60). The Kirghiz themselves favor the first interpretation which they take to mean the "descendants of forty maidens." This is also the meaning that their myths of origin attempt to explain (see Khan 1963, p. 32;

28. The reason behind the smaller population in the Great Pamir is not its smaller size. The loss of a greater number of inhabitants (by death or immigration to Badakhshan where most of them also died of disease and heat) is the result of their greater vulnerability to Soviet raids in the past, and also because winters bring heavier snow and more severe weather conditions, which cause greater loss of livestock. These two factors discourage some Kirghiz from going to the Great Pamir from the more densely populated Little Pamir. For details concerning Kirghiz present population see Shahrani 1978 and chap. 5, this work.

Schuyler 1876, pp. 135-38). The Kirghiz were also called *Burut*
(moustache) by their traditional enemies, the Terma Qalmaqs, during
the seventeenth century (Barthold 1924, p. 1025).

There are two main groups of Kirghiz known in the literature:
the Qara Qirghiz or Kara Kirghiz, the "genuine" or "true" Kirghiz
(not Black Kirghiz as has been suggested; Krader 1963; Jochelson
1928); Kirghiz or Kirghiz-Kazakh, an appellation adopted by the
Russians to distinguish the Kazakhs from the Cossacks. The Kirghiz
of the Afghan Pamirs consider themselves to be the Kara Kirghiz,
the "genuine" Kirghiz, and the Kirghiz-Kazakh are referred to by
them as Otez Oghul (thirty sons), the explanation of which is given
in the Kirghiz myths of origin.

The Kirghiz living in the Afghan Pamirs (about 2,000), the Fergana
and Osh district of Soviet Tajikistan (approximately 26,000), and
those of Sinkiang Pamirs in the People's Republic of China (over
100,000) make up the Kara Kirghiz. The Kirghiz-Kazakh occupy
the Kirghiz S.S.R., Uzbek S.S.R., and Kazakh S.S.R. The Russian
census of 1970 put the total Kirghiz population in the Soviet Union
at 1,452,000 people (Riasanovsky 1965; Krader 1971; Jochelson
1928; Wheeler 1966; Allworth 1971; Chen 1977).

The Tashkili

The term *Tashkili*, a Persian word meaning "organizational"
or "administrative" refers to the nonindigenous population of the
Wakhan and the Pamir—the non-Wakhi and the non-Kirghiz. Historically all government administrative personnel were made up of
nonindigenous people, but this is no longer true since during recent
decades a number of educated Wakhi have been incorporated into
the lower echelons of the bureaucratic structure. However, in this
discussion *Tashkili* is intended to include two general categories of
nonindigenous peoples.

Administrative personnel: civil servants, police, schoolteachers,
and units of frontier military guards. Membership of this group is
ethnically quite heterogeneous and may include members of the
various linguistic and ethnic groups found in Afghanistan. It is necessarily transient. *Free agents:* immigrants and itinerant traders in the
area. Among the permanently settled immigrants are a number of
retired military and civilian personnel and some traders who have
bought land and settled in Wakhan as well as some who have married
Wakhi women. A larger number of traders, however, have a shop
in Khandud as an established base but spend most of the summer and
early fall in the Wakhi hamlets or among the Kirghiz. Their time is

spent engaging in new transactions or collecting their debts. The members of this group belong to only three ethnic groups—Pashtuns from Kabul and Jalalabad, and Uzbeks and Tajiks from Badakhshan province, of which Wakhan is a part. At the time of this research this growing group of entrepreneurs numbered about thirty individuals and families.

THE NEW CLOSED FRONTIER CONDITIONS

This prolonged discussion of the topography, geography, history, and demography in the Wakhan Corridor and the Afghan Pamirs was designed to draw attention to a number of main points. First, the topography and geography of the region have played an important part in the history of this frontier area. Second, the historical processes in the region have in turn considerably altered the significance of the physical environmental realities. Third, both history and geography as interdependent factors have had a remarkable influence upon the population composition, density, and dynamics, and their ecological adaptation systems in the Wakhan and the Pamirs. Finally, the present inhabitants of the Wakhan Corridor and the Afghan Pamirs are, in addition to the harsh physical restrictions, burdened by a new set of sociopolitical and economic constraints produced by recent historical developments.

The last point, that of the closed frontiers, calls for elaboration. The Communist revolutions in neighboring Russia and China drastically altered the former demographic, socioeconomic, and political conditions under which the population of this area previously lived. The revolutions caused many individuals, families, and larger groups to flee their homeland and cross into Afghan territory. As it was not possible to recross these new borders under the ensuing border policies, many social, economic, and kinship ties were permanently severed. The closure of the Russian border also cost the Kirghiz pastoralists the greater part of their former pasturage and they have become confined for year-round habitation to what were formerly their summer camping grounds. The flow of trade through this region (the Silk Road) between northern Afghanistan and Russian Turkistan in the west and Chinese Turkistan (Sinkiang) in the east, came to a complete halt. The Kirghiz, as well as the Wakhi, suffered a considerable loss of income when the caravans of Muslim pilgrims and traders no longer passed through their territory. They lost the privilege of not only serving, but controlling this important highway of communication and trade, and found themselves relegated to the most remote and forbidding frontier of Afghanistan. It is also im-

portant to note that the Kirghiz, as a Turkic group with sociocultural orientation toward towns and villages in Turkic Central Asia,
were also among the majority in that region, but became a minority
within Pashtun- and Tajik-dominated Afghanistan. It is the processes
of coping with, and adapting to, the constraints of these new closed
frontier conditions by the Kirghiz (and to some extent their neighbors
the Wakhi) that is the focus of the remainder of this study.

PART II

STRATEGIES OF ADAPTATION

Right, Wakhi carrying sheaves of wheat; *below,* Wakhi woman weaving indoors; *preceding page,* Wakhi reaping wheat.

3. The Wakhi
High-Altitude
Agropastoral Adaptation

THE WAKHI SOCIAL SYSTEM

ONE OF THE basic organizing principles of the network of social relations in Wakhi society is agnatic descent and kinship. Personal identity, group membership, unity and difference, conflict and harmony, within or between groups in Wakhi society, are expressed on the basis of cultural ideas grounded in agnatic-descent relations and kinship affinities.

The Wakhi ideas of descent and affinity serve as cultural guides for the organization of social allotments (e.g., agnatic-descent groups, domestic units, local community groups, and the larger society) as well as a means of interpersonal communication and social interaction within the context of their social system.

The Wakhi do not claim a common ancestry for all the members of their society. On the contrary, they acknowledge six different agnatic-descent categories (or groups) that recognize separate and distinct ancestral ties, with minor exceptions. Each of the six is assigned and referred to by a particular distinctive title commonly used throughout the society.

Sayyed

The group claims direct descent from the Prophet Mohammed,[1]

1. It is very common in the Muslim world to find among peoples of all linguistic, regional, and racial origins a few who claim ancestry from certain impor-

and consists of only four families residing in four separate villages. They keep close contact with other families and groups claiming similar blood ties with the Prophet outside Wakhan. In the Wakhan the total membership in this group does not exceed seventy persons.

Khuja

About five families, all living in the same hamlet, acknowledge descent from Sayyed Sorab Aowleya, who was allegedly also related to the Prophet Mohammed. However, this claim is disputed by some members of the community, who consider their ancestry traceable to the first caliph of Islam, abu-Bakr, and not to the Prophet himself.

The senior leading male members of both Sayyed and Khuja groups are addressed by the same honorific title, *shah* (monarch or king). Both are rival spiritual leaders with different semihereditary followers or disciples from among the rest of the society. In practice, they are the theocratic lords of Wakhan.

Mir

The descendants of the former Wakhi Mirs, or chieftains and feudal lords, whom the early travelers in Wakhan have described as the then rulers of the territory, comprise this group. At present, there are only three domestic units, about thirty persons, occupying the old Wakhan stronghold at Qala-i-Panja. As a small group they are comparatively land rich. Politically, however, they now exercise little or no authority.

Like many of the nineteenth-century, and earlier, rulers of Badakhshan and Amu Darya region, the Mirs of Wakhan allegedly claimed ancestry from Alexander the Great, locally known as Iskander (see Wood 1872, p. 244; Olufsen 1969, p. 86).

Sha-ana

These are the descendants of those male members of the Mir

---

tant Islamic leaders and saints. Some groups have gone so far as to prepare a family pedigree tracing their alleged ancestry to the Prophet Mohammed or the Caliphs of Islam, and certain saints. The origin and perpetuation of this phenomenon is certainly a fascinating research topic in itself. For our purposes, however, I am concerned only with the sociological significance of the make-believe of such alleged ancestry, and not whether their claims are supported by evidence.

agnatic-descent group who broke the prescribed rules of endogamy and married women of the Kheek (commoner) group. As a result they lost their membership in the Mir descent group, thus creating a new kinship group with a new place in the social hierarchy of Wakhi society. There are only two domestic units, about fifteen persons, living in a different settlement from that of the Mirs.

Khyberi

About seventy individuals claim descent from the courtiers of the former Mirs. Their common ancestor is believed to have been a man from Khyber, who had joined the service of one of the Mirs, and later married the Mir's daughter.

Kheek

These are the remainder of Wakhi society, the largest but the lowest ranking group—the Wakhi commoners. They reckon descent from an unknown, but common ancestor for all the Kheek. Collectively they are the least organized, thus lacking group characteristics. They are divided into numerous small agnatic-descent-based groups who play significant parts within their social system.

As mentioned in chapter 2, the term Kheek has two meanings. The first meaning is described above; a second meaning (when used by the Wakhi in a different social context, such as distinguishing themselves from others, e.g., Kirghiz, etc.) denotes the entire Wakhi population (i.e., Sayyed, Khuja, Mir, Sha-ana, Khyberi, and Kheek).

The same agnatic-descent ideas have a direct bearing upon the principles of marriage and affinity in Wakhi society. The agnatic-descent groups and categories prefer endogamy, and the exchange of women is permitted only between certain groups and forbidden between others. For example, it is possible for Sayyed, Khuja, and Mir to exchange women with each other and Khyberi, Sha-ana, and Kheek to do the same, but it is strictly forbidden for the first three groups to exchange women with the last three.

This social structural dichotomy in Wakhi society is explained by the cultural notion of the "quality of blood." The Wakhi consider the first three agnatic-descent groups as *asl* (original, pure) or of "high blood and birth" and the last three as *ghareeb*[2] (poor) or

2. The term *ghareeb* in Iranian Persian means "stranger." In *Dari* or Afghan Persian, the primary meaning attached to the term *ghareeb* is "poor and lowly." Among

of "common blood"; not equals, they may not intermarry. However, this social differentiation is relevant only in so far as the Wakhi choices of marriage partners are concerned. Other kinds of structural differentiation and group integration become significant in other contexts (see fig. 1). For example, the Mir group is lumped together with the Khyberi, Sha-ana, and Kheek as members of a larger category referred to as *mereed* (disciples, followers, or subjects, etc.) vis-à-vis the category of the *peer* (spiritual leader, master, and savior), which includes only Sayyed and Khuja groups.

The *mereed* have traditional allegiance to only the head of either the Sayyed or Khuja group. The leader is referred to as the *peer*, who is also called the *shah*, thus forming yet another structural dichotomy. Each of the two new categories consists of a *peer* whose traditional following comes from among all of the four lower strata of the Wakhi society. The *mereed* membership in the two categories is not based on individual choice, rather it is determined by the traditional affiliation and allegiance of the family units to the head of either the Sayyed or the Khuja groups. Change of allegiance, when and if desired, is the privilege of the family as a group and not of its individual members.

The Sayyed and the Khuja descent groups are the ruling class in Wakhi society. The leaders of the two groups exercise a form of "patrimonial domain" (Wolf 1966) over the rest of the Wakhi population. It should be noted however that the right of domain exercised by each *peer* or *shah*, in this instance, is not based on legal claims over the land upon which subjects reside and work. Instead, claims to the right of domain are justified by descent from Rasul (the Prophet). By the same token they hold the position of *shah*, or spiritual intermediary, in the religious hierarchy of an Ismailia sect of Islam headed by the descendants of the Aga Khan (Stein 1928, p. 865). The annual tribute received by the *shah* is sanctioned largely by the Wakhi religious belief in the sanctity of the person of the *shah* by virtue of his descent from the Prophet. The Ismailite Wakhi also believe that the *shah* has the power to influence the fortune and misfortune of his followers in this world, as well as in the next. His spiritual guidance is sought in matters of faith and

the Wakhi, as well as in many parts of Badakhshan and northern Afghanistan, poor, landless people refer to themselves as *ghareeb kar*, those who do the work of poor men—perform manual labor and other menial tasks. My translation of *asl* as "high blood and birth" and *ghareeb* as "common blood" in the text is based on the connotations of the terms as they are used by the Wakhi. (I am grateful to Dr. Michael Fischer of Harvard University who brought the dialectical differences of the meaning of the word *ghareeb* to my attention).

Descent groups	Asl (high blood)			Ghareeb (common blood)		
	Sayyed	Khuja	Mir	Sha-ana	Khyberi	Kheek
Sayyed	XX	X	X	—	—	—
Khuja	X	XX	X	—	—	—
Mir	X	X	XX	—	—	—
Sha-ana	—	—	—	XX	X	X
Khyberi	—	—	—	X	XX	X
Kheek	—	—	—	X	X	XX

XX = preferred marriages

X = permitted marriages

— = prohibited marriages

Prescriptive Rules of Marriage in Wakhi Society

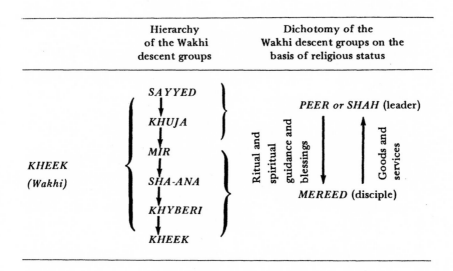

Fig. 1. Social stratification in Wakhi society on the basis of agnatic descent affiliation and religious status.

and in life crisis situations, and his help is expected either directly or through his representative, the *khalifa*. His happiness is desired by his followers, all of whom hope for his blessings, and the annual contributions to the *shah* by the *mereed* is part of their religious obligation (i.e., as alms) to their much revered theocratic leader. These contributions are not "rent" for the land. This particular right of domain is passed on to the next generation through the agnatic line as patrimony.

Each *shah*, as the head of his local theocratic organization, appoints *khalifa* as his personal representatives in each hamlet or group of neighboring hamlets (see fig. 2). *Khalifa* are chosen from among the devoted and pious Kheek families. They are responsible for carrying out all the religious and ceremonial functions (cure of illnesses, funerals, weddings, etc.) in their own constituency, and also act as the intermediary between the villagers and the *shah*. The *shah* pays annual visits each autumn to all hamlets where he has followers, during which time the *mereed* are obliged to present him with gifts (food, animals, etc.) in addition to paying him the annual tribute amounting to one-tenth of their earnings from harvest, livestock owned, and cash income from labor and services rendered to the markets outside Wakhan. The *mereed* are also expected to allocate a certain amount of annual labor to the personal services of the *shah* (plowing, sowing, harvesting, herding, etc.). The *khalifa* has a personal obligation to aid in the collection and transfer of the goods and services from his people to the *shah*. He usually keeps his share out of the accumulated tributes, before delivering them to the *shah*.[3] The *shah*, in his turn, is believed to convert part of the goods received in tributes to cash or valuable goods and send it as part of his contribution to the next person(s) above in the hierarchy in Pakistan or India. He may also redistribute a small portion of the collected goods to the poor, disabled, and needy who seek help, but it is a rare occurrence.

In 1921, during the time of the visit of General Nadir Khan, the names of the ancestors of the present *shahs* were not recorded in the list of the ten important and strong men of the area given by his secretary in his travel memoirs (Kushkaki 1923). It would appear, therefore, that the emergence of the *shah* as a dominant

3. I was told that in 1973 the *shah* of Qala-i-Panja alone received 400 head of cattle, 500 *gadek*, 10,000 *sairs* (equivalent to over 70,000 kilograms) of grain, mostly wheat, and 40 *sairs* (210 kg.) of cooking oil and fat. These figures contain additional contributions made by his followers to partially cover the cost of his second wife, whom he married in the fall of that year. I was unable to get an estimate of how much the various *khalifa* may have retained before passing the amounts mentioned on to the *shah*.

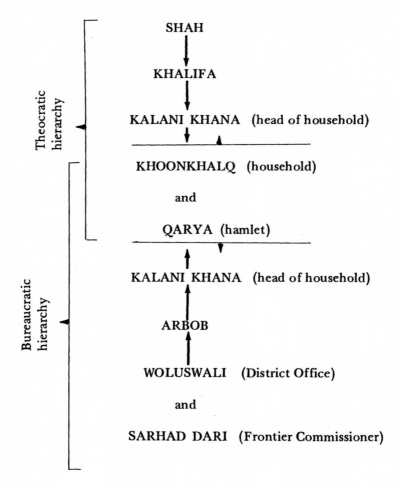

Fig. 2. The structure of theocratic and bureaucratic organization in the Wakhan.

force in the local sociopolitical scene is quite recent. It is possible, however, that they were serving as the religious functionaries under the Mirs, the political leaders of Wakhan.

The Mirs, during the national pacification efforts, either fled the area or were forced to emigrate to other parts of the new Afghan nation-state. The local power vacuum was filled by the heads of the Sayyed and Khuja groups who were more sympathetic towards the central authority in Kabul. Therefore, they were given the new role of the political mediators between the Wakhi and the government authorities, the role filled by the Mirs in the past.

Thus, their traditional religious authority and newly sanctioned political role by the government put the *shahs* into the local limelight. The relations of the *shah* with the main religious body to the south of the Hindu Kush have become weaker, but his economic gains locally have increased dramatically. Despite their economic power and religious influence, they have remained nothing more than local dignitaries, posing no threat to central authority.

SOCIAL SYSTEM AND ADAPTIVE STRATEGIES

The Wakhi agnatic-descent principles do not serve only to guide social interaction and personal and group identity within their stratified social system, but, as indicated earlier, they are also directly related to resource management and use, which in turn involves decision-making processes. There is no question that the upper social strata (Sayyed, Khuja, and Mir) are the major landowners. There are other differences in access to resources, power, and authority, based on the cultural principles of kinship and affinity, existing within the local and domestic groups and which involve the members of all of the six major agnatic groups. However, these guiding principles of social relations, powerful and prevailing though they may be, are at the same time subject to the influences of environmental constraints and the resources available. That is, if the particular local, domestic, social, and spatial organizations found in a society are ecologically viable, they are the product of the systemic processes of social, cultural, and environmental constraints (availability of resources and the types of subsistence strategies, etc.) as a whole rather than the consequences of a single dominant form.

Subsistence Structure

Wakhi subsistence depends upon agriculture, pastoralism, and manual labor, activities that are determined for individuals and groups by their particular types of resources.

Wakhi agriculture *(dehqani)* relies on the use of a simple plow with animal traction combined with human energy that fits what is called by Wolf "a paleotechnic peasant ecotype" (Wolf 1966, p. 30). Most Wakhi have access to some cultivable land, and secure their livelihood, at least in part, by working on the land. The size of landholding varies among families depending on the location of their residence and such other environmental factors as irrigation, water, terrain, and altitude.

Pastoralism *(maldari)* consists of two patterns of herding, based on the number of livestock owned, and the ecological zone(s) utilized by the productive units. The first type, a form that closely parallels pastoral-nomadism, is practiced only by a small number of land-rich Wakhi households (about twenty-five to thirty) that own large herds of sheep, goats (at least over one hundred head), and cattle or yak. Under this system, the herd and some members of the households spend the summer months on the fringes of the Pamirs and the rest of the year in various points in the Wakhan where adequate pasturage is available. The pastoral section of the family resides either in movable abodes, like the Kirghiz yurt, during the summer or in temporary shelters built by them in their traditional pasturage grounds. They may spend very little or no part of the winter months in their main agricultural settlements with the rest of the domestic unit, but instead live through the winter in the family agricultural outpost, where a small house and shelter for the animals has been built, and where fodder for the animals is stored for the bad weather periods. These outposts are located in a remote area in proximity to wide and open pastures where the large herds may forage for themselves in all but the most inclement weather.

There are no Wakhi pastoralists in the Wakhan ecological zone independent of their agriculturalist counterparts within a single productive unit. Furthermore, this pastoral-nomadic pursuit is only possible for the rich landed groups who have the means to participate in activities that call for use of the different resources available in separate ecological zones. Although the pastoralists of a household do not spend any of the winter months in "tents," this particular form of pastoralism, in conjunction with agriculture, seems to fit what is generally termed *agropastoral* subsistence.

The second pattern of pastoralism is the one found in most peasant societies with a paleotechnic ecotype, where the poorer agriculturalists keep a few cattle, sheep, and goats for traction, transport, milk, fleece, fuel, manure for their fields, or cash. The animals are generally kept in the agricultural settlement year round and are pastured nearby with a communally hired herder(s), or other ar-

rangements are made. Even the rich agropastoralists keep a small
number of their livestock in the village for their immediate use.

The third subsistence activity in the Wakhan is manual labor
(ghareeb kari) done by those who must earn at least part of their
living by such skills as smithing, or by doing manual labor within
or outside of Wakhan. The great majority of laborers are members
of either landless families or families who have a large number of able,
productive members but do not have access to sufficient amounts
of land and other agricultural means and/or livestock.[4] Therefore,
a part or the whole of their livelihood depends on their earnings
from services to rich Wakhi, the pastoralist Kirghiz, the itinerant traders,
or in the rural and urban labor markets in Badakhshan and northern
Afghanistan.

Settlement Patterns and Local Groups

The structure and distribution of the Wakhi settlements are
again a product of ecological and sociocultural factors working in
concert. They are generally composed of small dispersed hamlets,
located at irregular intervals throughout the inhabitable area or
the valley floors. This distribution makes possible a maximum use of
the very limited resources in the area. The two major components of
the Wakhi settlement pattern and social units are: (1) *qarya* (hamlet)
and *qoum* (the local community); and (2) *khana* (house) and *khoonkhalq* (the household).

Qarya and· qoum: Unlike settled agriculturalist communities in Badakhshan and other parts of Afghanistan, the Wakhi local communities are not large nucleated or centralized villages. Instead, the Wakhi
qarya consists of a number of residential structures, *khana*, scattered
throughout the tiny plots of farmland dotting the narrow high valley
oases. The *qarya* sites are located next to mountain spurs and alluvial fans in the valley, which provide a certain amount of protection
for people, animals, and the agricultural fields against the severe
bad-i-Wakhan, the Wakhan wind.

Hamlets are located not only to provide shelter from the violent
and persistent westerly wind but where ample amounts of irrigation
water from tributary streams, adequate pasturage, and other resources

---

4. Unfortunately I do not have quantitative data on the actual number of
landless and herdless Wakhi households. However, on the basis of my observations and discussions with the Wakhi and others I would estimate the number
to be less than 10 percent of the total Wakhi households.

such as brush for fuel are in proximity. The availability of arable land is the major factor in the choice of settlement sites and the eventual size of the settlements themselves.

The residents of Wakhi hamlets are often members of a common agnatic-descent group referred to as *qoum*. The *qoum*, because of its common descent and local residence, makes up the largest community group in Wakhi society. Members share many corporate rights and social responsibilities as a group. For instance, the pasturage *(maghzar)*, the brush-fuel resources *(jangal)*,[5] and the water for irrigation are communally owned and controlled. As a result, the maintenance of irrigation channels and protection and proper use of other resources is also carried out in collaboration with all members of the *qoum*. The local community usually hires several poor *ghareeb kar* from among their own *qoum* to serve as community herdsmen, water caretakers, or protectors of the community fields and pasturage. These individuals are hired each year with community consensus, and are paid a set amount of grain by each household on the basis of the amount of cultivated land and livestock each owns. In smaller hamlets, however, all domestic units may rotate these tasks. A group of neighboring small hamlets may join in a number of other communal activities such as weddings, funerals, and religious festivities. These ritual and ceremonial activities are often supervised by the *khalifa*, who is designated by the theocratic leader, the *shah*. The same local group also elects an *arbob*, who acts as liaison between the local community and the district administrative agencies. The elected *arbob*, who is approved by the government authorities, is usually a local strong man who plays a part in the community life that closely parallels the duties of the *khalifa*. The positions of *arbob* and *khalifa* are always filled by different persons. The *arbob*'s duties involve mediation between the villagers and the governmental organizations while the *khalifa* mediates between the villagers and the religious leader, the *shah* (see fig. 2). As such, the position of *arbob* is a recent creation and he is charged with reporting births, deaths, criminal acts, as well as aiding the district office *(woluswali)* in the process of conscription for military duty, collection of taxes, labor levies for the construction of public facilities, and the provision of hospitality. He also provides transportation and guides for govern-

5. Not all *maghzar* and *jangal* resources are owned by the villagers. The national government claims the right to a great deal of these resources (particularly where there are permanent government posts) and they are protected by frontier guard detachments in the area. Such claims are a source of frequent confrontation between the villagers and the military authorities, in which the Wakhi always lose.

ment officials when and if they frequent the hamlets. Many of these duties are assigned to the corporate community by the government, but they are in turn relegated to the Wakhi household. Each productive unit satisfies the community responsibilities following the procedure instituted by the community, such as taking turns in a rotation system or sharing them every time.

Khana and khoonkhalq: The *khana* is a mazelike structure, erected in an imperfect rectangular shape from mud and stone, covered with a flat roofing of mud and dirt, and supported by many vertical pillars and horizontal rafters, beams, and tree branches. Architecturally it is unlike houses elsewhere in Badakhshan and Afghanistan, with the exception of adjacent areas of the upper Amu Darya or Panj valley—that is, Ishkashim, Gharan, and Shighnan. Houses are generally located very close to, or in the center of, the households' landholdings. The Wakhi *khana* is built with three factors in mind: economy of space, so that a large number of household members can literally live under a single roof; maximum protection for residents against the stresses of the Wakhan wind and cold; and cost and availability of building materials.

The main residential quarters in the Wakhi house are almost identical in layout throughout the area but variation in size often reveals the past and/or present household economic strength. The room is rectangular, with high clay platforms built around all sides (see fig. 3). The highest platform (about one meter high), is located opposite the entrance, and it contains the family hearth. This platform is used for cooking and as a work area for the women. Other platforms (about 50 centimeters high) are partitioned by mud walls with their openings facing the center of the house. These small partitioned platforms are used as living and sleeping areas by the various nuclear families of the household. The lower central area is further divided into two sections. The area closer to the main hearth is elevated (about 30 centimeters high) and contains a small fire pit in addition to the ash pit at the bottom of the open cavity of the family hearth. The lowest portion in the center of the room is multipurpose. The main entrance to the house leads into it, so footwear is usually taken off here, and here the supply of fuel for immediate cooking and heating purposes is also stored. It is used for the family loom in autumn and at other times newborn, sick, weak, or aged animals are kept there and nursed at night. For poorer families who own very few animals this part of the house becomes a permanent night shelter for their few animals during most of the cold-weather periods.

The Wakhi house has a single direct opening to the elements,

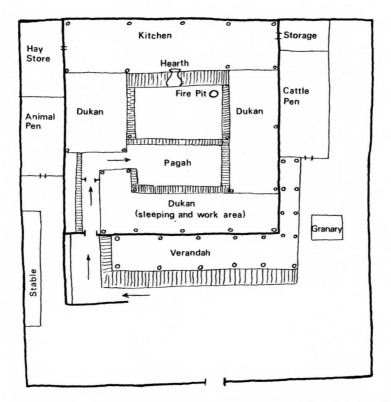

Fig. 3. *Above,* Wakhi house plan; *below,* bazaar in Khandud, district center and largest settlement of Wakhan

a skylight above the hearth that furnishes the room with light and allows the smoke to escape. The skylight is equipped with a wooden trapdoor that can be opened and shut from the hearth platform with the aid of a stick. On the roof the skylight is surrounded by the chimney wall to prevent the vicious wind from blowing down into the room.

The entrance(s) to the main room in the Wakhi house is never directly exposed to the outside elements. To reach the hearthroom one has to go through a mazelike passage, including two or three low wooden doors and interconnected chambers. The corridors and chambers leading to the room are usually used for storage or for animal shelters. The purpose of the design is to keep the hearthroom heat in, and the wind and cold out. Additional insulation of the house is achieved by the Wakhi practice of piling winter fodder for the animals on top of the house roof and building all the stables, sheds, verandahs, and so on (for their summer use) adjacent to the main room, so that it is completely surrounded by other structures.[6]

Very little wood is used in the Wakhan as fuel for cooking or heating since it is scarce and slow growing. Whatever wood can be procured is used for construction of the houses and other shelters that require a great number of beams for rafters, pillars, and other kinds of support. Only a few rich families, particularly in the Sarhad valley area, are able to use some tree branches for cooking or heating their houses. Since only a few hamlets have *jangal* near their settlements the Wakhi depend on another equally scarce fuel, animal dung, which is collected and made into cakes. Animal dung is usually supplemented with brush kindling gathered from the mountainsides.

All cooking is done on the clay hearth, which has a narrow vertical opening along its side facing the center of the room, so some heat radiates out to warm the rest of the house. The small fire pit in the lower platform is used for making tea and heating the house. The indoor temperature is higher than the outside and generally comfortable. For many undernourished and poorly clad Wakhi, therefore, the relatively well-insulated house is the main sanctuary against the suffering and stresses caused by the cold. The Wakhi spend minimal time outside during the long winter months, and are usually huddled close to the fire during the day, going to bed early in the evenings and sleeping in groups of four or five, with members

6. For a good description of the architectural characteristics of household dwellings in the region of the upper Amu Darya, including Wakhan, see Olufsen (1969, chap. 4).

of a nuclear family often under the same blanket. This practice is also noted among the Peruvian high-altitude and cold-climate inhabitants (see Baker et al. 1968, p. 18).

A large number of related natal-conjugal families often live in the same Wakhi dwelling as members of a single, corporate, domestic unit, referred to by the Wakhi as *khoonkhalq*. Ideally, the *khoonkhalq* is a patrilocal agnatic descent group that is generally endogamous and corporate. The size of a domestic unit at any given point in time depends upon the stage reached in the developmental cycle of domestic groups. Immediately after fission a household may have five to ten members, but, when it reaches maturity in its developmental cycle, through conjugal and natal processes, it may contain as many as twenty to twenty-five members.

At its largest the *khoonkhalq* is usually made up of two or more joint patrilineal extended families. The smallest domestic unit in Wakhi society consists of some type of extended family unit (i.e., joint or composite).

Independent households made up of a nuclear family, common to industrial societies, are rare or nonexistent in the Wakhan. The Wakhi *khoonkhalq* is usually composed of three to five adjacent generations, represented by several conjugal-natal families. This is particularly true of rich households and those groups occupying the upper social strata in Wakhi society.

The principal independent socioeconomic unit in Wakhi society is the corporate domestic unit in charge of production and consumption. The members of this kin-based domestic group are distinguished terminologically from one another on the basis of sex, generation, consanguinity vs. affinity, and lineality vs. collaterality (see table 1). While age and seniority seem important they are not reflected in the Wakhi kinship terminology system. Senior males and females in households enjoy a certain amount of respect but the exercise of absolute patriarchal power and authority by a senior male occurs only in Sayyed and Khuja households, and to some degree among economically better off domestic units. Generally, decisions concerning the household are made collectively by all adult male members of the *khoonkhalq*, and not a single dominant male. The eldest son, however, represents the household interests in community and societal affairs. The organization of production and consumption remains a collective task involving all members of the household.

The Organization of Production

Wakhi economy is perhaps best characterized as a marginal sub-

TABLE 1
WAKHI KINSHIP TERMS OF REFERENCE

Consanguineal Terms

Generation	LINEAL		COLLATERAL	
	Male	Female	Male	Female
2	*poop*	*moom*	*poop*	*moom*
	FaFa	FaMo	FaFaBr	FaMoSi
	MoFa	MoMo	MoFaBr	MoMoSi
1	*tat*	*nan*	*buch*	*vach*
	Fa	Mo	FaBr	FaSi
			MoBr	MoSi
0			*verut*	*khoey*
			Br	Si
	Ego			
			rutsaps	
			FaBrChi;	MoBrChi
			FaSiChi;	MoSiChi
-1	*putr*	*thegt*	*verut putr/ thegt*	*khoey putr/ thegt*
	So	Da	BrSo/Da	SiSo/Da
			rutsaps	
			FaBrChiChi	
			MoBrChiChi	
-2	*nepos*	*nepos*		
	SoChi	DaChi		

Affinal Terms

    shuy—Hu; *kund*—Wi
    khors—WiFa; *khush*—WiMo; *baksht* (or *kund khoey*)—WiSi;
    kheseirs—WiBr, SiHu; *baja*—WiSiHu; *damaad*—DaHu, SiHi, FaSiHu,
    MoSiHu; *stukh*—SoWi; *baksht*—HuBr; *baksht* (or *verut kund*)—BrWi;
    vach—FaBrWi; MoBrWi; *deg-da*—SoWiMo+Fa; BrWiMo+Fa; DaHuMo+Fa;
    SiHuMo+Fa.

sistence production system involving high-altitude irrigated agriculture and livestock breeding—that is, agropastoralism or mixed farming. A certain amount of "surplus" labor is also made available to outside economies by some Wakhi households, at least during part of the year, depending on their economic needs.

Division of labor in Wakhi households is influenced largely by the demands of a short agricultural growing and harvesting season, and the long, cold, and idle winter months. This system requires a large and concentrated labor force during the brief agricultural season and a much smaller number during the rest of the year. Because of these labor requirements there is no sharp sexual division of labor, unlike the male activities versus female tasks among the low-altitude agriculturalists in other parts of Afghanistan. Instead, their activities complement each other in agriculture, herding, and domestic services. Some of the major undertakings of males and females in their productive activities are as follows:

ACTIVITIES	MALE	FEMALE
Agriculture	Irrigation tasks; reaping and transporting the harvest on the back to threshing grounds; threshing, winnowing, carrying chaff and threshed straw to the hay storage, and transporting the grain.	Carrying manure to the fields; guarding the crops against birds and beasts; weeding the fields; tying reaped harvest into sheaves; gleaning, sifting, and cleaning the grain; and carrying chaff and threshed straw on the head in large willow baskets to hay storage.
Livestock care	Supervising grazing, making hay, and shearing.	Milking, feeding the animals in their stable, looking after the sick and the young.

The youth cooperate extensively in herding activities, while much of the late autumn and winter care of livestock is shared equally by both adult males and females, as well as the youth.

Domestic chores	Collecting brush and wood fuel; building fires.	Collecting dung from outside; making dung cakes from animal droppings in household stables; cooking.
Clothing	Much of household weaving, some spinning, with a drop spindle; sewing some male garments.	Spinning—with spinning wheel as well as drop spindle; sewing and knitting.

The upkeep of the house interior as well as the exterior and the construction of all shelters involve both male and female labor. In a household with a large number of adult women and a smaller male labor force, it is not uncommon to see women and their male partners doing the same tasks.

The division of labor in Wakhi society is not, therefore, sex-determined, but is influenced by the practical needs of each household and the uneven nature of the seasonal labor demands.

Agriculture

Wakhi agriculture is highly demanding. Not only does the thin, sandy, and porous topsoil yield poorly, but the area is highly subject to natural calamities. Agricultural work begins in late April or early May with the spreading of a compost of human and animal excrement and ash on the small terraced plots of farmland. At the same time, irrigation channels damaged by avalanches and winter ice are repaired. In May and the early part of June the fields are irrigated and plowed, generally by two oxen pulling a light wooden plow equipped with a detachable cast-iron tip for furrowing. Large clumps of dirt are broken down in two ways. Sometimes men and women walk behind the plow and break up earth with a small club. At other times a long heavy board *(mala)* is attached to the yoke and pulled over the freshly tilled soil to even out the land surface as well as to break down lumps of earth. Fields are plowed at least twice in a crisscrossing manner, and then the seeds are broadcast.

Barley, or the Wakhi *kaljow,* is the first crop sown, followed by the most common Wakhi mixed crop—barley, lupine, lentils, and horsebeans all mixed and broadcast in the same field. Some of these crops are also grown separately, but not in large quantities. Wheat is cultivated next, followed by flax and millet. Best suited to the sandy soil and least vulnerable to the extreme weather are barley, lupine, and lentils. The return even for these relatively high yielding crops in this area is barely more than ten to twelve times the amount of seed sown. Wheat has a fairly low return ratio; about six- to ten-fold, under normal conditions, depending on the nature and location of land under cultivation. In addition to the low yields, the high-altitude Wakhi crops suffer tremendously from periodic damage by early frost in the autumn, or prolonged cold and snow during the plowing season.

As soon as the crops germinate and surface, the fields have to be irrigated at least two times a week until about two weeks before harvest. In the meantime, repeated weeding and intensive protection of the fields against village livestock and birds, particularly in the few weeks prior to harvest, must be maintained. The location of the Wakhi house close to the household fields is necessary because of the constant attention that must be given to the fields during the cultivating and growing season.

Wakhi agriculture is based on a short fallow system, under which a piece of land is cultivated only every other year, particularly if the land cannot be fertilized. Because of the need for animal dung for fuel, it is often not possible to fertilize all of the fields. Whatever land can be fertilized is then cultivable for at least two consecutive years, leaving it fallow for the third. After the plowing and sowing of plots under cultivation is completed, the fallow plots are also tilled to help recondition the land. This short fallow system, in the face of the limited arable land, puts an additional burden on those households with small landholdings.

Tilling of the fallow land, and cutting, drying, collecting, and storing fodder for the winter is done during the growing season. Agricultural work is concluded after the peak labor demands during the harvest in September, the culmination of a highly concentrated work period of five months. The next seven months are fairly unproductive. The major occupation for households with livestock becomes care of the animals, and the spinning, knitting, and weaving of the sheep fleece into the woolen material *(tan)* that is used for many of the heavy warm Wakhi garments. Goat and yak hair are spun and woven into unknotted carpets, the Wakhi *palaas*, which cover the floor of the houses.

Other winter occupations include the treating and softening of the sheepskins acquired from the Kirghiz through trade during these months, and turning them into coats and sheepskin mats. Goatskins and yak hides are also locally treated and used for making high boots, without high heels, which are worn with high thick woolen stockings as the main footgear. After treatment, goatskins are also made into hide bags, used to hold and transport grains and flour.

"Surplus" Labor

Most adult males, particularly those in households that do not own large herds and with inadequate landholdings, have very little or no productive work to engage in during the long winter months. In such cases, the household income from agriculture is not sufficient to permit them to acquire, through the exchange of agricultural and livestock products, the market goods they must have. Some adult men from these households then go to the villages and towns of Badakhshan and northern Afghanistan in late autumn and winter to earn cash to buy their household needs. Generally employed as porters, manual laborers in construction, and in agricultural work, they return to Wakhan in time for the new agricultural season in the spring. The men from land-poor or landless Wakhi households, the *ghareeb kar*, also engage in similar work in Badakhshan during the summer months and work as farm laborers (reapers, hay makers, etc.), moving from one area to another following the harvests from the lower, warmer areas to those higher and colder. The men from these households often alternate between a year in household agricultural work and a year in "migratory" wage labor outside Wakhan. Not all *ghareeb kar* go to Badakhshan, however. Some Wakhi, particularly those living in the Sarhad River valley and the extreme upper Amu Darya areas who are closer to the Pamirs, seek employment among the Kirghiz during part of the year, earning livestock or livestock products to be used by their household or exchanged for market goods with traders.

Livestock

Wakhi livestock consists in part of two types of sheep, a dwarf native breed, *gadek*, and the large Central Asian fat-tailed sheep known as *turki*. A small number of *gadek* are owned by a large number of households, while the *turki* are possessed only by the rich. *Gadek*, which lamb twice a year, are also known for their twin, and sometimes multiple, births. They supply little milk, but have a very fine, soft fleece, which is used for many of the Wakhi garments and much of their bedding. The small *gadek* provides little meat, and since they are not able to make the distant markets on foot, their exchange value is generally small. A smaller number of goats are also kept along with the sheep in Wakhi flocks. Goats are kept for their skin and hair as well as for their milk and moderate exchange value.

More important in the Wakhi productive system are common cattle, and most households own a few. The cows are the main source of milk besides being a good source of cash, and the oxen are used as draft animals and for threshing the harvest. Cattle, both cows and oxen, have a high rate of exchange and are taken by traders to villages and towns in Badakhshan, where they are kept for breeding and traction, or are slaughtered for meat. Cattle provide most of the fuel and fertilizer in the Wakhi subsistence system.

Yak are kept only by the rich and those who live in the upper part of the Sarhad River valley. Unlike common cattle, yak are not very useful for agriculture, except for their manure. Oxen are used as pack animals as well as for transportation, and the female gives very rich and tasty milk. Yak hair is used to make the Wakhi carpets *(palaas)* and yak tails are sold to traders for fairly high prices.

The hides of both cattle and yak are tanned and treated locally and used for making foot- and other gear, besides having a good exchange value if sold. In the past, yak had only a marginal value in the markets of northern Pakistan, but with the increased demand for meat in the towns and cities of northern Afghanistan, the market value is rising sharply in Wakhan and in the Pamirs. Although the hybridization of common cattle and yak has been accomplished in Zebak, near the entrance to the Wakhan Corridor, to date there are no hybrids in the Wakhan.

A few donkeys are also owned by most Wakhi households. Rather small but sturdy animals, they are used as beasts of burden and for transportation throughout the area. Donkeys are used in agricultural transportation, as well as in threshing the harvest.

Horses are less numerous than donkeys and are regarded as very valuable possessions, to be used as both mount and pack animals, but almost exclusively by the richer households. Rental of horses to traders and travelers brings in a considerable amount of cash, especially when they are rented to members of the hunting and mountain climbing expeditions that have been coming to the area almost every summer for the past decade. Horses have a very high rate of exchange among the Wakhi and an even higher value among the Kirghiz.

A small number of Bactrian camels are owned by the very rich Wakhi households, including those of the *shah*. The camels have little function in the Wakhi economy at the present time, other than for their wool. They are rarely, if ever, used for transportation, and are too valuable for slaughter. Therefore, they are basically a sign of wealth and prestige for those households that own them. Occasionally, however, they are traded with the Kirghiz, who need and employ them for transportation. It should be pointed out that the Wakhi have only recently acquired the Bactrian camels, the yak, and the *turki* sheep from the Kirghiz pastoral nomads of the Afghan Pamirs.

The Organization of Disposition

The Wakhi household or *khoonkhalq* is the corporate domestic unit in charge of the disposition of its earnings in order to meet its needs and obligations. The *khoonkhalq* as a group pays the national land tax for its landholdings in wheat or barley. This land tax is a uniform amount, levied throughout the country without regard to the productivity of the land, the varying fallow systems, or the natural calamities that may affect agricultural productivity. Therefore, the payment of this tax puts a much heavier burden on the low-yielding, high-altitude Wakhi agriculturalist than on farmers in lower altitudes. During poor harvest years, this tax alone claims much of the meager wheat harvest of the *khoonkhalq*, and it has to pay one tenth of all its annual earnings as tribute to its theocratic leader, the *shah*. Again, wheat and barley are preferred for payment of the tribute, but cash, livestock, livestock products, market goods, and services are also used for tribute by all members of the lower social stratum, the *mereed*.

A certain amount of the proceeds of the annual harvest is spent for the feeding and care of the draft animals, as well as for the maintenance and renewal of agricultural tools and implements. One item required for agricultural work that is not locally produced is the detachable cast-iron plow tip, which the Wakhi buy from traders who bring them from Badakhshan. Most of their other agricultural equipment is produced locally by members of the household themselves, or acquired from local craftsmen. Households pay the community herder a stipulated amount of grain depending on the type and number of animals he has herded for them during the year. Also paid are the community-hired water caretaker, and the protector of the community fields and pastures.

Some of the major costs incurred by the Wakhi household are related to life cycle rituals—ceremonial costs. The Wakhi celebrate childbirth, particularly the birth of males, and deaths in the household, especially deaths of adults, are very costly. Wakhi funeral ceremonies involve several commemorative feasts, particularly during the first year after the death. Funerary costs can be very high among members of the upper social stratum, particularly if they are rich. The graves of the rich and pious are often enshrined in mud and stone structures and marked with flags and Marco Polo sheep horns. Although the Wakhi emphatically deny it, it is believed by many non-Wakhi who have lived in the area for a long time that armaments, clothing, carpets, and other expensive personal effects of the deceased are placed in the crypt with the corpse. A common practice among all the Wakhi is to leave food by the graveside on a number of occasions during the year, and to light candles made of cloth smeared in oil and wrapped around kindling sticks.

Marriages are also costly and are an economic strain for many

Wakhi households because they are not only prolonged festivities but involve the exchange of many goods over a period of time. Both a bride-wealth and dowry are exchanged. Many of the goods exchanged are imported commodities bought from traders or market towns for high prices, and include quantities of rice, tea, opium, candy, and cloth as well as livestock and agricultural and animal products. Bridewealth and dowry vary with the resources of the households and the relations (kinship, locality, and social stratum) between the two families or households involved. Marriages outside the *khoon-khalq* cost from five to ten thousand Afghanis (the equivalent of about two hundred U.S. dollars at least), a sum large enough to prevent the young men from many poor households from establishing conjugal families of their own, or at least to delay their marriages. If a household lacks an eligible marriage partner—that is, first cousin—it is not uncommon to find an adult man in his forties who has never married because of his inability to pay the bridewealth required for marriage outside his own domestic unit. This economic constraint is partially alleviated, however, through the Wakhi preferred endog-amous marriage practices.

In addition to paying taxes, tributes, renewing and replacing agricultural tools and implements, and meeting ceremonial costs, the *khoonkhalq* also has the responsibility of feeding and clothing its members and keeping the household productive, and Wakhi dietary habits and practices have a profound effect on household costs and economic patterns. The Wakhi have developed a habit of consuming large quantities of a concoction made from Indian black tea, *shur chai*. The term literally means "salty tea." It is a brew of a very strong, bitter, black tea, produced by boiling a handful of tea to about a quart of water with a small addition of salt and a cup of cream and milk (sometimes butter is added if available) to modify the taste.

Several gallons of *shur chai* are consumed by most Wakhi house-holds every day. It is drunk particularly during early morning and noon meals, which are supplemented with some bread made of a milled mixture of barley, lupine, lentil, and millet. The midmorning meal is taken about 9:30 to 10:00 a.m., and consists of only black tea and the same kind of bread, or milk products for those who have them. The evening meal generally consists of *aash-i-baqla*, a gruel made of milled horsebeans, and a mixture of peas and barley, or pasta made out of the same mixed flour and boiled in a large amount of water. Wheat bread is rarely consumed in Wakhi households, for it is considered a luxury and only a few people, such as the *shahs*, or members of a few other rich units can afford it. Meat, fruits, and sweets are rarely part of the Wakhi diet. Milk products are consumed by most households during at least part of the year.

For a majority of Wakhi households bread, made of a mixed flour of millet, barley, lupine, and lentil, and *aash-i-baqla*, are available only during the autumn and winter months. In spring and summer the main Wakhi staple consists of boiled wild vegetables weeded out from the cultivated fields. The Wakhi do not plant vegetables, but rely completely on what they can weed out of their fields. Milk and milk products supplement their diet while they last, and *shur chai* is drunk if the household can manage to buy tea on credit during this period.

Wheat and barley, and particularly wheat in recent years, have become the Wakhi "cash crops" that enable them to buy from the Kirghiz, the shopkeepers, and the itinerant traders those goods they do not produce themselves. For many Wakhi households wheat is the only means through which they can acquire not only tea and opium, but all other market goods they want. Thus, low wheat consumption by a household is directly related to the use of large amounts of tea in their diet and to the widespread opium addiction among the Wakhi. Both the traders and the Kirghiz accept wheat and barley in exchange for goods while linseed is accepted in exchange by the traders alone. As a result, most of the annual wheat, barley, and linseed (and particularly wheat) harvested by a household is used for exchange purposes and for the payment of taxes and tribute rather than for household consumption.

The increasing need and desire of Wakhi households for new market goods, especially tea and opium, has decreased the volume of their domestic subsistence crops—mixed barley, lupine, lentils, horsebeans, and millet. Every year more and more agricultural land is being used to cultivate wheat in place of the mixed crops to meet increasing Wakhi demands for market goods and agricultural commodities not produced locally. This trend is taking place even though wheat has proved to be the lowest yielding crop in the Wakhi agricultural production system. To date, the one and only safeguard against the loss of grain food in Wakhi households has been the continuation of "mixed crop" cultivation, but these mixed crops have little or no exchange value among the traders. The Kirghiz will accept the mixed crop of barley, lentil, lupine, and millet from the traders or the Wakhi only when wheat or barley are not available.

This specialization in wheat cash cropping is, then, a recent development that has arisen as a result of the new frontier situation in the Wakhan Corridor. It is closely tied to the needs of the Wakhi for market goods and the unbalanced nature of their trade and exchange, and dependence on outside economies. The consequences of these new economic processes on the marginal economy of the Wakhi have been an increasing loss of resources, economic dependence, and growing poverty throughout the area.

ECONOMIC DEPENDENCE

Wakhi economy has always been marginal. However, over the past several decades a marked difference in the Wakhi economic processes has taken place whereby there has been a gradual shift from near self-sufficiency to an irreversible dependence upon other economic systems lying outside the Wakhan.

Before the closure of the borders of the Soviet Union, the People's Republic of China, and Pakistan to trade and traders in this area, the Wakhi household depended on the outside for very little. Each household produced all the family garments it required from its own livestock and almost all of its agricultural products were used for its own subsistence. Most of the other goods required for domestic needs could be met through intracommunity exchanges of goods and services.

In the past Wakhi trade with merchants passing through their territory was minimal, being limited primarily to the provision by the Wakhi of a quantity of barley needed by the traders to feed their pack animals during their passage through the Wakhan. Merchants were not interested in trading with the Wakhi since their meager agricultural and animal products had little or no value and were not in demand in distant markets. However, the services of the Wakhi were hired by members of the trade caravans, who paid for these services in such goods as black and green tea, muslin and silk and other fabrics brought from Chinese Turkistan, and/or opium, which was taken in large amounts from Badakhshan and northern Afghanistan, where it was produced, to be sold in the markets of Chinese Turkistan.

The many centuries of opium and tea trading between northern Afghanistan and Chinese Turkistan through the Wakhan Corridor have resulted in the widespread use of opium and tea among the Wakhi. The addiction of many Wakhi to opium is directly related to the harsh environment of the Wakhan and to the absence of any kind of medical services. Impoverished, disease-ridden, and weather-beaten, the Wakhi have relied on the numbing effects of opium to help decrease their suffering from illness as well as to give temporary comfort at night after the stresses of cold, hard work, and travel in the rough terrain. According to the Wakhi, the consumption of large amounts of tea in the form of *shur chai* is related to opium addiction. They say that *shur chai*, if consumed in large quantities, enhances the effects of opium as well as decreases the pains of withdrawal for the addict in its absence.

There are a few Wakhi who have become addicted to opium out of their own desire to smoke for pleasure, as well as those who claim they were hooked by ill wishers in the society. The use of tea started in earlier times as a luxury but has now reached the point of addiction for most people throughout the area. The constant use of both tea and opium is also directly related to their availability, made so by the traders because of their high value and small bulk and weight.

The effects of these habits were not fully realized in the Wakhi economy and society until after the success of the Chinese Communist Revolution in 1949 and the consequent closure of the borders. Under the new conditions some of the old enterprising traders found their highly profitable opium and tea trade (among other goods) with Chinese Turkistan halted, so they initiated trade relations with the Wakhi and the Kirghiz, whom they knew well. The traders were aware that the Kirghiz now had to rely completely on the Wakhi for their needed cereals. Both the Wakhi and the Kirghiz needed certain market goods such as tea and some cloth, and the Wakhi also needed opium. The traders therefore offered their new trading partners large quantities of Indian tea and opium and a selection of manufactured merchandise, for which they quickly created a need among the Wakhi and Kirghiz, in return for animals and livestock products for which there was an increasing demand outside the Wakhan Corridor.

For example, the traders, who were aware of the rising demand for raw wool, animal skins, furs, and hides, encouraged the Wakhi to trade these livestock products for market goods. Consequently, Wakhi households that had relied for centuries on their own home-spun garments, fur coats, and animal hide footwear, soon found themselves in need of manufactured textiles, ready-made garments, leather, and shoes. The traders also introduced other market products such as metal and plastic household utensils, which to some extent have replaced the traditional, locally produced Wakhi wooden and clay ware. Transistor radios, guns, sewing machines, cigarettes, and a small selection of haberdashery and other items (needles, thread, buttons, scissors, matches, mirrors, vaseline, chemical dyes, etc.) have also become part of the trade goods sold to the Wakhi.

This increased dependence on market commodities has had three major effects on the Wakhi. First, there has been an increasing trend toward wheat cash cropping, with the consequent change in the Wakhi diet. Second, a triadic system of trade and exchange involving the Wakhi, the Kirghiz, and the itinerant traders has developed, in the course of which the Wakhi have become increasingly dependent economically upon the Kirghiz. Finally, the heavy dependence of the Wakhi on market goods, particularly upon opium, has become a source of tension in many domestic units, leading to their premature division. Grudges over the allocation of household resources between members who are opium addicts and those who are not (or between the heavy and chronic users and the occasional users) are common to most domestic units at present.

DOMESTIC DEVELOPMENTAL CYCLE AND CULTURAL ECOLOGICAL CONSIDERATIONS

The common form of domestic unit in Wakhi society, two or more patrilocal joint extended families, may, when matured, contain members of three to five generations represented by several conjugal-natal families. The development of the Wakhi household, therefore, is aimed at creating and maintaining such a viable unit of production and disposition.

The adaptability of this form of household is directly related to its effectiveness as a resource management group within the organization of the Wakhi adaptive strategies. By effectiveness is meant the ability of the household to maintain the large productive labor force needed by high-altitude Wakhi agriculture, and to safeguard against the dispersion and diminishing of the household productive resources through domestic fission.

Some of the major factors influencing domestic fission and fusion in the Wakhi society are: (a) limitation of existing and potential resources in the area; (b) rights of access to resources (e.g., rules of inheritance and marriage); (c) patterns of resource allocations (e.g., marriage practices and trade); and (d) the interpersonal relations within the household (e.g., level of tension). The effects of these factors on the domestic developmental cycle can be both cohesive and divisive. The particular end gratified at any given time may depend upon the choices of the individuals and groups involved, and the circumstances and constraints under which these choices are made.

The limitation of resources in the Wakhan influences all phases of the domestic cycle in the society. For instance, it determines the size of the productive unit and influences the recruiting of new members for the domestic unit through conjugal and natal processes.

The scarcity of productive resources also has significant effects upon the choice of marriage partners and the composition of the household membership.

A good example of the effects of limited resources upon the size and development of Wakhi domestic units is the Wakhi house. Its construction, proper heating, and maintenance is usually a major economic undertaking for most households in the face of the scarcity of building materials, fuel, and other requirements. Built as it is with maximum safeguards against the Wakhan cold, the Wakhi house helps to keep the household unit together and families who break away from the household prematurely because of other stresses usually end up living in former storage rooms, hay shelters, and so forth, and suffer greatly because of it.

In Wakhi society the ownership of such productive resources as arable land and livestock rests with the natal family units within each domestic group. Thus the household, as indicated earlier, is the corporate resource management unit for its total membership, who have differential rights of access to the resources. Within the natal families Wakhi rules of inheritance allow only the male members to be real or potential owners of property. A woman without male siblings can inherit part of the patrimony but may pass it only to her male offspring. Male siblings have, in principle, equal rights of access to the family property upon the death of their father. In case of household fission, however, the eldest brother inherits the choice agricultural land while the youngest brother inherits the paternal house. Female siblings receive a dowry of livestock (sheep, goats, cows), but only upon the birth of their first child. With some exceptions, therefore, the exchange of women through marriage in Wakhi society has a minimal effect upon the domestic ownership of agricultural land through inheritance. The exchange of women through marriage, however, always has a profound effect on the household economy and the perpetuation and maintenance of a viable domestic unit.

Marriages are necessary for the recruitment of new members to the household productive labor force and perpetuation of the domestic units. Carefully arranged marriages can enhance the development of the Wakhi household and its economy but if not well planned can be an economic drain, particularly when the payment of a high bridewealth is involved. Such marriages also create tension among the household members and eventually lead to the dispersion of the domestic unit. As a result, the planning and arrangement of marriages in Wakhi society is a crucial function of the domestic unit as a group, and is not relegated to the individuals involved.

Marriages between the two major groups of people in Wakhi society, the traditional aristocratic descent groups—Sayyed, Khuja, and Mir—and the nonaristocratic descent groups—Sha-ana, Khyberi and Kheek—are proscribed. This proscriptive marriage rule, devised to protect the purity and sanctity of the *asl*, draws support from the principle of homogamy, or marriage between those of equal status, found throughout the Muslim Middle East (see, e.g., Ayoub 1959; Barth 1954). This practice has certain other social and economic implications. For instance, it keeps the exchange of resources, through bridewealth and dowry, and the right of domain (tribute) over the commoners, within the *asl* group. Further, it encourages marriages that do not jeopardize rights of domain and rights of access to productive resources.

Apart from these proscriptions, Wakhi marriage rules permit conjugal relations with anyone outside of the small category of people who are considered in Wakhi society as within the realm of incest.[7] Polygyny is allowed but is not frequent, and generally occurs in aristocratic families. Child betrothals and marriages are also practiced, but most common among members of all strata in the Wakhan is the preferred bilateral first cousin marriage in the following order: FaBrDa, FaSiDa, MoBrDa, MoSiDa, and more distant classificatory cousins.

This preferred first cousin marriage, however, when considered along with the organization of the Wakhi domestic unit (which consists of two or more agnatically related patrilineal joint extended families made up of several conjugal-natal groups), promotes domestic unit endogamy. Given the composition of the Wakhi household, it is very likely to contain a number of bilateral first cousins of both sexes. When such prospective marriage partners are present in the household, marriage between them is considered by the domestic unit the most suitable and it is generally contracted. Endogamous marriage in Wakhi society is essential for a number of reasons: It eliminates the potential alienation and the loss of economic resource through marriage in which payments of bridewealth and dowry are necessary; it keeps the household's productive labor force intact; it decreases the tension between members of the household (through sentiment); and it ensures the future solidarity, economic viability, and political strength of the domestic unit both in the local community and in society (cf. Barth 1954; Ayoub 1959; Keyes and Hudson 1961).

---

7. The incestuous category in Wakhi society consists of: parents, siblings, children, FaBrWi/Hu, MoBrWi/Hu, WiSi, and WiSiDa.

There are other forms of marriage in Wakhi society. They include sister exchange and choosing a spouse for a household member from among paternal relatives, close maternal kin, the hamlet, the regional community, the linguistic and religious sectarian groups, and the non-Wakhi, respectively. The Wakhi household gives careful consideration to the selection of conjugal partners, *who* and from *where* prospective household members are is essential. Their calculations are based on immediate and short-term, as well as long-range, effects such decisions may have on the economy, the integrity, and the power of the household as a corporate productive unit.

However, despite the many constraints favoring the development of larger productive households, often the centrifugal tendencies overcome these processes, and households break down into smaller groups. Some of the most common causes of household fission are those concerning interpersonal relations—for example, disputes among brother's wives or betweeen adult males themselves. Disputes are often centered around the allocation of family resources, particularly when one or more members of the household try to use its corporate resources to satisfy their individual needs (e.g., opium addiction) rather than the household requirements. Division and distribution of productive labor can lead to bitter feuds between brothers as well as to personal animosity between brothers' wives, particularly if one or more of them have joined the household through exogamous marriages. Many of the cases of domestic breakdown follow the occurrence of fierce fighting and frequent disagreements between its members and involve the weakest agnatic link between or among patrilineal joint-extended family units within the maturing households.

The outcome of domestic fission is hardly a happy beginning for members of the new units, who find themselves left with little productive capital, fewer productive members, and insufficient tools and implements with which to work. Fission in domestic groups where the possibility of opening new agricultural land exists often leads to expansion of land resources, but in the Wakhan this prerogative belongs to the rich, united, and strong households alone, for only they have the time and resources necessary to construct dikes, irrigation channels, and terraces to make the new land productive. Even for the rich agropastoralist households this enterprise is difficult, because it is very costly and time consuming. The opening of new agricultural land usually begins with the securing of winter pasturage for the family herd in an area remote from the regular household. Once it is found, winter shelter for the pastoral segment of the domestic unit is constructed, and then the gradual clearing of land

and building of irrigation networks and terraces follows. Following the fission of the domestic unit, this new outpost, with its additional land, becomes the permanent residence of one of the new units and eventually the site for a new Wakhi hamlet.

This particular process of resource expansion, however limited, is a statement that the availability of productive labor and supporting capital rather than the physical environment are the real limitations to new resources in the Wakhi ecological system. It is the goal of most Wakhi domestic units, at least in principle, to control and overcome the divisive forces and to utilize and manipulate the cohesive cultural ecological factors in their continuing efforts to create a viable productive unit that would be able to expand their access to more new land and pasturage resources.

Above, winter camp in Little Pamir; *below,* same camp after a snowfall.

 # 4. The Kirghiz Pastoral Subsistence System

THE PAMIR ECOLOGICAL zone, as described in chapter 1, lies well above the altitudes of agricultural production, and so is at best a marginal high-altitude, mountain-plateau zone in which resources for the support of the human population can be best utilized only through nomadic adaptation. The ecological relationship between the human population and this marginal environment is mediated by a particular subsistence strategy: the raising of, and caring for, specific types and breeds of animals adapted to the stresses of severe cold, high-altitude effects (hypoxia), and the meager vegetation.

The ecological conditions in the Pamirs are dominated by altitude, which in turn affects the climate and vegetation. The climate is, of course, influenced also by latitude, the extent of daily and seasonal insolation, location within the continental mass, seasonal hemispheric movements, and local topography. It is characterized by extremes of daily and seasonal fluctuations in temperature, and sudden changes in wind direction and velocity. The amount of precipitation varies tremendously from place to place, season to season, and from one year to the next. Other physical factors affecting the growth and perpetuation of organisms in the Pamirs are the relative scarcity of oxygen, low barometric pressure, and ultra-violet radiation. Plants, animals, and human beings are subject to the strains and stresses of all of these elements in the process of adapting to this high-altitude environment.

Since clinical data on the biological and physiological responses of the human and animal population to the environmental constraints

were not obtainable,[1] this discussion of adaptability is based on
my own field observations. Substantiation of the remarks about
animal adaptability lies in the reproductive success or failure of each
type of animal, and the demographic data that was obtained about
the Kirghiz supplements my empirical conclusions about the responses
of the human population.

HERD COMPOSITION, VIABILITY, AND UTILIZATION

Unlike most low-altitude nomads, the Kirghiz of the Afghan
Pamirs do not specialize in herding a particular type or species of
animal. The composition of Kirghiz herds is influenced by environmental limitations—the adaptability of each species to extreme temperatures and to hypoxia, as well as its ability to exploit efficiently
the meager and diverse pasturage—and its socioeconomic value and
use to the Kirghiz herders. The Kirghiz, like most Central Asian,
Turkic-speaking nomads, have mixed herds, consisting of yak, sheep,
goats, Bactrian camels, and horses, each of which differs in its adaptability to the environment. As a result, the care required for the
survival and multiplication of each species varies a great deal.

The animals best adapted to high altitude are the yak and the
sheep, which are protected by their long, thick, and heavy coats.
Goats, although less able to tolerate the cold and wind, are agile
animals capable of utilizing a wide range of pasture. While Bactrian
camels can withstand cold, the ill effects of hypoxia limit their reproduction. Horses are the least adaptive of the Kirghiz animals. They
cannot survive the cold without the care and help of man, and cannot
successfully reproduce in the altitudes of the Afghan Pamirs.

Of the animals kept by the Kirghiz, sheep, goats, and yak constitute the largest proportion, and form the basis of their pastoral
subsistence. Camels, raised in decreasing numbers under the present
conditions, are of secondary importance. The Kirghiz buy horses
and the few donkeys they keep from Wakhi agriculturalists or itinerant traders since they cannot breed their own in the Pamirs. Each
species has its particular value: in capital, in prestige, and in wealth
for its owners. A more detailed discussion of the Kirghiz domestic
stock as units of pastoral capital resource is essential for an understanding of the Kirghiz system of subsistence and adaptation to the
high altitude and the closed frontiers.

1. For bibliographic information on the physiological effects of the stresses
of cold and hypoxia from the Andean studies see fn. 5, chapter 1 (also see chapter 5).

Sheep and Goats (qoey *and* echki)

At the time of this research the mixed goat and sheep herds of the Kirghiz numbered about forty thousand. The sheep, the most important of the three animals that provide the basic subsistence of the Kirghiz, outnumbered the goats by about three to one. The proportion of any type of livestock in a pastoral subsistence system is influenced by a multitude of inherent ecological and economic constraints as well as by the group's socioeconomic and cultural interdependence with the larger society. The number of sheep in Kirghiz herds is an indication of the sheep's superior adaptability to both ecological (temperature and altitude) and economic (subsistence and exchange) factors both within and outside Kirghiz society.

The Kirghiz sheep are all of one variety, the Central Asiatic fat-tailed strain known in the region as *turki qoey* (Turkic sheep). It is large, with long legs, a long neck, and a large, round, fat tail (see the illustration on p. 96), and is found throughout northern Afghanistan with only minor variations in the length, thickness, and texture of its fleece. It is particularly hardy, with a long, thick coat of coarse wool that protects it well against the extreme cold and the harsh climate of the high Pamirs. Its high resistance to prolonged frost and continuing bad weather and its sustained productivity makes it economically indispensable to the Kirghiz.

Kirghiz goats have a coat of long hair with a soft, fine undercoat (cashmere) that gives them some protection against the extreme temperatures. However, it is not adequate during prolonged periods of extreme cold weather, when goat losses are heavy. Sheep and goats are always herded together, their different grazing habits making the herd a formidable team for exploiting a wide variety of pastures under both the worst and the best range conditions. Goats generally browse and graze, moving with agility at the forefront of the flock. Sheep, on the other hand, tend to crop and often stay closely bunched together, ruining the best pasturage in a very short time if they are not kept moving. When herded with the quickly moving goats, however, they are good followers, and extensive damage to the range is avoided. During heavy snowfalls their roles are reversed, and the sheep lead the flock and expose the parched and dried grass by pawing the snow. Goats, which do not themselves paw to expose the grass, can feed only in the company of sheep and on what grass the sheep can uncover. This interdependence is highly significant given the ecological conditions of the Pamirs, as it necessitates mixed herding of the two animals.

The presence of goats, particularly several dozen large buck goats *(serke)*, in a herd to be taken to the Kabul market is of great importance during the two-month-long trek from the Pamirs. Buck goats are excellent leaders with a moderately fast pace during these long journeys and without them the itinerant traders and the few Kirghiz who accompany them would probably find the trip a great deal more difficult if not impossible.

Ranging in size from 200 to about 1,200, the herds of sheep and goats demand year-round care. A herd of two hundred to five hundred animals requires a mounted herder (generally on a yak) and one or two dogs. Larger herds require two mounted herders and two or more dogs.

In the spring and summer the lambs and kids are herded separately, as are the rams *(qochqar)* and buck goats *(teke)* designated for breeding purposes. Annually sheep and goats to be used as stud animals are separated from each household herd and are given to a few poor households hired to herd them in geographically isolated areas. Through this mechanism the Kirghiz prevent any mating of the animals during the first two natural rutting periods (June and August/September) in order to ensure that early and untimely births do not occur. The Kirghiz keep one ram for about every twenty ewes and one buck goat for about every thirty or more does.[2] Breeding animals are introduced to the herds in October, the time of their last annual rutting cycle.

The Kirghiz select the rams and buck goats for sires each year from among the lambs and kids during their first summer of life and geld all other males. This selection is generally based on the promise of desired size, color, and length and thickness of fleece. Kirghiz sheep are white, grey, brown, and black, though the Kirghiz prefer the lighter colors for making felt covers for their *aq oey* (the white house), which are uniformly light-colored felt on the outside and dark or black on the inside. Light-colored wool also more readily lends itself to dyes for making woven and decorated felt.

Lambs and kids drop in May, a critical period when the dried and parched pastures are exhausted after the long winter and the weather is extremely unpredictable. It is often a time of severe local

2. My informants have cited different figures regarding the ram and ewe ratio. The figure of 30 rams for 700 ewes was given by one of the most successful herders, the khan. A ratio of 1 ram for 60 ewes was also cited by some herders as the maximum limit. And there were those who gave figures in between the two. In the Badakhshan area I know of a practice of keeping 1 ram for about every 50 ewes. Fredrik Barth has suggested about 1 ram for every 5 ewes among the Basseri tribe in South Persia (1961, p. 6).

blizzards that can kill off the weakened females and devastate the newborn. The lambs and kids drop in large numbers in the pen where the ewes and does are kept at night, as well as in the cold and frozen pastures during daylight. They are transported to the camp inside felt bags fastened on the backs of camels and yak. In the camp the more affluent Kirghiz set up a separate yurt to keep the young animals warm and well protected, while the poor share a portion of their own yurt with the newborn animals. The lambs and kids are assisted in suckling twice a day, and are taken to graze near the fringes of the camp after they are one week or more old, weather permitting. On bad days dried hay is tied in small bundles and suspended from the yurt roof so that the young animals can supplement their daily suckling. In return for the hay given to the lambs and kids, the ewes and does are milked a little to provide the family with some fresh milk.

Livestock losses from *joot* (spring blizzards with wind gusts) are generally quite severe. Animal losses are not uniform throughout the Pamirs because of the wide variations in the weather, but are unpredictable and uneven. Lambs and kids may be devastated in one microenvironment, resulting in near total loss, while in other areas the losses may not run to more than 10 to 15 percent of the births. Losses of weakened ewes and does run very high during such bad weather. In the springs of 1971 and 1972 (during a severe drought in most parts of Afghanistan) prolonged bad weather during the lambing season caused up to 70 percent losses in livestock in some areas of the Pamirs, particularly in the Great Pamir. Other major threats to Kirghiz livestock are disease, lack of adequate forage, and predators, particularly wolves. Herd losses from these threats vary considerably from herd to herd, place to place, and time to time, but general estimates, in the absence of major *joot* and with normal vegetation growth, may run from 5 to 10 percent of the animal population. Since *joot* and poor pasturage conditions generally occur in some localities every year, the losses are often considerably more.

Kirghiz flocks of sheep and goats within the Pamirs are moderately fertile. There are a certain number of twin births, but reproduction, unlike flocks at lower altitudes, is limited to a single annual pregnancy. The ewes and does become productive during their third year and are expected to bear young an average of four to five times before being removed from the breeding stock. The Kirghiz ordinarily sell or slaughter any ewe or doe that remains barren for more than a year during their reproductive years, since such animals are automatically considered low yield animals. Ewes, after the age of seven or eight, are also used for domestic consumption or exchanged for market commodities along with all neutered males prior to or during their fourth year. Rams and buck goats are sent off to the market or used in exchange with the itinerant traders during their fifth or sixth year.

Despite heavy, unpredictable losses of livestock from natural calamities, disease, predators, bad pasturage, and negligent herding by some individual herders, the Kirghiz of the Afghan Pamirs have been able to maintain fairly large flocks of sheep and goats that have not only adequately provided for their needs but have also supported a lucrative system of trade and exchange for a small, but increasing, number of itinerant traders who frequent the area. These mobile merchants connect the Kirghiz to the national market economy of the country while satisfying Kirghiz needs for market and agricultural products.

Reproductivity of Kirghiz sheep and goats is, to a large extent, limited to the Pamirs. They lose vigor and fertility when taken to "hot" lowland towns and villages. As a result, they only leave the Pamirs to be sold for meat and not to be kept for breeding. The local strains of sheep and goats fatten very quickly during the short Pamir summer, a time of relatively abundant pasturage. This is a significant characteristic for a number of reasons: first, the fattened animals stand a much better chance of surviving the long, cold winter foraging on the meager vegetation; second, animals sold to the traders reach the Kabul market in fairly good physical condition and bring a good price after a sixty-day trek; and finally, the Kirghiz favor meat with a high proportion of fat and the enlarged tail of the Kirghiz sheep is much relished by the Kirghiz in their winter diet. This ability of the Kirghiz sheep to achieve good physical condition over a short period of time and to sustain fat and meat over a long cold winter is especially adaptive to the environment of the Pamirs, as well as being valuable to the subsistence and exchange of Kirghiz society.

Sheep and goats and their products either directly or indirectly provide most of the basic subsistence requirements of the Kirghiz. Both sheep and goats are milked for about four to five months of the year and no attempt is made to keep their milk separate during milking (yak milk is also included). Kirghiz do not consume fresh milk but convert it into a wide variety of milk products for use during the milk season as well as over the long milkless winter months.

The staple milk products among the Kirghiz during the milking season are *ayran* (sour milk) and *jughrat* (yoghurt). *Ayran*, a thin, curdled, sour milk that is reasonably palatable, is made from milk by adding a certain amount of water, bringing it to a boil and, after cooling, adding *oytuqi* or starter. For starter the Kirghiz use either fresh or dried *ayran*. *Jughrat* is made in the same manner as *ayran* except that no water is added to the milk. It is a rather thick, curdled substance with a mild, sour, but quite palatable taste. Both *ayran* and *jughrat* are consumed in diluted form as a drink, as well as eaten fresh in large amounts during the spring and summer.

Ayran and *jughrat* are also made into a number of other products that are kept for use when fresh milk is not available. For instance, *qroot* is made by placing *jughrat* in a large cotton bag to drain and then sun drying the solidified curd, which is then consumed during the winter or traded for agricultural and market goods. The drained curd from *jughrat* may also be converted to *suzma* by adding salt and placing the substance in *chanoch* (goatskin bags). *Suzma* is usually frozen and consumed locally during winter months. By boiling *jughrat* until the whey has evaporated the Kirghiz get a solidified sweet called *ayjgai*. It can be consumed immediately or dried and kept for later use.

Ayran is used for making *peshtaq* (cheese). The Kirghiz *peshtaq* is made by warming fresh milk very slowly and gradually adding *ayran* to the warming milk until it reaches boiling point. The boiled mixture of milk and *ayran* turns into solidified curd and whey. The curd is put into bags and compressed into flat round loaves resembling Kirghiz bread and is consumed throughout the spring and summer months in place of bread by most Kirghiz. *Peshtaq* keeps very well over a long period during the summer, and can be dried and kept for the winter months. By boiling the whey remaining after making *peshtaq*, they get *sherne*, a sweet that looks and tastes like unrefined sugar.

The Kirghiz employ absolutely no method of churning their *ayran* or *jughrat* in order to obtain butter. Their production of milk fat is limited to collecting *qaymaq*, the solidified layer of cream on top of unboiled milk left overnight, or the top of freshly made *ayran* and *jughrat*. The layer of cream collected from the top of unboiled milk is called *kham qaymaq*, and it is consumed by itself or with bread, or added to tea to make the Kirghiz brew known as *qateghdagan chai*. A very thick and solid layer of cream usually covers the top of all containers in which *ayran* or *jughrat* are made. This cream is known as *peshegh qaymaq* (i.e., cream from boiled milk) and from which cooking fat is produced. Because of the relatively high fat content of yak milk, the thickness of the Pamir cream is legendary among the lowland agriculturalists of Wakhan and Badakhshan.

Qaymaq may be eaten fresh, or mixed with *ayran, jughrat,* or bread, and is very much appreciated by the Kirghiz. It is stored in large amounts by households for later consumption or exchange. The *qaymaq* not for immediate consumption is collected over a period of time and then thoroughly washed in cold water to rid it of all its milk, *ayran,* or *jughrat* content to prevent spoilage. *Qaren* (cleaned and dried sheep and goat stomachs specially prepared for the purpose) are filled with the mixture and securely fastened to keep them airtight. The mixture thus prepared is called *meshka,* and can keep for over a year. *Meshka* can be eaten with bread, but it is not fit for use as shortening until it is purified and turned into *sari mai* or *mai.* The purification process involves melting the *meshka,* adding a certain amount of wheat flour and boiling the mixture for a period of time. It is then left to settle and solidify. The clear, yellowish substance on the top, called *nakhtagan mai,* can be stored in new *qaren* and kept for several years. It is excellent for cooking and is a prime trade commodity.

A fair number of male sheep and goats, particularly lambs and kids, are slaughtered for meat during the latter part of the summer and fall. Meat is eaten fresh and generally boiled and seasoned with salt. The Kirghiz never dry, smoke, or preserve sheep and goat meat, but yak and horse meat is often smoked and dried for use on special occasions, or when it is to be eaten over an extended period of time. Goat meat is in low regard because of its lack of fat, but mutton, especially if the animal is in good condition, is the favorite food of Kirghiz society.

The hides of sheep, goats, lambs, and kids are utilized in many ways: for clothing, bedding, containers, and in exchange for other goods. By treating and softening wool-covered sheepskin the Kirghiz make long fur overcoats, essential for protection against the subarctic climatic conditions of the Pamirs. Sheepskins are also used to make fur mats that are used as mattresses. The Kirghiz fur hat, *tumaq,* is made from lambskin. *Takhta postak,* fur mats used during the making of felt, are made from goatskins. The wool to be converted to felt is laid on top of the *takhta postak,* skin side up, and beaten. When the hair is removed from goatskins, and the skins treated, they can be used as *chanoch* for dairy products. Sheep and goat stomachs are also used as containers for *meshka* and *mai.* Goat hide is used in making various parts of horse tackle, including the whip, and for the making of bellows.

Sheep fleece is one of the most essential animal products of the Kirghiz. Soft lambswool is used to thickly pad jackets, pants and overcoats. Since lambswool is an excellent insulator it is used as the filler for most of their bedding and the coarser sheep fleece, mixed with some yak hair, is made into the felt that covers the Kirghiz yurt, the *aq oey*. Felt is also important for making covers for horses, camels, and yak, as well as for making the knee-high socks worn with high boots by the Kirghiz. Felt is used to cover the floors of the yurt and for bedding in Kirghiz households and particularly sought after by the Wakhi. The demand from outside for both wool and goat hair is increasing—in recent years the Turkmen carpet weavers from northern Afghanistan have been coming to the Pamirs themselves to buy high quality wool directly from the Kirghiz. With the prices of Afghan carpets rising internationally there is the prospect of an even better market for Kirghiz wool.

The Kirghiz themselves spin (using a spindle) and weave wool and goat hair to make *qop* (sacks used to store and transport grains and flour), *khurjun* (saddlebags), *qaqma* (material used for making horse, yak, and camel covers), *palaas* (matting), and *bow*, a variety of colorful, long straps and bands used to fasten and decorate both the inside and outside of the Kirghiz yurt. From goat hair the Kirghiz make sturdy ropes *(arqan)* that are used to tie and tether their animals, and to fasten loads of goods and supplies for transportation. Many of these latter products, such as horse covers and ropes, can also be exchanged with the Wakhi and traders for other goods.

Also very important to the Kirghiz are the droppings of sheep and goats. Penned during the long winter months in high mud and stone or mud-brick enclosures, the animals trample and compress accumulated droppings into a thick layer. In the spring the compressed manure is cut with spades into irregularly shaped blocks that are dried during the summer. This dried *qegh* is the main fuel for cooking and heating during most of the year. The only other fuels available are yak dung, which is used during the summer and fall, and peat, which is cut and dried over the summer. These are supplemented by a limited amount of low wormwood shrubs found in certain areas of the Pamirs.

Sheep and goats are significant to Kirghiz needs in local, regional, and national market exchange systems, where sheep serve as the standard medium of exchange, that is, the value of all local, agricultural, and market goods are computed on the basis of the value of *qoey*, a ewe. The value of *qoey* within the Pamirs in relation to other animals and animal products and goods is relatively constant (see table 2). However, its rate of exchange against agricultural and market goods and cash is subject to fluctuation influenced by the laws of supply and demand. Rates of exchange for Kirghiz livestock and livestock products for agricultural and market goods will be

Turkic sheep: *right*, Kirghiz
child with ewe and lamb; *below*, Kirghiz woman milking.

TABLE 2

THE EXCHANGE VALUE OF QOEY COMPARED TO OTHER ANIMALS AND GOODS IN THE PAMIRS

	Equivalent in *Qoey*
4 kids	1
2 she-goats or neutered males	1
1 buck goat	1
2 lambs	1
1 two-year-old male sheep	1
1 three-year-old+ wether	2
1 one-year-old yak (male or female)	1
1 two-year-old yak (male or female)	2
1 three-year-old yak	3
1 cow or gelded male yak (depending on age, size, and physical condition)	4-7
1 horse	6-16
1 camel	20-30
1 *kegiz* (felt piece, about 5 square meters)	1
1 sack of *qroot* (dried yoghurt, about 35.300 kg.)	1
1 *sair mai* (clarified butter, 7.60 kg.)	1
1 *werama* (horse cover made of goats hair)	1

Yak: *left*, woman milking; *below*, yak bull.

discussed in some detail in chapter 8. Suffice it to say here that sheep and goats are always in demand as exchange for all the agricultural and market commodities the Kirghiz need and cannot produce themselves.

The slaughter or exchange of sheep and goats are a common means of paying social obligations among the Kirghiz; they are given, received, and/or slaughtered in all life crisis rituals. They are presented as gifts by relatives to children at their birth or naming *(yenchi)*, slaughtered during *khatna toy* (circumcision festivities), given at marriage as *qalen* and *seyi* (bridewealth), and *jayzi* (dowry). They are also slaughtered by the families and kinsmen of the bride and groom as hospitality *(qunoq)* for those from distant camps attending a wedding. Slaughtered livestock are distributed as alms during illness and funeral rites and consumed during such religious festivities as breaking of the Ramadan fast, and the Feast of Sacrifice. Animals are exchanged during rituals of *dostlik*, bond of friendship, which establishes fictive kinship. Sheep and goats are also used for payment of alms, settlements of disputes, and other such social obligations.

Yak (qutas)

The only bovine herded by the Kirghiz of the Pamirs is the yak[3] *(bos grunniens)*. Since common cattle do not live in the high Pamirs, hybrids of the yak and common cattle are also nonexistent there.[4]

According to the reports of early travelers in the Afghan Pamirs there were wild yak until the latter part of the nineteenth century (see Shaw 1871, pp. 109-21). There are also petroglyphs in the Pamirs that suggest that wild yak have long lived in the area (see chapter 2). However, it is not known whether present Kirghiz herds of yak are a locally domesticated breed or were introduced. There are no wild yak in the area at the present time and none has been observed by the present generation in the Pamirs. They do know, however, that their ancestors hunted them in the past.

Yak are extremely well adapted to the thin air of the Pamirs because of their large lungs and their ability to move with great

3. In agreement with Robert Ekvall and the rules of the Tibetan language concerning nouns, I will not use *s* to form the plural for *yak*, which is a loan word from Tibetan. Therefore *yak* is used to denote both singular and plural (see Ekvall 1968, p. 13, fn. 3).

4. For a discussion of yak and common cattle cross see Ekvall (1968) in Tibet and Lattimore (1962a) in Mongolia. Also, I have discussed this achievement in chapter 2 with reference to the Zebak District immediately to the southwest of the Wakhan Corridor in Afghanistan.

agility in the rough and unusually steep, stony terrain throughout the year. With the help of their very thick and long coats of hair they have sufficient protection against weather conditions that debilitate other animals.

Yak can exploit the most meager and otherwise unusable resources in the area. During the summer they are pastured in remote areas of inner tributary ravines that are inaccessible to other less hardy and agile livestock. With their relative speed and ability to climb to higher elevations, yak, particularly those not obliged to return to camp daily for milking, can utilize the highest pastures. During the summer these more remote areas sometimes have quite good vegetation near the snow and glacier line. In winter yak can graze where the snow is fairly thick since they can easily expose the dried grass with their protruding snout. Besides being able to chew up the scanty, short grass, they can browse where taller grasses and small shrubs are found.

About four thousand yak, the third largest group of animals, are herded by the Kirghiz. They are the most widely owned and/or herded animals among Kirghiz households and are essential if the marginal high-altitude range resources are to be used efficiently. They flourish at the Pamir altitudes (from 4,100 to nearly 5,000 meters) but are less adaptive to lower elevations and warmer climates, where they lose both vigor and reproductivity.

Yak bulls *(buqa)*, especially those kept at stud, grow to over five feet at the shoulder and may weigh up to six hundred kilograms. There is sexual dimorphism between the yak cow and the ox—the cows *(eenak)* are smaller and less muscular than both the *buqa* (bull) and *waguz* (gelded yak) (see illustration on p. 98).

The reproductive processes of yak are quite regular. The yak rutting season occurs during July and August, and the nine-month gestation period brings calving in April and May. The young require about ten days of intensive care after birth, when they suckle only. The young calf *(turpoq)* starts grazing after this period and is allowed to suckle once or twice a day during the remainder of the milk season (six to nine months). Throughout the milking season the calves are separated from their mothers during the day and at night are tied securely in the camp to prevent unscheduled suckling. Calves and cows are herded together only after the milk has dried up completely and thus the young are weaned during the winter before the new calves are born. If a *tai turpoq* (one- to two-year-old calf) continues to suckle after the new calf is born, it is isolated and sent to a different camp to be herded, or a sharp stick is inserted through its nasal septum so that if it attempts to suckle it is avoided by the mother.

Male yak kept for stud are carefully chosen every year from among the best one- or two-year-old calves and those remaining are gelded. The *buqa* are used to service the yak cows until they reach eight or nine years of age, when they are gelded or slaughtered. Gelded yak, if physically well developed, will be gradually broken to the saddle and used as a mount and pack animal at the age of four or five.

Yak are generally short tempered and passively stubborn but not considered dangerous to people. Kirghiz view them as animals of low intelligence and not easy to train, but once trained, as indispensable for transportation in this high-altitude terrain, especially for households that cannot afford to buy horses. They are used to transport peat and other fuel, as well as yurts and household belongings during seasonal migrations within the Pamirs. Yak carry animal products to the Wakhi agricultural area for trade and transport cereal grains back to the Pamirs. They are used for riding while herding as well as for intercamp visiting. Yak are most suitable for short-term travel—no more than about twenty days at one time—even when they are in top physical shape.

Yak require little care to ensure their survival. They can manage to feed themselves under harsh conditions and lick up snow to quench their thirst in winter. They require no blankets for cover, corrals for protection from the cold and wind, or hay to eat. Yak do not have to be constantly watched while out to pasture, particularly during the summer. For the most part they are herded outside the camp area, directed to pasture, and later collected and brought back to camp for milking. They do, however, require a closer watch during the winter as they may be attacked by wolves, get stuck in deep snow, or become lost in a blizzard. A man, with the aid of a riding yak, can herd up to 150 head of livestock, pasture permitting. Yak herds are generally small, averaging from thirty to forty animals, but there are some herds as large as eighty to one hundred head.

There are a few yak that do demand special attention—the gelded males hired out for mount or pack animals. These *waguz* are covered during winter, and allowed water but once in twenty-four hours, usually in the morning, for irregular and untimely watering of working yak is considered particularly harmful. When working they are given hay on the basis of a prescribed schedule to ensure the best physical condition. These working beasts spend much time tethered on the edge of camp when not on the road.

Yak are not only the beasts of burden but also one of the most economically useful of livestock in the Kirghiz herd. The yak cow, for six to nine months of the year, gives almost as much milk as the common cow, but milk with a much higher butterfat content (see Lattimore 1962a, p. 49). Cows reach sexual maturity at the age of four, at which point they are called *peshti ghunajin,*[5] and remain capable of reproduction annually up to thirteen to fifteen years. Cows remaining barren for more than two consecutive years are considered nonproductive and, like the old and nonutilitarian males, are marked for exchange with traders or given as alms and bridewealth. In some instances they may be slaughtered and eaten during festivities or, occasionally, used for winter household consumption.

Yak produce milk over a longer period of the year than any of the other milk animals and provide most of the milk and milk products that the Kirghiz need. The milk is mixed with sheep or goat milk when it is available and is used for making all the milk products described earlier.

The thick and heavy coat of the yak is shorn annually in the early summer. The fine, fleecy undercoat is often mixed with sheep fleece to make felt and the long, coarse hair is spun and woven into *palaas,* camel and horse girths, and woven strips for tying the yurt. Yak hair is made into strings of various thicknesses that are used to sew equipment (such as felt covers) for pack and mount animals. It is also used in many hand-crafted items, such as yurt door screens and kitchen partitions, and is ideal for making the ropes that have a wide variety of uses among the Kirghiz. The long and bushy yak tails are much sought by the Wakhi and itinerant traders for trade items. They are often securely woven on to one end of nicely carved sticks and sold in towns and villages of Afghanistan, as well as exported to India, where they are used as fly swatters. It is said that white yak tails have sometimes reached western European and North American markets where they are made into beards for Santa Clauses!

Yak hide is very marketable to both traders and Wakhi, as well as having many uses among the Kirghiz. Untanned but treated (oiled and softened) hide is used for making the flat-soled, knee-high boots commonly worn by the poor, the young, and workingmen in Kirghiz society. Some important horse tackle—reins, bridles, girths, cruppers, whips, and stirrup leathers—are also made of the treated yak hide.

Yak have a commercial exchange value when traded with outsiders because of the increasing demand for meat in towns and cities of northern Afghanistan. They also have significant social uses among the Kirghiz. They, as well as sheep and goats, are slaughtered for festivities and exchanged during various rituals. They are exchanged among the Kirghiz themselves for other animals, or bought and sold

5. For the distinctions among yak made by the Kirghiz, see the glossary.

for cash or the equivalent market, agricultural, or livestock products. Except for communal feasts they are not generally slaughtered for food although the meat is not unlike beef and is quite tasty, especially if the animal has been slaughtered in the fall.

Given the scarcity of wood and other forms of fuel in the area, yak droppings are particularly important as fuel. In fact, the Kirghiz rely completely on dried yak dung for five to six months of the year, from April to September. The camp youth and sometimes the shepherds spend a great deal of time collecting and transporting dried dung from the nearby pastures to the camps.

Camels (tuwa)

Tuwa, the double-humped Bactrian camel *(Camelus bactrianus)* are fewer in number (less than ninety) than any other animal raised and herded by the Kirghiz. This number is less than a third of the camels they kept prior to the closure of the borders, when camels were the principal mount and pack animal of the Kirghiz in their long-range migration into the Russian and Chinese Pamirs and beyond. In those earlier times, camel caravans played a particularly significant role in trade and transportation. The present reduction in their number is the result of several factors. First, the year-round confinement of the Kirghiz in the high Pamirs has drastically increased the mortality rate among newborn camels, apparently from hypoxia. Second, in the past the Kirghiz had easy access to camel markets in towns in adjacent areas in Russian and Chinese Turkistan and were able to keep the size of their camel herd constant, particularly since camels were allegedly less expensive than horses. However, there is no such market now. Finally, the terrain between the Wakhan agricultural area and the Pamirs is extremely steep, rough, and quite unsuitable for camel transportation during most of the year, further diminishing their economic utility for the Kirghiz.

Currently, raising camels in the Pamirs has become economically less feasible because of their low rate of reproduction (the gestation period is one year), the extended period before reaching maturity (at least four years), and the high mortality rate of the newborn. Yet a lot of time and energy is devoted to their care by the thirty *oey* units that do own camels because, aside from their nominal economic use, camels are a social indicator of wealth and prestige to the herders. Indeed, of all the animals bred by the Kirghiz, only the birth of a camel is marked by preventive and protective ritual. If the calf survives, many months of intensive care, usually by a mature and knowledgeable woman, follows. Sometimes, in order to safeguard pregnant camels against hypoxia, the Kirghiz pay a household in Wakhan to care for the animals at the lower altitude.

Proper care of mature camels is also demanding in time and effort. During the winter they require thick felt covers to protect them against extreme cold, and during bad weather when snow covers the pastures they are fed hay and tethered inside the camp. They do not lick snow like other Kirghiz livestock and must be watered at a distant spring or given melted snow. During good weather, when the ground surface is exposed, they are taken to pasture in the morning and left to graze until dusk, when they are brought back to the safety of the camp. Only during the summer do camels require less attention; then they can be left uncovered and allowed to graze in ample pasturage some distance from the camp. They are checked only periodically to make sure none has gone astray and crossed into Russian territory, or has been attacked by predators. Of course, females with young are tended more closely at the camp, even during summer.

Economically, camels are the least essential of Kirghiz livestock under present circumstances. Camel milk, when available, is drunk fresh and never mixed with other milk. Wool is perhaps the camel's most valuable product—its softness, fine texture, and water-repellent quality making it the most desirable of wools. Its insulating quality makes excellent padding for garments and bedding. Camel hair is also spun and woven into lengths of material (*qoqma*) which the Kirghiz use in making high quality horse covers for their own use as well as for trade. Camel meat, although not well liked by the Kirghiz, is eaten, but camels are never slaughtered for meat except when an animal has to be destroyed for some other reason. Camel hides are used for making a flat-soled high boot (*chareq*) worn by most Kirghiz men.

Perhaps the camel's greatest economic utility, from the Kirghiz point of view, is its use for transportation. It ranks second only to the horse as a mount for short trips within the Pamirs. It is the strongest and largest of Kirghiz livestock, capable of carrying forty *sairs* (over 300 kilograms) of goods, almost as much as three horse loads. However, their use as a pack animal for transporting agricultural goods from the Wakhan is limited to only two round trips during the winter when the Sarhad River is frozen, permitting relatively easy progress for the camel caravan. Aside from these grain transportation trips to the Wakhan, which may last less than three months, their use in transport is restricted to local journeys and moving seasonal camps within the Pamirs.

In the Pamirs camels maintain a very high exchange value, although there is no real demand at present for either buying or selling. Among the Kirghiz a camel's value is twenty or more sheep, or twice that number of goats, or up to eight yak, or two to three horses. In the past, they were exchanged to satisfy various social obligations or traded for other livestock if needed, but now it seems that some Kirghiz regard the possession of a camel as more important than exchanging it for a larger number of sheep, goats, or yak, even when the family resources of such livestock have been depleted by natural calamities. Clearly, in these instances the prestige of owning a camel outweighs the economic advantages of an exchange. To these individuals and households the camel occupies a different economic sphere, so to speak, not comparable to, or exchangeable with, other animals.

Horses (aat)

The Kirghiz cannot breed horses, but they do keep about 320 of them. More than any of the other animals they keep, the horse is vulnerable to hypoxia and the stresses of cold. It cannot reproduce at the Pamirs' altitudes. As a result, unlike many Central Asiatic pastoralists, the Kirghiz of Afghanistan have no mares, breed no horses, have no mare's milk and do not brew *qemiz,* the traditional Kirghiz drink of fermented mare's milk, which is said to be mildly intoxicating.

The Kirghiz are probably one of the few pastoralist societies solely dependent on sedentary agriculturalists and traders not only for agricultural and market products but also for horses. Therefore, horses in Kirghiz society do not represent pastoral capital; instead they are one of their greatest capital expenditures since for many Kirghiz living in the Pamir without a horse is at best inconvenient. Buying one, however, is a heavy economic burden for many households as it may cost from six to fifteen sheep, or the equivalent in other livestock and animal products. The price depends on the type, age, and condition of the horse, and the credit terms involved in the transaction.

The Kirghiz get their horses from Wakhi peasants, who breed their own, and from traders who bring horses from Badakhshan and other northern provinces of Afghanistan. Wakhi horses, which the Kirghiz refer to as *tatu,* resemble the Tibetan pony in size, and have similar slightly long, shaggy coats. They are very agile and sure-footed in narrow trails and high passes. Their small size prevents them from carrying more than about twelve *sair* (a little over 91 kilograms), although they are hardier than Badakhshan horses on the steep trails and difficult passes leading to the Pamirs. Badakh-shan horses are slightly larger than the Wakhi horse (although not over fourteen hands high), and are capable of carrying heavier loads (16 *sair* or 121.6 kilograms) over longer distances.

What makes the horse so important and valuable to the Kirghiz is its fast pace and its suitability as a ready mount and pack animal in almost all weather, temperature, or terrain. The use of yak and camels for transportation is determined by type of terrain, distance, temperature, and so on involved, whereas horses serve all purposes and in all seasons. Without doubt, horses give the best ride and they also add tremendously to the prestige of the owner if they run fast and perform well in the traditional Kirghiz game of *olagh tartish* (*buz kashi* in Persian, literally, "goat snatching"). The game is played on horseback on festive occasions in the summer. During *olagh* games good horses are usually adorned with colorful, embroidered covers and tackle and publicly displayed by their owners and a great deal of time is spent praising exceptionally good horsemen, horses, and their owners. Although the Kirghiz can no longer breed their own horses, their traditional fondness for horses and "horse culture" strongly persists.

In the Pamirs, as elsewhere in the world, horses require a great deal of care and attention year round, particularly if they are expected to work. During the summer they are given long tethers in good meadows with their place of grazing being changed a few times a day. During this period they are rarely used except for short trips from camp to camp or for games. For the most part they are conditioned for future long journeys to the Wakhan and back. Grain is never fed to horses while in the Pamirs. Ordinarily, they feed on what they can forage, except during bad winter conditions when they are fed dried fodder two or three times a day. They are also given fodder if they are on the road or are expected to travel soon.

During the winter, on the road or not, horses are well covered and closely tended. Those not used to transport grain from the Wakhan are usually allowed to wander free and are periodically checked by a mounted horseman who wards off predators and sees that horse blankets are still in place, for without blankets the animals could die of the cold. Horses not used to pawing to uncover grass from under the snow blanket are particularly looked after when there are heavy snowfalls or when a heavy snow covers the ground for long periods. On the road horses are well fed and watered every day and when in the Wakhan they are given a certain amount of barley daily to keep them in good condition. On the road it is not enough to simply give feed and water to the horse, it is important to feed and water the animal at appropriate times in order to maintain its health.

Horses are very susceptible to all kinds of illnesses and back sores if not properly cared for. The danger of *tutak*, the high-altitude sickness that affects horses under excessive exertion and stress, is extremely high, particularly when a horse is very fat. Many horses die annually because of *tutak*, predators, sickness from lack of appropriate care, and, of course, bad weather, poor pastures, or lack of hay in the early spring. Many of these threats can be avoided if an individual is knowledgeable in the art of horsemanship, as many Kirghiz are.

When a family can hire a yak or a camel to do a task they do so to conserve the energy of the horse. But when other animals are not available or are inappropriate for the job the horse is used. The bulk of Kirghiz grain transportation is by horse and they are the most common and preferred mount for all journeys, local and distant.

The Kirghiz like horse meat very much. While they do not slaughter a horse for meat, when a horse dies of *tutak* or other natural causes, and if a man is around to perform the ritual slitting of the throat, the meat is consumed fresh, as well as smoked and dried to be used later for special occasions. Its hide, cut into narrow thongs, is particularly important in the making and repairing of the *kerega*, the lower wooden lattice frame of the Kirghiz abode.

Donkeys (eshak)

Like the horse, the donkey is not part of the Kirghiz pastoral reproductive livestock. There are only about a dozen donkeys in the Pamirs, and they are kept by large herd-owning units for menial tasks around the camp. They transport fuel—compressed sheep and goat droppings and peat—and the small shrubs collected from areas near the camp that are used for kindling. These small donkeys are bought from the Wakhi and require little attention, but also have a very limited use and represent the least essential livestock now kept by the Kirghiz.

Dogs (eet)

Herding households also keep one or more dogs to safeguard their herds against predators, although dogs are not used to herd sheep as they are in the West. The animals are well adapted to the environment and are capable of reproduction.

KIRGHIZ DEPENDENCE
ON NONPASTORAL FOOD AND GOODS

Hunting, Trapping, Fishing, and Collecting

Hunting, trapping, and collecting are very marginal economic activities among the Kirghiz. At the present time, hunting is limited to only a small number of men who have access to guns and ammunition and is generally carried out for sport as well as to obtain meat and fur. The most common prey is the *keyik* (ibex) and a certain number of *ghulja* and *arqar,* male and female Marco Polo sheep. Hunting is done alone or at most with a party of two or three men. The hunters generally use yak to climb the high mountainsides where ibex and Marco Polo sheep range, especially during summer; they use binoculars to find the prey. Sometimes these summer hunting trips may last two or three days.

Hunting during the winter months takes less time because the animals come down to lower elevations, nearer the camps. However, it is arduous at best and the meat and fur are not particularly well liked, especially when the prey is in poor physical condition toward the end of the winter months. Much winter hunting is done by a few poor individuals who are good marksmen and whose families need extra meat. I found at least two men in the Wakhjir valley (an area known to have a fair number of ibex and sheep) who claimed they hunted regularly during the winter for food since they could not buy enough grain to feed their families.

The Kirghiz, I was told, relied more heavily on hunting for their food in the past than they do now. The knowledge of traditional initiation rites surrounding the first hunt of a young man, the prohibitive and prescriptive rules regarding the hunters' conduct prior to, during, and after the hunt, and norms regulating the proper apportionment of the catch, and so on, are still very much intact in Kirghiz society. During my stay in the Pamirs, I had the opportunity to see a few Kirghiz hunters who attentively observed various rules and ritual behavior associated with the skinning, cutting, division, and consumption of their catch.

The Kirghiz never go out solely for the purpose of hunting animals regarded by Islamic doctrine as unfit for human consumption—wolf, fox, bear, or marmot. They shoot wolves and foxes if they run into them since their furs are used locally for making the Kirghiz fur hat, as fur linings for other garments, and are also exchanged with traders. *Quyun* (hare) are caught occasionally by poor families for food and recently their fur has also been bought by traders. A few years ago a trader from Kabul tried to encourage the Kirghiz to trap *sughur* (marmots), which infest the Pamirs from June to September. Kirghiz regard marmots as *haram* (polluting), and even though the trader offered goods in exchange for marmot pelts, the Kirghiz showed little interest. Over a period of about three years some poorer Kirghiz trapped and skinned, despite their reluctance, approximately two thousand animals. After this period the trader abandoned the idea since the Kirghiz would not trap enough animals to make it profitable for him. The Kirghiz's lack of interest in trapping marmots, although they are numerous during the warmer months when they are out of hibernation, does in fact save the herders much livestock since wolf packs feed on marmots rather than attack the Kirghiz flocks and herds.

Fishing in the Pamirs is even less important for subsistence than hunting. There are ample fish in the Pamirs' lakes and the runoff streams flowing from them, but only two persons in the whole area engage in even occasional fishing. One of those two Kirghiz had served in the Chinese Nationalist army in Sinkiang prior to the Communist takeover of Chinese Turkistan at which time he fled to the Afghan Pamirs with other Kirghiz. The other man recently had returned to the Pamirs after spending a number of years in towns in northern Afghanistan. Both men learned to fish and acquired a taste for fish from their association with non-Kirghiz. With a few other exceptions, such as the khan's family, most Kirghiz attach no value to the use of fish as food. The potential for fishing is present, and I am certain the Kirghiz will find it quite useful before long.

No vegetables are cultivated in the Pamirs and very few wild vegetables are collected by the Kirghiz. In fact, the only vegetable collected in small quantities by a few rich households is a wild onion that grows in small patches in a few areas near the summit of some of the passes of the main summer trails to the Pamirs. The onions are collected, dried, and used as seasoning and constitute the total vegetable consumption of any kind by the Kirghiz. The only other seasonings used are salt and red and black pepper, brought in from outside the area.

Agricultural and Market Goods

The bulk of the foodstuffs consumed by the Kirghiz consists of agricultural and market goods that they cannot produce themselves locally. They rely very heavily on cereal grains (wheat, barley, rice, peas, lentils, and horsebeans) for their winter diet. The bulk of their wheat flour and of their flour made from a mixture of barley, peas, lentils, and horsebeans is acquired from the Wakhi agriculturalists directly, or indirectly through itinerant traders, although a few rich Kirghiz households raise their own grain on agricultural land newly acquired from the Wakhi and sharecropped by Wakhi farmers. The cereal needs of the majority of the Kirghiz, however, are obtained through trade.

The Kirghiz staple for about five to six months during the winter is wheat flour, which is made into unleavened bread and consumed two or three times a day with tea and milk products preserved and stored for winter consumption. When it is available, bread is eaten all year, but most households are without it for several months during the spring and summer.

A moderate amount of rice, and a very little sugar, candy, and dried fruits (mulberries and apricots) are brought from Badakhshan and other parts of Afghanistan into the Pamirs by traders. Salt is also obtained through trade, as is a large quantity of black Indian tea, more than 6,300 kilograms per year.

In addition to various foodstuffs, the Kirghiz depend on outside sources for many other necessities. Such essential items as wood for the construction of Kirghiz yurt frames have to be brought in from long distances. Saddles, horseshoes, stirrups, bridles, and many metal articles are all purchased from the traders. Cooking pots, household utensils, china, glass, teapots, clothing materials, boots, shoes, galoshes, and some ready-made garments are all acquired through trade and exchange. Such luxuries as transistor radios, dry-cell batteries, watches, sewing machines, pressure cookers, sunglasses, cigarettes, tobacco, opium, jewelry, and countless other items are also obtained by the Kirghiz through trade.

LAND (PASTURE) USE AND NOMADIC PATTERNS

The vegetation of the Pamir ecological zone is at best meager, consisting of low shrubs, a few annual flowering plants, and a number of coarse grasses. Since the number of midsummer days without frost are from about twenty to thirty, all the vegetation in the area must be frost resistant. The type and density of plant coverage varies according to altitude, surface contour, soil composition, proximity to surface water, amount of precipitation, and exposure to wind and sunlight.

On the basis of local physiographic character and the types and nature of foliage coverage, the Kirghiz recognize nine general categories of pasturage, that is, microenvironmental niches, within the Pamirs (see table 3). Each category represents a specific kind of

TABLE 3

TYPES OF PASTURAGE (MICROENVIRONMENTAL NICHES) IN THE PAMIRS

Type	Physiographic character	Types of Vegetation	Density of Vegetation	Preferred by	Season of use
Shewar	ponds, marshes, and lakeside in central valley bottom	rushes	medium	horse and yak	winter
Sheber	plane along streams and springs with sufficient subsoil moisture in valley floor and inside *jelgalar*	sedge meadows	patches 20-30 cm. tall and dense turf (best pastures)	horse, yak, camel, sheep, and goats	all seasons, different areas
Toz jirlar	flat areas without sufficient constant moisture on the valley floor	mixed herbage meadow	medium	sheep, yak	spring
Cheqoor-ala	dry morainal ridges and rounded hillocks on the outskirts of valley	*tersken*, wormwood, and feather grass communities	10-20% coverage	sheep and camels	fall, winter
Sel-lar	screes found in both *kongey* and *terskey*	*tersken*-wormwood communities	less than 10% coverage	sheep, camel	all seasons, different areas
Adir	rubble-covered lower steep slopes in *kongey* and *terskey*	variety of shrublets and grasses with abundance of *godu*	about 15% coverage	sheep, goats	summer and winter, different areas
Sert	rubblelike, earthy, gentle high mountain slopes on *kongey* side	feather grass and *tersken* communities	20-30% coverage	sheep, goats	winter
Dunger sert	fringes of snow and glacier fields on *kongey* side	sedge meadows and feather grass	30-40% coverage	yak	fall and spring
Talang	rubblelike earthy slopes on *terskey* mountainsides	largely feather grass communities and meadow grass	about 40% coverage	yak, sheep, and goats	summer

range that, when available, is considered suitable grazing ground for one or more types of animals at different times of the year. Much of the land surface beyond about 5,000 meters is either covered by snow and glaciers year round or devoid of any kind of foliage. Also beyond reach are large areas of steep mountain slopes inside narrow tributary ravines, and some of the mountain slopes facing north on the *terskey* side of the valley.

The Kirghiz pastoralists' efficient utilization of meager but diverse and territorially limited range resources in the Pamirs is achieved because of the following: (1) extensive knowledge of Kirghiz herdsmen about the grazing habits of the various kinds of animals they raise; (2) the herders' thorough understanding, through shrewd observation, of the local microenvironments in the face of the most erratic and severe climatic conditions; and (3), the many calculated decisions the Kirghiz make, both individually and collectively, about the use of the various ranges available to them on both short-term (day to day) and long-term (season to season) bases.

A knowledge of livestock grazing habits is common among all nomadic societies, and is without doubt a necessary element in the art of pasturing animals. However, variations in grazing habits of the same animals under different conditions, as well as the significance of certain similar habits in different environments, may have varying implications for the survival and perpetuation of those animals. For example, the habit of pawing away the snow to uncover dried grass by sheep, but not by goats, is important in the Pamirs but may not be significant elsewhere. Such information and knowledge of the preferences of animals for different kinds of plants and grasses found in various ranges help the herders in deciding *which* pastures they should use at a given time during the year.

In the Pamirs all pastures mature at about the same time, and the over-all pasturage conditions throughout the area are uniform, so the Kirghiz migration schedule and pattern is not dictated by the quest for better pasturage and milder climates, as it often is among low-altitude pastoralists. Rather, the Kirghiz pattern of intensive use and short-distance seasonal migration is regulated by the actual and potential availability of pasture at different times during the year. The exploitability of various ranges depends on the local topography, the degree of exposure to sun and wind, seasonal climatic changes (particularly changes in wind direction and velocity), the annual snowfall, and the length of time the snow and ice cover remains on the ground. Therefore, the constricted migratory pattern of the Kirghiz involves a deliberate imposition of restrictions against the use of large areas of good fresh pasturage during the vegetation period so that the parched range can be exploited at a later date. However, the availability, that is, the likelihood of exposure from snow and ice, of the "reserved" pasturage is still subject to seasonal and local ecological conditions, as already noted.

The Kirghiz divide their pasturage into three overlapping sections on the basis of their seasonal use: *yaylow*, or summer camping and pasturage areas; *behar-o-kuz oterish jirlar*, or spring and fall camping grounds; and *qeshtow*, or winter encampment and grazing areas.

In the Little Pamir (Aqsu Onderi), with a few exceptions, *yaylow* lies on the southern side of the main river valley, as well as on the southern portion of a larger tributary river valley, the Wakhjir Jelga (map, p. 114). As described earlier, the Kirghiz refer to these areas of the valleys as *terskey* (shady face of the valley). Pasturage resources in the *terskey* areas are exploitable for the shortest length of time, from July through mid-September of each year. This limitation is imposed by two physical phenomena: the general northeast-southwest orientation of the Aqsu Onderi and the steeply rising Hindu Kush that forms the southern rim of the valley allow these areas to have little exposure to the sun during most of the year, and they thus remain shady; and the persistent northwest cyclonic wind blows most of the snow from northern portions of the valley during the long winter months, transporting it to the *terskey*, covering the pastures under a thick layer of snow and ice.

Therefore, the Kirghiz use these *terskey* areas and the higher reaches of some of the smaller tributary river valleys (e.g., Qerchin, Aq Jelga, and Ghorumdi) on the northern portions of the Aqsu Onderi during the short summer months when these pastures are most effectively exploitable. The Kirghiz camp close to the base of the mountains and near the entrance to small, narrow ravines from which small, glacier-fed streams flow into the lakes. During this period the Kirghiz avoid grazing their animals in areas more than about half a kilometer below (i.e., to the north of) their camp site, in an attempt to conserve the grass on the valley floor for later use. They make every effort to utilize those areas on the mountain-side and inside the ravines that will not be accessible at a later date. This is accomplished by efficient pasturing, the use of both the abilities and the range preference of each type of animal.

When temperatures fall and snow covers the higher mountain slopes on the *terskey* side, the Kirghiz move their camp further north to *suni boyi*, near the water, that is, the watershed area in the middle of the valley. This area is used for about a month during fall (September/October) and a month in spring (June). During the fall it is used in a final effort to make use of the pastures at the

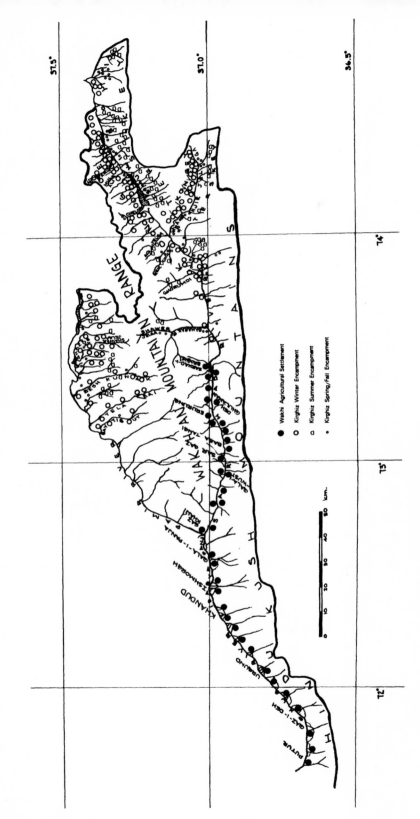

Distribution of some Wakhi settlements and Kirghiz campsites.

peidmont areas of the *terskey* as much as possible. It is also an attempt
to use the pastures near the banks of lakes and streams before the
waters and marshy grounds freeze, covering the pasturage under
a layer of ice. Many families stay longer in their summer camping
areas when possible and graze their herds in the valley floor to the
north of their camp, and then move directly to their *qeshtow*.

By about the first week in November most Kirghiz return to
their *qeshtow* on the *kongey* (sunny face of the valley) where they
spend the longest period of the year (November to June/July). The
camps are now smaller in size and more dispersed than in summer.
Encampments are well hidden in depressions, surrounded by hillocks
of glacial drift or mountain ridges, where the occupants and their
herds have some protection against the persistent gusty and freezing
wind. Careful use of the parched, frozen range during the winter
becomes essential to every herder. Attempts are made once again
to use pasturage higher up the mountainside before snow covers
it. The best pastures on the fringes of watershed areas are saved
for those days when heavy snow covers the ground, forcing some
animals (sheep and some horses) to paw, and yak to move the snow
with their snout in order to expose the frozen grass. If animals are
taken to poorer pastures under such weather conditions, the chances
of their returning to camp hungry are virtually certain and there
is a potential loss of livestock. The better pastures are also kept
in reserve during the winter months, when possible, for weakened
ewes during the lambing season. These reserved pastures are an important safeguard against possible early spring blizzards, which can result
in heavy losses not only of newborn animals but of the herd as well.

To save the better pastures for use when needed most the Kirghiz
take the herds to areas with less abundant pasturage during the days
when the weather is good, and whenever such areas are cleared of
snow by wind or sun. This kind of systematic and calculated use
of pasturage during the winter is accomplished by constantly taking
into consideration the peculiar grazing habits and tastes of each
type of livestock.

By the later part of May and early June, when the weather gets
a bit warmer and lakes and streams thaw, some Kirghiz herders move
their yurts to *suni boyi* to try to utilize the recently exposed frozen
pasturage by the watershed that they had not been able to use
in the fall. This change of camp is practiced by some herders and
lasts for about a month before moving once again to the summer
camps. However, many remain in their winter camps until the snow
has lifted from their summer pastures and new grass has sprouted.
After the Kirghiz have all moved to their summer campgrounds

some men return to the winter campgrounds to clear debris from the ground and to spread manure over those areas in need of fertilization. Then the irrigation channels are cleared and water from the nearby stream is diverted into the camp, which is periodically irrigated throughout the summer months. This investment of time and effort in the deserted campgrounds provides the herders with their only source of harvestable grass for winter fodder for their horses and camels. The grass is cut, dried, and stored in September before they return to occupy the camp once again.

In the Great Pamir (Pamir Onderi) where the entire area of Kirghiz occupation lies within the southern side of the main river valley *(terskey)*, the migratory patterns of the Kirghiz are slightly different from the Kirghiz of Aqsu Onderi. In the Great Pamir area the Kirghiz use the highest reaches of the various small tributary river valleys during the summer. During fall and spring they camp near the watershed areas, and spend the longest period of their residence at their *qeshtow,* midway between their summer and spring/fall camping grounds.

The basic local ecological constraints in the two Pamirs of Afghanistan are the same despite topographic variation, and methods of pasture use and the migratory patterns within them are also very similar. In other words, the Kirghiz are intensive pasturage users and the distance covered in their pendular migrations is relatively short but not uniform. The farthest distance between camps occupied by the same herding unit during a year may range from fifteen to thirty-five kilometers. However, the distance covered during a change of encampment (e.g., winter to spring), especially for those who reside in more than two places during a year, may be less than that suggested above. The actual travel time involved ranges from about three to seven or eight hours.

Kirghiz herders, for the most part, claim ownership (as individual *oey* units or a group of related herding units) to a narrow north-south cross-section of land in the Pamirs, which contains almost all the various ranges found in the area (those listed in table 3). It is within these narrow strips of privately or corporately owned range territory that the Kirghiz seasonal pendular oscillations take place. The Kirghiz migrations are not strictly a function of elevation variations in their territory, as is usual where extensive pasture use and vertical migratory patterns are observed. Variation in elevation between seasonal pasturage areas differs from one area to the next depending on local topography and in many places the variations in elevation between summer and winter encampment may not exceed about 300 meters. The greatest elevation difference usually exists between summer and spring/fall camping grounds, when they may range from 300 to 1,000 meters in a few places.

The processes of developing an efficient technique of range management and utilization and its systematic execution are carried out by the Kirghiz *oey* and their larger local aggregates, the *aiel* or *qorow,* the camp. It is to a discussion of the organization of the Kirghiz reproductive units and herd managing units that I shall turn next.

5. The Kirghiz People, the *Oey,* and the *Qorow*

THE PEOPLE

HUMAN BEINGS IN a high-altitude environment are as susceptible to the stresses of the severe climate and the effects of hypoxia as are domestic livestock and other organisms inhabiting the same ecological zone. It is worth noting

that at altitudes up to about 8,000 feet (2,440 m.) above sea level there is sufficient O_2 carried in the blood stream to support the normal physiological functioning of the body's various organ systems. At altitudes above this a lowland-living human faces ever increasing stress on his physiology as he ascends, unless various adaptive mechanisms come into play (haematological, cardiovascular, respiratory, etc.). [Hoff in Baker et al. 1968, p. 97]

The immediate and short-term effects of high-altitude or acute hypoxic discomfort experienced by most lowland sojourners, described in the literature as "mountain sickness" or "altitude sickness," is probably the most commonly feared and discussed effect of the highland environment. The common symptoms associated with altitude sickness are severe headaches, high pulse rate, nausea, short-windedness, and sometimes insomnia. Although altitude sickness is generally considered to afflict only the temporary lowland visitor, Hoff would qualify this position: "Even though the native highlanders may be adapted to a degree to hypoxia, a positive 1,000 feet (305 m.) differential at high altitude may exert a proportionately greater stress than a similar increment at low altitude" (ibid., pp. 97-98).

The Kirghiz acknowledge temporary hypoxic discomfort during activities that demand added physical exertion (shoveling snow, for example). This discomfort is felt especially when a person engages in physical activity after consuming large quantities of fatty food like *qaymaq* (cream) and fatty or fried meat. The Kirghiz are fully aware of the debilitating effects upon both people and animals of altitude sickness, or *tutak* (literally, "being choked").

Kirghiz cultural response to alleviate hypoxic discomfort, as well as to prevent attacks, is based on simple dietary prescriptions and advice. The afflicted are advised to rest and avoid rich and fatty food, and are given *chalop* (diluted *ayran* or sour milk), *aash* (noodles cut from wheat dough and boiled in water with some seasonings), and bread and green tea. Moderate food intake is generally advised to prevent *tutak,* and the Kirghiz themselves usually eat less food than low-altitude people in Badakhshan. This advice seems consistent with the research of Newsom and Kimeldorf (1960) that "animal experiments have shown . . . a decrease in caloric intake increases hypoxia tolerance by lowering oxygen consumption" (McClung 1969, p. 40).[1]

Recent studies of human adaptation to high altitudes have emphasized the long-term effects of hypoxia upon human populations, particularly effects on reproduction, fertility, and survival. Although an estimated twenty to twenty-five million people of the world are believed to live above 3,000 meters (10,000 feet) (De Jong 1968), systematic study of how man lives in high altitudes is comparatively recent, and generally limited to South American populations living in the Andes. (Similar studies may possibly have been done in Russia and China, but are not generally available.) De Jong remarks (1968, p. 72) that "very few demographic studies [have] . . . explicitly considered altitude as a variable." He claims that serious demographic dialogue, even in South America, began only in 1963 when Stycos (1963) attempted to explain the regional natality differences in Peru between the Indians and the mestizos on a cultural basis. His "cultural natality differential thesis . . . was tested by Heer (1964) for Ecuador and Bolivia as well as Peru" (ibid.). But it was not until 1966, De Jong says, that James hypothesized "that natality differentials between the Spanish and Indian-speaking population of Andean countries were [recognized as being] due to the physiological effects of altitude rather than to voluntary socio-cultural factors" [such

1. McClung also suggests that the "low blood glucose in the human high altitude population" may be caused by their decrease in caloric intake. She discusses the correlation between low blood sugar and low birth weight and the consequent increase in neonatal mortality at high altitudes. For further details see McClung 1969, pp. 37-50.

as mating patterns by Indians and mestizos] (ibid., p. 73). Most of the information on the effects of high altitude on reproductive processes comes from animal experiments rather than those on human beings (cf. Donayre 1966; Van Liere and Stickney 1963). On the basis of research conducted in actual or simulated high-altitude environments, De Jong states that "the natality-depressing effects of altitude seem to be related to circulatory system adjustments to hypoxia, to the functioning of the hypothalmic and endocrine systems, to germ cell production, to copulation, to gestation, to birth weight, and to early mortality" (1968, p. 74; also see Weihe 1962; Moncloa et al. 1965).

There have been a number of studies dealing with the relationship between infant mortality and high altitude. Jean McClung, in her book *Effects of High Altitude on Human Birth*, after a long review of literature and research findings on the subject, concludes that

animal experiments are in almost unanimous agreement that hypoxia—whether encountered naturally at high altitudes or artificially in chambers—adversely affects the developing fetus. Hypoxia has been found to increase fetal and neonatal mortality and the frequency of congenital malformations, and in some species [including human] it depresses birth weight. . . .

The mechanisms through which hypoxia affects the fetus are still unclear. Experimental evidence indicates that hypoxia can directly affect cell composition of the maternal blood stream, the placenta, and the fetus.[1968, p. 50; also see Grahn and Kratchman 1963; Mazess 1966; Cruz-Coke et al. 1967; Hoff 1968; Tominaga and Page 1966]

It is stated that "Spanish chroniclers of the sixteenth century noted no child of Spanish blood was born during the first fifty years of Spanish occupation of the Peruvian highlands" (De Jong in Baker et al. 1968, p. 74). This phenomenon led to the subsequent decision of the Spaniards to move their capital from the highlands to the seacoast.

Of some help in understanding my own demographic observations among the Kirghiz is a brief mention of some of the demographic findings of a report on "Reproduction and Viability in a Highland Peruvian Indian Population" prepared by Charles Hoff (in Baker et al. 1968, pp. 85-152), a member of the Dr. Paul T. Baker project studying a highland Peruvian ecosystem (see Baker et al. 1965, 1968; Baker and Weiner 1966). The Hoff study was carried out in the Nunoa district located in the altiplano of the southern highlands of Peru, where human habitation lies between 3,960 and 4,880 meters. The population under study includes the mestizos, Cholos, and *indigena*, with the *indigena* comprising the greater part of the population in the district. For the study a sample of 136 married women and their offspring were selected for an analysis of fertility statistics. Hoff's findings on reproductive patterns in Nunoa are as follows:

The sample demonstrates a high fertility with a concomitant high mortality. . . .

Evidence that high altitude and hypoxia affects post natal mortality is demonstrated by the prevalence of respiratory complications (with a probably combined pulmonary-cardiovascular etiology) reported as cause of death in the Nunoan sample and Andean highlands of Peru at large. Thus it would appear that the high wastage is a function of hypoxia, as well as lack of proper medical facilities. [Baker et al. 1968, pp. 130-31]

Hoff further claims that "the most extraordinary phenomena observed in this sample are the differentials in reproduction and viability of males and females" in Nunoa (ibid., p. 132). Their sample has shown the highest recorded ratio of 129 males to 100 females at birth and 133 to 100 males to females of the surviving sex ratio.[2] It is suggested by Hoff that "The higher surviving sex ratios are a result of a higher net female mortality throughout the lifespan from birth through adulthood. Both the high SSR [secondary sex ratio or sex ratio at time of birth] and higher female mortality are unusual in comparison to the world norms" (ibid., p. 133).

A very large number (at least twenty-five) of factors are suggested to have influenced the unusual sex ratio. A few that are given consideration are sociocultural milieu, maternal age and parity, genetic systems, radiation and immunological factors, and hypoxia. However, an accurate assessment of their effects in determining sex ratios is difficult and subject to conjecture. What is generally accepted by authorities is that "there appears to be a strong relationship between total mortality and hypoxia" (ibid., p. 138). Hoff has concluded his study by adding that

this population has adapted to the exigencies of life at high altitude in terms of demographic resolution. In order to maintain population stability and temporal continuity in the face of high altitude-specific environment pressures this population maintains high fertility to offset the wastage of a high mortality. The latter appears to have manifest hypoxia-induced components. Although human biological adaptation throughout the life span from conception to late adulthood is severely stressed and viability as compared to lowland Western population is reduced, fertility variables suggest that this population is highly fecund. . . . It is still not known if this adaptation is genetic in nature or entirely due to acclimatization. [Ibid., pp. 138-39]

2. The sex ratio of any given population, according to Clarke (1965, p. 73), often varies from between 90 and 110 males per 100 females. Kirby et al. (1967, p. 139) puts the world sex ratio at 106 males per 100 females (see Hoff 1968 for further details).

My own observations and the population statistics I was able to obtain show that the reproductive and viability trends among the Kirghiz population are very similar to those found by Hoff among the Nunoans in Peru. I would like to point out that, unlike those of Hoff and his associates, my data were not collected solely for the purpose of assessing natality and mortality rates, the mortality and fertility rates, and the over-all reproductive trends and viability of human population in the Pamirs. Rather they were collected to determine the population composition by age and sex, and the increase or decrease in Kirghiz population during the past half century, since the closure of the borders. Because of my uncontrolled data gathering on the subject, and the inherent problems of taking ethnographic censuses in a nonliterate society, the figures given below, while suggestive of the general demographic trends in Kirghiz society, should be viewed as tentative. The Kirghiz do not keep records of births and deaths, and figures provided as to age of mothers, as well as offspring, are estimated and generally given in round numbers (i.e., 5, 10, 15, 20, etc.). There was much uncertainty as to the age, and sometimes the sex, of deceased offspring. Also, underreporting on stillbirths, miscarriages, prenatal deaths, and even deaths occurring during the early days after birth, is suspected. Because of some uncertainty about the accuracy of the ages of mothers and some children, I will present the statistical information according to broad age blocks and use gross statistics, such as means or averages, in order to decrease the degree of error.

The Kirghiz population statistics indicate a relatively high fertility rate and a very high mortality rate. From among 475 consummated marriages in the present generation, 380 married women reported giving birth to 1,674 live offspring. Some 50 women had died, leaving young children. The remaining 330 living women who had given live birth ranged in age from 15 to 70 years with the average age of 35.5 years. Of these 330 women 160 were 45 years old and over, that is, beyond the menopause.

A very high mortality rate during the entire life span in Kirghiz society is evidenced by the deaths of an estimated 46.7 percent (or 776) of the offspring. Close to 30 percent of the wastage occurs during the first year. A greater part of deaths of offspring occurs prior to the age of reproduction. The causes of death are many. Most of the deaths during early days *post partum* are from prematurity[3] (most likely induced by hypoxia) and respiratory complications,

---

3. From my own observations I found Kirghiz newborn consistently smaller than the infants in the lower altitudes of Badakhshan.

especially during the long winter months. Poor diet for both mothers and offspring during the winter, lack of any kind of medical help, and unsanitary conditions all contribute to the high mortality.

The differential in sex ratios in Kirghiz society, particularly the surviving sex ratio of 120 males per 100 females, is comparable to the unusually high surviving sex ratio of 133 to 100 reported for the Nunoan communities (see Hoff in Baker et al. 1968, p. 124).[4] The secondary sex ratio in Kirghiz society is 106 (the same as the world ratio, see Kirby et al. 1967, p. 139). This seems quite low compared to the SSR ratio of 129 found in Nunoa. However, since there was a high degree of uncertainty about the sex of their deceased infants, especially among Kirghiz women over 35 years of age, both figures on the sex ratio are tentative, but suggestive of a higher male ratio. The differential in the surviving sex ratio reflects the higher female mortality during the early years, as well as through the reproductive period, especially during pregnancy or at childbirth.[5]

4. The sex ratio among the Kirghiz population is based on the total number of reported births (1,674) within the living generations. The actual figures for the survivors and deceased of each sex is as follows:

Total number of males born = 851; number of deceased = 361 (42.4%); number of survivors = 490.

Total number of females born = 823; number of deceased = 415 (50.4%); number of survivors = 408.

5. The death rate of women at childbirth is especially high, which causes much fear and concern in Kirghiz society. Most of the 50 women who were reported deceased, leaving young children, very likely died either giving birth or from other birth-related complications. During my own fieldwork several women died at childbirth or from problems associated with the placenta.

In Kirghiz society the high maternal death rate is explained by most in cultural or psychological rather than physiological, biological, and medical terms. The Kirghiz attribute the cause of maternal death to a female demon called Albarste. Albarste is personified as a small, short (midgetlike) female with extra long breasts which she swings over her shoulders when moving. She is said to have crooked feet *(tetri taman)*, i.e., her heels face each other. She is also said to have a fair complexion, yellow (blonde) hair, blue eyes, and a foul smell.

Albarste may be provoked if spoken of or when called by her name. However, she may not need provocation since she likes to cause the death of pregnant women. She is believed to appear when pregnant women are in labor. Her method of killing is to pull out the lungs of the expectant mother. If, once she has extracted the lungs, she takes them to a pile of ashes the woman in labor will faint. If Albarste puts the lungs into water, the woman will die. A number of prophylactic and curative measures are also provided. For example, to avoid provocation, her name is not spoken, but she is referred to as *tetri taman* (crooked feet) or *ziandash* (the cause of damage, death at childbirth). Firing guns and provoking the dogs to fight and bark is thought to scare off Albarste. Dogs are thought to be able to see Albarste, but she usually remains invisible to man. Sprinkling cold water on the patient's face, holding the holy Quran over her head, and reciting aloud passages from the Quran are also prescribed to help the patient.

The higher mortality among females in Kirghiz society is also reflected in the population composition of the society as a whole (see table 4). It is important to note that there is a higher ratio of females than males in the 0-9 age group. After that point, however, because of the high incidence of maternal death at childbirth, the figures for females fall consistently below those of males until the end of the female reproductive age of forty-five and above. After the age of forty there seems to be an acceleration of male mortality in Kirghiz society.

The Kirghiz, like the Nunoan communities, have offset the high mortality in the population by a very strong procreative drive with emphasis upon having a large number of male children. This urge is based on their need to have at least three sons to manage their daily routine comfortably. In order to achieve this goal Kirghiz women marry as early as thirteen years of age, and a very high percentage of all women over the age of twenty are married (see table 5). Therefore, most females remain exposed to the risk of pregnancy throughout their reproductive years. Because of the lack of adequate data on the age of mothers and offspring it is hard to give, or correctly assess, fertility estimates. However, I was told by one woman that she had had twenty-one pregnancies, nineteen live births, but only one child survived. Many women have given birth to more than eight and up to sixteen children. The Kirghiz practice levirate whereby the wife of a deceased male is very often married by a younger sibling of the deceased. As a result the time a woman may remain unexposed to pregnancy is even further decreased.

In Kirghiz society men may marry as young as fifteen years of age and most are married before the age of thirty-five. Polygyny is practiced by a few (at the time of this research 25 marriages out of a total of 334 involved two wives and only one involved three wives). Because of the lower ratio of available females and polygynous practices, some younger women marry older men, but the number of such marriages is low, and counteracted by the restriction of levirate to younger men only.

Because of the consistently high rate of mortality in Kirghiz society, population growth has been almost nil during the past fifty years or so. If the 1921 estimate by Kushkaki (1923) of 2,000 people is correct, then the present number of 1,825 persons I found through my household census indicates that a balanced demographic trend has been maintained by the Kirghiz despite hypoxia, cold, exposure, and other high-altitude-specific factors influencing population dy-

TABLE 4

COMPOSITION OF KIRGHIZ POPULATION BY AGE AND SEX

Age	Total	Male	Female	Sex Ratio Male	Female	Percentage of total
0-9	476	234	242	49.2	50.8	26.2
10-19	399	223	176	55.9	44.1	22.0
20-29	289	149	140	51.6	48.4	15.9
30-39	233	130	103	55.8	44.2	12.9
40-49	172	87	85	50.6	49.4	9.4
50-59	108	52	56	48.1	51.9	5.5
60+	148	71	77	48.0	52.0	8.1
	1,825	946	879	51.8	48.2	100.0

Kirghiz Population Pyramid

TABLE 5

MARITAL STATUS OF KIRGHIZ POPULATION BY AGE GROUPS

Age	Male	Married	Widowed	Divorced	Female	Married	Widowed	Divorced
0-9	234	—	—	—	242	—	—	—
10-19	223	13	1	1	176	35	—	—
20-29	149	71	—	—	140	124	4	1
30-39	130	84	9	2	103	89	9	1
40-49	87	77	4	—	85	66	15	1
50-59	52	38	3	—	56	31	25	—
60+	71	47	21	—	77	23	51	—
Total	946	330	38	3	879	368	104	3

namics in the area.[6] My statistical and observational demographic data from the Afghan Pamirs, even though they were not gathered in a fully systematic manner, still reveal patterns very similar to those found among Peruvian and other South American high-altitude populations. I believe that further clinical, experimental, and better demographic research among the Kirghiz is essential for an understanding of their biological adaptation mechanisms in their recently restricted environment. Comparison with data from other areas of the world would also lead to a better understanding of human reproduction and viability in high altitudes in general.

The high cosmic radiation at altitudes above 4,000 meters (13,200 feet), which is considered to be five or six times more than at altitudes close to sea level[7] (see Hoff in Baker et al. 1968, p. 135), is believed to influence human reproductive processes, particularly sex ratios. Whatever effects radiation and cold may have on the reproductive biology of the Kirghiz population is open to further investigation. However, there are some apparent and observable health problems that are countered by cultural means.

The vast majority of Kirghiz, especially males, suffer from chronic eye irritations and other eye problems during most of their adult lives. This problem is for the most part, related to the exceptionally high exposure, glare, and reflection from the snow-covered surroundings during much of the year. As a result, shades and dark glasses of any kind, introduced by the itinerant traders, have become an important item of trade. The Kirghiz still attempt to make eye protectors from any pieces of dark glass they can find, but in its absence, they

---

6. Respiratory ailments including tuberculosis and coughs and gastrointestinal and digestive problems are common among the Kirghiz. The high incidence of digestive complaints is evidently related to the loss of teeth during their twenties by a great majority of Kirghiz, male and female. A certain amount of mental illness was also observed among both sexes. All of these factors contribute to the high mortality rate among the Kirghiz. The relationship between their high-altitude environment and the various health-related problems in the society is yet to be investigated fully.

7. The amount of cosmic radiation at 4,000 meters (13,200 feet) above sea level is reported to be nearly 200 mr/year (Cruz-Coke, Cristoffanini et al., 1967, p. 423), while cosmic radiation at sea level is computed at about 33 mr/year (Graham and Kratchman 1963). For further details and comparisons with the total environmental radiation at low and high altitudes see Baker et al. 1968, pp. 135-36).

use the traditional means—strands of yak hair worn in front of the eyes and fastened under the fur hat worn by Kirghiz males.

The Kirghiz cultural techniques of ameliorating the stresses of cold seem quite effective,[8] the most conspicuous being the Kirghiz houses, the *aq oey* (yurt) and the *tom* (a single-room adobe structure), heated by fire, and their clothing. The Kirghiz *aq oey* is the mobile abode used year round by the Kirghiz. It is a round tent made up of a circular, perpendicular wall of collapsible wooden latticework and a domed roof. The roof is formed by light poles that are tied at one end into the lattice wall frame and the other end fitted like spokes of a wheel into the rim of the circular chimney frame. The chimney frame, which is the highest point of the domed structure, stands about three to four meters from the floor of the yurt, which varies from about four to eight meters in diameter. It is covered first by a layer of straw mats around the latticework and then by a layer of thick felt especially made for the yurt. The entrance to the yurt is always placed opposite the persistent northwesterly wind, and fitted with a flexible felt-covered reed mat door. The structure is also equipped with an adjustable piece of felt for a chimney cover. By adjusting the cover it is possible to control the level of indoor lighting and the amount of smoke in the yurt, and to prevent snow and wind from entering.

When the yurt is covered with new felt and is well kept, it is a very well-insulated and comfortable shelter. It is fairly airtight during the winter and easy to adjust for air circulation during warm days, of which there are very few in the Pamirs. During the winter a fire is kept going on the floor in the center of the yurt for most. of the day from sunrise to late in the evening. Generally the Kirghiz have a single yurt per household unit so that all of the household cooking is done in one place. This is particularly important with the extreme scarcity of fuel. With the help of fire and the relatively airtight and well-insulated felt-covered yurt they have created an adequately protected microenvironment for the household against cold. Even at night during the winter the indoor temperature rarely seems to fall below the freezing point, while the outside temperatures are always at least twenty degrees centigrade below freezing.

Recently a few richer Kirghiz have built a very limited number

8. For a study of the effects of cold stress and additional bibliographic in-formation see Hanna in Baker et al. 1968, pp. 196-326; Hanna 1974.

(about fifteen) of permanent stone and mud abodes in a rectangular shape. Most of these houses, called *tom*, are in the winter camping grounds and are used only when heated by means of a peat- and *qegh*-burning metal stove built locally from kerosene drums, with an exhaust pipe leading outside. These are at present luxuries limited to few and are not practical housing for most. There are also at least three *tom* in the summer camping grounds, built during the past five years by rich herd owners, excluding the khan.

Probably the most effective means of protection the individual Kirghiz has against cold is clothing. They literally encase themselves in layers of clothing, even during the summer months. Their dress consists of fur-skin coats, wool-filled jackets and pantaloons, and thick woolen stockings worn with high leather boots. The traditional Central Asian heelless and thin-soled boot *(maseh)* is worn with rubber galoshes; the locally made thick-soled heelless boot, *chareq*, and more conventional boots, *otek*, are worn without galoshes. The below-the-knee-length pantaloons are tucked into the boots, and sashes are tied around the waist to prevent loss of body heat. Gloves are not commonly used, but the sleeves of the overcoat are made longer to protect hands, especially needful when riding. Men are equipped with fur hats that can cover the ears and the back of the neck when unfolded.

Men's and women's garments are similar except in color and type of material and thickness of padding. Women's clothing, in various shades of red, is made out of velvets and other fabrics. The heavily insulated garments for men are always made of a darker colored fabric, generally black corduroy or denim for the jackets, pantaloons, and overcoats. There is no difference in the footgear for men and women. Children are clothed very much like their elders. Girls, like the women, wear a round cap topped by a shawl that covers the head and shoulders.

In general, the individual Kirghiz has a well-insulated micro-climate in his clothing that protects him well from the cold. Men, between herding and the trips back and forth to Wakhan during winter to trade for grain, are more exposed to the outside cold. Women, who spend most of their time in the yurt, can be a little more lightly clothed. Most Kirghiz have a more than adequate supply of wool-filled blankets, quilts, and fur mats to keep themselves comfortable at night. They sleep very close to each other, generally retiring early in the evening and rising not long before the sun. Indeed, their daily activities are largely regulated by daylight.

It is apparent from this discussion that the Kirghiz have maintained, with some success, their human population balance despite high mortality in general and higher female mortality in particular. They have also safeguarded themselves fairly well against other hazards of high altitude, such as radiation and cold, by cultural adaptations. Directly influenced by the environmental stresses and responding to counteract them has been the reproductive and economic productive unit, the Kirghiz *oey*. It is the organization and viability of the *oey* that needs further explication.

ORGANIZATION OF REPRODUCTIVE AND HERD MANAGEMENT UNITS

The Oey

The smallest independent herding unit in Kirghiz society is the *oey*, the physical structure of a yurt (the Kirghiz house) and the group of people living in it. The *oey* very often contains one or more conjugal units of reproduction (family), and is generally also an independent unit of production and consumption (household). Members of an *oey* generally own and occupy a single yurt, and only the very rich have an extra yurt to use as a guesthouse. Most polygynous families also have two yurts, but polygyny is, for the most part, practiced only by the rich herd owners.

The arrangement of space in a Kirghiz *oey* is simple and uniform. A section of the yurt to the left of the entrance is always partitioned off by a high screen for use as the kitchen area and storage space for household pots, pans, milk, and milk products. Opposite the entrance the family chests (wooden, leather, or tin), containing the possessions of individual household members, are lined against the yurt wall. These chests are generally topped by a pile of family bedding that is placed there each morning after use. Saddles and other riding tackle, and sometimes skins containing various milk products, are stored on the right, close to the entrance. The fire is built on the ground in the center of the yurt, directly below the chimney hole. All the cooking is done on top of an iron tripod, common among most central and southwestern Asian nomads. Most of the household activities, including weaving on a long, horizontal loom, are done within the yurt, particularly during the winter. The family activities take place during the day around the fire. At night household members make their beds close together with heads toward the yurt walls and feet toward the center.

Many household items, particularly light articles in common use, are tucked into, fastened onto, or hung from the lattice frame of the yurt walls, in clear view of the occupants (see p. 131). For most households the yurt is an all-purpose abode for living, sleeping, and storage. Only recently, however, have some Kirghiz taken to building small mud and stone structures in their winter camps as storage areas, while a few have built *tom* as winter living quarters for some of their members.

All Kirghiz *oey* units own most necessary household utensils, such as cooking pots, pans, pails, containers, and riding tackle and there is little lending and borrowing of such items except on special occasions. Most household items are of cast iron, copper, brass, or tin, bu⁺ recently a certain amount of plastic, china, and glassware has been introduced. The Kirghiz have a few wooden utensils acquired from the Wakhi peasants, but pottery is not generally used. Much of what is presently in use in Kirghiz households came from towns and cities of Chinese and Russian Turkistan decades earlier and has passed from generation to generation. Most of the rather limited number of articles are used for a variety of different purposes.

As an economic unit the *oey* claims right of ownership over all movable property, including the yurt, the products of the herd, often, but not always, the herd itself, and sometimes pasture, encampment grounds, and any permanent structure built on the camp site(s). The *oey* very often acts as an independent political unit and is represented in public matters by the senior male or, occasionally, the senior female member of the household (in the absence of an adult male).

The Kirghiz *oey* is the basic unit of herd management, and the herd is the main source of subsistence. Unlike most nomadic societies, however, the Kirghiz household, for the most part, does not own its own animals, although it earns a livelihood from the products of the animals herded. This is done through a number of herding arrangements between the large herd-owning *oey* units and households without livestock, the organization of which will be discussed in chapter 7.

At this point, it is sufficient to note that among the 333 *oeylar* that make up the entire Kirghiz community in the Pamirs, only 105 or about 31.5 percent own all, or part, of the sheep and goats they herd. The number of households who own all or part of their yak herd number 228, or about 68.4 percent of the total households. However, the number of *oey* units that have animals for herding, regardless of right of ownership (disposal) over the animals, is much higher. That is, 255 *oeylar* (76.6 percent) have herds of sheep and goats, while 276 households (83.0 percent) of all domestic units have yak at their disposal.

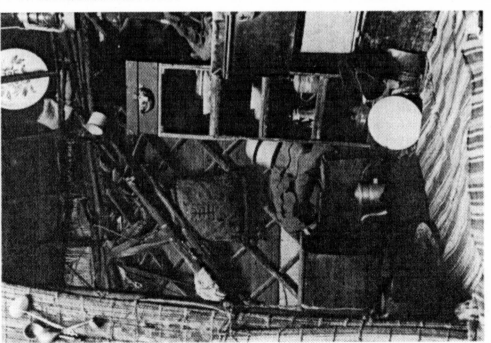

Inside a yurt: *left*, kitchen and storage area; *right*, baking bread.

The number of animals herded by the individual *oey* varies, ranging from only a few sheep and goats to an estimated 1,400 head, and from 1 yak to over 180 (see table 6). Generally a household herd consists of sheep and goats and yak, but there are families that herd only mixed sheep and goats or yak. As may be expected, those households herding large numbers of sheep and goats also very often herd a proportionately larger number of yak as well. The figures in table 6 indicating 78 *oeylar* are without a herd of sheep and goats, and 57 households without yak, needs some clarification here. These figures mean only that those families do not have access to animals all year round. Almost all of the families, however, receive milking yak, ewes, and does during the milking season from those who have

TABLE 6

SIZE AND DISTRIBUTION
OF KIRGHIZ HERDS AMONG *OEY* UNITS

Number of herding units	Size of herd	Total animals herded
Sheep and goats		
11	500–1,400	9,825
35	201–500	11,237
28	151–200	5,227
30	101–150	4,165
66	51–100	5,405
85	3–50	2,741
78	0	0
333		38,600
Yak		
9	51–186	696
32	21–50	1,048
26	16–20	485
30	11–15	388
69	6–10	592
110	1–5	335
57	0	0
333		3,544

larger herds in their own camp or from other encampments. Therefore, all Kirghiz *oey* have access to herds and animal products, especially during the milk season. Those who do not possess livestock
year round lack an adequate labor force or are not dependable
herders, at least in the eyes of rich herd owners who could supply
them with animals.

From the Kirghiz point of view, those households that receive
only temporary charge of milking animals for *saghun* during the spring
and summer are "small herders," and are those who possess less than
about one hundred sheep and goats and less than ten yak. Most,
or in some cases all, of such herds are milking animals, since the
male and unproductive animals are annually exchanged for other
needs, taken away by the herd owner, or not owned or given by
the herd owners in the first place. Such *oey* units with small (temporary or permanent) herds are not independent herders. In fact, a
number of them usually join together and form a corporate herding
group to save labor for other needs, or a smaller number of them
may join a household with a medium-sized herd under a different
arrangement. These small herding units demand a minimum labor
force of one adult male, an adult female, and at least one child over
ten years of age.

For the Kirghiz a medium-sized herd ranges from one to five
hundred sheep and goats and about twenty yak. About 40 to 50
percent of such herds are nonmilking. Such herding units require
the help of at least two adult men, two adult women, and one or
two children over ten years of age. *Oeylar* with a medium-sized
herd in Kirghiz society are, in essence, the independent herders.
They camp alone for about eight or nine months during the winter
apart from other herders, but generally join others during the summer.
These units very often have at least one hired man whose help is
needed year round, while the services of others may be needed intermittently.

Large herds of sheep and goats are those over five hundred head;
the large herds of yak are those over fifty head. At least 50 percent
of such large herds consist of nonreproductive or nonmilk-producing
animals. Such herds are divided into milking *(saghun)* and nonmilking
(swy) sections and herded separately. The labor force required is
large, consisting of at least four or more adult males, four adult
females, and three or more youths. The labor demand in *oey* units
with such large herds is quite high and several men, and sometimes
families, are hired as herders, often to look after the nonmilk-producing portion of the herd. This portion of the herd may be kept

in a separate camp, at least during the winter. Because of the labor demand the rich herding units, whenever possible, consist of what Samih K. Farsoun (1970, pp. 257-307) has called "functional extended families" rather than residential ones. That is, married sons or brothers who live in a separate yurt from that of the head of the *oey* and who maintain their own kitchen, either in the same encampment (at least part of the year) or in a different camp, act as a single herd-owning and/or managing unit. This particular *oey* organization is also found among poor households to whom large numbers of animals are farmed out by the rich herd owners. *Oeylar* with the maximal herd size camp alone and apart from other herders all year round.

Economic productivity of the Kirghiz *oey*, its economic needs, and means of satisfaction are influenced by a variety of factors. These include such basic means of pastoral production as the size and composition of household herds, the annual condition of pasture and weather, the size and composition of household membership, their skills, interests, and competence in herding activities, and so forth. The economic costs of the household depend very much on the size of the *oey*, its earnings in livestock or livestock products, its demand for different types of nonpastoral foodstuffs and other commodities, and the personal habits of its members (e.g., use of tobacco, opium), and so on. There is no easy way of presenting a simple and clear picture of Kirghiz domestic economy and their general standard of living.

One way of approaching this subject is, of course, by means of gross statistics. On the basis of a household economic survey I was able to obtain a picture of an average Kirghiz household economy (see table 7).

A comparison of the figures in table 7 with the figures on the distribution of the composition and size of Kirghiz households (in table 9, p. 140) shows that more than 50 percent of the Kirghiz *oeylar* consist of five persons or less. By the same token, a comparison of the average herd sizes given above with those presented earlier on the actual distribution of herd size among *oey* units (table 6), shows that the majority of Kirghiz households have access to less than one hundred sheep and goats and the ten yak stipulated for the average herding unit.

However, despite the predominance of small herds, the products resulting from the animals seem to satisfy not only the subsistence needs of the group but also provide a surplus since most households report earnings from livestock products above the average mentioned above (see table 8). Much of these livestock products that are in

TABLE 7

AVERAGE SIZE, ASSETS, EARNINGS, AND CONSUMPTION OF IMPORTED FOOD OF THE KIRGHIZ *OEY* IN 1973

(Based on data from 333 households)

Size of *oey*	5.5 persons
Size of herds and flocks	
sheep and goats	120 head
yak	10 head
horses	1 head
Major livestock products	
mai (clarified butter)	3.9 *sair* (ca. 30 kg.)
qroot (dried yoghurt)	6.2 *sair* (ca. 49 kg.)
kegiz (felt)	4.6 pieces* (ca. 23 m^2)
werama (horse cover)	1.2 pieces
Consumption of imported food	
grains (wheat, barley, lentils, etc.)	120 *sair* (912 kg.)
tea (Indian black)	2.6 *sair* (ca. 18 kg.)

*The average Kirghiz felt measures about five square meters.

TABLE 8

KIRGHIZ HOUSEHOLD LIVESTOCK PRODUCT EARNINGS

(During 1973)

Product	Number of *oey* reporting earnings	Estimated amounts	Estimated totals	Average per *oey*
Mai	278	1-20 *sair* (7.60 kg.-150.0 kg.)	1,323 *sair* (10,055 kg.)	4.7 *sair* (35.7 kg.)
Qroot	276	1-30 *sair* (7.60 kg.-228.0 kg.)	2,100 *sair* (15,960 kg.)	7.5 *sair* (57.0 kg.)
Kegiz	242	1-50 pieces (5-250 m^2)	1,540 pieces (7,700 m^2)	6.3 pieces (31.5 m^2)
Werama	167	1-10	418	1.5

excess of household needs are traded for agricultural and market commodities. Most large herd owner/herders do not produce much livestock produce for sale since they entertain large numbers of visitors (Kirghiz and non-Kirghiz, i.e., Wakhi and traders) year round, which exhausts their milk and milk-products. In the same manner, their felt products will cover the two or three *oey* they own, and the many horses, camels, and yak they use. They generally pay with livestock for their grain and market goods while medium and small herders attempt to cover much of these costs by their earnings from livestock products. Usually, families that do not have their own herd, but have extra manpower, earn animals (four to six *qoey* or equivalent per adult male per annum) by working as hired shepherds for other *oey* units. There are many other occasions, such as cutting peat, *qegh*, or fodder, when human labor can be exchanged for animals. The poor also receive annual alms of livestock and goods for their use. Some of the herdless *oey* units also include members who specialize in such crafts as shoemaking, silversmithing, blacksmithing, or building yurts. Such craftsmen are paid with animals for their services.

In general, the lot of most Kirghiz *oeylar* is much better, and their living standard much higher, than that of their neighbors the Wakhi or even many lowland agricultural villagers in Afghanistan. This is largely because of the increasing demand for meat and other animal products in the market towns and cities of Afghanistan, and the consequently high prices paid for livestock. Kirghiz livestock brings comparatively low prices in the Pamirs and the Wakhan because of the inherent nature of the "frontier economy." Nevertheless, they are still quite high for pastoral products, especially when compared with those of agricultural commodities in the Wakhan and in the country in general. Some of the average rates of direct exchange (not delayed credit) for sheep (ewes or two-year-old wethers) and livestock products in the Wakhan and in market towns in 1973 are as follows:

	Wakhan	Market towns
1 sheep	500 Afghanis (Afs.)*	1,000 Afs.
	20 *sair* (152.0 kg,) grain**	
	3 *sair* (22.8 kg.) rice	
	30 meters of inexpensive cotton cloth	
	5 meters of velvet or corduroy	
	4-6 *pow* (about 2-3 kg.) tea	
	3 pairs of galoshes	

	Wakhan	Market towns
1 sheep	1 *maseh* (heelless leather boots worn with galoshes) 10 sets (4) horseshoes	1000 Afs.
1 *sair mai (ghee)*	400 Afs. 8-10 *sair* (60.8-76.0 kg.) grain 4 *sair* (30.4 kg.) salt	800 Afs.
1 *sair qroot*	60 Afs. 2-3 *sair* (14-21.6 kg.) grain	120 Afs.
1 *werama* (horse cover made of goat hair)	10 *sair* (76.0 kg.) grain	700 Afs.
1 *werama* (camel hair)	15 *sair* (114.0 kg.) grain	1,000 Afs.
1 *kegiz* (felt)	7 *sair* (50.0 kg.) grain	400 Afs.
1 *arqan* (rope)	20 Afs.	
1 sheepskin	30 Afs.	

*Approximately 55 Afs. = U.S. $1.00
**Grain = wheat, barley, millet, lentils

These rates of exchange for pastoral and market goods have gone up during the past two years, while the price of grain in the Wakhan has remained almost the same. To give the reader better grounds for comparison let me quote cash prices in the Wakhan for some of the agricultural products and market goods.

1 *sair* (7.6 kg.) wheat	30.0 Afs. (U.S. $0.55)
1 *sair* barley	20.0
1 *sair* salt	25.0
1 *pow* (.453 kg.) black tea	90.0
1 meter poor quality cotton cloth	25.0
1 *sair* rice	180.0

With these exchange rates, the estimated average annual cost of nonpastoral subsistence products and goods (excluding the cost of horses) for an average Kirghiz *oey* with about 5.5 members runs to about twenty sheep, or its equivalent in other animals and animal products. The average annual cost per person will be, then, about four sheep:

20 *sair* (152.0 kg.) grain	= 1 sheep
8 *pow* (3.6 kg.) black tea	= 1½ sheep
salt, cloth, footwear	= 1½ sheep

This amount is reasonably low in view of the man-animal ratio of about 1:21 sheep and goats and 1:2 yak in Kirghiz society. On the basis of these statistics the average individual Kirghiz' assets and the costs of nonpastoral products consumed can be estimated as follows:

Average assets per person	Local value in cash	
	Afs.	U.S. $ (approximate)
15 sheep	= 7,500	136.30
6 goats	= 1,500	29.00
2 yak	= 3,000	54.50
Ca. 1 *sair mai*	= 400	7.50
1.3 *sair qroot*	= 100	1.80
1+ pieces *kegiz* (5 m^2)	= 250	4.50
	12,750	230.00

Average costs per person		
4 sheep	= 2,000	37.00

Of course, as with the average household herd size and earned livestock products, there are tremendous differences in consumption costs and actual earnings and productive assets of individuals and *oey* units. Many poorer households spend much less than four sheep per person per annum while many others spend a great deal more for luxury goods such as sugar, rice, radios, sewing machines, watches, readymade garments, and boots. A great many individuals smoke tobacco or use *naswar* (a powdered mixture made of green tobacco leaves, lime, and ashes that has a numbing effect when held under the tongue) and about one hundred persons are believed to use opium. The costs of obtaining nonpastoral commodities are higher for those households that do not have the means for direct exchange and use credit arrangements.

The total annual cost of all the nonpastoral subsistence and market luxury goods to the Kirghiz *oey* units is considerable. It amounts to an annual export of an estimated 5,000 sheep and goats, 200 yak, about 800 to 1,000 *sair* (6,080-7,000 kg.) of *mai,* about 200 to 300 horse covers, about 600 pieces (3,000 m^2) of felt and a large number of sheep- and goatskins, ropes, and so forth. The organization of trade and exchange will be discussed in a later chapter, but it may be worth noting that as a result of their relatively high productivity the Kirghiz *oey* in general enjoys a higher standard of living at the present than many households in many agricultural villages in Afghanistan. They also own a very high per capita number of transistor radios, sewing machines, watches, and other luxury items not commonly found in such numbers in rural communities.

The size of the Kirghiz *oey* ranges from 2 to 14 individuals with an average of 5.5 persons per household (see table 9). Over 79 percent (i.e. 265) of Kirghiz households consist of a nucleus of one married couple and their children. This nucleus is often augmented by a parent, occasionally a widowed uncle or aunt or unmarried siblings of the husband or wife. There are also a few "incomplete families" (Barth 1961, p. 19) consisting of a widowed parent and children or a single man and mother. Patrilineal extended families consisting of two or more monogamous conjugal units of siblings (horizontal) or of different generations (vertical) account for about 13.5 percent (45) of the Kirghiz households. The remaining 7.0 percent (23) of Kirghiz *oey* units are made up of composite or polygynous (two or three wives) families of either the nuclear or extended type.

The organization of an *oey* varies considerably, depending upon its size, composition, and access to livestock. Both the structure of authority and the division of labor is quite flexible in the Kirghiz household. All *oeylar* have a recognized *oey bashi* or "head of the household" who represents the interests of the herding unit in the community and who may be either male or female. Generally, the senior male member of the *oey* is recognized as *oey bashi* by its members. This person is the father (i.e., husband or widower), or an elder brother who is married. Widowed women with young unmarried, or young married, sons also commonly represent the interests of the unit directly. Only when an older married son is present does the widowed mother relegate the position to him. Aunts, uncles, and in-laws, who are part of the household but not primary members of the family, are not usually considered heads of households even if they are senior members.

The head of the household in the Kirghiz *oey* is the spokesperson,

TABLE 9

COMPOSITION AND SIZE OF KIRGHIZ *OEY* UNITS

Type of *Oey*	Number of Persons in *Oey*													
	2	3	4	5	6	7	8	9	10	11	12	13	14	
Elementary families														
Nuclear families	25	15	28	22	24	12	6	3	1	1				
Nuclear families with additional relatives		7	15	18	24	7	8	3		1				79.5%
Incomplete families, widow(er)+ children, etc.	2	13	10	7	7	2	4							
Patrilineal extended families			3	2	11	9	9	4		3	3		1	13.5%
Composite (polygynous) families														
Nuclear		1		2	1	5	3	1						7.0%
Extended				1		1	3	1	1			2	1	
Total	27	36	56	52	67	36	33	12	2	5	3	2	2	

manager, and executor of the collective will of all of its members. He enjoys a certain amount of respect from the members of the *oey*, as well as from the community, but he does not have absolute authority in making decisions without the consent of all adult members of the family, regardless of sex. All significant decisions concerning household marriages, livestock allocations to herders, acceptance of animals for herding from a particular family or families, moving camp, changing membership from one camp group to another, hiring help for the *oey*, or rendering services to other herding units, as well as many other decisions regarding the management of production and consumption are reached through agreement among all adult members of the domestic group. Women in Kirghiz society are quite assertive in all matters of importance to the domestic unit, though their role varies a great deal from household to household. Among the poorer households, male-female equality is in evidence in domestic affairs but in richer *oey* units males tend to dominate.

Division of labor in the Kirghiz *oey* is, to some degree, based on age and sex but it is always subject to the influences of the seasonal and daily labor requirements of the domestic units. There are, however, a number of tasks that are carried out exclusively by men, either because the tasks demand heavy physical exertion or because they involve travel away from the camp. Such tasks include trading and transporting cereals and other goods from the Wakhan, digging irrigation ditches, clearing and irrigating *khoreq* pastures (those needing irrigation), and cutting fodder. Most activities related to herding are generally carried out by males, and boys over ten years of age are expected to help with the herding. Activities involving the building of enclosures and platforms for drying milk products, loading and unloading during moving, making and repairing footwear (leatherwork), collecting dung, cutting *qegh*, and making fires are also done by males. Such domestic chores as milking, making the milk products, cooking, spinning, weaving, sewing, mending and repairing garments and animal covers, and carrying water, are all done by females. Scores of other tasks—feltmaking, ropemaking, dismantling the yurt, packing and setting it up again, and milking require the participation of all members of the household. Looking after lambs, kids, and calves are chores usually assigned to young boys and girls, when they are available. The family herd of sheep and goats is very often tended by a hired adult male or a younger member of the household, not usually by the head of the household.

During the winter the herds are taken to the pastures at sunrise and returned at about sundown. During the milk season, however, the herd is taken about one hour before sunrise and brought back to camp at about eleven-thirty in the morning for milking and to allow the lambs, kids, and calves to feed. The animals are taken to pasture again at about two o'clock and returned about one hour after sunset. The yak are milked early in the morning and then herded out to the pasture to be brought back at about three-thirty in the afternoon for the second milking of the day. The calves are also allowed to suckle a little at both times. The milking of yak is done by women who move from cow to cow with a pail while the calf is tethered at the yak's side. The calf is allowed to suckle intermittently for a short time during milking in order to increase the flow of milk.

The ewes and does are milked by women who sit in one place with pails while animals are brought and held for them, either by children or by adult males. Alternatively, the ewes and goats are loosely tied by the neck along both sides of a long hitching rope, and are milked in a rather systematic manner, leaving no confusion as to which animals have been milked. Unlike yak, which are milked from the side, sheep and goats are milked from the rear (see photographs on pages 96 and 98).

In this discussion the Kirghiz *oey*, its varying size and composition, and economic and reproductive tasks are treated as givens, rather than the products of an ongoing social and biological process. The differences noted in the composition and size of Kirghiz households reflect different states of the developmental cycle at which the *oeylar* are found at any given point (see Goody 1958, p. 3). In other words, the structure of Kirghiz domestic units is basically the same when observed (if it were possible) at a time when they are all at the same stage of the developmental cycle. However, such conditions are not likely to be found in an actual social system since, in reality, there are at least two main constraints that influence the *oey* composition and size. They are the uncertainty of human reproduction in the high-altitude conditions, and the access of domestic groups to productive, and thereby to reproductive, resources. It is through consideration of the impact of these constraints of the process of the domestic developmental cycle that both the variation and the viability of the Kirghiz *oey* may be understood.

As stated earlier, the Kirghiz *oey* is structured around one or more conjugal units, and close to 80 percent of all households contain only one married couple. The marriage of a son and/or sibling in a Kirghiz *oey* is generally an occasion for the fission of households. The new household is usually created one month to a year after the consummation of the marriage. Kirghiz weddings take place in the encampment of the bride's family where the groom and his bride spend three days in a yurt specially set up by the groom's family. After this the groom returns to his own parental household. The new *oey* is established when the bride is physically brought to join her husband at his parental camp, which may be one month to a year after the date of the wedding.

The main household of the groom customarily pays for the cost of the wedding festivities and the bridewealth *(qalen),* the total cost of which varies from one to twenty *jambu* in livestock and animal products. A *jambu* is an early Chinese silver ingot, once widely used in Central Asia. Although no longer in use as a medium of exchange, it remains the standard for determining bridewealth among the Kirghiz, and is valued at the present at ten sheep.[9] In addition to these costs, the groom's household is expected to provide the newlyweds with an *aq oey,* a yurt. The bride's family furnishes its daughter with a dowry that consists of most of the household utensils needed by the young couple, including bedding and furnishings. Thus, the immediate and basic requirements for a new household are provided by the families of the bride and groom. This new household is usually located at the groom's paternal camp (patrilocal-virilocal) or it may make a neolocal residence not very far from the paternal camp, at least during certain seasons.

Access to capital and means of production by or for the new *oey* may be obtained by a number of means. The Kirghiz, like many other western Asian pastoral nomadic communities, give animals to their young children on the occasion of their birth, circumcision, and as gifts at times to test the interest and luck of the youth as a future herder (see Barth 1961, p. 18). Young children may also receive animals during their initial visit to relatives or family friends or on special occasions. These animals remain the private property of the child although the rights of disposition remain in the hands of the head of the household until the young person marries or decides to move out for other reasons. At any rate, the young couple may have acquired some animals prior to their wedding.

After the marriage the groom is also usually given his share of the family herd as *yenchi,* or what Barth has called in the case of Basseri "anticipatory inheritance" (ibid., p. 19). This division is carried out in accordance with the Islamic rules of inheritance whereby the married son has no legal rights over the family herd at the time of his father's death, although he may claim rights over

9. The value of *jambu* for other animals is as follows: One *jambu* = twenty goats, four yak, or one horse; two *jambu* = one camel.

property other than livestock (c.f. Bates 1973, pp. 87-120). In addition, when the bride is formally brought into her husband's parental camp (whether setting up a separate household or not) she is invited by close relatives of her husband's household and presented with at least one or more animals. Another opportunity for capital for the new *oey* is when the bride is taken, after a year of residence with her husband's household, to her paternal household. At the end of her one-month-long stay with her natal family she is returned to her own new conjugal household with some animals. This is never formally acknowledged to be her inheritance from her paternal household, but it is somewhat similar to the anticipatory inheritance sons receive on the occasion of their marriage. The Kirghiz insist on the Islamic provision for women's rights to inheritance of property, but in practice many women do not claim their share from their siblings after the death of their father in order to guarantee male sibling support in the future.

For the new *oey* that does not obtain enough capital through these processes, there are two other alternatives available to help establish the new household. First, the man may hire himself out as a paid shepherd so that he can earn livestock and eventually start his own herd. Secondly, the *oey* can ask a rich herd owner for animals to herd under the *saghun* arrangement (temporary milk animals) or *amanat* system (long-term herding). When a lack of labor force does not permit such an arrangement, it is likely that the newlyweds will remain with the groom's paternal household at least until a younger brother is married. The newly extended family may then use the extra labor force to arrive at some kind of herding arrangement with a large herd owner. Similar kinds of extended family households may develop when a household with a large herd requires additional labor. The married son or sibling may be kept in the household and the *oey* fission delayed or a kind of "functional extended family" formed by dividing the herd and camping at different places, but remaining a single economic unit.

Access to additional labor is approached by the Kirghiz in several different ways. Incomplete families, such as a widow(er) left with young boys but with a marriageable daughter, may bring in a son-in-law through what is known as *kuch keyaw*. Under this system the man is obliged to stay and work for his bride's household for seven years; after that period he and his bride may choose to stay or leave and set up their own *oey*. In some instances the *oey* requiring the additional labor may adopt a son-in-law, especially if they have no sons of their own. Adoption of both girls and boys, particularly orphans of one's close agnatic relatives, is very common in Kirghiz society and is particularly desired by households with no offspring. Another method for the richer households both to acquire offspring and to alleviate demands on female labor is polygyny, leading to the creation of composite *oey* units. Acceptance of widowed relatives and their small children is not only regarded as a kinship obligation by the Kirghiz household, but is also a promise of additional labor for the *oey*.

For those not capable of finding capital and who are short of labor a further alternative is to camp with a relative or friend with a large herd or with a group of smaller herders. In such camps mutual interdependence is rewarding to both sides, and it is in this regard that a discussion of Kirghiz herding groups is significant for our purposes.

The Aiel or Qorow (Camp)

In the Kirghiz language the two terms *aiel* and *qorow* are used interchangeably in reference to encampments. It is important to point out, however, that in their literal form the two Kirghiz terms denote only certain components of a pastoral camp. The term *aiel* commonly means a group of people who reside in a spatially defined place. *Qorow*, on the other hand, means the pen or walled-off enclosure in which herds of sheep and goats are kept at night. When used by a Kirghiz in everyday conversation both *aiel* and *qorow* refer to a group of people who live in the same camp and keep their herds in the same pen. Therefore, by definition, those herding units that maintain common residence also herd their animals together and form the smallest social unit, or camp community, in Kirghiz society.

The organization and size of Kirghiz *aiel* is influenced by the seasonal availability of pasturage and the condition of the range in a particular area, as well as the size of the herd and the number of people required for tending the animals. Also important are the ties of kinship, marriage, and friendship, and the rights of private or corporate ownership by individual *oeylar* or a group of *oeylar* over the encampment site(s) and/or pasturage ground.

The effects of seasonal variation are obvious, as noted in the discussion of the efficient utilization of pasturage. Kirghiz camps are most numerous (about 118 total) and widely dispersed throughout the *kongey* area of the Pamirs during the winter (see p. 114). Winter camps are generally small, ranging in size from a single *oey* to about six or seven in the largest camps and rarely change from one year to the next. *Oey* units residing in the same *aiel* are very often related to one another by blood, marriage, or *dostlik*, a form of "ritual"

or fictive kinship established by public oath. In most cases encampment sites and the surrounding pastures are owned privately by one
oey or claimed as joint property by some or all of the families occupying it. Some encampment sites and their associated pasture(s) are
owned by a rich herder who may ask or allow those herding units
to whom he has given animals for herding under the *amanat* system
to use the land. In many instances, however, people who occupy
the camp site at the present are also the former owner(s) of the land,
which they or their parents sold to the rich herd-owning families.

The right of private or corporate claim over a camp site or pasture
is important in the decision of an *oey* as to whether or not it should
change camp membership. For the most part, however, camps are
not local corporate land (pasture and camp site) owning groups; rather
they are cooperative herding groups and, as such, a significant interdependent social unit. The Kirghiz *qorow*, as a herd management
group, is generally structured around an *oey* unit(s) that has access
to a relatively large herd. Many *aiel*, particularly during the winter,
are made up of a single large herding *oey* unit.

The larger *aiel* often consists of an *oey* with a medium or large
herd and some relatives with small or no herds. Despite such differences in access to livestock among the *oeylar* in the camp, the
relationship is based on equality as neighbors and mutual interdependence. There is no servant-master relationship in Kirghiz society.
Those who serve others see it as an economic transaction that can
be terminated when and if they see fit. In the same manner an *oey*
can change its membership from one camp to another at any time
but must first get the consent of the member(s) of the camp it plans
to join.

Both the poor herder and his family and the herdless families
are important to the rich herder, for they are his most intimate companions for many months of the year or, indeed, for the entire year.
Poor men help their richer neighbors to transport grain, or aid them
by caring for their livestock during the winter. The women of poorer
households may help those of richer households with their spinning
and weaving and other household chores. Such help is usually repaid
with foodstuffs and other goods, as well as the use of animal droppings for fuel. *Oeylar* sharing the same camp also depend on each
other in times of need for transportation, food, garments, tools, and
utensils, as well as for comfort and celebration during times of grief
or joy. Sharing is common between members of the camp, and indeed,
whenever an animal dies or one is slaughtered for some reason, it is
customary to apportion some of the meat to all neighbors. Camping

with a large herd owner during winter also assures the poorer family of *saghun,* or milk animals, during the summer.

Summer camps are larger in size (up to twelve *oey* units in one camp) than winter camps and are concentrated mainly in the areas of abundant pasturage on the *terskey* side of the valley and the upper reaches of the larger *jelgalar,* or tributary river valleys (see p. 114). They are formed by the aggregation of two or more winter camps and as a result there are only about eighty-six summer camps in both Pamirs.

Most households have access to the wool and milk products of some animals owned by rich herders. Whether such animals are given by the *oey* units with whom they camp or not, summer camp members cooperate by taking turns daily in herding throughout the summer months. This allows time for participation in wedding festivities and other summer activities that demand cooperative effort.

Summer in the Pamirs is a time of plenty, relaxation, feasting, and visiting among relatives and friends. There is little or no friction about the use of pasturage and most summer pastures are either public property or corporately owned by kinship groups.

Aggregation of larger numbers of *oey* units during the summer is important, not only for social but also for economic reasons. Many people are required at this time of the year to help with the daily milking routine, and the feeding of the lambs and kids. A large number of men are also needed to help shear the animals during the summer season while a good many men and women are needed to help in the making of felt. Yet another activity during the summer is the preparation for the long winter months. A large labor force is needed for the cutting, collecting, and storing of winter fodder, as well as peat for fuel. Some of these tasks are carried out with the help of hired labor (either Kirghiz or Wakhi) but many are accomplished through cooperation between members of each camp.

Daily internal activities of the camp are generally coordinated by the heads of the member *oey* units through discussion and consultation. Each camp is also represented by a *be,* or camp elder, who looks into all matters concerning his camp's relations with other camp groups, or local sociopolitical affairs. The *be* is usually the head of the most influential, and often the economically best off, *oey* unit, and is a male over thirty years of age. In cases where the *oey* units are all members of the same lineage group, the senior male in the camp is the person most likely to fill the position of *be.* The *be* mediates any dispute within the camp and is often consulted by the Kirghiz khan on any matters concerning the welfare of the camp or its members.

The Kirghiz camp as a localized social and herding group does not always represent a united political unit, unless all its members belong to the same patrilineal descent group. In such cases, it is clear that descent, and not residence, is the basis for political unity. However, camps defend their pasture rights against the neighboring camps through quarrels and/or negotiations. Such discussions are carried out publicly by the *be* of both camps, or in the presence of either an *aqsaqal* (lineage elder) or the khan.

The Kirghiz camps act as independent social units and are treated as such by other such localized groups. There are many social obligations of the camp as a unit that are met by its members jointly or by rotation. For example, provision of hospitality for strangers and government officials is the duty of the camp members collectively. Even when a guest arrives and enters a specific *oey*, he is viewed as a guest of the entire camp membership and not of the specific *oey*. Although it is customary to take the camp guest to the home of the *be*, especially when the guest is an outsider, food provisions are brought by other units and consumed together in the *oey* of the *be*, or the guest(s) and adult men of other *oeylar* are invited to eat at different households for the midday and evening meals, particularly if the visit lasts more than a day. If the guest happens to be an Afghan government official, the camp *be* is also responsible for finding rides and guides from his camp to take the official to the next camp, where it becomes the obligation of another *be* to continue these services. Accommodation of animals and men is always rotated among the *oey* membership within the camp.

During such life cycle rituals as birth, circumcision, weddings, illness, deaths, and funerals, *oeylar* within the Kirghiz camps act as interdependent social units. Camps with a single *oey* usually rely on neighboring camps or relatives for help on such occasions. During childbirth, illness, or death, members of the affected *oey* are helped with their necessary daily chores for as long as possible by their neighbors. During the summer, when weddings take place, many relatives may join camp. Neighbors actively take part in every stage of the wedding festivities and offer hospitality to wedding guests in accordance with the *qunoq* system, on the basis of which each neighbor is assigned a certain number of guests to feed and shelter for one or two nights during the final wedding celebrations. During rituals people are also called upon or invited on the basis of proximity to an *oey* or camp group as much as on the basis of blood and affinal ties. However, the significance of camps as local groups is very often augmented by the many ties of marriage, blood relationship, friendship, and economic interdependence that govern their internal structure and external continuation over a period of time. At this point it is imperative to our understanding of both Kirghiz herding units (the *oey*) and cooperative herding groups (the *aeil* or *qorow*) as the ecologically adaptive herd management institutions, to view them in the broader frame work of the Kirghiz sociocultural system (i.e., kinship, ideology, and polity) that has helped sustain and perpetuate their structural configurations through time.

6. The Kirghiz
Sociocultural System

THE KIRGHIZ SOCIAL structure is organized on agnatic-descent principles. All Kirghiz living in the Afghan Pamirs claim common descent
from the same male ancestor, whose name and identity is generally
unknown to the majority. The most commonly known relevant ancestors are four men who were allegedly brothers, called Teyet, Kesak,
Qepchaq, and Naiman, all of whom presently serve to identify the
four main patrilineages or *zor oruq* among the Kirghiz.

During my research in the field I found an incomplete hand-
written document in Kirghiz (Arabic script) containing at least three
different explanations of the Kirghiz origin and the meaning of its
ethnonym, along with a genealogical pedigree of the writer and
relevant others traced to twenty-six ascending generations. Ata Bai
Qazi, I was told, had died in the Little Pamir about twenty years
before. He was said to be a Muslim functionary prior to taking refuge
in the Afghan Pamirs, and carried the title of *qazi*, or judge; he was
a member of the Jamanang section of the Teyet *oruq*. In this document he traced the ancestry of the four renowned male ancestors
of the Kirghiz to an even higher apical father, as shown at the top
of the following page.

The information and explanation found in Ata Bai Qazi's manuscript is without doubt based on research and his own special interest.
Its contents are significant for the study of Kirghiz kinship, but
not particularly relevant to the purpose of this study. The written

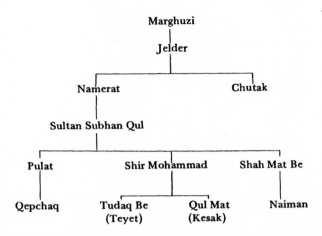

genealogy, however, is consistent with a very important principle of Kirghiz kinship, for traditionally the ability of individual Kirghiz to trace ancestry for seven ascending generations in the male line was necessary as a proof of identity and claim to membership in a particular Kirghiz *oruq*. Those unable to do so were considered *qul* or slaves, just as were the descendants of those born of mixed marriages between Kirghiz and non-Kirghiz/non-Kazakh, and the offspring of Kirghiz married to slaves.

Every Kirghiz is regarded as being a member of one of the four *chung* or *zor oruq* (major or great seed or root, i.e., maximal lineage). The affiliation to the *chung oruq* may be direct or through membership in a smaller named section of the main patrilineage. Each of the *chung oruqlar* have up to four additional segmentary levels, hierarchically arranged from less inclusive to more inclusive membership groups. All levels of these kinship groups are referred to by the same Kirghiz term, *oruq* (seed or root), preceded by the modifiers *zor* or *chung* (great or major) to signify the more inclusive or higher level groupings, and *kechek* (minor or small) to indicate the lower and less inclusive membership groups. The number of named patrilineage groups at each level, as well as the number of levels involved, vary with the size of membership acknowledged in each of the four major *oruq*. The structure of the *chung oruqlar* and their component membership groups are outlined in table 10.

For the most part, the Kirghiz of Afghanistan are members of only two of the four major groups, with the majority of the Kesak *oruq* residing in the Great Pamir area and the Teyet in the Little Pamir. The head of over 200 *oey* units, with a total population of over

TABLE 10

The Organization of Kirghiz *Oruq* Structure

Four major *oruqlar* (Level I)	Subgroups (Level II)	(Level III)	(Level IV)	(Level V)

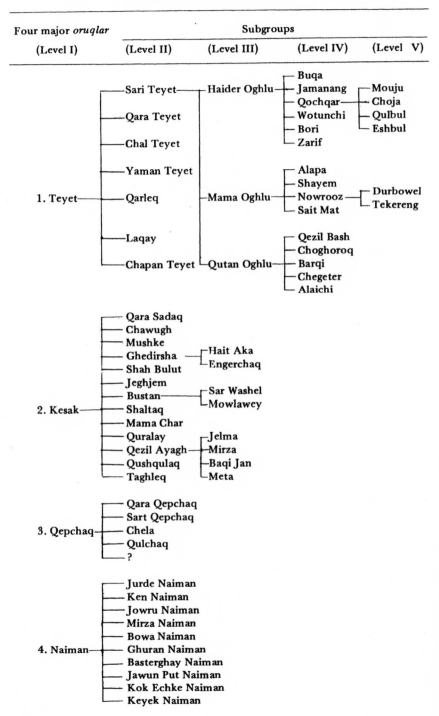

1. Teyet
   - Sari Teyet — Haider Oghlu
     - Buqa
     - Jamanang — Mouju
     - Qochqar — Choja
     - Wotunchi — Qulbul
     - Bori — Eshbul
     - Zarif
   - Qara Teyet
   - Chal Teyet
   - Yaman Teyet
   - Qarleq — Mama Oghlu
     - Alapa
     - Shayem
     - Nowrooz — Durbowel
     - Sait Mat — Tekereng
   - Laqay
   - Chapan Teyet — Qutan Oghlu
     - Qezil Bash
     - Choghoroq
     - Barqi
     - Chegeter
     - Alaichi

2. Kesak
   - Qara Sadaq
   - Chawugh
   - Mushke
   - Ghedirsha — Hait Aka / Engerchaq
   - Shah Bulut
   - Jeghjem
   - Bustan — Sar Washel / Mowlawey
   - Shaltaq
   - Mama Char
   - Quralay — Jelma
   - Qezil Ayagh — Mirza
   - Qushqulaq — Baqi Jan
   - Taghleq — Meta

3. Qepchaq
   - Qara Qepchaq
   - Sart Qepchaq
   - Chela
   - Qulchaq
   - ?

4. Naiman
   - Jurde Naiman
   - Ken Naiman
   - Jowru Naiman
   - Mirza Naiman
   - Bowa Naiman
   - Ghuran Naiman
   - Basterghay Naiman
   - Jawun Put Naiman
   - Kok Echke Naiman
   - Keyek Naiman

1,100 persons, claims to be a member of the Teyet descent group (see table 11). The Kesak group, the second in size, consists of 112 *oey* units with a population of about 579 persons. There are only a small number of Naiman (8 *oeylar*, 66 persons) and Qepchaq (5 *oeylar*, 30 persons) living in both the Little and the Great Pamirs. The majority of the members of Qepchaq and Naiman are believed to be residents of the Pamirs in the Soviet Union and the Sinkiang Pamirs of the People's Republic of China. There are only about 4 *oey* units with 18 members who identify themselves as Qalmaq, who are not members of the four major Kirghiz *oruq* structures. In fact, the term *Qalmaq* implies their Mongol or Chinese ancestry; their forefathers are believed to have been *qul*, or slaves, of the Kirghiz. At present, however, they are free and Turkicized members of Kirghiz society. There are also two Uzbek households with 20 members living among the Kirghiz, one of whom

TABLE 11

DISTRIBUTION OF KIRGHIZ POPULATION
BY MAJOR AGNATIC KINSHIP GROUPS

Kinship group (*oruq*)	Total number of *oey* units	Percentage of *oey* units	Total population	Percentage of population
Teyet	201	60.0	1,111	60.8
Kesak	112	34.0	579	31.7
Naiman	8	2.4	66	3.6
Qepchaq	5	1.5	30	1.7
Others (Uzbek and Qalmaq)	7	2.1	39	2.2
	333	100	1,825	100

is a recently nomadized former trader from a village in Badakhshan. A number of *sart*, or Wakhi, households also reside with the Kirghiz but are not considered an integrated part of Kirghiz society, and are thus not included in the figures.

The Teyet *oruq*, the largest of the Kirghiz patrilineage groups, is segmented into seventeen minimal lineages *(kechek oruq)* of varying sizes. The Kesak recognize about fourteen such minimal lineages or sections within their group, while the small Naiman and Qepchaq do not acknowledge any segmentation in their membership. The names of the significant *kechek oruq* of the two major *oruq*, Teyet and Kesak, are listed below and seem to be selected by the descent groups from levels one through four of the *oruq* structure presented in table 10. However, it was also noted that some households address themselves on occasion by the least inclusive names from level V.

Chung oruq	Kechek oruq	Number of oey	Number of people
Teyet	Qochqar	35	218
	Alapa	26	137
	Shayem	23	131
	Nowrooz	20	106
	Wotunchi	19	111
	Qezil Bash	18	90
	Qutan	17	87
	Alaichi	9	48
	Jamanang	8	39
	Qara Teyet	8	40
	Buqa	6	35
	Bori	3	21
	Chegeter	3	19
	Yaman Teyet	3	12
	Chal Teyet	2	15
	Barqi	1	5
	Choghoroq	1	7
Kesak	Qezil Ayagh	31	157
	Ghedirsha	19	98
	Jeghjem	14	68
	Kesak	13	65
	Shaltaq	9	46
	Mama Char	7	43
	Bustan	4	27
	Mushke	4	17
	Shah Bulut	4	17
	Quralay	3	16
	Hait Aka	1	5
	Qara Sadaq	1	12
	Chawugh	1	3
	Qushqulaq	1	5

All these groups are considered structurally equal to one another by the Kirghiz, regardless of the level of pedigree from which their names are drawn. It is these structural units that serve as points of reference to identify individuals and *oey* units, and that serve the needs of the individuals and groups on the basis of segmentary principles as socioeconomic and political entities (see Evans-Pritchard

1940; Fortes 1953). Indeed, the Kirghiz *kechek oruq* are very often corporate groups with common pastures and camping grounds. Therefore, such groups are to some degree spatially definable. In these instances, it is quite common for the Kirghiz to refer to certain camps, or the area where camps are located, by the name of the *oruq* of those who occupy it. *Oruq* names are usually added after personal names for purposes of specificity. Groups of individuals are also both referred to and addressed by the *kechek oruq* name.

Membership in an *oruq* is ascribed by birth or bestowed through adoption,[1] and is traced through the male line only. The rights and obligations of members towards each other are numerous and binding throughout life. Both individuals and groups are reminded regularly of the significance of the principles of descent as guides for interpersonal and intergroup relations. This is achieved during socialization processes by the domestic unit, and through repeated and recurring participation and observation by the individuals of rituals, ceremonials, and feasts surrounding such events as birth, marriage, illness, conflict, death, and so on. At these times food is provided and reinforcement given to keep these basic normative and structural principles in perspective. It is also during such situations that the boundaries of these structural units are best realized and maintained.

Kechek oruq in Kirghiz society are the most significant agnatically defined kinship groups, which, among other things, act as independent political units. The strength and influence of each group is based upon its membership size, its collective wealth in livestock, pasture, camping grounds, and of course the willingness of its membership to act as a unified interest group. The internal structure of each *oruq* is based on the recognition of the equality of the heads of member *oey* units, and an emphasis on respect for seniority, knowledge, and proven skill as a persuasive orator. Very often, the economic status and the size of an *oey* membership determine the sociopolitical standing of its senior male member. Each *kechek oruq*

1. The most striking example of gaining membership in an *oruq* in Kirghiz society, especially for a non-Kirghiz, is the case of a family of former slaves who are fully enfranchised members of Alapa *oruq* in the Little Pamir. In fact, Hait Be, head of Mama Oghlu, of which Alapa *oruq* is one section, is a member of one such adopted family. His ancestors were allegedly the slaves of some Alapa families who later freed and adopted them into their own descent group. It is also believed that the parents of Hait Be were of mixed Chinese and Kunjuti blood.

is, therefore, headed by a senior male of one of its member *oeylar* (membership permitting) who is generally referred to as *aqsaqal* (elder, or, literally, "white bearded").

There are at least twenty lineages with recognized *aqsaqal* in the Pamirs. The *aqsaqal* is expected to be a man over forty years of age, known for his impartiality and good judgment. The position is not elective or hereditary. Rather a man is acknowledged by the members of the group as they turn to him for help, advice, or the mediation of conflicts. Therefore, the position is attained through public approval and maintained as long as such consent continues without public challenge from another member. The *aqsaqal* is treated in public gatherings with such special attention as seating him in the place of honor. He acts as the spokesman for his group in all matters of public or private concern, and represents the interests of his membership to the khan, and through him to the local government.

The *aqsaqal* usually has previous experience as a *be,* camp elder, and may be acting as such in his own camp. However, his position as the lineage elder supersedes local groupings and is concerned with its descent group membership regardless of their local residence. The *aqsaqal* serves to resolve any jural disputes among his *oruq* members through mediation and persuasion by himself or in concert with the heads of *oey* units. In disputes with members of other groups he is responsible for negotiating with the individuals and the *aqsaqal* of the rival group. *Aqsaqal* do not have absolute authority or means of enforcing their decision except through community pressure or referral of the case to the Kirghiz khan, or the local government authorities. Very often the public recognition of the *aqsaqal* as the lineage elder of a group by the khan gives a certain degree of legitimization and this is usually done by asking the designated *aqsaqal* for consultation in matters concerning his specific group or the public matters of the Kirghiz as a whole.

There is no doubt but that the existence of the position of lineage elder such as *aqsaqal,* and its relations with the higher political constellations has an important effect on the structural continuation of kinship groups in Kirghiz society. However, the processes that have the greatest effect on the perpetuation and the structural integrity of the Kirghiz *oruq* and its political leadership are generally nonpolitical in nature, although never without political implications in practice. Specifically, I refer to the importance of the exchange of goods and services during Kirghiz funeral rites, questions involving the choice of a marriage partner, and rules of inheritance.

During funeral rites, presumably in accordance with Islamic tradition, the Kirghiz distribute some of the possessions of the deceased adult. I use the term *presumably* here because there seems to be no clear statement in Islamic law as to the amount and the nature of *esqot,* or alms, given out during the funeral rites. The practice varies considerably from one place to the next in northern Afghanistan. However, the purpose of such distribution of goods is to help the poor and needy and through this to gain merit and salvation for the deceased. The Kirghiz way of fulfilling this religious duty is particularly significant and has very important social, structural, and political implications.

The Kirghiz use the Persianized Arabic phrase *sadaqa-e-fedeya soum wa salot* ("penance paid for omissions of fasts and prayers") to refer to goods given as *esqot.* When the deceased is a member of a wealthy household, the amount given can be fairly large. But the important aspect is not only the amount given but the *way* in which it is presented, and to whom. To give an example, I shall describe a case in which I was involved. The deceased was a woman of thirty-seven who had died in childbirth. She and her husband were both members of Qezil Ayagh *oruq,* a section of the Kesak major *oruq.* Before the burial a crowd of over a hundred relatives and friends from neighboring camps had gathered. Also present was the Kirghiz khan and a few *aqsaqal* of other lineages. The khan and elders were seated on quilts outside the yurt, and I was placed next to the khan (a high honor), and treated as an elder despite my age. Soon, the brother of the deceased woman appeared in public with the halter of a horse in his hand and announced that the deceased's husband was presenting three *toquz* (three sets of nine, nine being the magic number in Kirghiz) of animals and other items. One set included a horse as the "head" plus eight sheep and goats, the second set was headed by an *eenak* (yak cow), and the third set by a *turpoq* (yak calf) plus eight other items from among the deceased's personal possessions in the household (e.g., a chest, a mirror, a bowl, etc.). The bereaved brother said that he was presenting the first set of items to the Haider Oghlu, who were represented by the khan *Haji* (the khan, who has been to Mecca, is also *Haji*), the second set to the leaders of Mama Oghlu *oruq,* and the third to the *aqsaqal* of Qutan Oghlu *oruq* who were also represented. At the same time I was given 200 Afghanis in cash and a ceremonial *chapan* or gown.[2]

---

2. There are a large number of these *chapan* made out of colorful and sometimes expensive fabrics, but they are not filled with any kind of padding. They are

This was very surprising since it was my understanding that *esqot* was given only to the poor and needy.

It was later explained to me that traditionally *esqot* is given to rival *oruq* and that the goods were presented to their leaders as a group. It was the responsibility of the *aqsaqal* to dispose of the animals among his own membership as he saw fit. As table 10 shows, Haider Oghlu, Mama Oghlu, and Qutan Oghlu are related agnatic groups belonging to the Teyet major *oruq*. No goods were presented to any member or elder of Kesak *oruq*. I was told that they would receive goods upon the death of an adult from the Teyet *oruq* and that in the past this was an occasion for economically outdoing the opposite *oruq* since "offerings" at such times are expected to be reciprocated in an equal amount, or more.

The Kirghiz insist that in the past (prior to some thirty years ago), *esqot* had little to do with the deceased or his spiritual welfare, but had a lot to do with the living and their losing or gaining prestige. This is still true to some extent, although not quite as much as in the past because since the closure of the borders there have been consistent attempts on the part of the Kirghiz elders to curb any such lineage rivalries. This is seen as possible by the Kirghiz through a return to the orthodox (Sunni) practices of Islam, despite the tremendous decrease in religious education since the frontiers were closed. The distribution by the *aqsaqal* of *esqot* goods among the poor and needy of his own *oruq* is very much in accordance with the spirit of Islam.

The Kirghiz principles of descent and *oruq* structure are major constraints influencing both individuals and *oeylar* in the choice of marriage partners for members. This is not, however, because of any specific prescriptive rules of exogamy or endogamy governing the lineage groups. Indeed, Kirghiz have no such rules, and the only sexual relations not permitted are those between the members of one's immediate blood relatives—parents, their siblings, siblings, children, and siblings' offspring. The Kirghiz in general deny any particular preference as to whom they should marry. In practice, however, there seems to be a very high occurrence of bilateral first cousin marriages, *kechek oruq* endogamy, and marriages between related *kechek oruq* members within a major *oruq* (see table 12).

Information on over 420 marriages shows a very high occurrence

---

never worn as garments except ceremonially, but are circulated among people on different occasions as a sign of friendship and appreciation or gratitude, and must be returned in the same way at another time.

of endogamous marriages. Two hundred and ninety (69 percent) of the marriages contracted took place within the major *oruq*, while only 131 (31 percent) marriages involved exchange of women across major *oruq* lines. The total number of *kechek oruq* endogamous marriages alone accounted for almost 29 percent of the contracted marriages. A very high number of these endogamous marriages are patrilineal cross and parallel cousin marriages. There is an equally high incidence of matrilineal cross and parallel cousin marriages, some of which are not reflected in the statistics in table 12, especially if the parents were exogamous in the first place.

TABLE 12

EXCHANGE OF WOMEN AMONG MAJOR *ORUQLAR*
IN KIRGHIZ SOCIETY BASED ON ALL REPORTED MARRIAGES
OF LIVING GENERATIONS

		Wives given						
		Teyet	Kesak	Qepchaq	Naiman	Qalmaq	Uzbek	Uyghur
Wives taken	Teyet	199	43	5	5	6	1	1
	Kesak	42	87	1	6	1	1	1
	Qepchaq	2	4	0	0	0	0	0
	Naiman	1	8	—	3	—	—	—
	Qalmaq	1	1	—	—	1	—	—
	Uzbek	—	1	—	—	—	1	—
	Uyghur	—	—	—	—	—	—	—

The question one has to raise, and which has been raised by other anthropologists (see Barth 1954; Ayoub 1959; Keyes and Hudson 1961), is how can one explain a very high incidence of lineage endogamy and first cousin marriage in the absence of any prescriptive rules of marriage in the society. In chapter 3 I commented on this issue in relation to the Wakhi practice of preferred bilateral first cousin marriage. Some of the major arguments are economic. In Kirghiz society, as in the Wakhan, the cost of bridewealth and wedding expenses are proportionate to the closeness of the relation (blood and previous marriage) between the two *oey* units, and their respective *oruq*. Part of the marriage expenses are contributed by the relatives of the groom and redistributed by the family of the bride, especially if the union is exogamous. Such economic exchanges

are kept to a minimum at all levels, particularly among the poor.
While young men and women in Kirghiz society have some voice
in their choice of spouse, such decisions are largely affected by the
economic status of their *oey* and their respective *oruq*. Of course,
the consent of the heads of households is also essential in this matter.

In addition to economic constraints, the segmentary nature of
Kirghiz *oruq* structure requires a reaffirmation and strengthening
of the existing blood ties between lineage members. Also considered
is the maintenance of a sufficient labor force for *oey* and local herding
groups. Without doubt, the provision of Islamic *Shari'a* for women's
rights of inheritance in many cases figures quite strongly. Equally
important is the desire of parents to bring to their *oey* or camp
a woman who will help to ease their work load and who will not
create tension and quarrels between members of an *oey* or a *qorow*.
Endogamous marriages in Kirghiz society seem to serve all of these
concerns very well.

Nevertheless, the value of exogamous marriages between lineages
as a means of establishing alliances between different *oruq* are also
appreciated and practiced by the Kirghiz. Such marriages, however,
are usually the prerogative of the rich and ambitious who look for
political gains. Many, but not all, exogamous marriages between
influential households and elders of different lineage groups serve
such a strategic purpose. Indeed one of the most common means
of ending an ongoing political tension or animosity between lineage
groups in Kirghiz society is by exchange of women. There are many
examples of exogamous marriages for political purposes among
the Kirghiz. Perhaps the most noteworthy are a few marriages contracted recently by the family of the Kirghiz khan. The khan himself,
who has been married three times, contracted his third marriage
about fifteen years ago. The woman he married is the daughter of
the second most wealthy and powerful man among the Kirghiz of
the Afghan Pamirs. He is the *aqsaqal* of another sizable *oruq*, the
Qezil Bash, a different section of the Teyet under Qutan Oghlu.
Two of the khan's sons are married to younger daughters of the
same man's deceased brother and a son. His other sons are married
to girls of leading families of Alapa and Qezil Ayagh *oruqlar*, both
large and strong groups. He married his only daughter of marriageable age to his younger half-brother's son for no other reason than
to reaffirm the existing good relations within the family and to
strengthen the continuation of family ties.

Therefore, marriages and the consequent maternal blood relations between households and *oruq* are very important in Kirghiz social relations, an importance reflected in their kinship nomenclature. Kirghiz kinship terms are quite similar to the terminological systems used by other Turkic groups of Central Asia—Kazakh, Uzbek, Kalmuck, Turkman—varying only in details (see Krader 1963). They generally distinguish between three categories of relatives terminologically—agnatic, uterine, and affinal. The kin terms used for agnatic relations make up the core terminology system of the Kirghiz, and reflect the significance attached to the age of relatives, particularly in their terms of address (see fig. 4).

The Kirghiz use the same core terminology in referring to the uterine and affinal categories, with the addition of the prefixes *ty* and *qayn* respectively to indicate the nature of the relationship. Of course, there are some additional terms but the numbers are very small (see fig. 5). The importance of maternal ties is second only to those of agnatic descent, especially in the areas of economic help and cooperation between individuals and groups. In exogamous marriages, the term for mother's brother, *tagha,* is applied to all male members of the mother's *oruq,* and the relationship between the two groups is, for the most part, cordial.

Marriage relations are not very important until a child is born to the new *oruq.* Once a marriage is consummated and a child born, the woman is expected to remain within the *oruq* and bride inheritance is acknowledged within the patrilineage. The levirate rule followed by the Kirghiz dictates that the next youngest brother or close agnatic relative of the deceased shall marry the widow, but her consent, or that of her close male relative, is essential in the new contract.

The traditional rules of inheritance exclude women from any share, while among male siblings age is a determinant in the division of property. On the basis of traditional customs, the passage of office, prestige, and pasture land is channeled to the eldest son, while the father's yurt and much of his herd at the time of death remains with the youngest. Married sons are generally given an *oey* and part of the herd after marriage, but if they live in a different camp at the time of the father's death they cannot customarily claim any part of the herd. However, those living in the father's camp as part of the extended family divide the herd equally, making allowances for the cost of the marriages of younger brothers. Presently, however, the Kirghiz insist on the Islamic rules of inheritance and that the division of property should be carried out in the presence of a mullah and a group of Kirghiz elders.

The discussion of Kirghiz segmentary lineage principles so far

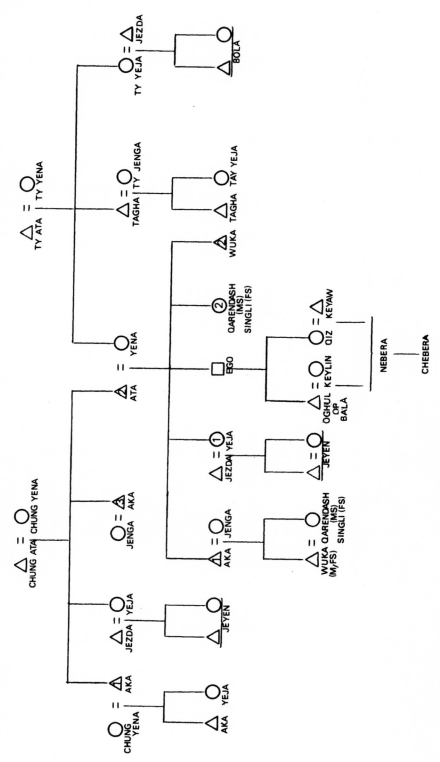

Fig. 4. Kirghiz kinship terms of reference (agnatic and uterine)

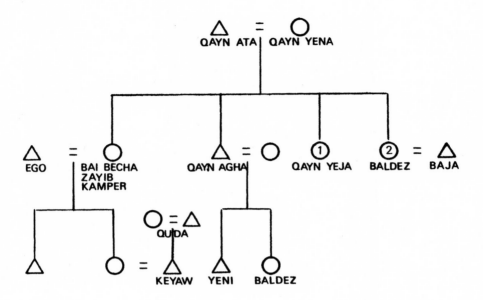

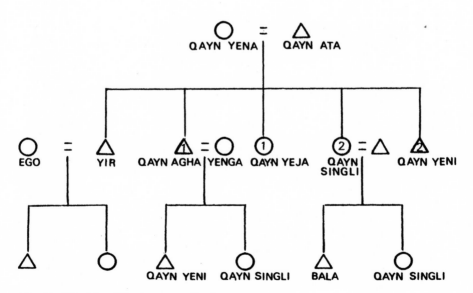

Fig. 5. Kirghiz affinal terms of reference

has been limited to its normative functions regarding the jural and property rights of the individual within the *oruq* structures, and the maintenance of these descent groups as independent political entities. I have talked about the significance of the Kirghiz *oruq* as the most important independent political unit in Kirghiz society, and that although *oruq* differ in their membership size, economic riches, and political influences, they are nevertheless structurally equal to one another. As such, the Kirghiz are indeed a "tribally" organized society headed by the khan.

The Kirghiz tribal structure at the community level is realized by the office of the khan, who occupies the highest political office and has the support of the general population and that of the *oruq* leaders, the *aqsaqal,* as well as the backing of the *qorow* leaders, the *be.* The office of the khan is the single vehicle through which the unity of the Kirghiz community is achieved. Doubtless, the Kirghiz political structure at the highest level is also based on kinship ideology and receives its support and legitimization from the kin-based group and the principles of agnatic descent.

The rank of khan is nonhereditary in principle nor is it elective or ascribed. Instead, it is generally assumed by the most obvious candidate, usually the *aqsaqal* of one large and powerful *oruq,* and is legitimated through public consent by the Kirghiz and/or recognized by external forces—local government authorities or outsiders such as the neighboring Wakhi, traders, visitors, and so forth.

The qualities necessary for the candidate for the office of khan vary only in magnitude from those of the single *oruq* leader. That is, strong and effective leadership qualities in Kirghiz society entail bravery (military prowess in the past), honesty, abilities in public persuasion and oratory, sound judgment, being a good Muslim, membership in a large *oruq,* and of course success as a herdsman, with a large flock and wealth in other tangible goods. Perhaps at present as well as in the past, wealth in livestock and other items has been one of the most crucial factors in the effectiveness of a leader's performance and maintenance of influence, but what is important in this instance is not the possession of goods and animals, but how they are used to help the community. Hospitality, generosity, and the offer of help to one's relatives and to the needy and poor, stand out as the signs of being a good Muslim and are the personal qualities desired among the politically ambitious in Kirghiz society. Indeed, all political officeholders must, and do, have these qualities. During a household survey of the Kirghiz *oey* units I asked them to whom they would turn for help in times of need. The answer followed exactly the political hierarchy pattern; first the *be* (camp leader), then the *aqsaqal* (the *oruq* leader), and finally, the khan.

The present khan is in his mid-sixties, and is the head of one of the largest *oruq*, the Qochqar, which is a branch of the largest major *oruq*, the Teyet. His father had been a large herd owner and quite influential but not an acknowledged khan. The present khan is both knowledgeable and capable in the true sense of the word. He is also a very successful herder who owns more than 16,000 sheep and goats and over 700 yak. He is equally successful as a father; he has nine sons, five of whom are married.

The main function of the khan is to maintain internal order among individuals and groups, and to protect the interests and integrity of the Kirghiz community in relation to the outside world. Dispute settlement is one of his most important functions in keeping internal order, particularly in instances where disputes have broken out between two *oruq*, thus threatening the integrity of the community. His role is very often reconciliatory and mediational in such cases and he usually approaches his task in two ways. First, he may attempt to persuade the members of the disputing parties to exchange women with one another through marriage contracts. Or, he may seek the taking place of *Quran dostlik* (Holy Quran friendship ritual), a means of establishing a fictive kinship between two individuals who are members of different *oruq*. This ritual involves an elaborate exchange of goods and public embracing by the two individuals while holding a copy of the Quran between their chests. Once performed, a formidable alliance between the two groups is established. The newly created pseudo kinship is signified by the use of the regular agnatic kinship term preceded by the prefix *ayesh*, denoting its ritual nature. This ritual kinship is also created for alliance purposes between groups without the existence, or threat, of a conflict.

The khan resolves all other disputes, quarrels, jural or political, through mediation and persuasion on his own or in concert with *aqsaqal* through *qureltay* (the council of lineage elders) and if necessary the religious teachers, the mullah. He does not have a police force and does not bring individuals to trial. He does, however, send men after an accused if a complaint is filed. Most conflicts are usually resolved at the lower levels of the political structure by the *be* or the *aqsaqal* (see table 13). Therefore, issues brought to the khan are often those not resolved or resolvable at the lower levels. Very often his judgment is redressive and reconciliatory and not based on punishment. Generally, however, the number of offenses involving theft,

sexual offenses, assault, or murder are very low. In fact, during the
past twenty years only two homicides were reported, neither of
which was premeditated. Most disputes involve pasture rights or
quarrels over other property rights in trade and exchange matters.
In all issues requiring religious decree the khan consults the mullah.
A new position was recently created by the government of the Republic of Afghanistan, called *qaryadar* (village headman), which
is integrated with the office of the khan in the Little Pamir, and
that of the *aqsaqal* in the Great Pamir. Therefore, the authority
of the khan is sanctioned by the government to serve as the liaison
between the Kirghiz and government authorities and to refer individuals who, for whatever reason, did not agree with his judgment in
their case to the local government.

TABLE 13

KIRGHIZ HIERARCHY OF POLITICAL STRUCTURE

Head or leader	Group
Khan (*qaryadar*)	Tribe or community
Aqsaqal	*Oruq* or lineage
Be	*Qorow* or camp
Oey bashi	Household

The Kirghiz have indeed had considerable success in establishing
social stability and economic prosperity in their adaptive efforts
in the Pamirs of Afghanistan. It has been achieved through a long
process of social structural change during the past thirty years or
more and has been facilitated by the segmentary lineage system,
as realized in the Kirghiz *oruq* structure and its accompanying normative principles, in concert with certain elements of Islamic ideology.

PART III

CLOSED FRONTIERS

Left, Little Pamir valley, showing extent of seasonal migration; *below*, living and sleeping area in a yurt; *preceding page*, sandstorm in the Amu Darya valley.

7. Territorial Loss: An Intracultural Adaptation

THE CONCEPT OF *frontier* as it is used here has a much broader implication than generally accepted in anthropological literature, where its implication is restricted to cultural frontiers (e.g., see Bohannan and Plog 1967 and other acculturation and adaptation studies). For frontier historians such as Owen Lattimore, the concept has geographic (spatial), temporal, social, and cultural referents (see 1962b, pp. 469-91, and 1951; also see F. J. Turner 1961, p. 38, and 1962). I find the frontier historians' view of the concept of the frontier more comprehensive, dynamic, and more relevant to my own discussion of social change in Kirghiz society (from a diachronic perspective) than the more restricted anthropological interpretation.

Owen Lattimore distinguishes between at least three types of frontiers and frontier processes. The earliest, according to Lattimore, was the *Inner Asian frontier,* the frontiers between the despotic states of the great river basins (in China, Western Asia, and the Middle East) and the pastoral nomadic societies of the steppe, the desert, and the highlands of Central and Inner Asia. By the end of the fifteenth century, the opening of the era of great navigators, the second type, which Lattimore has called the *overseas frontier,* or colonial frontier, was created (1962b, pp. 488-89). The third type, the *new frontier,* was created for the most part after the First and Second World Wars. Both the Inner Asian and the overseas frontiers were free and open zones, subject to territorial expansion and loss with considerable socioeconomic and cultural consequences for the neighboring societies over a period of time. The new frontiers are, however, marked by linear closed boundaries and are absolute in theory and practice, which both restrains and excludes those who live across the lines (Lattimore 1951, p. 241). The new linear boundaries, particularly in Asia, have resulted in territorial losses (especially by pastoral nomadic groups), as well as the severance of long established and ongoing socioeconomic and cultural relations between numerous adjacent communities that were part of a single "key economic" and/or "key strategic" region(s) (see Lattimore 1962b, p. 498). These are what I refer to as the *closed frontiers* that have characterized the external situation in the Wakhan Corridor and the Afghan Pamirs during the past thirty years or so. Internally, because of its distance and remoteness from the regional (provincial) and national market and administrative centers, as well as the lack of reliable communication and transportation systems because of the terrain, this area of Afghanistan has remained isolated, and as a result a frontierlike socioeconomy has prevailed.

The major constraints, therefore, that have influenced the direction of change and provided the impetus for the adaptation processes in Kirghiz and, to some extent, Wakhi societies under these closed frontier conditions have been the severance of former socioeconomic and cultural ties with the peoples of Chinese and Russian Turkistan (i.e., the reverse of the cultural contact situation), the loss of territory to the Soviet Union, and the self-imposed confinement to the isolated Afghan Pamirs. The kind of change Kirghiz society has experienced under these conditions is not radical but accumulative, which I have characterized earlier as disjunctive structural change without accompanying cultural change—or a pastoral nomadic involution. It is therefore the aim of this section (Part III) to explore and explain the processes through which the structural refinement, complication, and specialization in the Kirghiz social and ecological adaptation system has been achieved, and the means by which the Kirghiz have been able to retain their high-altitude pastoral nomadic mode of subsistence.

OPEN BORDERS: BEFORE 1949

It is not possible to understand the direction, the nature, and the magnitude of the adaptive success or failure of any kind of systemic change unless the relationship between and among various component parts within a given system, as well as its relations within the total environment, are assessed under different conditions at different times. It is only then that the study of " 'change' becomes a mode both of explaining and experiencing the working of the institution

and its milieu, including, of course, its social and cultural milieu"
(Bohannan 1967, p. xviii). Therefore, to clarify the dynamic process
of sociocultural and ecological adaptation of the Kirghiz under the
closed frontier conditions, it is necessary to recapitulate briefly
some pertinent aspects of their adaptive strategy and socioeconomic
and cultural relations prior to the closure of the borders more than
a quarter of a century ago.

Before the 1930s the Afghan Pamirs were frequented by only
about thirty Kirghiz *oey* units during the summer months. These
Kirghiz were extensive pasturage users, with a vertical pattern of
migration oscillating between the high Pamirs and the lower altitudes in their winter pasturage ground, in what is now the Soviet
territory of Tajik S.S.R. The Kirghiz did not remain in the Afghan
Pamirs during the winter months except when they had to avoid
trouble with the local and state authorities, or a confrontation with
other feuding Kirghiz groups.

Kirghiz households universally owned smaller herds than those
owned today, averaging no more than seventy or eighty animals per
oey unit. Almost every household owned its own herd, and no herd
was larger than fifteen hundred animals. There was very little or
no demand from the outside for Kirghiz animals or livestock products. The poor obtained most of their needed cereal and market
goods in return for services rendered to the caravan traders passing
through the area on their way to and from India, northern Afghanistan, and Russian Turkistan (also known as Western Turkistan) to
Yarkand and Kashgar in Chinese Turkistan (Eastern Turkistan).
The rich received their needed goods as gifts from the traders in return for their hospitality and for other assistance to ensure safe passage through the area.

The political hierarchy of Kirghiz society, organized on the basis
of a segmentary lineage system of *oruq,* was more egalitarian both
in principle and practice under these earlier conditions than it is now,
and the structure of authority was more diffused. In fact, the Kirghiz
contend that there was not a single powerful khan in control of a
large area or group of people. Rather there were a number of contending, influential khans representing smaller groups of kinsmen.

The Kirghiz did very little trading except for a certain amount
of grain generally obtained from low-altitude villages near their
winter pastures in the adjacent areas that are presently parts of
Soviet Central Asia or the Sinkiang Province of the People's Republic
of China. The grain was usually obtained in exchange for the cash and
goods the Kirghiz earned from the traders, or for small amounts of livestock products or a very few animals. As such, the Kirghiz were an in-

tegrated part of a general "key economic" and cultural area of the Osh and Fergana valleys (in the U.S.S.R.) to the north and the adjacent Kashgar and Yarkand oases in Sinkiang to their northeast. The Kirghiz cultural and socioeconomic ties with the predominantly Turkic-speaking and Sunni Muslim population of this area were very strong. A few Kirghiz from various groups were sent to Andijan, Kashgar, Yarkand and other urban centers to get religious and/or professional training in crafts such as silver-, metal-, and woodworking (especially yurt building) to serve the needs of their groups, needs that were in some other instances filled by trained sedentary religious specialists or craftsmen from these regions who had joined the Kirghiz.

Prior to the closure of the Chinese and Russian borders, the Kirghiz were familiar with the Wakhi peasants of the corridor, and on occasion visited the area in the service of traders. Generally, however, they did not initiate continuing socioeconomic relations for two reasons: although, in terms of travel time the Wakhi villages were about the same distance from the Afghan Pamirs as the nearest settlements in Sinkiang, the trails were far more dangerous and trying; and the Wakhi are a radically different linguistic, cultural, and religious-sectarian group from the Kirghiz and other Turkic peoples of Central Asia.

It is, therefore, the changes from these previous conditions in the Afghan Pamirs and the altered relationships of the various elements within the sociocultural environment of the Kirghiz since the closure of the borders that will be discussed in this and the following chapter. These changes necessarily emanate from the system of pastoral nomadic adaptation and the Kirghiz social and cultural organization that prevailed at the time of the closure of the frontiers. As a result, we will see that in this process of accumulative social and ecological change, the pre-existing socioeconomic and cultural realities have influenced the direction and development of the new adaptive system as much as the ecological and sociopolitical constraints resulting from the closed frontier.

CLOSED BORDERS: AFTER 1949

Loss of the greater portion of their pasturage has had a marked effect on the Kirghiz in the high Pamirs. The Kirghiz could not expand their territory in order to maintain their extensive range use and vertical migration patterns in a different area. It was not possible for them to move south to the northern tip of the British-Indian Empire (Gilgit, Hunza, and Chitral areas) because of the difficult passage over the Hindu Kush, where the lowest pass is over

5,500 meters in altitude. The Kirghiz were also unwilling to enter non-Muslim territory because of their fear of the infidel Kunjuti who, before the establishment of British rule in the region, had at times crossed the high passes to raid the Kirghiz summer encampments in the Little Pamir (see Younghusband 1896).

The only alternative open to the Kirghiz at the time was to seek pasturage in the Wakhan Corridor within Afghanistan. That, however, was not negotiable because most Wakhi villagers owned livestock and a few rich Wakhi owned large flocks of sheep and goats. The Wakhi claimed not only the lower agricultural areas but were also using, at least part of the year, the pasturage between the limits of the agricultural zone and the Pamirs proper—that is, between the village of Sarhad and Buzai Gumbaz. In recent years, however, because of the reduced number of animals owned by Wakhi peasants (see chapter 3) and the tremendous increase of Kirghiz livestock in the Pamirs, the Kirghiz have gained access to some former Wakhi pasturage, but it has added friction to the already strained relationship between the two societies.

After the closure of the Russian and Chinese frontiers, the Kirghiz who had taken refuge in the Pamirs—a much larger group than had ever occupied them before—were confined year-round. For subsistence in the high pastures, the Kirghiz of Afghanistan introduced and developed the following measures: (1) adoption of a highly regulated, intensive pasturage use; (2) introduction of a short-distance pendular, seasonal, migration pattern; (3) acceptance of the right of individual families, groups of related families, and small patrilineage groups to claim private or corporate ownership of pasturage and encampment sites; and (4) the improvement of pasturage by irrigation and, where possible, the growing of a limited amount of winter fodder. These new methods were developed over a period of time and are interdependent measures that have had very broad economic and social structural consequences in the development of Kirghiz high-altitude nomadic adaptation. Indeed, some of these methods, such as claiming rights of ownership over range and camping grounds, are still in the incipient stage, and are presently a very common cause of dispute and friction among the Kirghiz.

The Kirghiz pattern of intensive pasturage use and short-distance seasonal oscillations within the Pamirs, as an effective and efficient means of exploiting the meager resources, were discussed in some detail earlier. With the limited resources and the large number of herders, the maintenance of intensive use was possible only through a certain territoriality on the part of the individual herding units and groups. Those Kirghiz who were using the Afghan Pamirs regu-

larly prior to the closure of the borders were the first to claim territorial rights. The majority of the newcomers established residence
in areas that were not claimed by others, or they paid to set up
camps on already claimed land. Kirghiz who did not have such notions
of total ownership rights over pasture and camp sites soon came to
grips with the concept. Buying and selling of both pasturage and
camp sites claimed by individual families is either arranged with another herder or, in part, with relatives who have corporate ownership rights to the property. Generally, all corporately claimed land and
camping grounds are inherited lands from the original claimants,
who had obtained it without payment. At any rate, all pastures
and camping grounds are either privately or corporately claimed and
territorially defined and defended in the Pamirs.

Private ownership undoubtedly helps the efficient use and management of the pasture ground. However, with the increasing value of
the limited pasturage, and the increasing numbers of livestock, certain
difficulties concerning the transmission and disposal of land through
inheritance or sale have also arisen. For example, I found a large
number of disputes resulting from SiSo claims over their mother's
right to the use of pasturage previously sold to another person by
their MoBr. In one case the conflict was so bitter that the disputant
SiSo attempted, by an unprecedented measure (presenting a copy
of the Quran accompanied by a bullet), to break up the existing
Holy Quran friendship (fictive kinship relationship) between a
member of his patrilineage and the patrilineage of the man who earlier
had bought the camping and pasturage grounds from his MoBr,
with whom he shared a winter camp. The measure was taken to open
the way for the final resort, the use of force or violence, which is not
culturally approved of between individual members of *oruq* related
through *ayesh* or the Holy Quran friendship relationship. This particular attempt was thwarted for the time being by the khan's mediation,
but no final solution was in sight.

Other disputes involve grudges between those who had bought
land from men who later died, leaving young children. These offspring, who are now mature, contend either that their land was not
sold by their father, or that the price paid at the time was too small.
They now claim the return of their paternal pasturage or compensation for it. Since in most cases the earlier transactions were without
the written agreement that is customary now, the disputes are particularly hard to settle. There are also a number of difficulties between
paternal first cousins or other closely related family members, who,
for one reason or another, cannot get along with each other and who,
even when they have resorted to fission of the *oey* and camp, are

still disputing rights to pasture land. All of these conflicts over land are very new to the Kirghiz, and hard to resolve. In the past such grudges would have been grounds for the dispersion of the *oey* units and the larger groups, and would also have resulted in a change of range territory. Such a solution, under the new conditions, is no longer possible.

Another major consequence of private ownership in the Pamirs has been the increasing interest in capital investment in the camp-grounds and efforts to cultivate fodder and improve pasturage. Some anthropologists have thought that this phenomenon did not occur in nomadic societies, with minor exceptions (see Spooner 1973, p. 4). Yet for the Kirghiz this development was absolutely essential if they were to maintain a viable pastoral economy. For instance, the Kirghiz have had to build high stone and mud enclosures in their winter encampments to keep their flocks of sheep and goats protected against both cold and predators. Some Kirghiz have also built permanent structures *(tom)* in their *qeshtaw* that are used either as living quarters during the winter months or as storage areas.

All winter camping grounds are cleared, manured, and irrigated during the spring and summer to grow winter fodder. Many large herding units have invested a great deal of time and money building long irrigation ditches to sluice water into suitable patches of land near their winter camps that they have prepared for hay "cultivation." Such patches of land, *khoreq,* are valuable properties among the Kirghiz. Cultivation of both winter camping grounds and the *khoreq* require a lot of annual work. While the Kirghiz do not seed cultivated patches, the work involves building and clearing the irrigation channels, spreading manure, clearing the fields, and irrigating them.

In addition to these intensive hay-growing efforts, the Kirghiz, especially the khan, have improved, and indeed created, large areas of better and thicker pasturage by diverting water from the high tributary streams into piedmont areas where there was no running water. Over the years this process has created many new large and small lakes and ponds in the center of the valley, and in some areas has improved pasturage enormously. The khan has been the pioneer in introducing this idea in the Pamirs, and he very often encourages others to carry out this scheme. The practice has indeed proved to be very successful and many other people have begun to invest in it. There are still large areas where the vegetation could be improved considerably by irrigation. Although irrigation has caused salts to build up in the soil in certain areas, some vegetation is visible, even there.

All of these developments have had further significance in the articulation of Kirghiz socioeconomic and political organization during this period of adaptation. One of the most obvious consequences is the present distribution of herd ownership. A large portion of the livestock herded in the Pamirs, particularly sheep, goat, and yak, are owned by only a small number of *oey*. About 16,000 sheep and goats and over 700 yak of the 39,000 sheep and goats and the 3,500 yak, are owned by only one *oey*, that of the khan. Of the total livestock remaining, over 17,000 sheep and goats and about 1,200 yak are owned by only thirteen *oey* units. This leaves some 228 *oeylar* with neither sheep nor goats, 105 without sheep, goats, or yak, and 70 with no animals of their own (see table 14).

One has to seek an understanding of the relationship in Kirghiz society between the concentration of herd ownership and the development of a restricted type of nomadism and the concomitant phenomena of intensive pasturage use, private ownership of range and camping grounds, hay production and improvement of pasturage, and other capital investment activities. These two developments are indeed related in many ways and have been part of one and the same cultural ecological adaptation processes in the Pamirs.

It is important to recognize that the Kirghiz who came to live in the Afghan Pamirs were not equally wealthy in animals. They also differed from one another as individuals, as well as in kinship groups, and in prestige and strength. Within the new territory they occupied areas that differed from each other to some degree in climate and pasture, and such ecological variations in the Pamirs, even within short distances, are sometimes enormous. A blizzard that might wipe out the animals in one area may not occur in another. The Kirghiz remember repeated occurrences of such incidences in the area. For example, during my research I was told that in the winter of 1972 the loss of livestock in the Great Pamir from bad weather was more than three thousand sheep and goats and over two hundred yak. But the people in the Little Pamir suffered no heavy losses during the same period. However, during a return visit to the Little Pamir in the summer of 1975 I learned that in the winter of 1974-75, livestock losses suffered by the khan alone, because of lack of pasturage and the occurrence of *joot* in certain areas, amounted to about four thousand sheep and goats and over one hundred yak.

During the initial period of settlement in the Pamirs the more powerful herders used their influence and/or wealth to secure the better pasturage and camping grounds. A few either own or have bought pasturage in different parts of the Pamirs, so that in case of bad weather or poor pastures in one area they will have another

TABLE 14

DISTRIBUTION OF LIVESTOCK OWNERSHIP AMONG THE AFGHAN KIRGHIZ

Number of *oey*	Sheep/goats owned by each unit	Total sheep/ goats owned by all units	Yak owned by each unit	Total yak owned by all units	Horses owned by each unit	Total horses owned by all units	Camels owned by each unit	Total camels owned by all units
1		16,400		720		15		18
6	1310-3640	12,285	40-277	954	1-6	22	1-7	23
7	500-940	4,920	12-60	214	1-3	15	1-10	22
13	120-430	2,755	8-70	318	1-4	23	1-5	17
14	50-100	1,090	2-30	161	1-2	18	1	1
64	1-40	1,150	1-25	600	1-2	82	1	2
123	—	—	1-40	577	1-3	105	—	—
35	—	—	—	—	1-2	38	—	—
70	—	—	—	—	—	—	—	—
		38,600		3,544		318		83

place to turn to. For most, however, with the private ownership of range, the traditional freedom of nomads to search after better weather and pasture within their restricted environment has not been possible. Therefore, if a natural disaster befalls a particular locality it is likely that all those who live in the area face either total, or a very heavy, loss of their livestock. Unpredictable and erratic weather had significant effects on the distribution of herd ownership during the early periods of confinement, especially for those *oey* units that owned relatively small herds.

During the early years after the closure of the border the small herders' reproductive capital in livestock faced continued depletion with the new and excessive economic demands upon their herds. Since the Kirghiz could no longer obtain agricultural and market goods through serving the traders as they did prior to the closure of the frontiers, they had to pay for grain and market commodities in animals and livestock products. Although in the long run this demand on the household herd served as an incentive to increase the number of livestock in the Pamirs, it also perpetuated the poverty of many small-herd-owning *oey* units during that period. Although the large herd owners also had to buy commodities they had sufficient capital left to build larger herds later. The differential access to herd ownership was, without doubt, owing in part to decreased mobility, the development of private ownership of range territory, and new economic costs, but other factors such as shrewd herdsmanship, diligence, innovation (particularly the introduction of irrigation to create new pastures and improve existing ones), and at times the sheer luck of individual herders were involved.

The initial inequalities in herd ownership, as well as the ecological constraints in the Kirghiz high-altitude habitat, have necessitated new methods of herd management that, in turn, have resulted both in a tremendous increase in livestock and in the further concentration of wealth, in herds and other tangible goods, in the hands of a few. Kirghiz herd owners are traditionally obligated to help their poor kinsmen and those relatives who do not have their own livestock and, under the new conditions, raising large herds in a single small area was, at best, risky. Therefore, the Kirghiz have made extensive use of a simple rule in their herd management technique—to disperse their capital as widely as possible throughout the area to ensure against the total loss of their herd. Furthermore, given the marginal quality of the ecological conditions it is impossible for any single *oey* to raise or manage a very large herd on its own.

In addition to the hiring of shepherds by the rich, the Kirghiz have employed two systems of herd management, *saghun* and *amanat*, through which they are able to distribute their concentrated wealth of livestock among the poor herders. The first system is a limited means of aiding the poor and needy among the Kirghiz and has been used for a long time. The second is a refinement of the first system, a recent development based on the same cultural principles.

1. *Saghun:* Under this system poor families who do not own animals and do not have the labor force to herd livestock year round are provided by the rich *oey* units with ten to thirty ewes and does, with their lambs and kids, shortly after the lambing season, or one or two yak cows with their calves. These animals are given only for the use of their milk and wool during the spring and summer and are to be returned to their owners by autumn. This temporary arrangement is contracted anew every spring and concluded in the autumn. In return, as I discussed earlier, the poor herders cooperate in herding at the camp in which they live.

2. *Amanat:* In this arrangement, a large number of animals, ranging from ten to five hundred head of sheep and goats and one to twenty yak or more, are given into the custody of poor *oey* units according to their needs and herding abilities. The herders exercise all rights over the products (milk, wool, and fuel) that can be earned from the herd while they are in charge of raising them. But the rich Kirghiz retains the right of ownership (i.e., disposal) over the herd. Reciprocally, the herders must give an annual accounting to the owner and must show an increase in the size of the herd to ensure the continuation of the arrangement. It must be made clear, however, that this arrangement is not the same as hiring an individual or a family as shepherds. Over 17,000 sheep and goats are herded by the owners with the aid of shepherds and almost 22,000 head of sheep and goats are distributed among over 200 families under the *amanat* system.

There are clear and explicit rules and understandings that govern these herding arrangements. The individual shepherd, or a whole *oey,* is hired and paid a predetermined number of sheep (ranging from four to six sheep, or the equivalent, plus food and some clothing) per year for services. However, in both the *saghun* and *amanat* systems the head of an *oey* without animals comes to the large herd owner and asks for animals. The number and type of animals are negotiated between the herd owner and the prospective herder and such decisions are influenced by many social and local ecological factors. Under neither herding arrangement is the herder responsible for any loss of livestock in his charge from disease, bad weather conditions in his locality, lack of adequate pasturage, or predators. However, loss of large numbers of livestock because of negligence by the herder warrants the return of the surviving animals to the owner on demand, though under such circumstances the herder is not asked to replace the animals lost. If the labor force of a herding family decreases, or if for any reason the household lacks a labor force adequate for the number of animals in its charge, the *oey* is free to return any number of animals to the owner to prevent unnecessary losses. Similarly, if poor pasturage or bad weather threatens livestock in a particular locality the herd owner expects to be notified by the herder so he may seek alternate pasturage, if possible, to prevent loss. To maintain a balance between the herd size, the herder's labor force, and pasture resources, the herd owner annually collects a number of male sheep and older ewes from the herder to be sold or exchanged. In some cases the herd owner may take some of the livestock and give it to another household in need of animals.

The distribution of herds as *saghun* is practiced by most of the 105 families who own sheep and goats, and the 228 *oey* units who own yak. However, there are only about 20 households with large enough herds to distribute some or most of their animals under the *amanat* system. It is these few large herd owner-managers who have benefited tremendously, both economically and politically, from this type of herd management. The economic advantage of the *amanat* system lies in the dispersal of the herd owner's livestock over a wide area, so if animals are killed off in one area, the owner will still have a source of capital. Indeed, those who have spread their herds among the largest number of *oey* units and geographic areas through the *amanat* system enjoy rights of ownership over the largest number of livestock (see table 15). Under the environmental conditions in the Afghan Pamirs, this particular herding arrangement is not only the sole way of preventing total loss of livestock by individual owners, but is also a means of increasing the total livestock population.

This concentration of the ownership of herds in the hands of a few *oey* units has developed over the past thirty years, mostly as a consequence of the ecological constraints prevailing in the area, but also as a result of shrewd observation, keen perception, and manipulation of these factors by a few successful herders. For at least two important and related reasons this process has proved to be a very successful mechanism for the retention of pastoral economy in the Pamirs. First, the concentration of the ownership of livestock has given rise to the emergence of a very small group of herd owner-managers. This small group, through extremely efficient herd management systems, has helped increase livestock population, as well as the

TABLE 15

RELATIONSHIP BETWEEN INDIVIDUALLY OWNED HERD SIZE
AND THE DISTRIBUTION OF LIVESTOCK THROUGH AMANAT SYSTEM

Herd owner	Size of herds		Number of livestock herded by hired shepherds		Number of oeylar with amanat	Number of animals given as amanat	
	Sheep/goats	Yak	Sheep/goats	Yak		Sheep/goats	Yak
Kh. H.	16,400	720	2,250	309	135	14,150	411
M. H.	3,640	162	1,400	97	24	2,240	65
B. H.	2,600	150	800	140	29	1,800	10
A. S.	2,000	130	950	26	18	1,050	104
S. Q.	1,600	110	1,280	115	6	320	5
Mh. H.	1,135	135	700	70	13	435	65
Kh. W.	1,310	40	1,000	40	4	310	—
M. A.	940	32	700	30	4	240	2
A. F.	850	20	640	20	5	210	—
Q. H.	830	60	770	45	5	60	15
A. J.	500	12	250	12	6	250	—
Or. H.	430	70	200	51	4	130	19
Asl.	350	21	200	20	4	150	1
T. B.	270	27	160	26	5	110	1
A. Q.	260	8	150	8	2	110	—
M. I.	170	17	160	16	2	10	1
Os. H.	135	13	95	13	2	40	—
J. B.	130	27	100	25	2	30	2

distribution of the animals, among all strata of Kirghiz society. Second, these few herd owner-manager *oey* units have in turn insured the provision of a reserve of livestock, and have acted as nodes of herd distribution for those households afflicted by natural calamity in any area of the Pamirs, at any time. Consequently, this socioeconomic process in Kirghiz society has prevented the drift of the poorer pastoralists to sedentary agricultural or urban adaptation.

The development of radical differences in the rights of access to the ownership of pastoral capital has fostered a stratification in Kirghiz society that is based on wealth and which has definite political implications. To date, however, this stratification has not caused any serious confrontation or conflict between the very rich and the very poor. On the contrary, the existing ties of kinship, friendship, and affinity in many cases have been strengthened through herding arrangements between rich and poor relations, while new ties based on economic interdependence have developed. In other words, when rich herd owner-managers allocate animals to the herding *oey* under the *saghun* and the *amanat* arrangements, the agnatic segmentary descent principles, uterine relations, affinal ties, and the political support and allegiance of individuals are given thorough consideration. This is true in almost all cases, since most of the rich herders are political officeholders at some local, lineage, or tribal level. These political considerations are indeed reflected in the dispersal of herd owners' livestock among the poor Kirghiz (see table 16). The allocation of the number of animals per herding unit, as well as the number of households who receive animals, shows a pattern of concentric circles determined by the herder's relation to the herd owner-manager, influenced, of course, by the size of the original herd and the political rank and ambition of the allocator. Whether smaller herd owners, heads of local encampment groups *(be)*, heads of *oruq (aqsaqal)* or finally the khan, each seems to allocate animals in descending order, first to close blood relations, affines, and friends, and then to members of more distant or unrelated kinship groups in respectively decreasing numbers of animals per *oey* unit. These choices are consistent with the basic cultural tenets of Kirghiz society, as they are realized in the form of Kirghiz *oruq* structure and principles. Perhaps the best example of this phenomenon is to be found in the distribution of the khan's livestock among the Kirghiz (table 16). He is by far the largest herd owner-manager in the Afghan Pamirs. He has allocated more than fourteen thousand sheep and goats, and over four hundred yak among more than 130 *oey* units. Naturally, the size of his herd gives him the means to satisfy the needs of both close

TABLE 16

DISTRIBUTION OF LARGE HERD OWNER/MANAGERS' LIVESTOCK THROUGH AMANAT SYSTEM ON THE BASIS OF KINSHIP AFFILIATIONS

Herd owner	Oruq	Number of animals given to own kechek oruq			Number of animals given to closely related kechek oruq			Number of animals given to own zor oruq			Number of animals given to all other oruqlar		
		oey	sheep and goats	yak	oey	sheep and goats	yak	oey	sheep and goats	yak	oey	sheep and goats	yak
Kh. H.	Qochqar	21	3,275	163	25	2,860	70	41	4,245	68	48	3,770	110
S. Q.	Qochqar	2	280	–	–	–	–	3	30	5	1	10	7
M. H.	Qochqar	4	310	2	1	200	–	12	1,190	56	7	550	7
Or. H.	Qochqar	2	100	12	1	30	–	1	–	4	1	–	3
A. S.	Shayem	14	920	99	2	70	–	–	–	–	3	60	5
B. H.	Qezil Bash	6	380	3	12	570	2	6	590	1	5	260	4
Kh. W.	Qutan	2	150	–	–	–	–	1	100	–	1	60	–
M. I.	Alaichi	1	10	–	–	–	–	–	–	–	1	–	1
T. B.	Alaichi	–	–	–	2	30	–	2	30	1	1	50	–
J. B.	Alaichi	1	30	–	–	–	–	–	–	–	1	–	2
Mh. H.	Qezil Ayagh	4	215	18	–	–	–	5	50	40	4	170	7
Q. H.	Qezil Ayagh	4	60	11	–	–	–	–	–	–	1	–	4
Os. H.	Qezil Ayagh	1	20	–	–	–	–	–	–	–	1	20	–
A. J.	Shaltaq	–	–	–	5	210	–	–	–	–	1	40	–
Asl.	Shaltaq	2	55	1	2	90	–	–	–	–	–	–	–
A. Q.	Shaltaq	–	–	–	2	110	–	–	–	–	–	–	–
A. F.	Jeghjim	3	150	–	1	30	–	–	–	–	1	30	–
M. A.	Jeghjim	2	190	–	1	–	2	–	–	–	1	50	–

and distant kin as well as those of many unrelated Kirghiz. Because of his prevailing economic influence he enjoys far greater power and prestige than any other man in recent memory among the Kirghiz in the Pamirs of Afghanistan.

Indeed, because of this tremendous economic power of the khan, and that of a few other leaders, the traditional egalitarian and rather loosely structured Kirghiz political organization has gradually given way to an increasingly more centralized, mildly authoritarian and "feudal" structure in which the khan figures prominently. The development of a nomadic feudal-like political and economic structure under closed frontier conditions has been further encouraged by the sanction of the office of the khan by the central government of Afghanistan under a different name, that of *qaryadar* (village headman). This development seems to support views expressed by frontier historian Owen Lattimore, who contends that historically in the struggle between nomadic societies and settled agricultural states, the nomads or

the retreating people lose, but their chiefs gain; the tribal structure is tightened up and the authority of the chief is enhanced. . . .
    The new character of authority seems to be directly related to the function of the chief as representative of his tribe, recognized by the [central government]. . . . The fact that the [government] . . . make him their go-between reinforces the power of the chief over his people. . . . Frontier phenomena of this kind are probably one of the origins of feudalism. [Lattimore 1962b, p. 476, see Schram 1954, and Ekvall 1939]

The impact of both the central government of Afghanistan and of national and regional socioeconomic realities upon the Kirghiz has not been limited to the reaffirmation and sanctioning of the khan's political authority—the entire development of Kirghiz adaptation has been continually influenced by events outside the Pamirs. For example, the very basis of the Kirghiz system, the maintenance of a viable number of livestock, although achieved internally through efficient herd management systems, well-regulated use of available range resources, and the creation and cultivation and improvement of new pastures, is also subject to outside constraints. Two in particular have encouraged the increase in herd size.

First, with the closed frontiers, the Kirghiz could no longer obtain their needed agricultural and market goods through serving the traders as they had done in the past. Therefore, they had to increase their herd size in order to produce the surplus livestock necessary to pay for the grain and other commodities they do not themselves produce. The Kirghiz must also trade livestock for horses, which they cannot breed in the Pamirs but need to carry on their daily routine.

Second, the increasing demand for meat and livestock products in the cities and towns of Afghanistan and the increased market prices have encouraged a large group of itinerant traders to frequent the Pamirs on a regular basis. These traders have introduced a whole new range of market goods (e.g., sewing machines, transistor radios, cigarettes, tobacco, tea, opium) for which the Kirghiz have to pay, again in livestock and animal products.

Therefore, Kirghiz adaptation to their loss of pasturage and its concomitant developments has been influenced not only by the environmental stress of the Pamirs and sociocultural and economic developments within Kirghiz society itself, but has evolved simultaneously with their responses to the socioeconomic and cultural pressures imposed from without.

8. Adaptation to Socioeconomic and Cultural Restrictions

THE SEVERANCE OF Kirghiz socioeconomic ties with the agricultural population of a "key economic" region to their north and east, brought about by the closure of the Soviet and Chinese frontiers, forced the Kirghiz to look for alternative sources of agricultural and market goods. Their alternatives were, however, limited and the choices difficult to make. Growing their own grain was an unlikely prospect, but the Kirghiz attempted to do so, with limited success. Some twenty years ago in the Great Pamir area, a few families spent a great deal of time digging irrigation ditches to sluice water into a large flat area. After completion of the irrigation work they sowed barley, which grew tall but produced no harvest. The irrigation work and plots are still visible, and a constant reminder of the impossibility of agriculture at these altitudes. Similar attempts have been made in the Little Pamir, but only two families have succeeded in getting a small harvest of barley from a number of small terraced plots in the area of Langar, at the bottom of a narrow river valley at an altitude of close to 4,000 meters.

The other alternative available to the Kirghiz has been to obtain their needed products through trade and exchange. Under the circumstances, there were two places they could turn to for trading. One, the area to the south, the region of Gilgit and Hunza, in the northeastern tip of the area in dispute between the governments of India and Pakistan (presently under the control of Pakistan), was not possible. The passes between the Afghan Pamirs and Hunza and

Gilgit permit only limited travel during late summer; absolutely no commuting is possible at other times. Even when accessible, travel across the mountains is extremely hard on both men and animals. The Kirghiz dependence on cereals from this area has, therefore, been minimal. During earlier years, however, Hunza traders came to the Pamirs bringing Indian and Pakistani-made sewing machines, tea, cloth, and other luxury items (such as transistor radios), which they exchanged for yak, goats, and *mai* only. According to the Kirghiz, these Kunjuti traders (Kunjut is apparently the name of a principal village in the area) offered a much better rate of exchange for their livestock than the Afghan traders, mainly because of the higher price paid on the market for animals and animal products in Pakistan and the relatively lower price of Pakistani goods, which the Afghan traders brought from distant Kabul and other northern cities in Afghanistan. This rather lucrative trade opportunity for the Kirghiz and their Kunjuti neighbors, even for a short period during each year, has now been completely denied because of the chronic political problems between the governments of Afghanistan and Pakistan over what is generally called the Pashtunistan issue, or the dispute over the Northwest Frontier.

The Kirghiz have thus had to depend upon the Wakhi villagers in the corridor for almost all of their agricultural commodities. Initially, the Kirghiz were in need of grain, which they obtained from the impoverished, but somewhat self-sufficient, Wakhi agriculturalists. Wakhi self-sufficiency did not last very long under the new frontier conditions, however, as described in chapter 3. Consequently, the relationship that began with the dependence of the Kirghiz pastoralists upon the Wakhi has gradually evolved to one of increasing economic interdependence. This is evidenced both in their direct exchanges of goods and services and in indirect means mediated by the itinerant traders. It should be made clear, however, that the evolution, development, and continuation of this economic interdependence is affected not only by the satisfaction of the economic needs of the Kirghiz and the Wakhi through each other, but by the necessity to satisfy newly created needs instigated by the outside traders and the increasing economic demands of the national economy. This same process has resulted in the depletion of resources and the growing poverty of the agricultural Wakhi, which has in turn produced their unprecedented dependence upon the Kirghiz pastoral economy.

The majority of Kirghiz adult men annually spend most of the winter months in the Wakhan engaging in trade and exchange with the Wakhi agriculturalists and the thirty or more Wakhi and non-

Wakhi shopkeeper-traders, who are based in the district center, Khandud, during this period. The Kirghiz bring to the Wakhan loads of livestock products, such as dried yoghurt, horse covers, wool, goat and yak hair, sheep- and goatskins, yak hide, felt, and *mai*, most of which they exchange directly with the Wakhi households for wheat and some barley, lentils, lupine, and millet. Despite long-time trade relations between the two groups, I found less than a dozen Kirghiz who claimed to have permanent Wakhi partners for exchange of their goods. Most of the Kirghiz move freely in the Wakhi hamlets until, after long negotiations, they find a reasonable rate of exchange. The rates of exchange for their pastoral and agricultural products are similar to those presented on pages 136-38. Most of the Wakhi who participate in direct trade with the Kirghiz are members of households that do not have their own livestock, and therefore need the animal products of the Kirghiz in order to be able to make their heavy woolen and fur garments, floor covers, bedding, and footwear. Kirghiz milk products also supplement the Wakhi diet. Exchanges between the Kirghiz and the Wakhi are conducted almost exclusively on a direct barter basis of livestock products for grain, and rarely involve the exchange of animals.

During late summer, that is, after the beginning of the harvest in the Wakhan, some Wakhi take certain amounts of wheat and barley flour into the Pamirs. The grain is transported in goatskin bags on the backs of men or are loaded onto donkeys and yak. The Wakhi who take part in this extremely timely trading with the Kirghiz are from Wakhi households without livestock who go to the Pamirs to obtain the specific livestock products and/or animals they need. These summer trading journeys are particularly profitable to the poorer Wakhi as most Kirghiz households, even the rich, are in need of cereals at this time since their reserves have long since run out. The Kirghiz do not, or cannot, make the trip to Wakhan to bring grain themselves, either because of the fear of lowland heat and/or because they are taken up with activities, such as felt making, peat cutting, collecting of fodder, or transporting of fuel to their winter camps in preparation for the winter ahead. By taking flour to the Kirghiz, the Wakhi succeed in receiving a better rate of exchange for their agricultural products than any other time of the year. The value of flour sold during the summer is two to three times higher than that sold during the winter, and even higher than that negotiated through credit transactions with traders at other times of the year. In addition to flour, some Wakhi and a few Zebaki[1] take salt (a

1. *Zebaki* is a term used for a group of people living in the area to the south

rare commodity in the Pamirs during this time of the year) which they generally exchange for such products as *mai*, dried yoghurt, wool, and yak and goat hair, or felt. The rate of exchange for salt is exorbitant: five or six times its cash value in Khandud. However, the higher returns for the flour and salt carried to the Pamirs by the Wakhi and their neighbors, the Zebaki farmers, are justified not only by their strategic timing, but also by the transportation costs and the time and effort involved for those who make the trip. Indeed, transportation costs are a major concern for the Kirghiz, especially during their several winter journeys between the Wakhan and the Pamirs. The Kirghiz report an average cost of about one sheep per round trip for every man and two of the pack animals involved in the journey. Some of these costs involve buying grain feed and fodder for the pack animals while in the Wakhan, horse-shoes, special food for the road, and presents of tea for the Wakhi with whom they lodge overnight.

Many poor Wakhi, who do not have access to sufficient agri-cultural or pastoral resources to meet their needs, have to look for temporary work, at least for part of the year. As the Kirghiz are economically much better off than the Wakhi as a community and able to employ outside labor, particularly during the summer months, some Wakhi seek summer work, or even permanent herding jobs among the Kirghiz. The tasks the Wakhi are hired to do during the summer usually involve repairing and constructing sheep pens and storage shelters, digging or clearing irrigation channels, and cutting peat sods and hay. Other short-term services the Wakhi are hired to undertake in the Pamirs include helping in and around the camp with milking, collecting fuel, and other daily chores within the camp. The payment for these services is usually in the form of animals or animal products, which the Wakhi may use for payment of debts to the traders or for other family needs. There are a number of very poor Wakhi, and some individuals from villages in Badakhshan, who come to the Pamirs solely for the purpose of seeking alms and dona-

---

of Ishkashim, the entrance to the Wakhan Corridor, in the subdistrict of Zebak. They are related linguistically and racially to the Wakhi and are also Ismailite. The Zebaki are known among the Kirghiz for their specialization as salt traders. Salt is a particularly cumbersome commodity to transport to the Pamirs because of the dangerous trails and high passes, and is, therefore, very precious. I was quoted an exchange value of 4 to 6 *sair* of salt (valued in Khandud at 100-120 Afs.) for 1 sheep (valued at least at 600 Afs. in Khandud), or its equivalent in livestock products.

tions, mostly in the form of animal products or, in some cases, small animals.

There are also a number of Wakhi individuals and families who, for many years, have been living year-round in the Pamirs. All are former agricultural villagers who have become nomadized and are attached to specific rich Kirghiz households, whom they serve and with whom they camp. The reasons for the nomadization of these Wakhi families are very much the same in all instances. They were all poor peasants and, in some cases, members of large impoverished households with whom they still maintain very close ties. Generally, one or two adult male members of the family were initially hired as shepherds, receiving six sheep, or the equivalent in other animals, per year. Through continued service the Wakhi shepherd built a small herd over the years. Later, in accordance with Kirghiz practices, he asked his employer for milk animals *(saghun),* and brought his female family members to the Pamirs to set up household during the summer only. Finding the Wakhi female help in the Kirghiz household chores indispensable, the rich Kirghiz offered more compensation, which in turn resulted in the year-round residence of nearly ten Wakhi households in the Pamirs. All of these Wakhi families still continue to serve a Kirghiz household as well as caring for their own livestock. Some members continue to receive payments in animals or goods, while the family is helped by the provision of extra milk animals, camping, and pasturage rights for their privately owned and acquired herds. There is only one Wakhi householder who has recently become an independent herder. He owns some animals and has also received others from a rich Kirghiz herd owner as *amanat.* There are at least two Wakhi families who own more than seventy goats and sheep and about ten yak, but who continue to work for Kirghiz households.

In almost all cases the Wakhi pastoralized families still operate as single economic units with the farming segment of their household in the Wakhan. That is, the pastoralist section furnishes the agricultural segment with the animal products it needs, and receives grain in return. Sometimes the female members of the household will alternate their time between the village and the Kirghiz pastoral camp. In one or two cases, additional women and children are brought from the village for the summer milk season to help with the making of dairy products and with the herding activities of the family. The limited nomadization of the Wakhi agriculturalist is then clearly caused by poverty and is a deliberate decision by the Wakhi individuals and families to seek herding jobs among the Kirghiz, and to gain access to pastoral capital through their services. This is a gradual process and intended to complement the larger Wakhi agricultural household economy and not to act as a separate and independent unit of production and consumption. In this regard, the nomadization of the Wakhi peasants differs from that of the people of another high-altitude environment, Tibet, where Robert Ekvall (1968, pp. 21-23) reports that the mixed herder and former *Sa Ma aBrog* take up pastoral nomadism by switching their economic productive system completely to *aBrog* or pastoral nomadism by taking their own herd to the high pastures.

Another area of direct interdependence between the two societies lies in the purchase of agricultural land from the Wakhi by a number of rich Kirghiz, who then give the land to the Wakhi to cultivate under various kinds of arrangements. Some fifteen Kirghiz *oey* units have invested in agricultural land, most of which is located in hamlets near Sarhad, the agricultural area closest to the Little Pamir. The amount of capital spent on land ranges from as little as three thousand to several hundred thousand Afs. The amount of seed sown in Kirghiz-owned land also varies considerably, ranging from only six to nearly two hundred *sair*. However, the return for most of the Kirghiz land is minimal or nil, except where the Kirghiz landowners can maintain close supervision of the agricultural activities. Fourteen Kirghiz landowners who claim to own enough land to sow close to six hundred *sair* of seed, half of which they could cultivate under the Wakhi fallow system, reported annual harvests amounting to about one thousand *sair* of grain. This is a very low return for the seed and labor costs they have to pay to the Wakhi who work on their land. In some cases the Kirghiz provide the draft animals and seed, and pay for the labor so they can retain all the harvest. In other instances they give the land and seed to a Wakhi farmer who will do the work and use his own oxen in return for half the harvest. The Kirghiz contend that the reason for the low harvest return is that the Wakhi cheat them by reporting low yields, mixing part of the harvested crops from the Kirghiz land with their own, or by simply not looking after the Kirghiz fields as well as their own. All of these accusations are justified to some extent when one compares the size of the average harvest to that of the Kirghiz khan, who is not only the most successful herder, but also the largest Kirghiz landowner and cultivator. His success in farming is owing to his supervision of the activities of his Wakhi farmers during the critical periods of agricultural work. One Kirghiz *oey* is located in the hamlet of Petukh, near Sarhad, and is charged with overseeing the khan's agricultural activities.

He has also hired two or three Wakhi who do the farming. In addition, the khan sends one of his sons during cultivation to properly distribute the needed seed and to allocate appropriate plots for different crops, and again during harvest to prevent any theft of his harvested crop at that time. All of these activities involve heavy costs but, in the case of the khan, the size of his landholdings and the final harvest of over twenty-five hundred *sair* of grain justify the expense. This amount, although substantial in the context of Wakhi economy, is not sufficient for the khan's needs, and he usually buys additional grain from the Wakhi and from traders. Despite the khan's success, the total Kirghiz earnings from their agricultural investments in Wakhi territory is only a fraction of the cereal needed by Kirghiz society.

With the exception of one Kirghiz family hired by the khan and sent to live near most of his acquired agricultural land, no other Kirghiz, either poor or rich, has yet decided to take up permanent residence in the Wakhan, or to pursue agriculture and a settled way of life. For a number of sociocultural, as well as economic reasons, it is also unlikely that it will happen in the near future, for despite intensive economic interaction, Kirghiz and Wakhi entertain strong mutual feelings of contempt. This is mostly because of the religious-sectarian, linguistic, and cultural differences between the two groups rather than their economic modes of production. The Kirghiz, who are Sunni Muslims, generally consider the Wakhi Ismailite practices heretical. Their feelings are aired verbally as well as in their interactions. For example, during their long winter journeys in Wakhan the Kirghiz are obliged to stay in the homes of the Wakhi, but on such occasions most refuse to eat food cooked by the Wakhi. They either cook their own or bring cooked food with them. There are absolutely no cases of intermarriage between them. In one instance during my research, the corpse of an old man, who died during his trading trip to Wakhan, was brought back to the Pamirs on horseback to be buried. Such an action is very unusual in other parts of Afghanistan, and the Kirghiz explanation was that they could not bury a Muslim Kirghiz in the land of the heretic Wakhi. It was by no means an easy task to carry the body back to the Pamirs in winter, but it was fully approved of by all the Kirghiz.

The close association, under the new conditions, between the Wakhi and the Kirghiz over the past three of four decades has, however, had at least two results: a very large number of adult males, and even some females, from both groups have learned to speak each others' language and the use of opium and large amounts of black Indian tea, which has been widespread among the Wakhi agriculturalists for a long time, has been adopted by the Kirghiz. Although the introduction of the use of opium and tea was the result of the Kirghiz' constant interaction with the Wakhi, its continued use is nurtured by the traders who supply these commodities to both societies. Indeed, the activities of outside agents, particularly the itinerant traders, are the cause of the development of much of the intense direct economic interaction between the two groups, which I have discussed so far, and the many indirect trade relations between them which I will explore next.

KIRGHIZ INTERDEPENDENCE
WITH THE LARGER AFGHAN SOCIETY

The closure of the borders and termination of the caravan trade between northern Afghanistan and Chinese Turkistan had a major impact on the regional economies of adjacent areas in the Soviet Union, China, Pakistan, and Afghanistan. The effects of the abrupt end to the trade and exchange of specialized market commodities in Afghanistan was, however, most severely felt by the traders who took part in the exchange system, and the Kirghiz and Wakhi populations, who not only lost their share of the revenue, but also lost ready access to a variety of market goods they needed. Many traders from northern Afghanistan were trapped in the towns of Chinese Turkistan and were for many years not allowed to return to Afghanistan.[2] A few had to give up their caravan trading ventures, while others opened up shops in towns and villages. A small number of these enterprising traders, mainly those from the central Badakhshan area, who were aware of the rising demand for animals and animal products in the cities of Afghanistan, particularly Kabul, took the opportunity to establish trade relations with the Kirghiz and the Wakhi. The traders provided the Kirghiz and the Wakhi with market goods in exchange for the livestock and animal products that they took to the Afghan markets. This was found particularly promising

2. I know of several traders from the general area near my own home village in Badakhshan, including one man from our village who was not allowed to leave Sinkiang after the Communist takeover. In the mid-1960s, however, because of public pressure the government of Afghanistan negotiated the release of Afghan citizens and their dependents from China. At that time the young son and wife of the then-deceased man from our village came to live in the village. At the same time close to 7,000 people were reported to have immigrated to Afghanistan, most of whom came through the Pamirs and the Wakhan Corridor.

by the traders because they recognized the Kirghiz dependence on
Wakhi cereal products and horses, and the need of both Kirghiz and
Wakhi for market goods and opium from the outside. This small
number of early entrepreneurs organized the basic structure of an
elaborate system of trade and exchange that involves both direct
and indirect transactions between the traders, the Kirghiz, and the
Wakhi, and which ultimately connects the economies of the two
communities to the regional and national economic system of the
country. The organization of this system of trade is strongly influenced by the frontier character of the area—its isolation from
the rest of the country and market centers as well as the presence
of less experienced or dishonest administrative staff often sent to
the area as a punishment for their deeds elsewhere.

The frontier character of the Wakhan Corridor and the Afghan
Pamirs is emphasized by the absence of any permanent communication infrastructure, and the sheer geographical isolation and in-
accessibility of the area. These conditions have also made the development of any large-scale business and trade enterprise impossible.
As a result, most of the trade and exchange is still carried out by
a group of traders and tinkers using pack animals. Because the Wakhi
local communities are dispersed into small isolated hamlets, maintaining permanent shops and stores in the form of a bazaar has been
limited. A small but increasing concentration of shops exists in one
place only, in the village of Khandud, the district center of Wakhan.
Apart from Ishkashim, at the entrance of the corridor, Khandud
is the only village with small shops (about thirty in all) serving the
entire district of Wakhan, which includes the Afghan Pamirs. Most
of these shops are, however, owned and operated by the itinerant
traders who have to remain mobile most of the year, moving throughout the Wakhi villages and the Pamirs to contract new transactions
or to collect debts for previous credit exchanges.

These same frontier conditions in the Wakhan Corridor have
made the civil and military administrative posts in the area extremely
unattractive to the better qualified officials. Consequently, the least
qualified individuals with no previous work experience, and often
those well known to be corrupt, are sent to the Wakhan, frequently
as a form of punishment. This policy has served only to further encourage such officials in their corrupt practices, the very distance
of these frontier regions from the seats of central government serving
to shield their activities from constant inspection. Many rich Wakhi
households have suffered the loss of their belongings because of
the actions of these officials, who have allegedly staged and provoked

conflicts between people, or have indicted certain people on false charges. Many officials and/or their friends, dependents, or relatives have engaged in the illegal sale of opium and have acted as traders or partners to traders during their tenure in office. This misuse of administrative power by government officials in the area existed long before the closure of the borders and it still continues to some extent, despite the occasional close scrutiny of the activities of officials in the frontier regions maintained by the provincial authorities in Faizabad. These corrupt and illegal activites have had great effect on the nature of the organization and execution of trade and exchange in the area between outside traders and the local inhabitants.

THE ORGANIZATION OF TRADE AND EXCHANGE

Outside traders have played the dominant role in the establishment and continuation of the existing triadic network of trade relations. They have all the characteristics of entrepreneurs in their roles as economic and cultural brokers in the area. They are all motivated to maximize their personal socioeconomic interests, and to this end are willing to undertake certain risks in their ventures. They have adequate prior knowledge of the Wakhi and Kirghiz socioeconomic systems, or are willing to learn about it in the course of their trading activities. Most of them can understand, and some speak, either one or both of the local languages in addition to Dari (a dialect of Persian spoken in Afghanistan) and their own mother tongue. All of the itinerant traders operating in the region are rural- and urban-based individuals from other parts of the country. A few of them, however, have become permanent residents of the Wakhan with large landholdings, and farm as well as trade. The majority (about fifteen individuals in all) are from the central areas of Badakhshan province, and are members of the Tajik or Uzbek ethnic group. Many of the Badakhshi traders are either descendants or relatives of some of the early caravan traders. The newcomers into the area are a group of ten Pashtun, who claim residence in a village near the city of Jalalabad, the provincial capital of Nangarhar province in the eastern part of Afghanistan. They seem to be all related to one another and a few of them work together as partners. During this research there were also two other recent recruits from Kabul, one of whom had not been successful in his new endeavor. In addition to these regular and continuing mobile traders and shopkeepers, there are a number of irregulars who pay occasional visits to the area, and their number has been rising as the economic pressures in the urban centers have risen. All of these outside traders were individuals who had been less than successful in their trading activities within the context of their own original communities, and their success in their new venture has varied tremendously from one to another.

The traders maintain regular and direct contact with the individuals and communities participating in the networks of exchange and are, therefore, well aware of their clients' economic needs, demands, and interdependencies at the local level. They also have an exclusive, firsthand knowledge of the regional and market demands for agricultural and pastoral products. The successful traders seem to be those who have made full and effective use of local political realities to further their own interests. They are also able to translate and mediate the exchange of commodities between different types of specialized economies, as well as between different spheres of commodities within these economies. They provide the major link between the primary producers of goods and the consumers in the local as well as the regional and national market economies (see fig. 6). Lastly, they are very active agents of not only social change and dynamics, but are also important forces for the development and continuation of both Kirghiz pastoral and the Wakhi agropastoral subsistence strategies.

The full impact of the entrepreneurial roles played by the small number of outside itinerant traders and shopkeepers in the economy and society of the Wakhan Corridor and the Pamirs can perhaps be best illustrated by a discussion of the basic strategy employed by them for the organization and perpetuation of the triadic network of trade and exchange in the area. Their strategy has been based on the following principles. First, to maintain strict control over the supply, type, and amounts of different market goods, and to select what pastoral and agricultural products are exchangeable commodities for market goods.

Second, to create new and greater dependency among the farmers and pastoralists upon market goods, with the result of more specialization and more interdependence between the two adaptive systems. Third, to rely almost exclusively on conversion as a means of exchange between the different economies, instead of dealing in cash prices in such transactions. Finally, to use credit, or delayed exchange of various lengths and terms, rather than direct and immediate transfer of goods. All of the above measures have served to maximize the interests of the outside traders and have also helped to promote change and the continuation of the local economies under the new frontier situation.

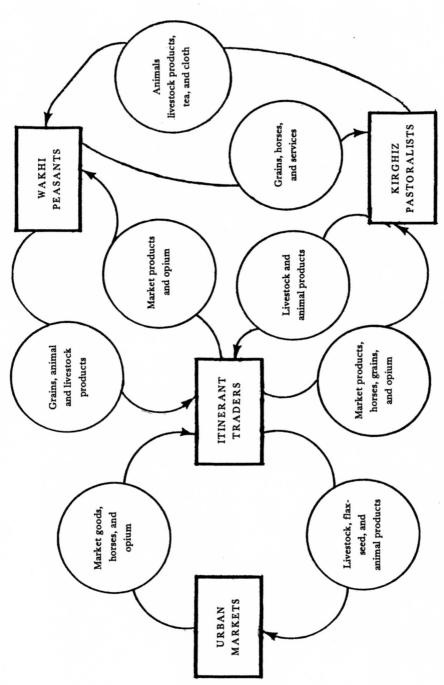

Fig. 8. Flow of goods and services in the triadic network of trade in the Wakhan Corridor and the Pamirs.

The traders' choice of trade commodities from outside the Wakhan Corridor, as well as the goods taken from the area, are influenced by two major factors common to any frontier region: (1) the cost of transportation of exchangeable goods per unit of weight and/or volume between the point of origin and the place of disposition; and (2) the potential or actual margin of profit to the trader per unit of measure after the transactions are completed. As a result of these very basic rules of frontier economy, the composition of imported trade goods from outside economies has been disproportionately dominated by such harmful "luxury" items as tea and opium. Trading in tea and opium has its roots in the early history of the corridor, when it was one of the main trading routes between northern Afghanistan and Chinese Turkistan and beyond. The wide use of opium and tea, especially among the Wakhi, are habits acquired long before the closure of the borders. Indeed, the pioneer traders in the area were opium and tea traders who had taken part in the long trading journeys to and from Chinese Turkistan through these valleys before the borders were sealed. There was a certain demand for tea and opium in the Wakhan and since the closure of the frontiers itinerant traders, visitors, and government officials have exploited this opportunity to its maximum so that at the present time these two items account for more than half of the total exchange of goods in the region.

Production of opium in Afghanistan was legal for a long time. However, during the past two decades certain restrictions on the growing of opium poppies have been periodically imposed and lifted, depending on the weight of international political pressures. Since the summer of 1973, a new ban has been ordered and to a large degree enforced. Even when its production was sanctioned by the government, domestic consumption of opium was banned, and producers were expected to sell only to the appropriate government agencies. As a result, all nonofficial trafficking and sale of opium has been considered illegal. The Wakhi are not able to grow their own poppies because of the altitude, so the sale of opium in the area has provided traders with their highest profit margin (given its low production cost, particularly in the central areas of Badakhshan where opium is produced in large quantities, as well as its low transportation cost). The cost of opium in the Wakhan, during the time this research was carried out, was reported to be as high as six to eight times the original price paid by the trader per unit of weight. As a result, it has been one of the most prized items of exchange taken by traders into the Wakhan, and has also been a source of corrupt practices by the administrative authorities. Some officials even sell it themselves to the public through minor officials or soldiers. It is very difficult, because of its illegality, to get an accurate estimate of the amount of opium sold in the area, but the number of users, particularly among the Wakhi, is very high, although I was told it had been declining in recent years. The effects of the use of opium on the relationship between individual members of Wakhi domestic units, on their household economy, and on the Wakhi society are considerable.

Tea is without doubt the largest single item of trade in the Wakhan Corridor and its neighboring areas in the province of Badakhshan. Next to opium it brings the highest profit, and the demand for it is universal in the area at the present time. I was informed by older people, both in the Wakhan and the Pamirs, that although the use of tea in small amounts as an item of luxury goes back a long way, its consumption in large amounts began only about ten to fifteen years ago.[3] Drinking tea in the form of a concoction known among the Wakhi as *shur chai* (literally, "salty tea"), and among the Kirghiz as *qateghdagan chai,* is no longer a matter of pleasure or an occasional addition to the diet. For many people it is a clear case of addiction, and they admit to experiencing physical, as well as emotional, discomfort when they run out of tea. Among opium addicts drinking tea brewed in the local manner is believed to enhance the effects of opium right after it is smoked or eaten. It is also considered the only available means of easing the pains of opium withdrawal symptoms. In a number of instances, some addicts told me that when opium is not available, they use an extract of tea, which is obtained through a process of reduction by boiling large quantities of tea.[4]

3. During my own early years in the village of Shahran, only a few hours from the provincial town of Faizabad, tea was a very rare commodity. It was served occasionally and then only to house guests. The amount consumed by most well-to-do families did not exceed more than five pounds of black tea per year. I do remember the gradual increase in the tea supply in the area since the latter part of the 1950s, and its concomitant consumption by the people throughout Badakhshan. At the present time even the poorest of households consumes more than twenty pounds of tea each year. Tea is one of the most costly economic drains in the whole province of Badakhshan, and the major beneficiaries of this tea trade are the tea merchants from outside.

4. I am not aware of any studies on the physiological effects of tea consumption on human organisms under high or low altitude conditions. Tea may also have some nutritional or digestive effect that needs to be looked into. In the studies among Nunoans of Peru, for instance, chewing coca leaves is found to affect body water loss and to help retain body heat (for details see Baker et al. 1968 and Hanna 1974).

It is in response to this heavy dependence, and continuing demand for large quantities of black Indian tea among the Kirghiz and Wakhi population, recently created by outside traders, that the self-perpetuating highly profitable tea trade in the area is growing. The sale of tea, unlike that of opium, is free of legal restrictions, and involves only a minimal transportation cost per unit of measure compared to other market goods brought into the area. Its exchange value, depending on the kind of transportation, ranges from two to five times that of the original cost to the trader, adequate reason for it to be the largest part of the imported trade goods. During the year 1973 alone, traders claimed to have brought about 500 boxes of tea (a box contains either 30 or 40 kilograms) into the corridor. Assuming an average of 35 kilograms a box, the total amount runs to 17,500 kilograms (38,500 lbs.) of tea. I have noted earlier that on the basis of my own household survey, more than 14,000 lbs. of tea are consumed by the Kirghiz annually. About 400 of the 500 boxes of tea sold are brought from Jalalabad by Pashtun traders, making them the main tea retailers in the area. They buy the tea directly from tea importers from India and Pakistan and send it by truck to Khandud, where they have their main trading base. The remainder is sold by the Badakhshi traders who are, for the most part, third or fourth parties in the chain of exchange.

Essential food items such as rice, sugar, candy, and dried fruits, which are in demand, are rarely taken in any appreciable amounts into the area. This is because their bulk makes transportation costly and decreases the net profit. By the same token, the supply of cloth is for the most part limited to expensive materials, such as corduroy, velvet, and imported synthetics. Other items of import that have been on the rise during recent years include tobacco and cigarettes. A certain amount of used cloth, footwear, leather, plastic and metal household utensils, in addition to transistor radios, batteries, and a small selection of haberdashery and inexpensive jewelry, are brought in by the outside traders. Also sold, although only to the Kirghiz, are a small number of horses and horseshoes, bits, stirrups, and saddles.

The itinerant traders accept in exchange for their imported market goods only those local products that bring them the maximum profit in the market. Their choice is largely determined by market demands for certain pastoral and agricultural goods and, once again, the risks and transportation costs of taking such items to the market. In this respect, livestock, especially fat-tailed sheep and goats, are the most desired and profitable. The Wakhi *gadek* are not particularly valued because of their small size, short pace, and low tolerance of the sixty-day trek to Kabul. The cost of transportation for animals is very low since they cover the distance on foot and are pastured free of charge along their route to the market. There is, however, the risk of predators, animal thieves, and disease taking their toll during the trek, which could result in large losses. A small number of cattle and yak are taken to Badakhshan markets, but this has been only in response to a recent demand in the provincial towns there. Cattle and yak are not taken to Kabul or other distant markets because of their lack of tolerance for heat and the long distance involved. Among animal products *mai* rates very favorably, and brings the largest profit since it is considered the best and most expensive cooking oil in Afghanistan. Certain amounts of dried yoghurt, felt, horse covers, furs, sheepskins, and wool are also taken to markets. Again, the amount of these latter items is small because of the extremely difficult and costly transportation. The demand for wool, however, is very much on the rise because of the increasing international market for Afghan carpets. The need for high quality Kirghiz wool was realized particularly after the 1971-72 drought in northern Afghanistan (one of the main areas of the carpet-weaving industry), which devastated the animal population of the area. As a result, during the past few years Turkman carpet weavers have been coming to the Pamirs solely to buy wool. Wakhi agricultural products, with the exception of small amounts of flaxseed, have no outside market demand. This is owing partly to the assumed inferior quality of Wakhi wheat in Badakhshan markets, and partly to the very high transportation costs involved and the hazardous nature of the roads. Thus, Wakhi wheat and barley are not taken to lowland markets except when droughts in central Badakhshan reduce the local yield. Itinerant traders accept Wakhi wheat and barley solely to sell back locally to the Kirghiz for animal and livestock products, which they then take back with them to the lowland markets.

This selective demand imposed by market conditions upon itinerant traders, which forces them to seek pastoral products in their transactions, has had two further economic consequences in the region. One is that traders have encouraged the Wakhi to exchange their meager livestock products, such as raw wool, animal skins, and animals, for tea, opium, and other items they desire. By losing their raw material the Wakhi are no longer able to make their own traditional garments and footwear, so that they now have to buy manufactured clothing and shoes from these same traders. The latter have also introduced new tin and plastic household utensils, glass, and chinawear, which have replaced the traditional locally produced wooden and clay items. The second consequence is that the Wakhi now have to pay for their newly created needs, as well as for their older existing ones, with animal products, wheat, or barley. This in turn has resulted an increased "cash" cropping of wheat and barley among the Wakhi (see chapter 3), and increased economic interdependence between the Wakhi and the Kirghiz. The Wakhi have had to acquire animals or pastoral products they need through service or direct exchange of goods in order to be able to pay for their changed patterns. As for the Kirghiz, they were already in need of both the agricultural and the numerous market commodities that traders provide. The traders have further increased the volume of their exchange among the Kirghiz pastoralists by providing them with Wakhi grains and adding supplies of luxury items such as manufactured clothing, tobacco, radios, and so forth.

All market commodities, as well as agricultural and pastoral products, have a cash value. A certain amount of currency is available in the area but its use is limited to the payment of services, and to those places where there are permanent shops. Most trade exchange in both the Wakhan and the Pamirs is based on direct conversion of goods for their equivalents for all purposes. This is both a matter of convenience as well as a practical concern, especially for Wakhi villagers and Kirghiz nomads who, under the circumstances, have very little use for cash. In return for living accommodations, or other required services, very often visitors will provide a certain amount of tea or even opium, both more acceptable than cash. In addition to the practical aspects of conversion as a means of exchange for the Kirghiz and the Wakhi, it ensures a much higher margin of profit for the traders. Therefore, the traders have not only adapted to the local demands, but indeed have promoted the practice to maximize their own interest in the process. Generally, the cash value of goods is not considered at all in arriving at a mutually acceptable rate of exchange; rather the discussion is based on the exchange value of other such commodities in the area at the time. For example, if the aim of the parties involved in a transaction is to exchange tea for barley, then they will consider the going exchange rate of tea for sheep, tea for wheat, and wheat for sheep and barley for wheat, and so on, to arrive at a comparable rate for the two items concerned. The rates vary on the basis of where the transactions take place, what time of year they took place, and the particular commodities involved. Distance from Khandud or Qala-i-Panja, where the motor vehicle road ends, has a definite effect on the exchange rates. In the Wakhan, negotiations are very often settled solely between the trader and the individual Wakhi. There are often noticeable differences of rates within the same hamlet depending on the economic and social status of the individual Wakhi. In the Pamirs, however, the rates of exchange between livestock and livestock products are traditionally recognized and strictly followed in local transactions as well as in exchange with the outsiders. These rates are stated in chapter 4, and if, for example, one had to pay a sheep but did not own one, though one did have goats or *mai* or felt, perhaps, then the equivalent must be accepted: two goats, one *sair mai,* two pieces of felt, and so on, instead of a sheep. Similarly, the exchange rate between agricultural and market goods bought from the traders, especially when transactions are contracted in the Pamirs (instant exchange or credit), is generally uniform. This is because the itinerant traders usually consult with the Kirghiz khan and other elders to reach a particular rate of exchange for their goods, and once such a rate is sanctioned it is followed without deviation. Any difference would result in disputes and termination of payments to the traders. This is without doubt another important area of the khan's political influence in protecting the economic interests of his group. His influence is also extended, with some success, to the discouragement and prevention of the supply of opium by the traders to the Kirghiz.

The final character of the trading system in the area is the widespread use of credit or delayed exchange. This is a practical means of facilitating the large volumes of exchange, and ensuring its continuation with the highest amount of profit for the outside traders. The credit system is structured so that market and agricultural goods are sold for more than three to five times their value during the fall and winter months in exchange for pastoral or agricultural products payable the following summer or early fall (see table 17). This is known among the Kirghiz as *kutarma,* and the Wakhi refer to it as *wardasht,* and it is generally contracted between traders and the Wakhi or Kirghiz, rarely between the Wakhi and Kirghiz themselves. This is a particularly attractive arrangement for acquiring goods when individuals lack the means to pay for them at that time. However, because of the exorbitant interest rates involved in the credit system, once individuals enter into such an arrangement, it is almost impossible to get out of it since it perpetuates itself year after year. When an individual does not have the kind of animals or the stated amount of products to pay at collection time, the traders often use force or the threat of it to collect. In such circumstances the trader may take possession of other more valuable animals or goods the person may have, particularly so if the debtor is a Wakhi. For example, a trader who was owed one sheep by a Wakhi who did not own any sheep took the man's cow instead, saying that although he had no need of a cow and he realized that the cow was more valuable, it was the only solution.

TABLE 17

EXAMPLES OF EXCHANGE RATES OF MAJOR TRADING
ITEMS IN CASH AND CONVERSION

Cash values

1 *pow* (0.453 kg.) tea	= 45 Afs. in market (about U.S. $0.85)
	= 90 Afs. in Wakhan (about U.S. $1.70)
1 *sair* (7.6 kg.) wheat	= 50 Afs. in market (about U.S. $0.92)
	= 25-30 Afs. in Wakhan
	(about U.S. $0.45-0.55)
1 sheep	= up to 1,200 Afs. in market
	(about U.S. $21.80)
	= 500-600 Afs. in Wakhan
	(about U.S. $9.00-11.00)

Conversion values

1 *pow* tea	= 3-4 *sair* (22.8-30.4 kg.) wheat
	(direct and immediate exchange)
	= 7-8 *sair* (53.2-60.8 kg.) wheat (credit)
1 sheep	= up to 10 *pow* (4.5 kg.) tea (direct exchange)
	= 4 *pow* (2.5 kg.) tea (credit exchange)
20 *sair* (152.0 kg.) wheat	= 1 sheep (direct exchange)
8 *sair* (60.8 kg.) wheat	= 1 sheep (credit)

This is but one of many such cases. In instances where no payment has been forthcoming, the amount due has been doubled and tripled over the years, and on occasion has only been cancelled when a daughter has been married off to a trader or one of his relatives. Many of the traders have taken a wife or wives from the area because of such credit transactions. One of the main reasons for the increasing sale of Wakhi agricultural land, both to the traders and the Kirghiz in recent times, is the need to pay off increasing debts incurred by repeated credit transactions. Very often the traders, through bribes, friendships, or relatives, have the backing and blessing of a corrupt government official in the area to aid them in the collection of debts.

In addition to using the threat of force to collect debts, some traders are known to engage in other forms of usury and deceit.

During the spring of 1973 a group of people from the Maydan province to the south of Kabul came to the Pamirs with large amounts of cash to buy sheep. They paid unprecedented prices for sheep and goats in the area. However, it was later discovered that they had passed a large number of counterfeit bills in the form of 1,000 Afghani notes. During the summer of the same year, another trader from Nangarhar province took advantage of the news of the coup d'état to tell some Kirghiz that the existing currency would not be honored after two weeks if not taken to a bank and exchanged for the new bills. He persuaded a few people who had cash from their spring sales to the earlier traders to give him the money in exchange for the promise of wheat that he was to bring them in the fall. He got about fifty thousand Afs. in cash, giving the Kirghiz notes for large amounts of wheat priced at forty Afs. a *sair* (twice the cash price of wheat in Wakhan at the time). He did not return to the Pamirs after that incident, or at least he had not been back by the summer of 1975. Other traders are known to have used scare tactics on rich Wakhi to make them sell their goods on credit for livestock. On at least one occasion it had involved tape recording the conversation of a Wakhi in which he had spoken of an illegal trade trip he had made across the borders to Pakistan. The trader then threatened to report the Wakhi to the government authorities unless he bought some of his merchandise.

I hope it is clear that the structure of the existing trade network in the Wakhan and the Afghan Pamirs is part of a much larger regional adaptation to the closed frontiers. The organization of this triadic system of exchange, between three different economies, is particularly influenced by increasing urbanization and the consequent rising demand for meat and animal products by the national economy for export. Also it should be noted that the economic exchange system in the area is based largely on luxury and consumer goods, a condition consistent with frontier economic processes in general (see Lattimore 1962b). Because of the increasing supply and consumption of tea, opium, and tobacco (particularly tea), both the Kirghiz and the Wakhi are, at the present time, experiencing a very serious loss of economic resources. Consequently, some richer Kirghiz, and a few Wakhi, have been moving toward participating directly by taking their livestock and animal products to Kabul themselves to ease the economic drain on the area. This effort on the part of the Kirghiz and the Wakhi, although very limited at this stage, could change future trends and it is worth looking into the development of this trend in some detail.

DIRECT PARTICIPATION OF THE KIRGHIZ
AND WAKHI IN OUTSIDE TRADE

For nearly a decade after the closure of the frontiers, no Kirghiz left the Wakhan Corridor for other parts of Afghanistan to trade or for any other reasons. The outside traders were, therefore, able to persuade the rich Kirghiz to sell their excess, unproductive animals on a credit basis for a cash price slightly higher than the direct exchange local value of the animal, which was to be paid after the animals were taken to Kabul and sold in the market. The payment was made at least six to nine months later in cash or goods. While this was a much better deal than that available to poorer individuals, the traders were still getting the best of the bargain. In many cases, however, the traders never paid the Kirghiz, since they were usually themselves already deeply in debt in their own villages or towns and their earnings from the Kirghiz livestock sales were used to pay these earlier debts. After making a sizable deal many traders did not come back to the area, and the Kirghiz were not able to go after them to collect their money. As a result of these early dealings two of the rich Kirghiz claim to have about 1,500,000 Afs. each in outstanding debts due from a number of Badakhshi traders. There are a number of other Kirghiz who also claim that much smaller sums are also owed to them by traders. Much of this money is no longer recoverable since one or both of the original parties involved are now dead.

The main reason for the Kirghiz lack of direct contact with the urban-centered market in Afghanistan during that period was the lingering political uncertainty of the Kirghiz elders as to the future of their people and themselves. This uncertainty had its roots in the events and rumors concerning the Kirghiz role in the frontier disturbances that had caused their flight to Sinkiang territory in 1947 and their return to the Afghan territory two years later, following the Chinese revolution. The Kirghiz, although welcomed on their return to the Pamirs in 1949 by a special representative of the provincial authorities, dispatched by order of the prime minister, were not quite sure of the future policies of the Afghan government, and so they remained aloof and watchful for about ten years.

As noted earlier, with the rediscovery of Marco Polo sheep in the area and the opening of a game reserve, the Kirghiz came into direct contact with a number of court and government officials in the process. They gradually became more confident and during 1959 the khan and a party of Kirghiz elders passed through Kabul on

their way to Mecca. On their return to Kabul from the pilgrimage
the khan and his party were well received, given an audience by the
king of Afghanistan, and met with several government officials.
Since then the khan and a few other rich Kirghiz have themselves
been taking about one thousand to fifteen hundred animals annually
to Kabul. Not all rich herd owners participate in this newly available alternative. In 1973 about six people sent animals to Kabul;
in 1974 only five herd owners took part. At least three or four herd
owners are still giving their animals to the outside traders on the
basis of the credit system described earlier. The only difference
is that they now have a much better chance of collecting their money.

Until very recently Wakhi with large herds did not take their own
animals to Kabul either. They sold their animals to the outside traders
as did the Kirghiz. Many of them, however, became progressively
poorer, or their herd size decreased markedly when the wealthy
became the target of exploitation both by their theocratic leaders
and by local government officials. Therefore the rich in Wakhan
maintain a very low profile and live no better than the very poor.
They often deny owning large numbers of animals, or wealth of
any kind, to protect themselves against avaricious officials. I was
told, by an allegedly wealthy Wakhi, that in the past government
officials had taken rugs, blankets, and even a wood-burning stove
he had owned. Only recently a few of the Wakhi herd owners decided
to take their animals, in the company of the Kirghiz herds, to Kabul.
Even these individuals try to hide the purchases they make in the
markets of Kabul to avoid being asked to give them as "gifts" to
a visiting official or their religious leader, the *shah*. One Wakhi told
me that on one of his recent trips to Kabul he had bought an expensive Iranian-made woolen blanket worth about 1,000 Afs. (about
$18.00) and had brought it home. A day after his return home,
the *shah* sent a man to ask him to send the blanket as a "gift"
to the *shah*. The Wakhi did not want to give the blanket so he
went home and cut it down the middle into two pieces. He then
took one piece to the *shah's* man and told him that his brother had
already cut it and taken half but that if the *shah* cared to take the
other half he was welcome. He also expressed his regrets that the
shah had not asked sooner so that he could have had the blanket
in one piece!

The very few Kirghiz and Wakhi who are active in this new trade
opportunity undoubtedly represent an emerging nucleus of a local
entrepreneurial group. They are motivated in their quest for outside trade by both economic and political incentives; by taking their

animals to Kabul they sell them at the highest possible market price, and in return they get all their needed market goods for the lowest possible cost. At least one rich Wakhi from Khandud has opened his own shop and brings most of his goods directly from Kabul, Faizabad, or other towns. There is one other poorer Wakhi who also maintains a shop in the same village. Other rich Wakhi are believed to convert their cash from livestock into gold and silver coins as an insurance for the future.

The Kirghiz entrepreneurial group is once again headed and encouraged by the richest herd owner-manager, the Kirghiz khan. For the Kirghiz the political significance of this new trade development is as important as the economic gains from it. The khan and his eldest son alternately make the annual trip to Kabul to sell their sheep and to meet old acquaintances and concerned government officials. It is also in part a ritual or reassurance of support and help by the government and an expression of allegiance by the Kirghiz to the central government.

The khan and other Kirghiz who take animals to Kabul also bring back a truckload of goods. Most of these goods are necessities for their own household use, but some of the smaller herders buy goods for local trading. The Kirghiz, like the Wakhi, have also converted large sums of cash into precious metals, but the khan and his only surviving father-in-law, the second richest Kirghiz, have taken a new step. Both men have bought shares worth 500,000 Afs. in a trading company in Badakhshan province. The company is owned and operated by a number of wealthy individuals, mostly from Faizabad and its neighboring towns. It is the largest in the region and exports regional commodities abroad as well as importing goods. This investment is only about four years old now, and it may open up the way for further and more profitable enterprises.

KIRGHIZ AND THE LOCAL AND NATIONAL GOVERNMENT

The relationship between the Kirghiz and the central authority has been minimal, and for the most part the Kirghiz have dealt directly with Kabul rather than going through normal administrative channels. The three basic matters that require a great deal of interaction between the local government authorities and the public in Afghanistan are: (1) collection of taxes; (2) compulsory military conscription; and (3) resolution of conflicts and legal and jural disputes. The Kirghiz paid livestock taxes until the abolition of the livestock tax laws by the Afghan parliament in 1966 (see Fry 1974,

p. 155). The Kirghiz are exempt from military duty. The exemption was apparently granted to them during the 1921 visit to the Pamirs of General M. Nadir Khan, then minister of defense of Afghanistan. The reason for the exemption was that the Kirghiz are the guardians and keepers of the Pamirs' frontier by reason of their occupation of the area.

As indicated earlier, all local disputes between the Kirghiz themselves, or with the Wakhi and outside traders, are resolved and adjudicated within the Pamirs by the khan and the Kirghiz elders. This is done for two reasons: (a) such settlements are both expedient and effective since the parties do not have to travel to the district center and back; and (b) people avoid contact with the local officials, who are known to exploit both parties. The only occasions that call for nominal interaction between the Kirghiz and local government authorities are those concerning border violations by individual Kirghiz. That is, the khan is expected to report to the Afghan frontier authorities any crossing of the borders to the neighboring countries by either Kirghiz or any others. During this research I was told of some ten cases of such violations by Kirghiz who had, in the past, entered Soviet territory for reasons ranging from feuds and fights between individuals to temporary lack of food, general frustration, and, in some cases, hope of receiving medical treatment. Only those persons returned by Soviet authorities have to pay the penalty and state their reasons, if any, for their actions. In general, therefore, the Kirghiz public and the local authorities have very little or no contact at all.

During continued drought, widespread poor pasture conditions, or repeated devastating blizzards causing heavy losses of livestock, the Kirghiz have asked for help directly from Kabul. Such petitions are generally filed with the authorities in Kabul by the khan, his eldest son, or those who go to Kabul annually. Orders issued by the central government for economic help are then carried out by the local authorities. At least in two instances the Kirghiz have received such help. Once during the 1960s when snow and persistent blizzards caused heavy animal losses throughout the Pamirs, the Kirghiz were given a large amount of cash to buy animals to replenish their stock. Again, in 1971-72, during the drought, the Afghan government officially requested the Soviet Union to provide the Afghan Kirghiz with food and clothing. At that time the Kirghiz khan was authorized to accompany some Afghan authorities to Soviet territory to accompany the Russian aid trucks bringing goods to them. In addition to this, until a year ago the Kirghiz were provided with food and lodging by the Ministry of Frontier Affairs during their visits to Kabul.

The cordial nature of the Kirghiz relationship with the central authorities in Kabul, as a result of recent trading missions to Kabul and the maintenance of regular contact with the authorities, especially by the Kirghiz khan, has further enhanced Kirghiz local interests. In other words, the khan's personal acquaintance with some of the high officials in Kabul has at times enabled him to exercise some influence over the provincial and local authorities. Of course, his personal wealth, prestige, deep concern for the preservation of the Kirghiz way of life, and skills as a local leader, have also been responsible for the development of good relations with government authorities at all levels. Locally, a major consequence of this has been not only the economic but also the political superiority of the Kirghiz over their neighboring Wakhi. This is particularly evidenced by the Kirghiz's gradual encroachment on Sarhad during the winter to set up camp. This area was traditionally claimed by the Wakhi as their pasturage, but they are not able to use much of it because of their lack of access to animals or distance from their villages. The Kirghiz have moved into the area in small numbers since 1970, during which time they have had one major confrontation with the Wakhi. The issue is yet to be resolved between them. The Kirghiz in the meantime are using the pasturage and the matter has not been referred to the government authorities by either side.

At the present, therefore, the Kirghiz political organization, which has evolved in response to local ecological and socioeconomic processes over the past three decades, has been in turn strengthened through the Kirghiz economic and political relationship with the Afghan society at large. It is indeed the dialectical processes between the local, regional, and national socioeconomic and political systems that have provided the basis for the development of a pastoral nomadic involution in Kirghiz society under the closed frontier conditions. There is no doubt its continuation depends as much on the socioeconomic and political environment outside the Pamirs as the ecological constraints of the high-altitude environment in the Pamirs.

The Kirghiz have not been as successful in coping with the deprivations resulting from the severance of their cultural and educational ties with their traditional centers of learning in Chinese and Russian Turkistan. There has been a gradual disappearance over the past three decades of skilled artisans and well-trained religious and ritual specialists (mullah and *bakhshi*) in Kirghiz society. Most of the tallented, skilled, and respected craftsmen and religious functionaries who were trained prior to the closure of the borders have either died or are nearing old age. Opportunities for training young Kirghiz locally have been very limited because of their pastoral nomadic lives and the Kirghiz have remained reluctant to send their young men to Badakhshan and other parts of Afghanistan to receive the necessary training. This lack of interest and hesitation are generally attributed to fear of lowland "heat" and the linguistic, cultural, and ethnic differences between the Kirghiz, the neighboring Wakhi, and the distant towns and cities of northern Afghanistan (see Shahrani 1978). By the same token, no mullah or craftsmen from the lowlands have come to the Pamirs to perform these services for the Kirghiz.

At present, the Kirghiz are faced with an acute shortage of both craftsmen and mullah. During this research, there were only four mullah with adequate training in the Little Pamir, three of whom were over seventy years of age, and the fourth, the khan, is in his mid-sixties. In the Great Pamir there were three individuals with sufficient religious training, including one *mowlawi* (someone who has completed the highest level of religious education), but the *mowlawi* died in the spring of 1974. The number of accomplished blacksmiths, gold- and silversmiths has decreased to only two, both of whom are over sixty years of age and nearly blind. A few younger men with a little religious education, or training in smithing, shoemaking, and woodcarving (yurt making), are, however, present and they satisfy the local needs for such services.

Training and education of the Kirghiz youth in general and the provision of basic religious education is a major concern of the Kirghiz elders. The khan is especially troubled by the prospect of the future Kirghiz generations not having any access to Islamic education, thus "losing their faith." He has been particularly active in teaching Islam to a small number of young Kirghiz, including his own sons, as well as instructing them in reading and writing in Persian and Turkic languages and basic arithmetic. His effort in this direction has been restricted only by the limits of his own knowledge and lack of educational resources. He has encouraged two of his sons to pursue their artistic interests, one in painting and the other in woodcarving and sculpting. They have developed great skill in their work, and recently have received much support and appreciation from both the artistic community in Kabul and government authorities. They held their first art exhibition in Kabul in the winter of 1973 and since then have had at least two other such opportunities during the winter visits they make to the capital.

The khan and other Kirghiz elders have repeatedly requested the government to provide them with schools. The authorities finally decided to open a school in the Little Pamir in 1974. A teacher was assigned to the job during the summer of 1974 but he found living in the high altitude of the Pamirs too difficult and returned to Wakhan after only a short stay, putting an end to the first attempt on the part of the Afghan government to provide the Kirghiz children with some form of basic education. The Kirghiz deprivation of opportunity for education, as well as their reluctance to directly participate in the learning institutions in other parts of the country, persists.

Above, Tajik trader selling trinkets in a Kirghiz winter camp; *below,* trader leaving with skins obtained in exchange for the trinkets.

Haji Rahman Qul

Mowlawi Murad

9. Conclusion

THE BASIC ASSUMPTION of the preceding analysis is that the present location of the Kirghiz and Wakhi communities and their particular adaptive strategies are strongly influenced not only by their responses to the constraints of high altitude, but also by their relationships with other societies in the context of larger regional, national, and international politico-historical processes. The habitat of a community is treated as an historical given in most ethnographic studies—distribution of different groups is often explained in reference to their particular adaptation and ability to exploit an environmental niche as one part of a larger regional complementary economic effort. There is a certain validity in this proposition although such an assumption often implies that different interdependent groups in a region had a free hand in choosing their habitat. In this work is is made clear that the initial occupation and continued habitation of the Wakhan and the Afghan Pamirs by the Wakhi and the Kirghiz are not the result of a free and unrestricted choice but the result of long and protracted competition among many different interest groups in the region for control of strategic resources.

The size, nature, and composition of the contending parties have differed considerably through time, ranging from centralized political entities of various magnitudes to the local and regional groups based on differing linguistic, religious-sectarian, and tribal-kinship allegiances. The place members of a group occupy in the

changing mosaic of populations in any culturally heterogeneous
environment is strongly influenced by at least two factors: first,
the groups' relative power vis à vis other such entities in the field
at any given time; and secondly, the location of exploitable resources in the relevant area at a given time.

The Wakhan Corridor and the Afghan Pamirs have always been
areas of marginal ecological resources. The Pamirs have high pasture land, suitable only for grazing. The Wakhan and upper Amu
Darya valleys are peripheral, high-altitude areas with a limited potential for both irrigation agriculture and livestock breeding. Both
zones are characterized by severe climate, cold, inadequate oxygen,
and by meager and often unreliable food sources. In addition to
the paucity of resources, two other factors have dominated the
sociopolitical and demographic realities in this area: the geographical
location and the imposing topographic character of the Pamirs that
separate the major agricultural societies of China and Chinese Turkistan to the east from Russian and Afghan Turkistan, India, southwestern Asia, and beyond to the south and west; and the strategic
role this area has played over the centuries as a major highway of
trade, communication, and cultural exchange between these two
regions.

The development of events in this inaccessible and ecologically marginal region has been, therefore, continuously influenced
by neighboring "primary societies formed within the primary environments" (Lattimore 1951, p. 249). Because of internal growth
and expansion of the adjacent primary societies these mountainous
areas have at various times become distant and insignificant frontier
zones of different empires and states. Consequently, politically
weak and numerically insignificant populations have been forced
to retreat into this harsh environment, forming "marginal, secondary societies" (ibid.).

This characterization is true of both the Kirghiz and the Wakhi.
The Wakhi are a small and distinct linguistic and cultural group
who are also adherents of an Ismaili sect of unorthodox Islam. As
a sectarian minority the Wakhi and most other Shi'a groups have
been historically subjected to continuing political pressures and
persecution in Western and Central Asia by the predominantly
Sunni majority, with whom they compete for political and economic resources. As a result the Wakhi, together with other Ismaili
groups (mainly Hazara, and the neighboring Shighni, Ishkashimi,
and Zebaki) are found to "occupy the most remote lands of the
Hindu Kush-Pamir mountain range between the centers of [polit-

ically and numerically dominant] Sunni and Imami influence" (Canfield 1973a, p. 115). This kind of population distribution, Canfield explains, "is due partly to the nature of the varied landscape itself, which provides shelter to the different interest groups, and partly to the sectarian nature of the Afghan state" (ibid.). State sectarianism in favor of Sunni populations, however, has not been limited to the modern nation state of Afghanistan. Indeed, such practices were common throughout most of Western and Central Asia for centuries. It should also be made clear that sectarian differences, while significant to the Wakhi in their regional context, have not been the only, or even the dominant, point of articulation for intergroup competition over resources and power. Sectarian difference, therefore, must be seen as only one of many factors responsible for the present mosaic of population distribution in Western and Central Asia.

The Kirghiz are one of the less numerous groups among major Turkic-speaking populations (i.e., Uzbek, Uyghur, Kazakh, Turkmen) of Central Asia (for population figures see Allworth 1971, pp. 282-83 and Chen 1977, pp. 366-72; Dupree 1973, p. 61). Historically, the Kirghiz have had to cope not only with the larger Turkic-speaking populations but also with powerful neighboring Mongol, Chinese, and Russian groups and/or states. During the sixteenth century they were forced by the Mongols to move southwestward from the Yenisei River region to present-day Soviet Kirghizia. In the seventeenth and eighteenth centuries they were under constant attack by the neighboring Djungar Oirat, also known as Kalmuck Tartars (a Western Mongol group), and had to leave the northern slopes of the Tien Shan. Crossing the mountains to the south they were confronted by the Uyghurs in the oasis of Kashgaria, and further to the west they were met by the Uzbeks in the Fergana valley region. Unable to win for themselves a more favorable niche in the fertile agricultural land, the Kirghiz began to occupy the high pastures of Kizil Su, Tekes, and Aqsu in the southern slopes of Tien Shan and the high valleys of Pamir and Karakoram east and northeast of the Wakhan and Fergana valleys (see Chen 1977, p. 118; also see Grousset 1970).

The Kirghiz, who began occupation of these marginal areas during the seventeenth and eighteenth centuries, were not able as a group to change the situation very much. Some of them engaged in mixed high-altitude irrigated agriculture and herding (similar to the present-day Wakhi) wherever possible, but most remained full-time, relatively long distance, vertical nomads until a few decades ago. There seems to have been a constant shift between agriculture and nomadism by isolated households as well as by small kinship groups among the Kirghiz in this general area. The degree of nomadic oscillation also varied from group to group as well as from one area to another. Influencing the degree of sedentarization and/or nomadization among the Kirghiz at all levels of social articulation were the internal power relationships among the various agnatic kinship groups within Kirghiz society. Power relationships between the Kirghiz and outside political authorities, both agriculture-based and nomadic chiefdoms and states, also influenced the Kirghiz choice between agriculture and nomadism.

Within the Kirghiz territory competition for agricultural land as well as better pasturage was rife among contending Kirghiz *oruq,* the agnatic kinship groups. The stronger and more powerful *oruq* that acquired access to agricultural land tended, therefore, to become sedentary agriculturalists with mixed herds; those who were able to appropriate favorable pastures did not have to oscillate over large areas. The weak *oruq,* on the other hand, in order to remain viable as a group, were forced to use the higher, marginal pastures, which involved greater mobility and hardship. This process was carried on only when no severe external political or military threat was directed toward the Kirghiz. On a few occasions when Turkic-speaking groups (mainly Uyghur in eastern Turkistan and Uzbeks in Afghan Turkistan) were able to control central political power, the Kirghiz seem to have enjoyed greater access to agricultural areas and better pasture lands. During such periods sedentarization of the Kirghiz seems to have increased and use of marginal high-altitude pastures reduced. Following the defeat of Turkic political authority by other groups, sedentary Kirghiz tended to return with their flocks to high pastures as full-time nomads to avoid the political and economic demands of alien authorities. As discussed earlier, during times of perceived danger from Chinese or Russian authorities the Kirghiz took refuge in the higher reaches of the Pamirs, even during the winter months, to avoid military and political confrontation. It was the realization of the gravity of the threat of Communist revolutions in the Soviet Union (1917) and the People's Republic of China (1949) that forced the small group of Kirghiz agriculturalists and pastoralists to take refuge once again in the high valleys of the Afghan Pamirs only a few decades ago.

The data on the dynamics of changing environmental conditions (including those sociopolitical and historical) and the relationships between the Kirghiz and other communities in this part of Central Asia, particularly during the Inner Asian and colonial periods of frontier history, seem to indicate a rather strong similarity to the dynamics of intergroup relationships in Western Asia and the Near East. However, this situation is quite different from the structural configuration of such processes further to the east and northeast (in China and the Inner Asian steppes) during the same periods, as discussed by Owen Lattimore (1951, 1962b). The differences in the articulation of the interaction among human populations in the two areas are the function of the environment and the consequent adaptation of contending societies. For example, Chinese irrigation agriculturalists confronted the Turko-Mongol nomads of the steppes to their north, and to avoid conflict the Chinese chose to limit their own expansion by building the Great Wall to separate themselves from the non-Chinese nomads (see Lattimore 1962b, pp. 477-78).

The mosaic nature of the distribution of exploitable natural resources in the Near East and Western and Central Asia, on the other hand, has simultaneously accommodated the development of agriculture, nomadism, trade, and exchange as specialized modes of subsistence throughout the region. Unlike the Chinese and Inner Asian situation *no* complete or clear-cut economic specialization based on ethnicity is present in the Near East and Western and Central Asia. Instead, one finds members of ethnic and cultural groups engaged (to varying degrees) in many different forms of subsistence strategies to complement economic activities. Consequently, peoples with diverse linguistic, religious, sectarian, and cultural backgrounds are involved in the exploitation of the same or similar ecological resources. This condition has been necessarily conducive to competition over control of strategic resources, and the lines of cleavage between contending groups have been generally based on ethnic and cultural affinities and rarely, if ever, solely based on the dichotomy of economic modes of adaptation—that is, the pastoral versus the agricultural and urban societies. In the Middle East and Western and Central Asia, therefore, competing factions organized on the basis of ethnic differences have often consisted of nomads and agriculturalists as well as urban elements on both sides. As a corollary it should be stated that the dynamic force in the social and political history of Western and Central Asia and the Near East has been the presence of diverse ethnic populations which have constantly competed with one another for access to important economic and political resources. In this respect, the traditionally assumed confrontations between nomads and agriculturalists (or agriculturally based central political authority) may not have been as significant as we are often led to believe.

This, however, in no way invalidates the significant role nomadic pastoralists have played as a political force in the historical processes within the context of ethnic and cultural confrontations in the region. It was observed that the Kirghiz hostility or allegiance toward neighboring sedentary groups and agrarian-based central authorities has always been influenced by the degree of their linguistic, sectarian, and cultural affinities, and *not* by their mode of ecological adaptation alone. Similarly, throughout the Near East and Western and Central Asia where, prior to the closed frontiers, when the military strength of regional and central governments was not substantially greater than that of their internal rivals, the magnitude of hostility or cooperation by a pastoral nomadic group toward the central authority was determined by the degree of perceived ethnic and cultural differences between the two groups (e.g., concerning the Pashtun nomads of Afghanistan see Tapper 1973 and Ferdinand 1962; on the Yomut Turkmen of Iran see Irons 1969, 1974, 1975, and Napier 1874; and other groups in the Near East and Western Asia see Nelson 1973).

It is indeed within the context of ethnic group conflicts that the significance of nomadism as a political adaptation comes to full realization. This is particularly true considering that armed conflict in this area has often resulted historically in the destruction and devastation of less powerful groups. Pastoral nomadism has thus served as a means of political and cultural viability for some groups militarily and numerically less strong.

The information presented in this study on the Kirghiz and, I believe, other data from Inner Asia (Lattimore 1962b, 1951) and some recent anthropological studies on the Near East and Western Asia and Africa (Dyson-Hudson 1972; Irons 1974, 1975; Gulick 1976; Bates 1973; Gellner in Nelson 1973) confirm the view that pastoral nomadism is not only a form of economic adaptation in marginal, isolated areas, but also a kind of political-ecological adaptation as well. This is best illustrated by a nineteenth-century account of the Yomut Turkmen, a reportedly belligerent group, who "never attack superior numbers, never attack twice, and never meet the resolute attack of an enemy" (Napier

1874, p. 5). Irons, in a recent ethnography of the Yomut, confirms that among the Yomut retreat and withdrawal (but never surrender) was the norm in cases where the threat of defeat seemed certain (1974, pp. 647-49; also 1969, pp. 33-35).

This example of a nomadic group that is on the defensive contradicts the commonly held belief that nomads have always constituted a militarily strong body capable not only of withstanding attack, but also of imposing their will upon sedentary societies. The example, I believe, is not unique, for there are several cases of Near Eastern and Western and Central Asian nomads who have been described variously as "enclosed nomads" (Rowton 1973) and "encapsulated nomads" (Fazel in Nelson 1973). These comparatively small, ethnically diverse, and spatially dispersed groups could not pose any real threat to sedentary communities.

Viewing mobility as a political strategy in pastoral nomadic adaptations helps to clarify another misconception about change in adaptive strategies. It is generally assumed that the direction of movement of populations is always from nomadism to agricultural or urban life, that the sedentarization of nomads is the only evolutionary course. This sedentarization is further believed to occur among very rich and very poor households. Contrary to these assumptions, it is found in this study that the direction of neither demographic nor economic change in Kirghiz pastoralist society has been toward agriculture, despite radical economic polarity among Kirghiz households. Data on the Wakhi and Kirghiz presented here, as well as data on the Yomut Turkmen (Irons 1969, 1974, 1975; Napier 1874, 1876), Tibetan groups (Ekvall 1968; Ekvall and Downs 1965, Downs 1964), and Inner Asian communities (Lattimore 1950, 1951, 1962b) clearly suggest that both nomadization of agriculturalists and sedentarization of nomads has always occurred in these areas for both economic and political reasons. Exploitation of marginal environments through nomadism as a part of a complex land-use system has made possible the continued survival and viability of politically weak and threatened ethnic groups. The peripheral territories therefore have allowed historically the movement of populations from one economically specialized sector of society to the other in times of excessive demographic, economic, or political pressures (see Bates and Lees 1977). Nomadization of agriculturalists has been as much a part of the Near Eastern, Southwestern, and Central Asian socioeconomic and demographic history as the sedentarization of nomads.

The closed frontiers and the growing military might of the national central governments committed to forging unified nation-states have altered conditions dramatically. Under these conditions, mobility as a means for group survival has a diminished value mainly because there are no real places of refuge left. Closed borders not only bar access to economic resources and opportunities but also affect interethnic relations and the cultural identity of individuals and groups. This is so partly because all groups, traditionally strong or weak, have been brought to some degree under the direct rule of the politically dominant ethnic group(s) who are generally supported by outside (international) forces in the name of regional political stability, and so forth. Yet the structure of sociopolitical and demographic dynamics in Southwestern and Central Asia is not radically changed. The rivalry for control over resources still continues along agnatic kinship, tribal, and ethnic lines; what has changed are the mechanisms of struggle.

The constraints that have influenced the nature and the direction of change and provided the impetus for the adaptation in Wakhi and Kirghiz societies to the closed frontiers have differed both in magnitude and, to some degree, in kind. The Wakhi agricultural and herding populations were forced to move into their present high-altitude marginal habitat at least several centuries ago. In the safety of their mountainous frontier the Wakhi developed an irrigated mixed-crop agriculture and herding subsistence economy that provided them with near self-sufficiency. Internally, Wakhi society was organized on agnatic descent principles that divided the population into six ranked kinship categories, each with certain rights and responsibilities toward one another. Access to strategic economic resources and political privileges was also directly related to the kinship ideology of the separate and distinct ancestry of the membership of the six ranked groups. As such, Wakhi society had a feudal-like structure where the lineage of Wakhi Mirs, or chieftains, exercised considerable local authority and often were able to maintain near-autonomy despite the strengths of neighboring states. The Mirs also controlled that part of the strategic Silk Road trade that crossed their territory and provided them with a large share of their revenue.

Two of the principal constraints imposed by the closure of the Soviet Union and Chinese frontiers upon the Wakhi were the termination of caravan trade through the area to and from Chinese Turkistan, northern Afghanistan, and the Indian subcontinent, and the severance of socioeconomic relations with the other Wakhi communities on the left bank of the Amu Darya. No caravans meant the loss of earnings for their services to the traders, which, for the average Wakhi, may have been negligible. The disruption and anxiety resulting from the loss of relations with the other Wakhi across the Amu was probably quite severe, though not easily measurable. The impact of the concomitant increased political and economic influence of the national government of Afghanistan, as well as that of the larger Afghan society upon the Wakhi, however, is discernible.

One of the consequences of the closed frontiers was the flight of the Wakhi Mirs, together with some members of their lineage, to northern Pakistan. Afghan authorities also relocated some other members of the lineage in other areas of Afghanistan in the 1940s. These two occurrences account for the small number of descendants of the Mirs in the Wakhan and the consequent emergence of the Sayyed group as the theocratic leaders of Wakhi society. Perhaps the most profound change is that the formerly almost self-sufficient Wakhi have become increasingly dependent for their needs upon the pastoral Kirghiz and the "invading" national market economy mediated by Pashtun, Tajik, and Uzbek traders from other parts of Afghanistan. The phenomenon may be characterized as exploitation of the Wakhi by outside traders with the tacit approval and sometimes cooperation of local government officials, rather than one of the traditionally described symbiosis between the center and the periphery. Its consequences are increased wheat cash cropping, despite the low yield of wheat, and the substantial loss of Wakhi economic resources to the opium and tea traders. For the Wakhi household it has meant increased poverty accompanied by increased potential for domestic turmoil. A few impoverished households have become nomadic, joining the rich Kirghiz herd owners in the Pamirs as shepherds and servants. The continuing presence of traders and government agents was assured in 1970 by the construction of a mosque in Khandud, the center of Wakhan *woluswadi*. Most traders and some officials speak about it as the triumph of true Islam—Sunni orthodoxy—in Shi'a Wakhan.

The closed frontiers have imposed two major constraints on the Kirghiz to which they have had to respond: the physical constraints of loss of pasturage and self-imposed, but externally induced, confinement to the Pamirs of Afghanistan; and the socioeconomic and cultural restrictions that ensued after the abrupt severance of former social, economic, and cultural ties with the societies of Turkic Central Asia.

The Kirghiz response to the constraints has not been one of radical social and cultural change. Instead, it has been cumulative, which I call a disjunctive structural change without accompanying culture change—or pastoral nomadic involution. This particular kind of social change has been achieved through structural refinement, complication, and specialization within the traditional Kirghiz social and ecological adaptive system. The aim has been to retain a nomadic mode of subsistence in a high-altitude, isolated, and closed-frontier environment (also see Shahrani 1978).

The chronic stress of hypoxia, cold, unpredictable climate, and meager pasturage, characteristic of the permanent high-altitude habitat of the Kirghiz, have had a significant effect upon the composition, size, and viability of Kirghiz herds. The Kirghiz have remained generalized herders with a variety of livestock, each with different degrees of adaptability to the new environment and of varying significance to the economy and survival of Kirghiz society. The ratio of different livestock in the Kirghiz herds is determined by the adaptation of each type of animal to the local ecology, the relative importance of its contribution to Kirghiz subsistence, and the outside market demands for it. The gradual increase in number of sheep and yak and decrease in the number of camels and horses in Kirghiz herds is the result of the new circumstances.

The loss of pasturage and the confinement to the high-altitude valleys has had a further effect upon the Kirghiz regime. Denied access to pastures in lower altitudes, the Kirghiz have been unable to continue their traditional extensive pasture use and vertical migration pattern. Their new habitat lay above the altitude of agricultural production, and the number of Kirghiz who took refuge in the area is much larger than the number who formerly used it for temporary year-round or summer pasturage. For efficient and effective exploitation of these high pastures, therefore, the Kirghiz have introduced and developed a number of important interrelated measures: adoption of a highly regulated system of intensive pasture use that has replaced their traditional extensive system of grazing; introduction of short-distance pendular seasonal oscillation; claims to private ownership of pastures and camping sites by individual families and small agnatic groups (right of use and disposal through sale, etc.); and, finally, attempts to improve poor pastures through capital investment in irrigation networks, and production of a certain amount of winter fodder where possible.

The establishment of these new measures and the demands of high-altitude pastoral economy have had a crucial impact on the structural dynamics of the Kirghiz *oey* and the *qorow*, the basic herd management unit, and on the articulation of the socioeconomic and political organization of Kirghiz society. The territory and encampment sites of the *oey* for example, have become almost fixed in time and space—from season to season and year to year. Similarly, the membership of the *qorow* does not alter much from one year to the next and is generally small and dispersed, particularly during the long winter months. The rather fixed nature of Kirghiz seasonal and annual nomadic patterns is now governed by a simple principle that has its justification in the climatic realities of high altitudes: use whatever pasture is available now, wherever it may be, if it will not be available later. This, of course, contrasts with other Near Eastern and Southwestern and Central Asian low-altitude desert and steppe nomads' attitude of seeking and using the best available pastures at any given time.

These new range-management practices and the increased demand upon the Kirghiz to pay for their nonpastoral needs with animals and animal products has produced a marked increase in the overall livestock population in the Pamirs. The initial inequalities in herd ownership and uneven effects of the erratic climate in the Pamirs, together with the differential access to quality pastures have resulted in an unequal distribution of herds among Kirghiz *oeylar*. Wealth in herds and other tangible goods has, therefore, become increasingly concentrated in the hands of a small number of *oeylar,* leaving a very large number without productive capital of their own. Such a concentration of wealth in turn has lead to the development of new, or the elaboration of traditional, systems of herd management between the large herd owner-managers and the poor herders. The new herd-management systems include the use of shepherds hired by the rich herd owner-managers, and the farming out of livestock under *saghun* and *amanat* arrangements. The distribution of herds through either *saghun* and/or *amanat* is based on the herding capability and competence of the herdless *oey* units, as determined by herd owner-managers, and mediated by the principles of Kirghiz segmentary agnatic lineage structure in conjunction with considerations of certain Islamic religious ideology. These same principles also serve as a normative framework for the jural, legal, and property rights both of individuals and of kinship and contractual (friendship and economic clientship) groups in Kirghiz society.

Saghun and *amanat,* which are based mainly on kinship and traditional community obligation of the rich toward the poor, combined with a great deal of economic and political self-interest on the part of a small number of rich Kirghiz herd owner-managers, have ensured the access of poor herdless *oeylar* in the community to the herds and animal products necessary to their subsistence. These arrangements not only constitute efficient management of herds but are also largely responsible for maintaining both the very rich and the very poor Kirghiz in the Pamirs. Ultimately, they are the basis of the viability of their pastoral nomadic subsistence strategy under the present conditions.

The Kirghiz herd-management system suggests two very important points about pastoral production: first, access to herds and the use of their products by each *oey* seems to be the crucial factor of viability rather than simply the ownership (right of disposal of the animals as well as their products as a precondition) of herds themselves; secondly, when the emphasis is put on access to rather than ownership of herds by nomadic households, it is apparent that the real unit of production in pastoral modes of adaptation is the "tribe" or "community" as a whole and not the individual herder.

The development of radical differences in the right of ownership over pastoral capital in the Pamirs has resulted in the emergence of an economic and political stratification that was previously unknown among the Kirghiz. The traditional, somewhat egalitarian, and rather loosely structured Kirghiz political organization, governed by the principles of an agnatic segmentary lineage system, has gradually given way to an increasingly more centralized and mildly authoritarian and feudal-like structure in which the nonhereditary khan plays a prominent role. All of these changes in Kirghiz society, including stratification, however, have been conditioned by the political and economic developments in the wider Afghan society.

A major impetus, for example, for the remarkable increase in the size of Kirghiz herds, especially in the number of sheep, is the growing demand for meat and animal products in the urban markets of Afghanistan. Traditionally, "ecological" studies stress interdependent (parasitic or symbiotic) relationships between men, animals, and the physical environment as a self-regulating feedback system in pastoral modes of production, but for the most part appear to have ignored the role of the external political and economic factors as another variable in the dynamics of pastoral ecological adaptations. Robert Paine, in an article on "Herd Management of Lapp Reindeer Pastoralists" (1972, pp. 76-87), discusses the interdependent relationship between herd, personnel, and pasture, "the principal factors of production" (ibid., p. 76), and acknowledges the significance of "such independent variables as external political regulation of pastoral relations" (p. 78), but he leaves consideration of it for separate treatment. Fortunately, however, at least two recent studies of nomadic societies have addressed the issue more fully. Daniel Bates, in writing of the Yörük of southeastern Turkey, for example, sees a direct link between the increased cash requirement for grazing fees paid by the nomads to the farmers (a practice externally imposed) and the increased size of Yörük herds (1973, p. 224). Also Donald Cole found that the Al Murrah Bedouins of the Empty Quarter, as well as other Bedouins in Saudi Arabia, are changing from the traditional herding of camels for subsistence to raising sheep and goats, in response to the demand for mutton by the prospering urban populations of Saudi Arabia (1975, pp. 158-63). There is little doubt that the number and type of animals in nomadic herds reflect not only the demographic and environmental constraints but also the constraints and incentives imposed by the larger social context upon the nomadic groups. Therefore I believe that the Kirghiz data, together with those of the Yörük and Al Murrah and other Bedouins in Saudi Arabia, strongly suggest that the major regulators of the nomadic production strategy are composed of not *three* but *four* interdependent variables: man (herder); animals (herds); physical environment (pasture and water); and *the outside economic and politicohistorical constraints and incentives.*

Indeed, the development, maintenance, and perpetuation of the adaptation system achieved by the Kirghiz has been possible through indirect (traders) and recently initiated direct participation in the regional and national economy and polity of Afghanistan. The Kirghiz response to the severance of socioeconomic and cultural ties with Chinese and Russian Turkistan has been generally a slow and cautious reorientation toward northern Afghanistan. The Kirghiz have come into close contact with the neighboring Wakhi, this purely economic relationship beginning with Kirghiz dependence upon the Wakhi for their agricultural needs. However, it soon evolved into a relationship of economic interdependence, and even the complete dependence of some Wakhi upon the Kirghiz economy, mediated by a new group of entrepreneuring traders from the towns and villages of Badakhshan, and from Kabul and Jalalabad in eastern Afghanistan. This highly complex, triadic system of trade and exchange between the Kirghiz and Wakhi and the Pashtun, Tajik, and Uzbek traders could not have developed without the increasing demand for meat and animal products in the cities and towns of Afghanistan. Through this network of trade the Kirghiz obtain market and agricultural goods, for a sizable price, but with only a limited direct participation in larger Afghan society. Kirghiz and Wakhi interaction, while intensified over time, has nevertheless remained purely economic and always restrained because of their mutual feelings of contempt, based mainly on their different religious-sectarian allegiances.

A few wealthy Kirghiz herd owner-managers who began themselves to take their herds directly to the Kabul market were able to establish contact and eventually develop a close personal relationship with some high-ranking government officials in Kabul and in the province of Badakhshan. Official Kirghiz relationships with government authorities are handled through the Kirghiz khan, an early political and economic entrepreneur, often at the higher level of government bureaucracy in the provincial center and Kabul rather than at the district level. Also, the position of the khan has been officially sanctioned under the new title of *qaryadar* (village headman), which has been integrated into the local Kirghiz political organization. The development of political relations between Kirghiz elders and the national government has further enhanced the processes of political and economic stratification that are still in the making.

The Kirghiz have achieved a measure of success in establishing new social, economic, and political relations with the larger society in Afghanistan, but they have not been able to find means of coping with the severance of their religious, educational, and cultural ties. They have remained reluctant to send their young men to other parts of Afghanistan for appropriate education and training, and specialists from lowland towns and cities have not offered their services. The acute shortage of religious, ritual, and traditional craft specialists is a major problem, and remains a subject of grave concern for at least some Kirghiz.

The Kirghiz social and cultural systems together with their subsistence strategy have shown a remarkable resilience in their response to the problems of territorial loss and confinement to high altitudes and the severance of social, economic, and cultural ties (i.e., a condition of social discontinuity). They have been able to retain a viable pastoral nomadic economy in the face of tremendous odds over the past several decades. The Kirghiz case further demonstrates that in the context of political developments in modern nation-states the direction of social change in a pastoral society need not be always toward an agricultural or urban way of life; the possibility of change within a pastoral regime exists and can provide a practical alternative.

One question still remains. How much of what has been described here concerning the Kirghiz involutionary adaptation is really the function of the particular conditions of high-altitude nomadism, and how much is a response to the closed frontiers? Comprehensive answers to this question must await further research on high-altitude nomadism and on how human communities, especially nomads, have responded to closed borders elsewhere. It is apparent, however, that both of these environmental factors have had a substantial part in the dynamics of Kirghiz and Wakhi systems of adaptation. Further, a better understanding of the place of nomadic communities within the complex multiethnic societies of modern nation-states is not possible unless greater attention is paid to the phenomenon of social peril and the response of retreat and refuge. We must also consider the magnitude and intensity of such threats, just as we are urged to pay attention to the severity and magnitude of different natural environmental threats in purely ecological studies (see Vayda and McCay 1975, p. 302).

Finally, it is clear from this study that the early settlement of the Wakhi agriculturalists and the recent flight of the Kirghiz nomads to the Wakhan Corridor and Pamirs of Afghanistan was induced by threats from outside. Their particular adaptations to the changing conditions are the outcome of multilateral interactions involving local environmental, national, and international forces over the past decades. There is no doubt that the continuation of the two societies and their cultural systems depends as much on the environment outside the Pamirs as on the ecological constraints of the Wakhan and the Pamirs.*

---

*Toward the end of 1978, following the change of government in Afghanistan, there were unconfirmed reports from *Tass* of a possible exodus of the Kirghiz from the Afghan Pamirs.

Epilogue: Coping with a Communist "Revolution," State Failure, and War

DURING THE SUMMER of 1975, while I was accompanying a British Granada Television crew to film a documentary on the Kirghiz of Afghanistan, an Afghan army officer and a soldier rode into the camp of Haji Rahman Qul, the Kirghiz Khan (chief). The officer produced a letter from the governor of Badakhshan province offering Kirghiz families the chance to receive recently reclaimed land at a location near the provincial capital, Faizabad, more than a week's journey (by horseback and truck) from the Pamirs. After discussing the matter with some of the Kirghiz elders, the Khan asked me to write a reply to the governor, thanking him for the generous offer, but saying that at the moment, no one was interested. Should any Kirghiz show interest in the future, the Khan's letter went on, he would notify the authorities promptly. The officer was sent off with the reply in hand and some personal gifts for his trouble.

This was not the first such offer that the Kirghiz had received from the Afghan government; they had been asked repeatedly to abandon the remote and inhospitable Pamirs. Villagers in central parts of the province of Badakhshan, where I grew up, wondered what kept the hardy Kirghiz herdsmen in that awesome land they referred to as *bami dunya,* "roof of the world." Some of the reasons why the Kirghiz preferred to stay in the high Pamir valleys have been discussed in the previous chapters at some length.

However, in April 1978, a military coup in Kabul installed a "revolutionary" regime in Afghanistan. In fact, this was the second such coup d'etat within the last five years. The first coup was staged in 1973, when Prince Muhammad Daoud toppled his cousin and brother-in-law King Muhammad Zahir Shah, abolished the monarchy, and pronounced himself the president of the Republic of Afghanistan (1973–78). The Kirghiz, like most other rural people in Afghanistan, viewed the change of regime in 1973 as a simple dynastic squabble over succession to the throne within the royal household. In 1978, it was President and Prince Muhammad Daoud who was killed. Most of his family members were also brutally murdered by the new coup makers, who were not related to Daoud by blood. This time the Kirghiz and countless others in Afghanistan were alarmed by the developments in the distant capital, Kabul.

Haji Rahman Qul was convinced that if the coup makers in Kabul were Communists, as he suspected them to be, his own and his family's safety would be in danger. He sent his eldest son, Abdul Wakeel, to the provincial capital of Badakhshan, Faizabad, to ascertain the true character of the political change in Kabul. After staying about ten days in Faizabad, Abdul Wakeel returned convinced, based on what he had seen and heard in the city, that the new regime in Kabul was indeed Communist and supported by the Soviet Union.

The Kirghiz, twice displaced and forced to take refuge in the mountain ramparts of the Afghan Pamirs following the Bolshevik and Chinese Communist revolutions, were faced once again with another Communist revolution, this time in Kabul. Haji Rahman Qul met with some of the Kirghiz elders and informed them of the news his son had brought from Faizabad. He also told them that he had to take his family to the safety of Pakistan, just south of the Pamirs. In order to do this, he asked his kinsmen to help him and his family to cross the mountains over to Pakistan. However, he advised the Kirghiz elders themselves and their families to remain in the Pamirs and keep the Khan's herds, as they might not be in any immediate danger from the new regime. He told them that because of his past opposition to Communism, the Russians regarded him as their personal enemy and would not leave him in peace. Recalling their earlier flights from Communist Russia and China, over 1,300 Kirghiz, members of some 280 families, chose to join the Khan in his flight to Pakistan territory over tortuous, high mountain terrain. Only about ten very poor and disgruntled Kirghiz households from the Little Pamir valley, numbering about fifty individuals, chose not to join the exodus with the Khan and stayed behind.

The Kirghiz of Afghanistan were, therefore, among the earliest refugees of the Communist coup in Kabul. The exodus from the Little Pamir valley was undertaken with utter secrecy, and in order not to alarm the watchful Soviet border guards, the Kirghiz left most of their yurts standing in their encampment as decoys. About five hundred Kirghiz living in the Great Pamir valley, separated from the Little Pamir valley by at least two days' travel over extremely difficult terrain, were not able to join the exodus. After a difficult journey through the high Hindu Kush-Karakoram mountains, the Kirghiz, together with their animals and household belongings, reached the Pakistani villages of Yasin and Eshkomen in early August 1978. They lost some of their animals while crossing glaciers and flooded streams. Some animals had to be eaten or sold to get provisions. After initially settling in scattered villages in northern Pakistan that lacked adequate pasture and fodder, the Kirghiz were forced to sell most of their remaining animals. The Khan and a few wealthier Kirghiz drove their herds to the Peshawar area and sold them to slaughterhouses; and a few of them, including the Khan's sons, opened a shop in Gilgit, where they sold cloth.

The heat and exposure to new diseases during their first summer in Pakistan took their toll on the Kirghiz, causing the death of more than one hundred people. To add to their problems, they were initially treated with suspicion by Pakistani officials, who curtailed their movements and subjected them to police surveillance. This treatment resulted from Pakistani uncertainty about the political leanings of the Kirghiz, about whom they knew absolutely nothing. Indeed, in May 1980, when Granada Television Limited, U.K., interviewed Haji Rahman Qul for the documentary film *Afghan Exodus,* Pakistani officials did not permit the Khan to speak in the Kirghiz language, since the Pakistanis could not monitor what he had to say. Therefore, the Khan had to speak in Tajik/Persian, which was apparently understood by the local Pakistani officials. Such security measures were deemed necessary because the Kirghiz had entered and settled in the politically sensitive Northern Areas of Pakistan. International refugee relief organizations were also prohibited from these areas, so the Kirghiz received only limited foreign assistance during their first couple of years of refugee life in Pakistan.[1]

1. For further details, see Shahrani 1980a.

Initially, the principal form of refugee assistance reaching the Kirghiz came from the Pakistani government: a daily cash allowance of four rupees (forty cents) per person. In addition, seventeen tents were distributed to the nearly 240 households. Cash allowances from the Pakistani government were not dispersed regularly; for at least seven months during the first two-and-a-half years of their refugee life, the Kirghiz received nothing. During the same period, the cash allowance of forty cents per person remained constant while the cost of essential goods rose dramatically. Unlike most other Afghan refugees in Pakistan, the Kirghiz received no food rations; they had to purchase all their food and buy clothing. Some basic foods, when available, were sold at subsidized prices by the Pakistani government. However, government prices, although relatively low compared to those of the bazaar, also rose precipitously. For example, from 1978 to 1980 the price of flour went up by 48 percent; tea, 60 percent; rice, 50 percent; and cooking oil, 38 percent. The refugees also had to buy cooking fuel, either firewood or kerosene. Forty kilograms of wood, not always available, sold for $2 in 1978 and $2.50 in 1980. There was more demand for kerosene, but by 1980, the price of a five-gallon kerosene drum had risen from $2.50 to $6. Bottled gas, although slightly less expensive, was not used because the initial investment of nearly $100 for a gas stove was prohibitive.

Since the Kirghiz had left most of their tents behind when they fled the high Pamirs, many families had to rent shelter in villages and towns. Rents for houses in Gilgit ranged from 100 to 1,000 Pakistani rupees ($10–100) per month. For single families, renting a house was impossible; three or more families usually rented a house together. As a result, while much of the meager cash allowance was spent on rent, living conditions were unusually crowded. Housing problems also resulted in the dispersal of families and relatives in different villages and towns within the Northern Areas of Pakistan, causing additional expenses for transportation and increased personal anxieties.

CHOOSING TO FLEE, NOT TO FIGHT

The Kirghiz collective decision, less than four months after the coup in Kabul, was to vote with their feet against the Communist regime and take refuge across the border in Pakistan. They literally were the first among more than five million citizens of Afghanistan who chose flight out of the country into neighboring Iran and Pakistan as the preferred alternative to fighting. Indeed, their exodus so soon after the establishment of a Communist government in Kabul, especially from such a remote and inaccessible part of the country, was clearly indicative of the seriousness of the emergent tensions between the new revolutionary Marxist state and the Muslim society in Afghanistan, which the state wished not only to govern, but also to transform.

The initial reports of the Kirghiz decision to leave the Pamirs came from *Izvestiya* (15 September 1978), under the sensational headline "The Bloody Path of the 'Independent Khan'" (Akhmedziyanov 1978), which was an important sign of Moscow's concern over the future course of events in Afghanistan. In this report, the Kirghiz leader, the "Independent Khan" Haji Rahman Qul, was depicted as a cruel, ruthless, and oppressive feudal lord, "fearing punishment for his [past] crimes" at the hands of the revolutionary and "progressive forces." The Soviet report also alleged that Rahman Qul was incited and armed by the "Peking envoys." The Khan had turned "bandit," launching anti-government activities before "ordering" his "fellow tribesmen to leave Afghanistan" (Akhmedziyanov 1978:J1). As popular opposition to the Russian puppet regimes in Kabul grew throughout the country in later months and years, these same arguments were presented in more elaborate form by Russian and Western experts sympathetic to the Kabul government (see Shahrani 1984a, 1984b).

The fact that the Kirghiz Khan and his tribesmen had left the Pamirs well in advance of any serious government actions threatening them puzzled me, especially in view of the fact that the regime was incapable of sending any kind of credible force against the Kirghiz in the distant Pamirs. Therefore, in my view, at least during the early months after the coup, there were no imminent government threats to Kirghiz welfare that could have justified the speedy exodus into Pakistan. The critical question then was, why? What motivated the Kirghiz Khan and his followers, as well as millions of other Afghans, to leave the safety and security of their homes for the uncertain future of refugee life in Pakistan?

With these questions in mind, and my concern about the plight of the Kirghiz as refugees in a radically different environmental and sociopolitical situation, I went to Gilgit during the summer of 1980. Gilgit is a town in the Northern Areas of Pakistan, the area closest to the Afghan Pamirs, where the Kirghiz Khan and his camp followers were living. Although the Kirghiz in Gilgit had been in Pakistan for nearly two years, compared with Afghan refugees near Peshawar and Quetta, they were offered little support from the government of Pakistan or the international agencies. They had suffered the loss of many members, mostly women and children, due to exposure to new illnesses, extreme heat, and unsanitary living conditions. Depressed, disillusioned, and frightened, some hundred and fifty of them had returned to the Pamirs in the late spring of 1980. Those continuing their refugee life in Gilgit were in desperate circumstances and required assistance.

The news of my arrival was apparently greeted with the expectation that I might have brought some form of tangible economic assistance for them.[2] Much to my own personal dismay, and so true to the anthropological tradition, the only tangible gift I was able to offer them was a copy of my then recently published first edition of this book, which detailed their former, happier lives in the Pamirs of Afghanistan—now, in retrospect, my salvage ethnography of the Kirghiz of Afghanistan. Under the circumstances, all I could promise to do was to prepare a written report about the seriousness of their situation and submit it to the office of the United Nations High Commission for Refugees (UNHCR) in Islamabad, Pakistan, urging it to assist the Kirghiz. This I fortunately was able to accomplish (Shahrani 1980b), which resulted in the establishment of a single official Afghan refugee camp, located on a riverbed near Gilgit. All the Kirghiz families lived together at the camp, and they were provided with appropriate economic, medical, and educational services for the remainder of their stay in Pakistan.

Although some United Nations refugee assistance began to reach the Kirghiz through the government of Pakistan, the frustration and disappointment of the Kirghiz grew because of their total dependence on charity. During my visit to Gilgit, many Kirghiz talked wistfully of their good life in the Pamirs, which was in the best of times not an easy one. They would say that Pamir was a "God given *na'mat* [blessing]," which they had not appreciated until it was taken from them; adding that no doubt because of their "thanklessness and countless misdeeds/sins," they were now paying by suffering as refugees in the heat of Pakistan.[3]

2. Earlier in the spring of 1980, two individuals, both of them Central Asian refugees from earlier Soviet and Chinese Communist occupation of Turkistan living in Turkey and Saudi Arabia, had distributed some cash among the Kirghiz refugees. The money was apparently collected from the Turkistani expatriate communities in Turkey and Saudi Arabia (see Shahrani 1980a).

3. In Muslim eschatology hell fire, thus heat, is considered one of the worst forms of punishment for sinners. The Kirghiz were implying that they were already receiving their punishment in life by becoming refugees in Pakistan.

An elderly Kirghiz put the nature of their losses and the sudden end of their pastoral way of life in the Pamirs in more concrete terms:

We Kirghiz did not really know how lucky we were in the Pamirs until we came to Pakistan. There we spent very little time tending our animals. Our herds naturally increased and gave us all the things we needed—milk, wool, meat, money and grains when sold or traded, fuel to cook our food, and a variety of other products. Here we find that money does not reproduce money unless you are a shopkeeper or something and know what you are doing.

The Soviet military invasion of Afghanistan in December 1979 convinced the Kirghiz that return to the Afghan Pamirs and resumption of their former lifestyle was an impossible dream. The eventual implosion and collapse of the Soviet empire a little over a decade later (1991) was difficult for them to even imagine. Therefore, the Kirghiz Khan, who was still able to provide a strong sense of community for the Kirghiz refugees in the Northern Areas of Pakistan, began to search for a new haven outside of Pakistan where they could rebuild a close approximation of their pastoral way of life. Indeed, during my visit, Haji Rahman Qul's hope was to be able to take his people to Alaska, and on April 7, 1980, he had applied to the United States Embassy in Pakistan for visas for his entire community.

IN SEARCH OF A PERMANENT HOME

By the time I arrived in Gilgit in late June 1980, the Kirghiz presence in Pakistan was known to some Western journalists, and a few brief reports about them were beginning to appear in the press. More significantly, a week before my arrival in Gilgit, a documentary film crew from Granada Television Limited, U.K., which had in 1975 produced an ethnographic film, *The Kirghiz of Afghanistan,* for their now well-known *Disappearing World* series, had visited the Kirghiz Khan in Gilgit and interviewed him for another documentary film called *Afghan Exodus,* which was released in Britain and Europe in late 1980. In 1981, the Public Broadcasting Associates (PBA) in Boston, the producers of the anthropological series *Odyssey* on PBS television, decided to buy the rights for *The Kirghiz of Afghanistan* (along with several other ethnographic films) from Granada Television Limited, U.K., with the intention of reediting and updating it with 1980 footage of the Kirghiz exile in Gilgit.

I was invited by PBA to participate in the reediting of the *Odyssey* version of the documentary, based on my earlier fieldwork among the Kirghiz. The film focused on the complex and intricate nature of Haji Rahman Qul's leadership role as the Kirghiz Khan. This new version of the film raised the prospects for the future permanent resettlement of the Kirghiz community outside Pakistan, possibly in the state of Alaska—a topic of immense interest to the Kirghiz during 1980 and 1981. This film was widely shown on American television and generated considerable media coverage and interest in the plight of the Kirghiz. Indeed, the film may have played a part in the eventual resettlement of the Kirghiz in the Van province of eastern Turkey in 1982.

My principal motive for going to Gilgit in the summer of 1980 was not to advocate on behalf of the Kirghiz (I had learned "real" anthropologists did not condone such involvements with native peoples!). Rather, I was there to conduct further anthropological research—that is, to explore the motivations behind the Kirghiz exodus so soon after the Communist coup and in the absence of any imminent danger to their well-being. This relatively brief period of research among the Kirghiz refugees opened entirely new vistas and concerns for my future research interests. It raised new questions about the purpose and relevance of anthropological knowledge and the responsibilities of the anthropological researcher in the field (see Shahrani 1994). Much to my surprise, the Kirghiz readily agreed that they had not faced an imminent threat to their safety from the central government in Kabul. They did, however, report Russian action against them across the border, but only during the last day of their flight from the Pamirs, after their intentions were discovered by the Soviets.

The Kirghiz decision to leave was, therefore, based entirely on their anticipation of future threats. Their anticipation was based on their recollections of the past, not just the evaluation of the immediate circumstances. They told me that once they had convincingly established for themselves that the new revolutionary regime in Kabul was Communist, they were absolutely certain of the future dangers both from the Kabul regime as well as from direct Russian military intervention in Afghanistan, a development they had correctly anticipated. Therefore, based on their considerable past experiences as victims of Communist revolutions, the fact that they were located in a small, distant frontier community adjacent to the Soviet and Chinese borders, and lacked the possibility of effectively defending themselves by means of a credible, sustained resistance, they simply sought to safeguard the future integrity of their community as Muslims by taking refuge in the neighboring Muslim state of Pakistan. In essence, the single most dominant motivating force for the Kirghiz exodus was said to be

Islam, that is, their desire to preserve the future continuity of their identity both as Muslims and Kirghiz. The centrality of Islam as the primary motivating force was consistent with their previous flights to Muslim Afghanistan in search of security from Soviet and Chinese Communist revolutions.

The suggestion that Islam was a cardinal motivating force for the Kirghiz was not new to me. They had mentioned it numerous times during my earlier research in the Pamirs in more peaceful and tranquil times, while discussing the events of the relatively remote past. The invocation of Islam by the Kirghiz before the crisis in Afghanistan, it seemed to me, was always used to explain past events or present circumstances and activities of members of the community. In Pakistan, under the uncertain conditions of refugee life, the invocation of Islam and Islamic religious and cultural symbols appeared to have gained a new focus, one intimately linked to the Kirghiz discourse about their future as a Muslim community. I soon realized that the phenomenon is equally pervasive among other Afghan communities, both those who sought refuge in Pakistan and Iran *(muhajireen)* as well as those who remained in Afghanistan and resisted *(mujahideen)*. Indeed, one of the most lasting impressions of my 1980 research among the Kirghiz in Gilgit, and later among other Afghan refugee communities in Pakistan, has been the overwhelming and forceful collective sense of loss (or the threat of impending loss) of personal, social, cultural, and national integrity as Muslims. The situation reflected the feelings of a people in a deep state of crisis, yet without the usual accompanying sense of despair or despondency about their future (see Shahrani 1996). Flight to a safe refuge or active armed resistance was, and still is, understandable not solely in terms of past memories or the assessment of the military and political realities of the Kirghiz. Rather, it is best explained in light of their powerful images of the future, both under Communism as well as in terms of the defeat of Communism and the establishment of an Islamic government.

As an anthropologist, a Muslim, and an Afghan, what impressed me most in studying the situation in Afghanistan was the appeal of Islamic ideas and cultural capital as a charismatic motivating force to believers. This motivating force not only helped shape and inform Muslims' social and political behavior (see Shahrani 1987), but also provided the vocabulary for charting the trajectory of their discourse on their future and political culture. My central research inquiries since 1980 have been, therefore, an attempt to understand the dialectics of the impact of Islam upon the social imagination of the Afghans concerning their future under the prolonged situation of societal crisis in the country (see references).

In this connection, I explored the impact of such images of the future upon the actions and activities of the Kirghiz and other Afghan communities. To the Kirghiz, and especially to their leader, Haji Rahman Qul Khan, contemplation about the future was not just an exercise in wishful thinking, devising a plan of action, or simply defining one's options. It was an intense moral act aimed at finding ways and means to ensure the future continuity and integrity of their Muslim and Kirghiz community. Based on their historical experiences of repeated victimization and spatial displacement by Communist revolutions during the twentieth century, the Kirghiz wished to move as far away as possible from Communist Russia and China in their search for a new homeland. They said that regardless of the outcome of Islamist resistance in the country, it would be unsafe for them to return to the Pamirs of Afghanistan—assuming at the time that the Soviet Union was there to stay forever. They imagined, therefore, that the United States would be the farthest away from their traditional enemies and thus the safest place for them to go. The idea of resettling in Alaska, however, was the result of encounters with an Alaskan zoologist, a staff member of the United Nations Wildlife Federation, who had spent time in the Pamirs in the early 1970s while setting up a Marco Polo sheep reserve for the government of Afghanistan. Undoubtedly, they had heard much from him about the cold climatic and ecological similarities between the Pamirs and Alaska.

As one who was living in the United States and as their concerned anthropologist, I was asked by the Khan to give advice and assistance towards their resettlement efforts. I tried in vain during the summer of 1980 to dissuade him and other Kirghiz elders from considering the United States as an option. I told them that the possibility of their admission as a community for resettlement anywhere in the United States seemed almost nil on the basis of U.S. immigration laws alone. Instead, I suggested that they consider resettlement in Turkey for historic, linguistic, cultural, religious, even ecological reasons, where their chances of admission would be much better. They told me that they wanted to go to the United States because I was there and I could help them. Besides, they argued, if the United States was good for me, then it could not be bad for them. So the Khan and other Kirghiz elders asked me to assist them in their efforts to relocate and settle in the United States.

Respecting their wishes, but strongly against my own better judgment, I worked with a number of interested individuals and

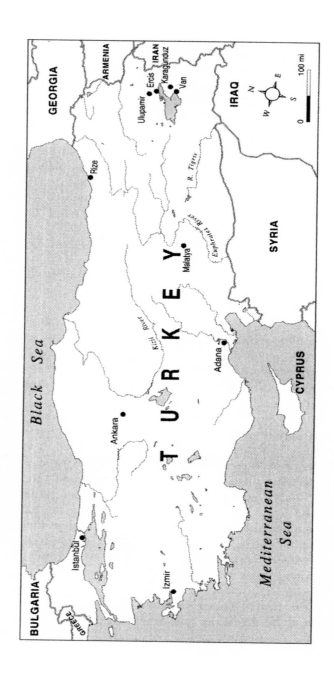

small organized groups, especially in Alaska, to promote the Kirghiz cause. It soon became clear to me that such an effort was doomed to failure. I kept the·Khan informed of the growing interest (by some people and the media) in their cause in the United States, especially following the airing of *The Kïrghiz of Afghanistan* documentary on public television (PBS) channels in the fall of 1981. But I also let him know that he should not expect any positive results in the near future, thus urging him to consider other alternatives. The plight of the Kirghiz, and their expressed wish to immigrate to the United States as a community, had received considerable worldwide media coverage, much of it as a result of the ceaseless and effective public relations efforts of the Kirghiz Khan himself.

RESETTLEMENT IN EASTERN TURKEY

Turkey, because of her historic, ethnolinguistic, and cultural ties to the peoples of Central Asia, has traditionally offered refuge to the Turkic peoples displaced by the Russian and Chinese Communist revolutions. The Kirghiz request for immigration to Turkey, however, received an especially favorable review when their plight was brought to the attention of General Kenan Evren, the president of Turkey, during his 1981 official visit to Pakistan. The Kirghiz community, along with nearly three thousand other Afghan refugees of Turkic origin (Uzbeks, Turkmen, and Kazak), were accepted for resettlement in Turkey. The arrangements for their transfer were made remarkably quickly. With help from the UNHCR, the Kirghiz were airlifted on August 3, 1982, to Adana, Turkey, and then taken by bus to temporary camps in eastern Turkey, thus ending their four difficult years as refugees in Pakistan.

The arrival of this small community of Turkic Central Asians in Anatolia may have marked the end of a significant historical process that began almost a thousand years ago—the westward migration of nomadic pastoral tribes from the Central Asian steppes to Anatolia. Yet, while the experiences of the Kirghiz community during this century demonstrate the continuity of this westward migration, they also exemplify the rapidly changing conditions in which nomadic pastoral societies continue their ardent, but generally failing struggle for cultural survival.

For lack of adequate residential facilities in a single location, the Kirghiz were temporarily settled in two separate areas. Some 202 families (776 individuals) were placed in the village of Karagunduz, in Van province, and 96 families (353 persons) in the village of Yeşiltepe, on the edge of the city of Malatya. The two groups were to be reunited after the construction of their permanent village in Altindere (Golden Valley), twenty-six kilometers west of the town of Erciş (pronounced Erjish), in Van province. The Kirghiz were promised that upon the completion of their new permanent settlement in Altindere, they would be given homes equipped with modern conveniences such as electricity, indoor plumbing, and hot water for each nuclear family. Each household was to be allotted fifty sheep and goats and three cattle to begin a new herding economy using the plentiful pastures of the surrounding hills. Like their temporary settlements, the new village would have public facilities such as a school, health clinic, telephone and postal service, a government-run store, police station, and a mosque.

In 1983, a year after their arrival in Turkey, when I spent the summer with them,[4] the Kirghiz spoke longingly of their good life in the Pamirs while carefully tending their small family gardens. Most of them, young and old, looked to their future in Turkey with feelings of certainty and expectancy. Since their arrival they had received monthly cash allowances of 4,000 Turkish lira (about $18) per adult, and half that for each child under eight years of age. They were also given food, clothing, medicine, household utensils, fuel, and other forms of assistance from a number of Turkish public and private charity organizations. All school-age children, some of whom had attended schools in Pakistan, were now going to an elementary school in the village, and seven of them had passed the necessary exams and been admitted to a middle school with boarding facilities in the city of Van, some forty kilometers from their village. About eighty adults, male and female, had already completed the first phase of an adult literacy program. A number of women had also completed courses in carpet weaving and embroidery sponsored by a private charitable organization, the Van and Environs Development Foundation. The same foundation had set up a kilim-weaving workshop with eight vertical looms, where some Kirghiz women were putting their traditional skills to use. Twenty young males had been trained to operate tractors and other farm equipment, and a number of them were hired for temporary work on state farms during the 1983 harvest.

Idleness, however, remained the principal source of frustration

4. My three months of field research in Turkey was made possible by the Social Science Research Council and a Pitzer College Faculty Research and Development award. Their generous support is gratefully acknowledged.

for many young Kirghiz, since they lived some forty kilometers from the nearest town, and work opportunities in the neighboring villages were almost nonexistent. A few youngsters hired themselves out as shepherds to the Turkish villagers, and the Kirghiz themselves were building small herds of their own. During the summer of 1983, the Kirghiz in Karagunduz village fielded a herd of about four hundred sheep and goats (1 percent of their 1972–74 total). As a result, the traditional Kirghiz practice of slaughtering animals for honored guests and communal feasts (at an average cost of $30 to $35) had become common again.

The five years of refugee experience had also produced some subtle but significant structural changes in the traditional forms and ideals of family organization, resulting in new sources of anxiety and tension. Specifically, the nuclear family and individual-centered allocation of refugee assistance, whether cash, food, clothing, tents, or houses, had effectively eroded the importance of the traditional ideals of patrilineal, extended family households. In the Pamirs, where it was considered the most desirable form, such cooperative family households accounted for about 20 percent of the domestic units. In 1983, not a single extended family existed, a trend that has persisted in Turkey during the past two decades. The proliferation of economically independent families of young married couples, which resulted from the egalitarian nature of the distribution of refugee assistance, has contributed to the rising tension, particularly among the members of previously wealthy extended households. The elders were, and continue to be, particularly disturbed by this and bitterly complain about the unreliability of their young sons as a means of support in their old age.

Another major source of community tension was directly related to the size and form of their new village life. The Kirghiz customarily were obliged to invite their close kinsmen and people from neighboring camps within a particular radius to attend weddings, funerals, and other public rituals. The number of people attending such events in the Pamirs varied from twenty people to a couple of hundred on rare occasions. Applying the same principle under the current situation meant entertaining the entire Kirghiz population, a virtually impossible task for a single family. Thus, commissions and omissions of individuals on such occasions had become a point of concern. The Kirghiz had, however, found an innovative, partial solution to this dilemma by coordinating several wedding celebrations simultaneously so that resources could be pooled to involve the entire community in such festivities, thereby avoiding any bad feelings. By the summer of 2001, during my most recent visit to their new permanent settlement, named Ulupamir Koyu (the Great Pamir Village), their numbers had reached two thousand people, but their problem of communal celebrations had been effectively addressed, as will be discussed later in this epilogue.

Considering the long and agonizing experiences of this small community over the last five years, the Kirghiz were in remarkably good shape and spirits. With the availability of better health care, decreased morbidity, and the continuation of strong pronatalist values, the Kirghiz had experienced a remarkable 4.2 percent annual demographic growth during the previous three years. That is, their actual numbers had grown from 1,040 in 1980 in Pakistan to 1,172 in 1983 in Turkey. This incredibly high birth rate has continued over the last twenty years of their resettlement in eastern Turkey.

Their arrival and resettlement in Turkey was widely covered by the Turkish media, and the Kirghiz enjoyed considerable public support, but not without occasional strong expressions of resentment towards them from the local Kurdish population. The placement of Kirghiz in the midst of a sea of Kurdish villagers in eastern Anatolia, although justified by the availability of state-owned pastureland in a cooler mountain setting, was perceived by the local Kurdish population to have been a highly political decision on the part of Turkish government. Living in relatively impoverished, arid parts of eastern Turkey, the Kurdish insurgency had many supporters in the area. Therefore, some local Kurdish hosts (especially low-ranking officials) resented the Turkish government's expenditure of state land and financial resources on the Afghan Kirghiz refugees, whom their local Kurdish hosts saw as a bunch of Turkic-speaking outsiders.

On the whole, however, the common Islamic, cultural, and linguistic heritage of the Kirghiz with that of their Turkish hosts had already proven an important asset within the first year of their arrival, a fact which enhanced their chances of future success immeasurably. The critical role of the Kirghiz Khan, Haji Rahman Qul Kutlu,[5] who in 1983 was referred to in the modern Turkish vernacular as Agha (chief), could not have been overestimated in the continual struggle of his community for survival. Through the strong will of this remarkable traditional tribal leader, the Kirghiz

5. Upon arrival in Turkey, all Kirghiz were given Turkish last names. Kutlu (meaning auspicious, lucky, fortunate, and happy) was assigned to the family of the Khan.

were able to preserve the integrity of their community, although in the process a way of life was vanishing forever.

EMERGENT PATTERNS OF ADAPTATION IN TURKEY

After being with the Kirghiz in Turkey in the summer of 1983, I returned three years later in the summer of 1986 to conduct further field research among the Afghan Kirghiz still living in their temporary camps in the village of Karagunduz, Van, and in the Yeşiltepe district, at the edge of the city of Malatya, a long day's bus ride west of Van. The single most important objective of this research project was to conduct a household demographic and economic survey of the Kirghiz community in order to obtain base data for the long-term study of the processes of their social, economic, and political adaptation in their new, and radically different, ecological and socioeconomic environment.[6] I completed a survey of all 301 household *oey* (ev) units (203 in Karagunduz and 98 in Malatya). The result of this survey data pointed to a number of important emergent trends in Kirghiz adaptation to sedentary refugee conditions.

First, a significant rise in the birthrate of children was continuing with a much-reduced rate of infant mortality, resulting in a rapid rate of population increase. Several Kirghiz women in their late thirties who had been married for more than a decade in the Pamirs and had never gotten pregnant were giving birth for the first time. By 1986, the Kirghiz population had reached 1,348, reflecting a demographic increase of about 19.4 percent over the last four years. The higher rate of survival of infants born during the four-year period of refugee life in Turkey became even more apparent when compared to the survival rates of those Kirghiz born during the four years of refugee life in Pakistan, and of those born during the last four years in the high-altitude Pamir valleys of Afghanistan before the Communist coup of 1978. That is, the number of children between the ages of 0 to 4 (born in Turkey) were 277 or 20.5 percent of the population, while those between the ages of 5 to 8 (born in Pakistan) were 156, or 11.5 percent of the population, and those ages 9 to 12 (born in the Pamirs of Afghanistan) numbered 107, or only 7.9 percent of the Kirghiz population. The indications were quite clear by then that the demographic survival of the Kirghiz in Turkey was assured.

6. My research was supported by a Fellowship Award from the American Research Institute in Turkey, Oriental Institute, University of Chicago; and a grant from the Committee on Research of the Faculty Senate, UCLA.

Second, more than 280 Kirghiz children, and some young adults, both boys and girls, were in schools. Among them were a group of eight students, who, having started school in Pakistan, were entering a high school with boarding facilities that autumn in the city of Van. Close to thirty Kirghiz youth of military age had been drafted and were serving in the Turkish armed forces. In addition, most of the adult males, and some females, between the ages of twenty and fifty had completed adult literacy courses, and many of them were able to read modern Turkish, however haltingly. All of these developments were likely to have significant consequences within the structure of social, economic, and political relations among the Kirghiz.

Third, all Kirghiz households, with the exception of those of Haji Rahman Qul Kutlu and his sister, Bibi Maryam Haji, which were considered wealthy, received the same amount of monthly cash allowances and other benefits. This new economic reality had created an unprecedented sense of social equality within the community and a general aura of freedom from dependence on the wealthier members of the community, which was so characteristic of the highly stratified Kirghiz society in Afghanistan. While the assistance given to them by the UNHCR, Turkish government, and a few private charitable organizations (NGOs) met the basic needs of most families, many Kirghiz households had begun, some very successfully, to take advantage of other economic opportunities in Turkey. For example, seventy households had bought sheep and goats from neighboring Turkish villagers, and together owned a total of some seven hundred animals. About thirty households had cows, and a number of these households were earning some cash from the sale of milk products within the community. Several men were working as shepherds in distant Turkish villages to earn extra cash. In both Karagunduz and Malatya, several Kirghiz families had opened small shops where they sold general goods in high demand within their own communities, much of which were sold on credit. In Malatya, almost 90 percent of the families with adult males had at least one member working as a porter in a dry fruits market, as a construction worker, or as a farm worker in or around the city of Malatya. More than 50 percent of the households in Karagunduz sent at least one adult male member to work for several months each year in Malatya and in other cities as far away as Izmir, Istanbul, Rize, and Adana to supplement their meager monthly refugee allowances of 6,000 Turkish lira per adult and 3000 lira per child less than eight years of age. In Karagunduz, women contributed to the family income by making traditional Kirghiz woven and felt crafts, which were bought by some foreign tourists, but largely by the Van and Environs Development Foundation, which runs a shop in the city of Van that sells Kirghiz goods. Differences in the availability of workers, as well as household strategies for making use of economic opportunities, were beginning to result in a new structure of economic differentiation among the Kirghiz, which would undoubtedly affect the long-term socioeconomic arrangements within the community.

Fourth, the critical significance of the role of the Kirghiz Khan, Haji Rahman Qul Kutlu, in managing Kirghiz relations with outside forces, including Turkish state authorities, appeared to have remained unchanged. In representing the interests of the Kirghiz to the Turkish authorities, the Khan took periodic visits to oversee the construction of the permanent Kirghiz village in Altindere, which was, at the time, falling behind schedule for completion. He also received a long stream of Turkish officials, international visitors, journalists, researchers, and well-wishers from all over the world. However, due to changes in the political economy of the community, important changes in the economic basis of his personal power had began to influence the nature of his leadership in the management of social relations within the community.

Finally, the construction of about 220 housing units, utilities, and public buildings (including a school, mosque, etc.) in Altindere was completed, while another hundred units were near completion. Turkish government authorities were planning to move those living in Karagunduz to Altindere either that fall or early in the spring of 1987. Those in Malatya were to move upon completion of the remainder of the housing units during the fall of 1987. At the time of their move to Altindere, the Kirghiz were to be given identical houses, an equal number of animals, and access to some 34,500 *dekar* (acres) of pasturelands to start a new herding economy. Upon relocation, their cash allowances were to cease. It is their long-term adaptation to these new conditions which I had hoped to be able to study later in their permanent village, with the help of the household demographic and economic survey data base collected during the summer of 1986.

A FRESH START IN THE ULUPAMIR KOYU
(GREAT PAMIR VILLAGE)

The Kirghiz had been extended Turkish citizenship by the end of the first year of their residency, and many of their young men were being drafted annually to serve in the Turkish armed forces.

Living in temporary shelters formed the last remaining aspect of
their refugee life in Turkey, and this ended with the completion of
their permanent village in Altindere. Fortunately for the Kirghiz,
their aging, charismatic leader, Haji Rahman Qul Khan, was able
to oversee the final move and resettlement of his community into
their permanent village, which he had named Ulupamir (the Great
Pamir), thus memorializing their place of origin in the Pamirs of
Afghanistan. Those living in Karagunduz were moved to the permanent village of Ulupamir in the fall of 1987, and the ones in
Malatya joined them during the spring of 1988. Haji Rahman Qul
Khan passed away in August 1990.

I had heard the sad news about the Khan's death shortly after
the event and very much wanted to pay my respects to his aging
sister, Bibi Maryam Haji, and to the family and community as soon
as possible. In Turkic Central Asian Muslim tradition, it is expected
of close friends or family members who cannot be present at a
funeral to visit the family of the bereaved as soon as possible to
offer condolences and to say the customary Muslim prayers on
behalf of the deceased. Given the fact that the Khan, with his usual
soft-spoken paternal affection, had often publicly spoken of me as
one of his sons and a member of his family, I felt duty-bound to
do what was expected of me: to visit the village and organize a
khatm-i Qur'an, a complete recitation of the entire Qur'an (the
Muslim sacred book) on the Khan's memory, and to feed a gathering of the elders of the community, at the least. This opportunity, much to my personal regret, did not avail itself to me until
August 1992, exactly two years after the Khan's death. I went to
Ulupamir Koyu in mid-August and spent about a week in the village commemorating the loss of a great community leader and
noticing the void his absence had left behind, which was still pal-
pably felt by the Kirghiz.

The death of the Khan, a man who had led his tiny pastoral
nomadic community through a tumultuous period that lasted
throughout much of the twentieth century; the shock of his loss to
the bereaved family and kinsmen; and the great honor with which
he had been laid to rest two years before were recounted to me
time and again. He had been mourned for an entire week, during
which some three hundred sheep had been slaughtered by the villagers in his honor. A huge stream of people coming to the village
to pay their respects from near and far in Turkey, especially members of the Afghan and Central Asian émigré communities, had been
entertained. The ritual surrounding the Khan's death had, indeed,
helped to formalize a major shift in Kirghiz funerary practices,

which was underway since their arrival in Turkey. This important change in Kirghiz social practices, to be discussed further in this chapter, has had very important economic and societal consequences for the newly sedentary Kirghiz villagers.

The Khan had been buried at the edge of the village in a preexisting cemetery, close to a small shrine said to be that of a local saintly shepherd. His tomb, marked by a well-polished, white marble tombstone (an innovation for the Kirghiz) and bearing his name (written in modern Turkish script as Haci Rahmakul Kutlu) followed by the dates 1913–1990, sat conspicuously amidst a tall, lush field of grass. By the spring of 2001, when I last visited the village,[7] his tomb was surrounded by the tombs of many a close kinsmen, including that of his sister, Bibi Maryam Haji, who had passed away in 1996. Two of the Khan's sons who are artists, Abdul Malik (a painter) and Muhamad Ekber (a sculptor), were in the process of erecting a small mausoleum of red sandstone over their father's tomb. The structure under construction, with its square base and planned cupola, appeared similar in design to the mausoleums built over the graves of important people in the Pamirs. The Khan, a tall, well-built, impressive-looking man who had towered over the living in his community during much of his life, appeared destined even in death to stand out among the deceased through his mausoleum, at least for the foreseeable future.

ULUPAMIR KOYU:
A MODERN VILLAGE IN EASTERN ANATOLIA

The new village, the site of which I had visited previously in the summer of 1986, while it was still under construction, consisted of 149 identical, two-storied, semi-detached, townhouse-style residential structures to accommodate members of the 298 Kirghiz nuclear families who had come from Pakistan. Two additional public structures with different architectural designs, a mosque and an elementary school, complemented the village structures. The whitewashed concrete buildings with gleaming tin roofs have the appearance of military barracks nestled within a narrow Alpine valley about

7. This ten-day visit to Ulupamir was made after attending a conference at Fatih University in Istanbul, May10–12, 2001. My travels to the conference and my brief research visit to Altindere were made possible by financial support from Indiana University's International Programs, Russian and East European Studies Institute, Department of Central Eurasian Studies, and the Inner Asian and Uralic National Resource Center. Their generous support is gratefully acknowledged.

5,750 feet (1,750 meters) above sea level. The village is located on the southern banks of the small snow-fed Zeylan River, which flows eastward into Lake Van, some 26 kilometers downstream near the town of Erciş. On the west, the new village, which looks ultra-modern especially compared with Kurdish villages nearby, is bounded by a small mountain spring–fed stream, which forks with the Zeylan River just west of the bridge that links the village to the road to Erciş. On the east, the village is abutted by a smooth, well-rounded grassy hill rising about 300 feet above the village. A small tributary valley opens up to the south for two to three miles and gradually rises to a rougher mountain range reaching a height of some 7,000 to 8,000 feet. To the north alongside the Zeylan River lies a high mountain range stretching westward into much greater heights. The side of this mountain range that faces south and the tributary valley across to the south of the village constitute the major pasture grounds for the Kirghiz villagers.

The Zeylan River, after passing Ulupamir downstream, continues to hug the mountain range to the south, while the northern banks of the river open up to a fairly wide plateau-like valley. The motor vehicle road, asphalted in 2000 from Erciş to Ulupamir, runs down the middle of the valley for about 15 kilometers westward from Erciş. The road then skirts the shores of the recently completed water reservoir/lake behind a dam on the Zeylan River for a few kilometers before approaching the Kirghiz village. The main road becomes a dirt track immediately after the Ulupamir turnoff, as it continues along the Zeylan River westward to many small Kurdish mountain villages located upstream. The road crossing over the bridge, which leads to the Kirghiz village, also becomes a dirt track beyond the village. It continues to snake up the mountainside and over a pass to other Kurdish villages in the next valley beyond the range south of Ulupamir.

Climatically, Ulupamir has some similarity with the Pamirs— long and cold winters, a very short spring and autumn, and hot and longish summers. The summer temperatures in July and August reach 37 degrees Celsius. Winter temperatures dip below freezing for months, and the valley is blanketed with several feet of snow and ice. The extremes of temperature and the scarcity of arable land in the vicinity of the village, especially irrigated plots, put severe limitations on the agricultural productivity of the Kirghiz villagers. Indeed, their ability to produce food grains has been, so far, negligible, and the possibility of raising large family herds is seriously curtailed by the necessity of stall-feeding the animals through the long winter months.

In 1988 the Kirghiz were given ten sheep per family at a cost of 105,000 Turkish lira on credit, to be paid back without interest at a rate of 8,750 lira annually over the next twenty years. By the spring of 2001, they had built a herd of some four thousand sheep and goats, several hundred cattle and horses, and a few yak.[8] They have been able to do so with a great deal of hard work, cutting and storing hay during the summer months from the rich pastures along the banks of the Zeylan River and the hills on the southern flanks of Ulupamir. The Kirghiz complain bitterly that they have already reached the capacity of the allotted pastureland by the Turkish government, and they hope they will be given some additional land so they can further expand the size of their current herds. Unfortunately for them, the prospect of gaining access to additional pasturage anytime soon does not seem likely.

SETTLING INTO THE VILLAGE

Each of the 149 townhouse-style buildings is designed to meet the needs of two families: the upper floors have three rooms, a small kitchen, and a toilet and a washroom for family residence, and the ground floors are intended to serve as stables or barns for the family herds and storage. Staircases at each end of the structures lead the families to their own homes, equipped with indoor plumbing and a dung- or coal-burning stove that also serves as a hot water heater. Each residential unit is also allotted 240 square meters of land for family gardens around the homes. The rows of residential structures, unlike traditional eastern Anatolian villages, are also separated by wide, straight streets.

The first challenge facing the Kirghiz community in their new village was the actual division of the new houses to individual families. Two critical considerations were at work in dividing the houses: a general concern that some locations within the village were bet-

---

8. An Irish gentleman named Peter Somerville-Large had met Haji Rahman Qul in 1982 in Gilgit, Pakistan, only days before the departure of the Kirghiz for Turkey. Much impressed by the Khan and deeply concerned about the Kirghiz's future in Turkey, Somerville-Large later arranged for the delivery of two wild female yak (in the summer of 1988) and two male yak (fall 1990) from the Whipsnade Zoo and animal farm in England to Ulupamir. The fascinating details of his project have been documented in a book by him (see Somerville-Large 1991). I am grateful to Mr. Doug Sparley of Vancouver, Washington, for sending me a copy of this book.

ter than others; and an equally important consideration that members of closely related lineages and clans wished to be able to live in the same neighborhood within the village. If the allocation of houses to individuals was not carried out in a transparent and fair manner, or if the wishes of close kin groups were not taken into consideration, it could have led to ill feelings and unnecessary tensions at the outset of their new, sedentary village life.

Therefore, in order to address both of these concerns, the Council of Village Elders (*Aksakaliler Majlisi,* literally, the "Council of Those with White Beards"), headed by Haji Rahman Qul, agreed to a common procedure involving two sets of lottery drawings. First, the 202 families residing in Karagunduz, who were relocated first to the new village, organized themselves on the basis of closely related, patrilineal descent groups (at the level of lineages and/or clans) into four equal groups of about fifty families, each of them headed by a named representative.[9] The 96 families living in Malatya, who joined the village last and were also mostly made up of closely related kinsmen, formed the fifth group. Second, the Council of Village Elders then divided the newly completed 202 housing units into four clusters (houses no. 1–50 as cluster #1; houses no. 51–100 as cluster #2; 101–150 as cluster #3, and 151–202 as cluster #4). In the first round of lottery drawings, the four group leaders were given the opportunity, in a public meeting, to draw a piece of paper bearing the numbers one through four, signifying one of the four clusters of houses. Once each of the four kin-based groups had learned their respective cluster of houses through the lottery, then each group held another lottery drawing for the actual house numbers within their particular cluster of houses. At the completion of this process, Haji Rahman Qul, representing one of the four groups in the first round, drew cluster #3 (i.e., houses no. 101–150) for his group of close kinsmen. In the second lottery for the assignment of actual units, he ended up with house no. 111 for his own family. Houses no. 203–298 were then assigned to the fifth group from Malatya. This five-tiered division of the Kirghiz village along descent groupings has since assumed even greater significance in the management of their sedentary lives as a community in Ulupamir, as will be discussed later.

Contrary to the Kirghiz's expectations, titles to the newly

---

9. These divisions closely followed the genealogical and demographic realities of Kirghiz *oruq* structures outlined on pages 152–154.

assigned homes were not free of charge. The houses were given to them for a fixed price of 7,500,000 Turkish lira (about $25,000 at a 1987 rate of about $1=300 Turkish lira). The heads of households were extended credit for the full amount and issued deeds for their houses in return for a promise to pay the Turkish government the constant sum of 375,000 lira annually for the next twenty years. This price included the lot measuring some 240 square meters of land around each unit, which was gradually walled off into gated compounds by the new owners.[10] Each family was also allotted, in principle, 2.5 dunum (940 square meters) of irrigated land along the riverbanks and 12 dunum of dry farmland on the hills south of the village. The assignment of these farmlands was made by Turkish officials. These lands also carried a price tag of 3,700,000 lira paid on equal annual installments over the next twenty years. Although these agricultural lands had been part of a Turkish government-owned *cheftlik* (agricultural farm) once assigned to the Kirghiz, the neighboring Kurdish villages disputed the government's claim of ownership in the courts. Although some of the land closest to the village is being used by the Kirghiz both as cropland and as pastureland, the court case against much of the rest of their agricultural lands remains unresolved. Land and water disputes with local Kurdish villagers as well as among the Kirghiz of Ulupamir Koyu appear to be one of the important sources of rising tensions in the village.

TURNING HOUSES INTO HOMES

By the spring of 2001, when I last visited the village, Ulupamir had the look of a mature and well-inhabited Alpine community. The bare blocks of rectangular house structures standing conspicuously on the Alpine valley, as I remembered during the summer of 1992, had been transformed into a honeycomb of walled compounds, tree-filled, gated courtyards, and decorated homes. The approximately six-feet-high walls enclosing each family yard to keep the animals either in or out were constructed of stone masonry or concrete cinder blocks. Contrary to the expectations of the village planners, very

10. Significantly, because of extremely high inflation rates in Turkey, by the spring of 2001 the value of the home loans to the Turkish government had decreased from the equivalent of $25,000 to less then $7, as $1 was valued at more then a million Turkish lira by 2001. Most Kirghiz families had already paid all their loans to the Turkish government by then.

few families used the lower floors of their houses as stables or barns. Many are in the process of converting them into living spaces for their growing families.[11] In a few cases the first floors are turned into work spaces and small shops. Families with herds have built separate animal shelters within their properties. Also, much to the disappointment of Turkish state officials, very few Kirghiz families have established kitchen gardens in their compounds. Instead, many of them have planted a few fruit trees and lots of fast-growing white poplars *(terek)*, which gives the village a very lush look during the spring and summer months. Poplars are much desired as construction wood within the village as well as in the region as a whole.

Given the high cost of bottled gas and the scarcity of coal, most families rely on animal dung for their winter heating fuel. As a result, the village streets and compound walls are covered with dried or drying cakes of animal droppings. The dried animal dung *(tezik)*, so critical to the Kirghiz's survival in the high Pamirs as principal fuel, is also now piled in large mounds in every courtyard and kept dry for use during the long winters. Every house was initially equipped with a coal- or dung-burning stove that also served as a hot water heater. The fire chambers of virtually all of the original stove/water heaters have burned through, but the water tanks have remained intact. Very few families have invested in new water heaters, so most of the old ones have been pulled out and are sitting in courtyards, where they are used as water storage tanks. But every household has newer models of coal- and dung-burning stoves, which can also be used for cooking family meals while heating the homes.

Inside the Kirghiz homes, with rare exceptions, one finds very few pieces of furniture such as couches, tables, chairs, or beds. Homes are organized and decorated in the traditional style of the Kirghiz yurt: floors are covered with rugs; instead of felt, quilts are laid along walls that are lined with stuffed pillows to lean against; and the walls are covered with colorful pieces of Kirghiz embroideries and appliqués, which used to adorn the Kirghiz's *aq oey*, or felt-covered yurts in the Pamir. Their bedding consists of traditional homemade, colorful quilts, mattresses, pillows, and blankets, and

11. A few Kirghiz, having worked in construction jobs in Malatya and other Turkish cities, have started businesses converting first floors of the original buildings into new family homes at a cost of about 300,000,000 to 400,000,000 Turkish lira ($300 to $400).

is folded into neat piles high against the wall during the day and taken down at night for sleeping on the floor. Every household, without exception, is completely wired to the outside world. They all now have a phone, a refrigerator, and a television set hooked into one or two satellite dishes (called *chenaq*) in their yards pointing to the heavens.[12] The virtual forest of dish antennas rising on poles from every yard gives the village an unusual look for this part of eastern Anatolia. The Kirghiz can get a wide variety of international channels, including MTV and those showing Indian movies they had come to appreciate while living in Pakistan. Many families also own expensive sound systems and video and CD players. A large collection of movies on video and DVD—among them *Gladiator, Titanic,* and Jacki Chan's *Shanghai Noon*—is widely circulated in the village. Some of them are dubbed in Turkish, but many are not. The pervasive use of electronic media worries the Kirghiz elders, who complained to me that the preoccupation with watching television and video has resulted in a serious decline in home visits amongst kinsmen and neighbors. More significantly, they also alleged that exposure to television and video had generated a widening gap between those who were born and raised in the Pamirs and those born after their exodus from the Pamirs. Abdul Wahid Kutlu, the late Khan's second eldest son, expressed the problem in the following stark manner:

The new generation of Kirghiz born and raised outside the Pamirs are increasingly disrespectful of their elders. Although they have attended schools and gotten education, they have very little to show for it. All they are interested in is television, video, and games. All the skilled craftsmen in the village—electricians, masons, tractor drivers, chauffeurs, construction workers—are those who were born and raised in the Pamirs. The newly educated young kids are for the most part idle and useless.

The men are also unhappy about the fact that their women are exposed to so much unseemly behavior on television.

THE NEW VILLAGE ECONOMY

One of the most striking economic realities apparent during my 2001 visit among the Kirghiz of Ulupamir is the relative prosperity and economic equality of all Kirghiz families. This is so in spite

12. Television and satellite dish systems are a relatively expensive one-time family investment amounting to some $150 to $200. What is remarkable is that in 1986, only twelve Kirghiz families owned television sets (three of them black-and-white). By 2001, owning television and satellite systems had become a necessity for every household rather than a luxury.

of the fact that the Kirghiz constantly complain about disparate economic conditions in their new village. The extremes of wealth and poverty which characterized the Kirghiz in the Pamirs during the 1970s have simply vanished from the community. This process of equalization of economic structure is due, at least in part, to two significant developments: a serious economic miscalculation on the part of Haji Rahman Qul, the wealthiest man amongst them; and equal treatment of all Kirghiz refugee families by their hosts in Pakistan and Turkey in terms of access to new economic resources regardless of previous status.

The Khan had reportedly deposited upon arrival in Turkey in 1982 the considerable sum of four hundred and fifty million (450,000,000)[13] Turkish lira, as well as some sixty thousand U.S. dollars ($60,000) in Turkish banks. He had hesitated to invest his wealth in income-generating commercial enterprises or to purchase land and real estate in Istanbul, as he had been encouraged to do by more established, earlier refugees from Central Asia (Turkistan). With rapidly rising inflation in Turkey, his millions of Turkish lira in the banks quickly diminished in value. Upon his death, what was left of his much-depreciated wealth was divided among nine sons and two daughters, leaving none of them wealthier than the newly emerging nouveau riche in their new village. His most significant investment in Turkey, aside from a small grocery shop in the village selling household necessities, was the purchase of a *dolmush* (mini-bus), which made a couple of trips daily between their camp in Karagunduz and the city of Van, mostly transporting the Kirghiz to the city and back. The income from these investments could not have been substantial by any measure.

New sources of income, hence wealth, are more diverse now than they were in the Pamirs. Although herds of sheep, goats, and cattle are becoming once again an important index of wealth, earning cash income from work, employment, or business has gained greater importance in the village. With rare exceptions, most families own a few small animals and cattle. About six or seven families, many of them among the very poor in the Pamirs, are now identified as rich herders. They each own between fifty and eighty sheep and goats, and a few cattle. The sheep are the most valuable stock in the village, selling for the unusually high price of

13. In June 1982, the value of Turkish currency hovered at about 150 Turkish lira to one U.S. dollar. Based on this rate, the Khan's fortune in Turkish money may have been worth about three million U.S. dollars.

between 280 and 300 million Turkish lira each. Some cows seem to fetch lower prices than sheep: from 250 to 300 million lira. The Kirghiz's most prized animal in the Pamirs, the horse, is now among the least valued stock in the village. A horse costs only about 30 to 50 million lira, virtually the price of a chicken. As a result, the number of horses in the village is on the rise.

The relative value of Kirghiz livestock is a reflection of the market demand for specific animals and their products in Turkey—milk, meat, wool, and skin—and the labor demands to care for them. Sheep ranks the highest in all indexes: mutton and lamb fetch a premium price at the bazaar,[14] sheep milk is sold fresh or as cheese, its wool is in great demand for use in Turkey's flourishing rug-weaving industries, and sheep and lamb skins also sell for a good price because of the thriving Turkish leather industry. In addition, sheep remain the most valuable animal for their social uses—they are slaughtered by the Kirghiz for hospitality, funerary rituals, and wedding celebrations. Sheep milk and milk products also continue to be a crucial part of the Kirghiz daily diet, when available. The five kin-based groups formed into residential neighborhoods in Ulupamir have also served as neighborhood shepherding associations. Each of the five kin-based neighborhoods hire two shepherds each spring to take their sheep and goats to pasture in return for a cash payment per animal. Each morning the families turn out their family herds to an appointed place in the village, where shepherds then take them to the pastures. The sheep are returned at dusk to the custody of their owners for the night. This is a very cost-effective way of herding sheep. The major labor input by the family in raising sheep is in making hay during the summer so the sheep can be stall-fed during the long winter months, a practice unknown to the Kirghiz in the Pamirs, where their sheep went to pasture year-round. The Kirghiz utilize the same neighborhood herding association scheme for pasturing the village cattle. Raising cattle is a more demanding, costlier option, especially providing large quantities of hay during the snowbound winter months. However, since the cows provide larger quantities of milk for a much longer period, they are desirable to keep, even if in smaller numbers.

During the milking season, which lasts three to four months for sheep and goats, the village is visited by representatives of outside dairy producing firms, who purchase fresh milk from the villagers. The purchased milk may be taken out of the village immediately

14. A kilogram of mutton is sold for about five million Turkish lira in the cities (about $5).

or made into cheese and then periodically trucked to towns and cities in western Anatolia. The heads of kin-based neighborhood groups negotiate the price for the milk with the purchasers, then collect the milk from their members and deliver it to the outside dairy merchant. During the spring of 2001, the representative of a dairy firm from the city of Erzerum had employed two Kirghiz in the village to make cheese and process it for him in a rented space. He disclosed that the total monthly payments for the milk he bought from the Kirghiz villagers[15] amounted to some twenty-five billion Turkish lira (approximately $25,000).

At the time of my trip, four villagers owned motor vehicles. One of them was an old Fiat passenger car that belonged to one of Haji Rahman Qul Khan's sons, Muhamad Ekber. He is a fine sculptor, and his older brother, Abdul Malik, a talented painter. Since their arrival in Turkey they have both been employed by the Van University, where they earn a monthly salary. Ekber is the more outgoing, entrepreneurial, and modernist-minded of the two, hence his willingness to drive his own car. The other three cars were mini-buses owned by individuals or jointly by a few persons. Like the Khan's mini-bus, these were used to generate income by carrying villagers to Erciş and back for a fee of one million lira per passenger each way. The three mini-buses made at least one round trip each day.

Another ongoing major form of income-generating activity in the village is shopkeeping. The village has four grocery shops, and all of them are doing a thriving business selling food and household goods, mostly on long-term credit. Three of the shops are owned by individuals. One of these is Muhammad Arif, the Khan's fifth son, who started the business in the Kirghiz's temporary camp in Karagunduz. Another is owned by a Mullah Ebrahim, who also is a large herder and owner of one of the three mini-buses. Mullah Ebrahim had started his enterprises with a modest capital of some 200,000 Turkish lira in the mid-1980s. In May 2001, his shop business was worth about eight billion lira, six billion of which was owed to him by villagers who had purchased goods on credit. The fourth

15. One liter of milk sold for 160 lira, and one kilogram of homemade cheese fetched 800 lira. About ninety metric tons of cheese were produced in the village during the year 2000. In the city, dairy product prices were much higher. A liter of milk sold for 300 to 400 lira; one kilogram of yogurt sold for 1.5 million lira; one kilogram of feta cheese sold for 2.5 million lira; and one kilogram of cheddar cheese sold for 4 million lira.

shop is a *shirkat,* a cooperative joint stock venture started by three individuals who contributed seven million lira to the initial capital. By 2001, the *shirkat* had one hundred members, and each share of stock in the shop was worth 135 million lira.

Two additional income-generating enterprises in the village that involve primarily the use of female labor have been the handicrafts of kilim (flat weave) or carpet weaving and leather works. The technique of sewing small pieces of leather together into larger sheets so that a garment or other useful article can be made from them was introduced to the village by the Kazak expatriate community in the Zeytunburun neighborhood of Istanbul. A few Kirghiz males who had visited Istanbul were encouraged by the successful Kazak leather merchants in Istanbul to work for them. The Kirghiz were given sacks full of leather strips, mostly left over from manufacturing leather products, to take with them to the village. The Kirghiz women were then asked to sew them together into square meter–sized pieces, which were returned to the merchant, who would make new, patched leather products from them. The male intermediary and the women in the village earned some cash income for their work. At one point some years back, when the leather business had been particularly lucrative in Turkey, a sizable number of Kirghiz men and a few families, numbering sixty to seventy persons, had been working in Istanbul in the leather manufacturing enterprises owned by the Kazaks. However, participation in this tedious work came to a halt a few years ago.

Carpet weaving, on the other hand, has been an important continuous activity in the village, although without substantial benefit to the Kirghiz women in Ulupamir village. As was mentioned earlier in this chapter, one of the Turkish charitable foundations, a *vaqf,* had started a small kilim-making workshop, which employed a few women in Karagunduz camp shortly after their arrival. More recently in Ulupamir, Sumerbank, one of Turkey's larger government-owned commercial banks, has converted an old animal shelter, which had preexisted the construction of the new village, into a carpet-weaving (*hali,* very fine knotted rugs with floral designs) *ataliya* (factory or workshop). This *ataliya* is very poorly lit, poorly ventilated, has little heat in the winter, and is damp and hot during the summer. It is also extremely noisy most of the time from the constant pounding done to tighten the knots on the new rugs. It is here that some sixty young, mostly unmarried Kirghiz girls crouch on very low wooden benches next to the vertical looms weaving some of the most beautiful Turkish carpets. Sumerbank had apparently installed twenty vertical looms in 1993 and hired three

Turkish instructors who taught the Kirghiz girls the art of Turkish carpet weaving. The Kirghiz carpet weavers are provided the yarn (at an estimated cost of about 100 million lira) by the Sumerbank, and they work in teams of three, each of them putting up to ten hours of work daily to complete a single rug (measuring about 5 by 10 feet) in two-and-a-half to three months' time. For all their hard labor, upon completion of each rug, the team of three young women is paid 300 to 350 million Turkish lira ($300 to $350) by Sumerbank. Their monthly paycheck amounted to less than about $45 for ten hours of work seven days a week. The Kirghiz were aware that their rugs, upon reaching the city of Van, fetched a price of over one billion Turkish lira, and in Istanbul twice that amount. The girls complained bitterly about the exploitative nature of their employment, but they also said that this was better then nothing. They are actively looking for a new investor who can offer better wages for their toil and a healthier environment in which to do their work. The oppressive working conditions in the rug-making factory are harming the health and well-being of many of these young women. I have promised to do my best to help them find more humane investors in their village.

In addition to these fancy new knotted Turkish rugs, most Kirghiz women produce traditional handicrafts for home use as well as for sale to foreign tourists, including weaving long strips of flat weave on their horizontal looms. On the whole, work opportunities both within and outside the village, especially for Kirghiz women, are very limited. Currently, there is only one woman who is working as a nurse *(hamshira)* and earning a regular salary. And only three Kirghiz women (and no men) are currently studying in college or university.

Finding gainful employment for the Kirghiz men remains one of the most pressing problems in the village. Some five hundred young men are said to be working away from the village for at least several months out of each year, in towns and cities as distant as Istanbul and Izmir. The remittances of these young men have become critical to the quality of life for their families in the village. In some cases, entire families have moved to Malatya and Istanbul looking for work.

At present, the most significant employment, and hence a major source of monthly income, for about 180 able-bodied men in Ulupamir is *koruçuluk/bekçilik*, or militia work. In the early 1990s, when the Kurdish insurgency led by the left-leaning Kurdish Workers Party, popularly known as the PKK, spread across eastern Anatolia, the government of Turkey declared the Altindere area, where the insurgents were active, a martial law region. Therefore, the Turkish army recruited many of the Kirghiz as government militia and provided them training, arms, and communication devices to help protect their own village and government installations in the area. In 1993, Ulupamir became a target of a PKK rocket attack, and the Kirghiz were able to successfully defend their village against the insurgents. Proving their loyalty and martial skills to the Turkish army in the region, more of them were recruited to defend their area. The recruits undergo periodic training and regularly patrol the village, as well as the surrounding hills at night and the mountain areas by day, often armed and on horseback. The *koruşu/bekçi* (militiamen) are paid a monthly salary of about 135 million lira, and as such, their wages constitute a substantial part of the villagers' income at present. The Kirghiz fear that the loss of these army jobs would drive an even larger number of them in search of jobs away from the village. Indeed, a number of families whose members were not fortunate enough to have a job as *koruşu/bekçi* have moved to Malatya (fourteen families) and Istanbul (ten families) looking for work.

Kirghiz participation in the military defense of the area on the side of the Turkish government, needless to say, has not endeared them to their Kurdish neighbors. Indeed, mutual suspicion and even contempt seem to characterize relations between the two communities. No Kirghiz women have been given in marriage to Kurdish men, and only two Kirghiz men working away from their village have married Kurdish girls so far. The Kirghiz complain that they are systematically and openly experiencing discriminatory behavior by the Kurdish majority in the region. The Council of Village Elders has, on occasion, considered the possibility of moving back to Central Asia—either to Kyrgyzstan, where they have been extended an invitation by the government of that newly independent country, or back to the Pamirs of Afghanistan, if and when peace returns to that nation. With the exception of a few Kirghiz youth—including the Khan's youngest son, Musadiq Kutlu—who have attended college in Bishkek, Kyrgyzstan, and another two or three young men who are working there, the idea of returning to Central Asia may be nothing but a dream, at least for the foreseeable future. Even then, it is a dream held only by the older generation of Kirghiz. The youth who have grown up in Turkey are completely immersed in the Turkish way of life and express no desire to go back to Central Asia.

CONTINUITY, CHANGE,
AND TRANSFORMATION OF SOCIAL PRACTICES

During the last quarter of a century of displacement, refugee life, and resettlement as sedentary villagers, the Kirghiz community has undergone some very important changes in certain aspects of their traditional social practices while holding on to others. The great majority of older Kirghiz women, and even many younger girls, have continued to wear the traditionally distinctive Kirghiz garments. On the other hand, with some exceptions on the part of the elderly, the men have adopted Turkish dress patterns.

Traditional Kirghiz wedding rituals and festivities have continued with some important changes. Weddings have become uniformly more elaborate and expensive undertakings, especially in recent years. In the Pamirs, weddings of poorer herders were very small and hardly noticed events, while those of the wealthy were grand occasions for extravagance. Now, with the relative economic prosperity of all Kirghiz, families tend to express their equality with others during their wedding rituals. Most weddings still take place during the warmer months of late spring to early autumn (May to September) and are very costly. The average bride price is estimated at about $1,500, topped by an additional $2,000 in the cost of festivities and the exchange of presents, including the slaughter of some eighteen sheep during various phases of the marriage proceedings. What is also new is the adoption of some Turkish practices in providing the bride with expensive gold jewelry. An important consequence of the inflation of wedding costs appears to be delayed marriages for the young men, who have to work in distant cities to raise money for their weddings. Some boys, having been away for extended periods of time, have married Turkish wives, leaving many Kirghiz girls without the prospect of marriage partners—a new predicament for Kirghiz families and one that was never known in the Pamirs.

Another significant social practice that has undergone important restructuring because of changed circumstances is the Kirghiz funerary custom. In the Pamirs, the family of the bereaved was obligated to offer a large number of animals as *esqat,* i.e., a Central Asian Muslim custom of offerings on behalf of the deceased's soul. These animals were distributed among members of lineages and clans not closely related to the deceased. The family also had to slaughter additional animals to feed those attending the funeral, as well as offer food to gatherings of people on certain dates following the burial. These practices required considerable expense for the family of the deceased.

In Pakistan, where the Kirghiz painfully recall burying some three hundred of their members in four years of refugee life, they simply ignored the observance of these customs. After arriving in Turkey, and with the gradual improvement of their economic situation, the Kirghiz began to shift the costs of funerary rituals from the family of the bereaved to the community at large. The new practice, which had begun to take hold after the move to Ulupamir village, apparently became crystalized during the funerary rites following the death of the Khan in 1990. In this new practice, the family and close kinsmen (neighborhood association) of the deceased are exempted from cooking for three days after the death. The other four neighborhood associations within the village each take responsibility for at least one day to provide all three daily meals for the family and kinsmen of the bereaved family. Members of the designated neighborhoods slaughter several sheep, boil the meat, and make sackfuls of fried dough *(boghursaq)*—the customary food for such occasions—and carry them in a procession of men and women to the house of the bereaved so that those gathered there are fed morning, noon, and evening. Only on the third day after death does the family and close kin of the deceased offer the villagers a similar meal. Within the three days, as many as thirty sheep and goats may be slaughtered. For Haji Rahman Qul's funeral, the Kirghiz claimed that the community slaughtered at least three hundred sheep. They reported that there was so much meat around that much of it went bad for lack of refrigerated space to keep it in the village. This restructuring of funerary rituals, while lightening the burden of the affected family, has nevertheless introduced a highly competitive, almost potlatch-like situation that has added considerably to the overall expenditures of the village community as a whole.

Another very significant and visible change in Ulupamir pertains to Kirghiz religious observances. Unlike in the Pamirs, where nomadic Kirghiz did not have a congregational mosque, Ulupamir is not only equipped with a mosque, but the Turkish government has appointed a Kirghiz scholar from the village to act as prayer leader *(imam)* and pays him a monthly salary. The *imam* leads the five daily Muslim prayers and the weekly congregational Friday prayers. He also teaches village children the basics of Islam and encourages an elderly female scholar to hold lessons for the girls. Indeed, many young boys and girls in the village are far better informed about Islam than they ever were. With their numbers rapidly increasing, they have built new lofts on both sides of their mosque to accommodate additional worshipers, especially during the Friday prayers.

The village elementary school has been elevated to a middle school, and a new structure has been built. The school enrollment in 2001 was 518 students (258 girls and 260 boys). Because of a serious shortage of classrooms, the school operated on double shift. About thirty graduates of the village middle school are said to be attending high schools in various parts of Turkey, with more than half of them attending the high school in Erciş. The village Council of Elders and their Mukhtar (chief) have petitioned the Turkish government to elevate their school to a high school.

In addition to providing the regular Turkish curriculum, the Ulupamir school teaches the Kirghiz language, music, and the performing arts. This innovative program was started a few years ago with the help of the government of Kyrgyzstan, which provides the school with a guest teacher from Kyrgyzstan. The presence of a dynamic and enthusiastic Kirghiz language and culture teacher has had an impressively positive effect on the Kirghiz children. Most of the Kirghiz youth who could not speak Kirghiz properly are now learning to speak it, and many have learned Kirghiz songs and dances, albeit choreographed during the Soviet era. Although very few of the school graduates have found lucrative jobs, the villagers are convinced that giving their children a good education is a must. A few families are spending considerable fortunes, at least by village standards, to support their children's higher education in distant Turkish cities.

The presence of the school, the increasing literacy among the Kirghiz, and considerable media exposure have combined to induce a remarkable shift in the reproductive behavior of the Kirghiz. As discussed earlier, the Kirghiz have experienced remarkable demographic success during the last nineteen years, and by the year 2001, nearly doubled their population, which stood at 2,200. Many of them are concerned about the costs of educating and caring for so many children, and three years ago the Council of Village Elders apparently invited Turkish family planning services to their village. According to the village chief, most married women have started using birth control devices such as the IUD (locally known as *sirghech*). Although a few women have experienced some complications, most families seem to be enthusiastic supporters of birth control.

DEATH OF THE KHAN
AND THE CRISIS OF COMMUNITY LEADERSHIP

The death of Haji Rahman Qul Khan in 1990 left the Kirghiz community without an effective leader. In retrospect, some Kirghiz elders admit that they seriously worried about their future without the Khan, a charismatic and compassionate man who had led them to safety and security in times of danger and uncertainty. The Khan had not formally appointed any of his sons to lead the community. However, the fifth-eldest son, Muhamed Arif Kutlu, a handsome, tall, well-built, and tanned young man, who resembled his father more than any of his brothers, had served for some time as his father's lieutenant. So the community turned to him for leadership, and he became known as the new Mukhtar or Agha of the village. Allegedly a bit full of himself, he give the impression that he did not care much about the needs or the feelings of the villagers, and was certainly not attentive enough to their concerns. But the community kept electing him without a challenge until 1998.

During the Turkish elections of 1998, Arif Kutlu was faced with two challengers: one woman and one man. The woman candidate was dismissed by some villagers as not being in good mental health. But the male candidate, Juma Taj, who came from a traditionally poor family, presented a credible challenge for the village leadership. The Khan's son, feeling a bit annoyed, publicly dismissed the contender as posing no problem to his election. On election day, however, Juma Taj won the election by a comfortable margin against the Khan's son and inaugurated a whole new era in the politics of Ulupamir village. Unlike Arif Kutlu, the new village Mukhtar, who is not literate, takes his responsibilities for protecting the interests of members of his village community to heart. He gives the impression that he takes great pride in having served his community well during the past three years (1998–2001). His detractors dismiss him as weak and ineffective. By some accounts, the Khan's son still behaves as though he is the village Mukhtar, especially in the presence of government officials For most ordinary Kirghiz villagers, however, both the Khan's son and the recently elected Mukhtar, Juma Taj, are very poor alternatives to their great leader, the late Haji Rahman Qul Khan. Confronted with a crisis of community leadership, the Ulupamir villagers face a long and complicated journey ahead as they continue to negotiate their place within the Turkish state and society at the dawn of the twenty-first century.

Much to my own personal disappointment, I have no firsthand ethnographic information to report about the Wakhi sedentary agricultural community as a whole and those Kirghiz who have continued to remain in the Pamirs of Afghanistan during the last quarter century of political turmoil in the region. Occasional media reports about the Kirghiz indicate that they have continued their herding way of life despite serious hardships due to disruption of their trade networks within Afghanistan. The Kirghiz of Little Pamir valley were reportedly gathered in a few camps near the Bozai Gumbuz area (at the westernmost end of the Little Pamir) by Soviet troops, where the Red Army had established their own military encampment during the Soviet occupation of Afghanistan (1979–89). During these years, the Soviet troops offered the Kirghiz provisions in exchange for animal products, thus minimizing their need for outside trade goods. Since the collapse of the USSR and the emergence of Kyrgyzstan as an independent nation-state in post-Soviet Central Asia, the Kirghiz of Afghanistan, both those in the Pamirs as well as the ones resettled in eastern Turkey, have been invited to resettle or "repatriate" in Kyrgyzstan. Both groups, while expressing some interest in the idea, have shown reluctance in taking up the offer so far. Reports of economic hardship among the Kirghiz in the Pamirs have been surfacing more frequently during the 1990s, and some help has been reaching them during the past couple of years by a non-governmental aid agency, Focus International, out of Tajikistan.

The Wakhi, on the other hand, have been the focus of very little media reporting. In the summer of 1996, when I returned to Badakhshan after twenty-one years, on enquiring about the Wakhi in the province I was told that they had not opposed the Soviet-backed Marxist regime in Kabul in any way. The reasons given were simple. The Wakhi are a small linguistic and Ismaili Shia sectarian minority who lived in close proximity to the former Soviet Union. While feeling neglected or oppressed and abused by the Afghan state officials, they had witnessed major infrastructural improvements on the other side of the Amu Darya river among their own Wakhi kinsmen in the Soviet Tajikistan. Besides, their sheer territorial closeness to the Soviet enemy made it impossible to stage a credible resistance against the Red Army. Therefore, they peacefully submitted to Soviet rule during the 1980s and were rewarded for their lack of opposition. After the implosion of the Soviet Union and the onset of Tajikistan civil war, their territory became an important transit route for opium trade between Afghanistan and Central Asian republics, especially to the city of Osh in southern Kyrgyzstan. With the end of the civil strife in Tajikistan in the mid-1990s and the beginning of rural development activities by the Agha Kahn Foundation (AKF)—an important international charitable organization headed by the spiritual leader of the world Ismaili community—in the predominantly Ismaili regions of Badakhshan (in both mountainous areas of eastern Tajikistan and Afghanistan), the Wakhi have become important beneficiaries of the AKF economic development efforts. The return of peace and political stability in Afghanistan combined with potential improvements in trade relations between the Indian subcontinent, Central Asian Republics, and China via the Wakhan corridor—the home of the Wakhi along the ancient Silk Road—hold other favorable prospects for the future of this long-suffering community.

REFERENCES

Akhmedziyanov, A.
1978 "The Bloody Path of the 'Independent Khan.'" *FBIS-SOV* 3, no. 189: J1, J2.

Shahrani, M. Nazif
1996. "Afghanistan's *Muhajirn* (Muslim 'refugee-warriors') in Pakistan: Politics of Mistrust and Distrust of Politics." In *Mistrusting the Refugees*, pp. 187–206. Edited by E. Valentine Daniel and John Chr. Knudsen. Berkeley, University of California Press.

1994. "Honored Guest and Marginal Man: Long-Term Field Research and Predicaments of a Native Anthropologist." In *Others Knowing Others: Perspectives on Ethnographic Careers*, pp. 15–67. Edited by Don D. Fowler and Donald L. Hardesty. Washington, D.C., Smithsonian Institution Press.

1991. "Local Knowledge of Islam and Social Discourse in Afghanistan and Turkistan in the Modern Period." In *Turko-Persia in Historical Perspective*, A School of American Research Book, pp. 161–188. Edited by Robert L. Canfield. Cambridge, Cambridge University Press.

1990. "Afghanistan: State and Society in Retrospect." In *The Cultural Basis of Afghan Nationalism*, pp. 41–49. Edited by Ewan W. Anderson and Nancy Hatch Dupree. London and New York, Pinter Publishers.

1988. "Jihad Against Communism in Central Asia: From Holy Wars to Islamist Revolutionary Struggles." Paper presented at the workshop on "Approaches to Islam in Central and Inner Asian Studies," Columbia University, New York, March 3–4.

1987. "Islamic Eschatology and the Kirghiz Interpretation of Modern Politics." Paper presented at the 86th Annual Meeting of the American Anthropological Association, Chicago, November 18–22.

1986. "The Social Bases of Islamic Movements in Afghanistan." Paper presented in a panel at 20th Annual Meeting of the Middle East Studies Association, Boston, November 20–23.

1985. "Revolutionary Islam in the Armed Resistance in Afghanistan." Paper presented at the 84th Annual Meeting of the American Anthropological Association, Washington, D.C., December 3–8.

1984a. "Introduction: Marxist 'Revolution' and Islamic Resistance in Afghanistan." In *Revolutions and Rebellions in Afghanistan: Anthropological Perspectives*, pp. 3–57. Edited by M. N. Shahrani and R. L. Canfield. Berkeley, Institute of International Studies, University of California.

1984b. "Causes and Context of Responses to the Saur Revolution in Badakhshan." In *Revolutions and Rebellions in Afghanistan: Anthropological Perspectives*, pp. 139–169. Edited by M. N. Shahrani and R. L. Canfield. Berkeley, Institute of International Studies, University of California.

1984c. "Kirghiz Refugee Experiences and the Concept of *Hijrah* in Islam." Paper presented at the panel "Cultural Interpretations of Refugee Phenomena," 83rd Annual Meeting of the American Anthropological Association, Denver, November 14–18.

1981. "Islamic Resistance to Russian Communism: The 'Basmachi' and the Afghan Mujahideen." Paper presented at the panel "Long-term Afghan-Russian Relations: Historical and Current Perspectives," 15th Annual Meeting of the Middle East Studies Association, Seattle, November 4–7.

1980a. "The Kirghiz, Now of Pakistan." *Cultural Survival Newsletter* 4, no. 4 (fall).

1980b. "Kirghiz Refugees of the Afghan Pamirs: A Report on Their Situation and Needs." Islamabad. Submitted to the United Nations High Commission for Refugees and other international aid donor agencies.

Somerville-Large, Peter

1991. *A Shaggy Yak Story: Forty Years of an Unfinished Journey.* London, Sinclair-Stevenson, Ltd.

Glossary

Language transliterated is shown in parentheses: W, Wakhi; K, Kirghiz; D, Dari (Afghan dialect of Persian or Tajik). Words set in capital letters are defined elsewhere in the glossary.

AASH [āsh] (K, W, D) Souplike wheat noodle dish

AASH-I-BAQLA [āsh-i-bāqlā] (W) Thin gruel of milled horsebeans; Wakhi staple

AASH KHANA [āsh khāna] (K) High, occasionally decorative, screen |of woven reed used for partitioning kitchen area in yurt; see CHEE

AAT [āt] (K) Horse

aBROG (Tibetan) Pastoral nomadism

ADIR [adyr] (K) Ecological niche in the Pamirs: rubble-covered lower steep slopes in KONGEY and TERSKEY

AFIUN [afyūn] (W) Opium

AIEL [ayil] (K) Camp residents; camp; see QOROW

AKA (K) Elder brother, father's younger brother

ALBARSTE (K) Female demon believed to cause death of expectant mothers at childbirth; see TETRI TAMAN and ZIANDASH

AMANAT [amānat] (D, K) Lit., things given for safekeeping; long-term herding arrangement

AQ OEY [āq oey] (K) Lit., white house; Kirghiz yurt

AQSAQAL [āqsaqāl] (K) Lit., white bearded; lineage elder or leader

ARBOB [arbāb] (W,D) Village headman

ARCHA (W, D, K) Juniper

ARQAN [arqān] (K) Ropes and tethers of yak or goat hair

ARQAR [arqãr] (K) Female Marco Polo sheep

ARZEN (W, D) Millet

ASL (W, D) Original, pure, of high blood ("pure bred"); upper-class Wakhi social stratum

ATA [ãta] Father

ATALIK GHAZI [ãtalik ghãzy] Turkic honorific meaning "supreme defender of the faith" (Islam); title claimed by Yakub Beg, a nineteenth-century ruler of Eastern Turkistan

ATASH-PARAST [ãtash parast] (D, W) Fire worshippers (Zoroastrians)

AYESH (K) Term denoting ritual or fictive nature of kinship relations

AYJGAI (K) A solidified sweet milk product

AYRAN [ayrãn] (K) A curdled milk product

BAD [bãd] (D, W) Wind

BAD-I-WAKHAN [bãd-i-wãkhãn] (D) Severe westerly wind of the Wakhan Corridor

BAI BECHA [bãy bicha] (K) Wife, see ZAYIB and KAMPER

BAJA [bãja] (D, W) WiSiHu

BAKHSHI (K) Kirghiz ritual specialist, shaman

BAKSHT (W) HuBr, WiSi, BrWi; see KUND KHOEY and VERUT KUND

BALA (K) Child, son

BALDEZ [bãldez] (K) Wife's younger sister; wife's brother's daughter

BAM-I-DUNYA [bãm-i-dunyã] (D, W) "Roof of the World," Pamirs

BAQLA [bãqlã] (D, W) Horsebeans *(Faba sutiva)*

BASMACHI, or basmaji [bãsmachy] (K) Lit., robber, plunderer; name used by Soviets for an armed uprising by various Turkic-speaking groups against the Soviets in Central Asia during the 1920s and early 1930s; see BEKLAR DIN QOZGHALESHI

BE [bi] (K) Camp elder or leader

BEHAR-O-KUZ OTERISH JIRLAR [behãr-o-kuz oterish jîrlar] (K) Spring and fall camping grounds

BEKLAR DIN QOZGHALESHI (K) Headmens' uprising or Beks (*Be's*) Revolt; Turkic term for BASMACHI

BOLA [böla] (K) MoSiChi and children of female members of mother's patrilineage

BORI [böri] (K) Large-eared Tibetan wolf

BOW [böw] (K) Decorative, colorful woolen woven straps and bands used to fasten yurt frames

BUQA (K) Yak bull; see QUTAS

BURGUT [bûrgût] (K) Eagle

BURUT (K) Lit., moustache; archaic name for Kirghiz used by others

BUZ KASHI (D) Lit., goat snatching; game played on horseback; see OLAGH TARTISH

CHALOP (K) Diluted ARYAN; sour milk

CHANOCH (K) Goatskin containers

CHAPAN [chapān] (K) Long quilted robe; ceremonial gown

CHAQMAQTIN KOL [chaqmāqtin köl] (K) Large lake in the Little Pamir

CHAREQ [chāreq] (K) High, flat-soled man's boot

CHEBERA [chibira] (K) Grand-mother's children

CHEE [chi] (K) A long, strawlike reed; woven for use in Kirghiz house-holds, e.g., around the yurt frame, in felt making, and in drying yoghurt

CHEM (K) Peat

CHEQOOR-ALA [cheqūr-ala] (K) Dry morainal ridges forming an ecological niche

CHERAGH [cherāgh] (W, K, D) Light; a kind of candle made of sticks wrapped in oiled cloth

CHOGUN [chögün] (K) Copper tea-pot of kettle

CHOP [chöp] (K) Meadow grass; hay

CHOP CHAPMAGH [chöp chāpmāgh] (K) Harvesting fodder

CHUNG [chüng] (K) Major, great, large, big, grand

CHUNG ATA [chüng āta] (K) Grand-father

CHUNG ORUQ [chüng örüq] (K) Major lineage; see ZOR ORUQ and KECHEK ORUQ

CHUNG YENA [chüng yena] (K) Grandmother

DALA KHAFAK (D, W, K) A stoat-like animal, probably mink

DAMAAD [damād] (D, W) DaHu, SiHu, FaSiHu, MoSiHu

DARGAW [dargāw] (D, W) Tributary stream, especially the mouth of such a stream where alluvial fans are formed

DARI [darī] (D) Persian dialect spoken in Afghanistan

DARZA (W, D) Sheaf of grain

DASHT (W, D) Desert

DA YAKA [dah yakah] (W, D) Lit., one-tenth; often of goods and services paid to the SHAH by Wakhi com-moners; tithe

DEG-DA (W) SoWiMo and Fa; BrWiMo and Fa; DaHuMo and Fa; SiHuMo and Fa

DEHQANI [dehqāni] (D, W) Agri-culture, farming

DEHQĀN KHĀNA [dehqān khāna] (W, D) agricultural outpost

DJUNGAR OIRAT Western Mongol group—Kalmuck Tartars

DOSTLIK [döstlik] (K) Ritual or fictive kinship established by public oath and feast; see QURAN DOSTLIK

DUKAN [dukān] (W, D, K) Small partitioned platforms in Wakhi house used as sleeping and working areas (W); also shop (D, W, K)

DUNGER SERT (K) Ecological niche: fringes of snow and glacier fields on KONGEY side of the Pamir valleys

ECHKI (K) Goat; she-goat or neutered male; see OLAGH, SERKE, TEKE

EENAK [inak] (K) Yak cow; see QUTAS

EET [iyt] (K) Dog

ER (K) Kirghiz epics

ESHAK (K) Donkey

ESQOT [isqāt] (D, K, and Arabic) Alms given during funerary rites by family of deceased

GADEK (D, W, K) Native dwarf sheep of Wakhan

GANDEM-I-SAFEDAK (D, W) Variety of irrigated wheat

GHAJIR (K) Snow vulture

GHALCHA [also GALCHA] Archaic Indo-Iranian dialect; "Pamir languages," e.g., Wakhi language

GHAREEB [gharīb] (D, W) Poor, lowly; of "common" blood; see KHEEK

GHAREEB KAR [gharīb kār] (D, W) Manual laborer

GHAREEB KARI [gharīb kāri] (D, W) Manual labor

GHULJA [ghūlja] (K) Male Marco Polo sheep *(Ovis poli);* see ARQAR

GHUNAJIN [ghunājin] (K) Two-year-old female yak; see QUTAS

GHUNAN (K) two-year-old male yak; see QUTAS

GODU [gödū] (K) A kind of grass found in ADIR areas

GUMBAZ [gumbaz] (K) Mausoleum

HAJI [hāji] (D, K) Title for one who has made the pilgrimage to Mecca

HARAM [harām] (D, W, K) Ritually polluting and polluted

HAZARA [hazārah] (D, W, K) A Persian-speaking, Mongol-looking population of central Afghanistan, mostly adherents of Imami and Ismaili sects of Shi'a Islam

HUN-T'O-T'O Chinese name for Khandud, district center of Wakhan

I-EYEN [ā-'iyyn] (D, W) Detachable cast-iron plow tip

IMAOS Ancient Greek name for Pamirs

ISKANDER (D, W) Alexander the Great

IZBOR Russian term for pasturage fee; see WOT POLI

JAMBU [jāmbū] (K) Early Chinese silver ingot used as a medium of exchange

JANGAL (D, W) Jungle, forest

JAYZI (K) Dowry

JEHEZ (W) Dowry

JELGA (pl. JELGALAR) (K) Narrow tributary valleys, ravines

JENGA (K) Father's younger brother's wives, elder brother's wives

JEYEN (K) FaSiChi, elder SiChi

JEZDA (K) FaSiHu, SiHu, MoSiHu

JOOT [jūt] (K) Spring blizzard

JUGHRAT [jūghrāt] (K) Yoghurt

JURAB [jūrab] (D, W) Sock; long thick woolen stockings

KAFILA BASHI [qāfilah bāshi] (D, W, K) Caravan leader

KAFIR [kāfir] (D, W, K) Infidel, non-believer (i.e., non-Muslim)

KALANI KHANA [kalāni khānah] (D, W) Head of household

KALJOW (D, W) Gymnospermous barley or naked barley

KALMUCK Mongol groups; see QAL-MAQ

KAMPER (K) Wife; see BAI BECHA and ZAYIB

KARWAN-BALASI [kārwān bālasi] (K) Lit., son (or child) of the caravan man; a small monument in the Darra Gorge where the son of a caravan man allegedly was buried

KASHT [kāsht] (W) Agricultural implement for carrying wheat sheaves

KECHEK (K) Little, minor, small

KECHEK ORUQ (K) Minimal lineage, minimal patrilineal kinship group

KEGIZ (K) Felt

KEREGA (K) Lower lattice frame of yurt

KESAK (K) A major Kirghiz kinship group (ORUQ)

KESHT GAH [kisht gāh] (W, D) Cultivated land

KEYAW [keyāw] (K) DaHu

KEYIK (K) Mountain goat, ibex

KEYLIN (K) SoWi

KHALIFA (W) Village religious representatives of the SHAH

KHAM QAYMAQ [khām qaymāq]

(D, K) Lit., raw cream; cream collected from top of unboiled milk

KHANA [khānah] (D, W) house

KHATNA TOY (W) Circumcision festivities and rites

KHEEK [khīk] (W) 1. Wakhi commoner 2. all Wakhi

KHESEIRS [khesîrs] (W) WiBr, SiHu

KHOEY [khûy] (W) Sister

KHOEY PUTR [khûy putr] SiSo

KHOEY THEGT [khûy şegt] (W) SiDa

KHOONKHALQ [khûnkhalq] (W) Wakhi household

KHOREQ (K) Irrigated pastures

KHORS (W) Wife's father

KHUJA [khûjah] (W) Wakhi kinship-based social category

KHURJUN (K) Saddlebag

KHUSH (W) WiMo

KHYBERI (W) Wakhi kinship-based social category

KIEN-KU Chinese name for the Kirghiz

KIRGH [qîrgh] (K) Forty

KOH [kûh] (D, W) Mountain

KONGEY (K) North or sunny face of the valley

KUCH KEYAW [kûch keyāw] Taking a bride in return for seven years of work for bride's family without pay

KUND (W) Wife

KUNJUT Principal village south of the Little Pamir in northern Pakistan; *Kunjuti*, people from that general area

KUTARMA (K) Credit system between Kirghiz and trader-shopkeepers; see WARDASHT

MAGHZAR [maghzär] (D, W) Marsh covered with fine meadow grass

MAI (or SARI MAI) [mäy or sari mäy] (K) Clarified butter

MALA [mälah] (D, W) Harrow, agricultural implement

MALDARI [mäldäry] (D, W) Animal husbandry, pastoralism

MANAS (or MANAC) Kirghiz epic about 16-century hero named Manas

MASEH (D, K, W) Central Asian thin-soled heelless boots worn with rubber galoshes

MENG BASHI [meng bäshi] (K) Military rank for commander of a thousand soldiers; also district officer or subgovernor

MEREED [merïd] (D, W) Disciple, follower, subject of a religious/spiritual leader

MESHKA (K) Cream mixture stored in sheep or goat stomach bag; unpurified butter

MIR (D, W) Chieftain; Wakhi kinship category

MIRAB [miräb] (D, W) Community water caretaker hired collectively

MOJUK (D, W) lentil

MOOM [müm] (W) FaMo, MoMo, FaMoSi, MoMoSi

MOWLAWI (D,K) One who has completed highest level of Muslim religious education; religious teacher and functionary

MULLAH (D, K, W) A low ranking Muslim religious functionary and teacher

NAAR [när] (D, K, W) Camel *(Camelus dromedarius)*; see TUWA

NAIMAN [näymän] One of the four major Kirghiz agnatic kinship categories

NAKHTAGAN MAI [nakhtagan mäy] (K) purified butter used as shortening; see MAI and SARI MAI

NAN (W) Mother

NASWAR [naswär] (D, W) Addictive mixture of green tobacco leaves, lime, and ashes dropped under the tongue or between lower lip and teeth

NEBERA (K) Grandchild

NEPOS (W) SoChi, DaChi

NONA Archaic Wakhi term for "count"

OEY (pl. OEYLAR) (K) House (yurt), family, household

OEY BASHI [oey bäshi] (K) Head of an OEY

OLAGH [olägh] (K) Kid; see ECHKE

OLAGH TARTISH [olägh tartish] (K) Lit., goat snatching; traditional Kirghiz game played on horseback; see BUZ KASHI

OLAR [olăr] (K) Mountain turkey of Pamirs and Wakhan

ONDER (pl. ONDERLAR) (K) Series of high plateaulike valleys; e.g., the Little and Great Pamirs

ORKHON Early eastern Turkic language

ORUQ [orŭq] (pl. ORUQLAR) or OROW (pl. OROWLAR) (K) Lit., seed, root, or shoot; also refers to the Kirghiz rules of patrilineal descent, descent groups, and categories

OTEK (K) Thick-soled boots with heels

OTEZ OGHUL (K) Lit., thirty sons or boys; refers to a Kirghiz myth of origin

OYTUQI (K) Starter for making yoghurt

PAGAH [păgah] (D, W) Area in Wakhi house closest to main entrance where footgear is removed

PALAAS [palăs] (W, K, D) Coarse, unknotted matting of yak and goat hair used for floor covering

PATUK (D, W) Lupine

PEER [pĭr] (D, W) Spiritual leader, master, savior; see SHAH

PESHEGH QAYMAQ [peshegh qaymăq] (K) Lit., cooked cream; cream collected from boiled milk or yoghurt; see KHAM QAYMAQ

PESHTAQ [peshtăq] (K) Cheese

PESHTI GHUNAJIN [peshti ghŭnăjĭn] (K) Yak cow that has just reached reproductive stage; see QUTAS

PESHTIQUTAS [peshtiqŭtăs] (K) Three-year-old yak; see QUTAS

PIZVAN [pizvăn] (W) Midmorning meal

POOP [pŭp] (W) FaFa, MoFa, FaFaBr, MoFaBr

POOSTAK [pŭstak] (D, W, K) Sheep- and goatskin mats

POOSTEEN [pŭstĭn] (D, W) Sheepskin overcoats

POW (D, W, K) Unit of weight equivalent to about .450 kg.

PUTR (W) Son

QALEN (K) Bridewealth/brideprice

QALMAQ [qalmăq] (K) Kirghiz term for a Mongol group (probably Kalmuck) considered a traditional enemy

QARA QIRGHIZ (or KARA KIRGHIZ) (K) Genuine or true Kirghiz

QAREN (K) Lit., stomach; bags made of sheep and goat stomachs

QARENDASH [qarendăsh] (K) Younger sister (male speaker as ego); see SINGLI

QARYA (D, W) Village, hamlet

QARYADAR [qaryadăr] (D, W, K) Village headman, an elective position

QATEGHDAGAN CHAI [qateghdagan chăy] (K) Brew of tea, salt, and milk or cream; see SHUR CHAI

QAYMAQ [qaymăq] (D, W, K) Cream; see KHAM QAYMAQ and PESHEGH QAYMAQ

QAYN (K) Kirghiz kinship term signifying affinal ties when used with consanguineal core terminologies; e.g., see QAYN-YENA and QAYN-ATA

QAYN AGHA [qayn ăgha] (K) WiBr, husband's elder brother

QAYN ATA [qayn āta] (K) WiFa

QAYN SINGLI (K) Hu younger SiDa; Hu elder BrDa; Hu younger Si

QEYN YEJA (K) Wife's elder sister, husband's elder sister

QAYN YENA (K) WiMo

QAYN YENI (K) Hu younger Br; Hu elder BrSo

QAZAN [qazăn] (K) cast-iron caldron

QAZI [qăzi] (Arabic, also used in D, W, K) Muslim judge

QEGH (K) Fuel of dried animal droppings

QEMIZ (K) Kirghiz traditional drink of fermented mare's milk

QEPCHAQ [qepchăq] (K) One of four principal Kirghiz ORUQ

QESHTOW (K) Winter camping grounds

QIZ (K) Daughter, girl, maiden

QOCHQAR [qŏchqăr] (K) Breeding rams; also a Kirghiz intermediate ORUQ or patrilineal descent group

QOEY (K) Sheep (ewe); see TURKI QOEY

QOMOCHDAN [qŏmŏchdăn] (K) Cov-ered cast-iron vessel used for baking

QOP [qăp] (K) Woolen sacks for transporting and storing

QOQMA [qăqma] (K) Narrow, woven, woolen strips for making sacks and horse covers

QOROW (K) 1. A walled enclosure for herds at night in winter camping sites 2. camping grounds; localized herd management group

QOUM (D, W) Localized kinship group (lineage) or community of relatives

QOZY (K) Lamb

QROOT [qrŭt] (K) Dried yoghurt

QUCH (W) Male Marco Polo sheep *(Ovis poli)*

QUDA (K) SoWiFa and Mo; DaHuFa and Mo

QUL (K) Slave

QUNOQ (K) Overnight hospitality extended during wedding festivities to guests from distant camps

QURAN DOSTLIK (K) Holy Quran friendship; fictive kinship

QUREGH MAL [quregh măl] (D, W) Communally hired protector of fields and pastures

QURELTAY [qŭreltăy] (K) Council of elders

QUTAN [qŭtăn] (K) High, mud, stone, or mud-brick enclosure for animals

QUTAS [qŭtăs] (K) Yak *(Bos grunniens); see* also BUQA, EENAK,

GHUNAN, GHUNAJIN, TAI TUR-
POQ, WAGUZ, PESHTI QUTAS,
PESHTI GHUNAJIN

QUYUN (K) Hare

RUTSAPS (W) FaBrChi; FaSiChi;
MoBrChi; MoSiChi; FaBrChiChi;
MoBrChiChi

RAIG (D, W) Lit., sand; also ecological niche of large sand tracts
on valley floor

RANG (D, W) Alpine ibex

SABAD (D, W) Large woven-twig
containers

SABZI (D, W) Vegetables; also a
Wakhi dish of wild vegetables

SADAQA-E-FEDEYA SOUM WA
SALOT Lit., penance paid for omissions of fasts and prayers; see ESQOT

SAGHUN [sāghǔn] (K) 1. milk
animals 2. short-term herding arrangement

SAIL (D, W) Alluvial fans at mouths
of tributary ravines and rivers in
Wakhan

SAIR (D, W, K) Unit of weight;
about 7.60 kg.

SA MA aBROG (Tibetan) Herder
of mixed flocks

SAMGHAT [samghāt] (W) Gift, particularly one given by a Wakhi commoner to his SHAH

SARAI (W, D) Caravan halting place

SARHAD DAR [sarhad dār] (D)
Frontier commissioner

SARHAD DARI [sarhad dāri] (D)

Office of the frontier commissioner;
the structure and the position

SARI EET [sari ǐt] (K) Yellow dog;
often contemptuously used by the
Kirghiz for Wakhi

SARI MAI [sari m̥āy] (K) Purified
butter (MESHKA); see MAI and
NAKHTAGAN MAI

SART (K) Non-Kirghiz, non-Kazakh;
also used pejoratively by Kirghiz
for Wakhi

SAYYED (D, W) Wakhi social category

SEAHPOOSH KAFIR [siyāh pǔsh
kāfir] (D) Black-robed infidels; i.e.,
pre-Islam inhabitants of Wakhan

SEL-LAR (K) Ecological niche in
Pamirs: screes in both KONGEY
and TERSKEY areas

SERKE (K) Buck goats and lead goat;
see TEKE

SERT (K) High flat or low gradient
grounds between tributaries

SEYI (K) Virginity price, i.e., additional bridewealth given by groom's
family to the family of a virgin
bride

SHA-ANA [sha-āna] (W) Social category of Wakhi

SHAH [shāh] (D, W) Monarch or
king; also used for spiritual leaders
of Ismaili Wakhi

SHAJARA (D, W, K) Genealogical
record; genealogical tree

SHARI'A (D, W, K) Islàmic law
based on the Quranic scripture and
"tradition"

SHEBER (K) Microenvironmental niche in the Pamirs: a plain with adequate moisture along streams and springs

SHERNE (K) Sweet solidified milk product

SHESHAK (K) Two-year-old neutered male sheep

SHEWAGH [shewăgh] (K) Variety of sagebrush in Pamirs

SHEWAR (K) Rushes; pastures near riverbanks and lakesides

SHIGHNI People from the district of Shighnan; language spoken by the Shighni

SHOWRA (K) Salt fields

SHUR CHAI [shŭr chăy] (D, W) Lit., salty tea; brew of strong, bitter black tea and salt and milk or cream; see QATEGHDAGAN CHAI

SHUY (D, W) Husband

SINGLI (K) Younger sister, older brother's daughter (female speaker as ego); see QARENDASH

SOOT [sŭt] (K) Fresh milk

STUKH (W) Son's wife

SUGHUR [sŭghŭr] (K) Marmot

SUNI BOYI (K) Watershed areas

SUZMA (K) Milk product

SWY [swăy] (K) Nonmilk-producing section of herd

TAGHA [tăgha] (K) Mother's brother; male members of one's mothers patrilineage

TAI TURPOQ (K) One- to two-year-old yak calf

TAKHTA POSTAK (K) Goatskin mats for floor coverings and felt making

TALANG (K) Rubblelike earthy slopes on TERSKEY mountainsides

TAN [tăn] (W, D) Fine woolen material woven by Wakhi

TASHKILI (D) Organizational; refers to two general categories of nonindigenous peoples living in Wakhan—traders/shopkeepers and government agents

TAT (W) Father

TATU (K, W) Small-statured horse native to Wakhan

TEKE (K) Buck goats kept for breeding

TERSKEN (K) A variety of sagebrush

TERSKEY (K) Southern, shady face of a valley

TETRI TAMAN [tetri tamăn] (K) Lit., crooked feet; euphemism for ALBARSTE: see ALBARSTE and ZIANDASH

TEYET (K) One of four principal Kirghiz kinship groups

TEZIK (K) Yak dung

THEGT [ṣigt] (W) Daughter

TOEY QARAR [toey qarăr] (W) Bridewealth/brideprice

TOM (K) Single room adobe or stone

structure used by some Kirghiz as living quarters or storage shelters

TOQUZ (K) Lit., nine; ceremonial gifts given in sets of nine at Kirghiz funerals and as SEYI at weddings

TOZ JIRLAR (K) Flat dry areas on valley floor

TUMAQ [tŭmăq] (K) Fur hat worn by Kirghiz males

TURKI, TURKI QOEY (K) Turkic sheep; Central Asian fat-tailed sheep

TURPOQ (K) Yak calf; see also QUTAS and TAI TURPOQ

TUTAK [tŭtak] (K) Mountain sickness, hypoxia

TUWA (K) Double-humped Bactrian camel *(Camelus bactrianus)*; see also NAAR

TY (K) Uterine blood relationships, i.e., relations through one's mother; see TY-ATA, TY-YENA

TY-ANA [ty-ăna] (K) MoMo

TY-ATA [ty-ăta] (K) MoFa

TY-JENGA (K) MoBrWi

TY-YEJA (K) MoSi, female members of one's mother's patrilineage

VACH (W) FaBrWi; MoBrWi; FaSi; MoSi

VERUT (W) Brother

VERUT KUND (W) BrWi

VERUT PUTR (W) BrSo

VERUT THEGT [verut sigt] (W)

BrDa

WAGUZ [wăgŭz] (K) Gelded yak; see QUTAS

WARDASHT [wardăsht] (D, W) Credit system between traders/shopkeepers and Wakhi; see also KU—TARMA

WERAMA (K) Horse cover

WOLUSWAL [woluswăl] (Pashtu) District officer

WOLUSWALI [woluswăli] District, district office

WOT POLI [wŏt poli] (K) Pasturage fee; see IZBOR

WUKA (K) Young brother, elder brother's son

YAYLOW [yăylow] (K) Summer camping and pasturage areas

YEJA (K) FaSi; Father's elder brother's daughter; elder sister

YENA (K) Mother

YENCHI (K) Anticipatory inheritance; also gifts given to children in various life crises

YENGA (K) Hu elder brother's wife

YENI (K) WiBrSo

YIR (K) Husband

YOBU [yăbu] (W, K, D) Pack horse

YUZ (K) One hundred

ZAGHIR (D) Flax

ZAYIB [zăyĭb] (K) Wife; see also KAMPER, BAI BECHA

ZIANDASH [ziyăndăsh] (K) Lit., cause

of damage; euphemism for ALBAR-
STE; see also ALBARSTE and TETRI
TAMAN

ZOR ORUQ [zör orūq] (K) Major
patrilineages in Kirghiz society; maximal lineage; see CHUNG ORUQ
and KECHEK ORUQ

 Bibliography

Abercrombie, Thomas
   1968. "Afghanistan: Crossroad of Conquerors." *National Geographic* 134: 297-345.
Alizadeh, Said Reza
   1927. *Turkistan.* Lahor, Matba-ha-i-Mufed-i-Aam (originally published in 1818 in Uzbek under the title of *Tarikh-i-Turkistan* [History of Turkistan] in Tashkent).
Allworth, Edward, ed.
   1971. *Soviet Nationality Problems.* New York, Columbia University Press.
Ayoub, M. R.
   1959. "Parallel Cousin Marriage and Endogamy: A Study in Sociometry." *Southwestern Journal of Anthropology* 15: 206-75.
Bacon, E.
   1958. *Obok: A Study of Social Structure in Asia.* Viking Foundation Publication in Anthropology, no. 25. New York, Wenner-Gren Foundation for Anthropological Research.
Baker, Paul T.
   1962. "The Application of Ecological Theory to Anthropology." *American Anthropologist* 64: 15-21.
Baker, P. T., A. R. Frisancho, M. A. Little, R. B. Mazess and R. B. Thomas
   1965. *A Preliminary Study of the Cultural and Biological Characteristics of a Peruvian Highland Population: Annual*

Progress Report. University Park, Pennsylvania, Pennsylvania State University.

Baker, P. T. and J. S. Weiner, eds.
  1966. *The Biology of Human Adaptability.* Oxford, Clarendon Press.

Baker, Paul T., Gabriel Escobar, Gordon DeJong, Charles Hoff, Richard Mazess, Joel Hanna, Michael Little, Emilio Picon
  1968. *High Altitude Adaptation in a Peruvian Community.* Occasional Papers in Anthropology, no. 1. University Park, Pennsylvania, Pennsylvania State University.

Barth, F.
  1953. *Principles of Social Organization in Southern Kurdistan.* Oslo, Universitetes Etnografisk Museum Bulletin, no. 7.

  1954. "Father's Brother's Daughter Marriage in Kurdistan." *Southwestern Journal of Anthropology* 10: 164-71.

  1956. "Ecological Relationships of Ethnic Groups in Swat, North Pakistan." *American Anthropologist* 58: 1079-89.

  1959a. *Political Leadership Among Swat Pathans.* London School of Economics Monograph, no. 19. London, Athlone Press; New York, Humanities Press.

  1959b. "The Land Use Pattern of Migratory Tribes of South Persia." *Norsk Geografisk Tidsskrift* 17: 1-11.

  1961. *Nomads of South Persia.* Boston: Little Brown & Co.

  1964. "Competition and Symbiosis in North East Baluchistan." *Folk*, vol. 6, no. 1.

  1967. "On the Study of Social Change." *American Anthropologist* 69: 661-69.

  1973. "A General Perspective on Nomad-Sedentary Relations in the Middle East." In *The Desert and the Sown: Nomads in the Wider Society.* Edited by Cynthia Nelson. Research Series, no. 21. Institute of International Studies. Berkeley, University of California Press.

Barth, F., ed.
  1969. *Ethnic Groups and Boundaries.* Boston: Little Brown.

Barthold, W.
  1924. "Kirghiz." In *The Encyclopedia of Islam.* 2: 1025-26. London, Luzac.

  1930. *Hudud-al-Alam.* Translated by Mir Husain Shah. Faculty of Letters, Kabul University, Kabul; Education Printing House. (Persian translation with the photostat of the original Persian text of 892 A.D.).

  1934. "Sart." In *The Encyclopedia of Islam* 4: 175-76. London, Luzac.

1956. *Four Studies on the History of Central Asia,* vol. 1. Translated from Russian by V. and T. Minorsky. Leiden, E. J. Brill.

1958. *Turkistan Down to the Mongol Invasion.* Translated from Russian. 2nd ed. London, Luzac.

Bates, Daniel G.

1973. *Nomads and Farmers: A Study of the Yörük of South-eastern Turkey.* Anthropological Papers, no. 52. Ann Arbor, The University of Michigan Museum of Anthropology.

Bates, Daniel G. and Susan H. Lees

1977. "The Role of Exchange in Productive Specialization." *American Anthropologist* 79: 824-41.

Beal, Sam

1869. *Travels of Fah-hsian and Sung-yan, Buddhist Pilgrims from China to India.* London, Trubner.

Becker, Seymour

1968. *Russia's Protectorates in Central Asia: Bukhara and Khiva, 1865-1924.* Cambridge, Harvard University Press.

Berrien, Frederick K.

1968. *General and Social Systems.* New Brunswick, N. J., Rutgers University Press.

Boehm, Christopher

1978. "Rational Preselection from Hamadryas to *Homo Sapiens:* The Place of Decisions in Adaptive Process." *American Anthropologist* 80: 265-96.

Bohannan, Paul and Fred Plog, eds.

1967. *Beyond the Frontiers: Social Process and Culture Change.* Garden City, N. Y., Natural History Press.

Bonvalot, Gabriel

1889. *Through the Heart of Asia: Over the Pamirs to India.* Translated by C. B. Pitman. London, Chapman & Hall.

Bretschneider, E.

1888. *Medieval Researches from Eastern Asiatic Sources: Fragments towards the Knowledge of the Geography and History of Central and Western Asia from 13th to the 17th Century.* 2 vols. London, Trubner.

Canfield, Robert L.

1973a. *Faction and Conversion in a Plural Society: Religious Alignments in the Hindu Kush.* Anthropological Papers, no. 50. Ann Arbor, The University of Michigan Museum of Anthropology.

1973b. "The Ecology of Rural Ethnic Groups and the Spatial Dimension of Power." *American Anthropologist* 75: 1511-28.

Cary, Max and E. H. Warmington
  1929. *The Ancient Explorers.* London, Methuen.
Chen, Jack
  1977. *The Sinkiang Story.* New York, Macmillan.
Chokaev, Mustafa
  1928. "The Basmaji Movement in Turkistan."   *Asiatic Review*
    24: 273-88.
Chu, Wen-Djang
  1966. *The Moslem Rebellion in Northwest China 1862-1878.*
    The Hague, Mouton.
Clark, G.
  1954. *Elements of Ecology.* New York, John Wiley.
Clarke, J. I.
  1965. *Population Geography.* New York, Pergamon Press.
Cole, John W. and Eric R. Wolf
  1974. *The Hidden Frontier: Ecology and Ethnicity in an Alpine
    Valley.* New York and London, Academic Press.
Cruz-Coke, R., A. P. Cristoffanini, M. Aspillaga, and F. Biancani
  1967. "Evolutionary Forces in Human Populations in an En-
    vironmental Gradient in Arica, Chile." *Human Biology*
    38: 421-38.
Dabbs, Jack A.
  1963. *History of the Discovery and Exploration of Chinese
    Turkistan.* The Hague, Mouton.
DeJong, Gordon F.
  1968. "Demography and Research with High Altitude Popula-
    tion." In *High Altitude Adaptation in a Peruvian Commun-
    ity.* Edited by Paul T. Baker et al. University Park, Penn-
    sylvania State University.
Donayre, J.
  1966. "Population Growth and Fertility at High Altitude." In
    Life at High Altitude. Scientific Publication no. 140.
    Washington, D. C., Pan American Health Organization.
Downs, James F.
  1964. "Livestock, Production, and Social Mobility in High Alti-
    tude Tibet." *American Anthropologist* 66: 1115-19.
Dunmore, The Earl of
  1893a. "Journeying in the Pamirs and Central Asia." *Geographical
    Journal* (London) 2: 385-402.
  1893b. *The Pamirs.* 2 vols. London, John Murray.
Dupree, Louis
  1973. *Afghanistan.* Princeton, Princeton University Press.

Dyson-Hudson, Neville
   1972. "The Study of Nomads." In *Perspectives on Nomadism*. Edited by William Irons and Neville Dyson-Hudson. Leiden, E. J. Brill.
Ekvall, Robert B.
   1939. *Cultural Relations on the Kansu-Tibetan Frontier*. Chicago, University of Chicago Press.
   1968. *Fields on the Hoof: Nexus of Tibetan Nomadic Pastoralism*. New York, Holt, Rinehart & Winston.
Ekvall, Robert B. and James F. Downs
   1965. "Animal and Social Types in the Exploitation of the Tibetan Plateau." In *Man, Culture and Animals*. Edited by Anthony Leeds and Andrew P. Vayda. Washington, D. C., American Association for the Advancement of Science.
Etherton, P. T.
   1925. *In the Heart of Asia*. London, Constable.
Evans-Pritchard, E. E.
   1940. *The Nuer*. London, Oxford University Press.
Farsoun, Samih K.
   1970. "Family Structure and Society." In *Peoples and Cultures of the Middle East* 2: 257-307. Edited by Louise Sweet. Garden City, N.Y., Natural History Press.
Fazel, G. R.
   1973. "The Enclosed Nomadic Societies in Iran." In *The Desert and the Sown*. Edited by C. Nelson. Institute of International Studies, Research series, no. 21. Berkeley, University of California Press.
Ferdinand, Klaus
   1962. "Nomad Expansion and Commerce in Central Afghanistan." *Folk* 4: 123-59.
Fortes, M.
   1953. "The Structure of Unilineal Descent Groups." *American Anthropologist* 55: 17-51.
   1958. "Introduction." In *The Developmental Cycle in Domestic Groups*. Edited by J. Goody. Cambridge: At the University Press.
Fowler, Catherine S.
   1977. "Ethnoecology." In *Ecological Anthropology*. Edited by Donald L. Hardesty. New York, John Wiley & Sons.
Frake, Charles
   1962. "Cultural Ecology and Ethnography." *American Anthropologist* 64: 53-59.

Frechtling, Louis
  1939. "Anglo-Russian Rivalry in Eastern Turkistan 1863-1881."
  Journal of Royal Central Asian Society 26: 471-89.
Fry, Maxwell J.
  1974. *The Afghan Economy: Money, Finance and the Critical
  Constraints to Economic Development.* Leiden, E. J. Brill.
Geertz, Clifford
  1957. "Ritual and Social Change: A Javanese Example." *American
  Anthropologist* 59: 32-54.
  1963. *Agricultural Involution: The Process of Ecological Change
  in Indonesia.* Berkeley, Los Angeles, and London, University of California Press.
  1965. "Religion as a Cultural System." In *Anthropological Approaches to the Study of Religion.* Edited by Michael
  Banton. Association of Social Anthropologists Mono-
  graphs, no. 3. London, Tavistock.
  1973. *The Interpretation of Cultures: Selected Essays.* New York,
  Basic Books.
Gellner, Ernest
  1973. "Introduction to Nomadism." In *The Desert and the
  Sown.* Edited by Cynthia Nelson. Institute of International
  Studies, Research series, no. 21. Berkeley, University of
  California Press.
George, Carl and Daniel McKinley
  1974. *Urban Ecology: In Search of an Asphalt Rose.* New York,
  McGraw-Hill.
Gibb, H. A. R.
  1923. *Arab Conquest in Central Asia.* London, The Royal Asiatic
  Society.
Goldenweiser, A.
  1936. "Loose Ends of a Theory on Individual Pattern and In-
  volution in Primitive Society." In *Essays in Anthropology
  Presented to A. L. Kroeber.* Edited by R. Lowie. Berkeley,
  University of California Press.
Goldschmidt, Walter
  1965. "Theory and Strategy in the Study of Cultural Adaptability." *American Anthropologist* 67: 402-7.
Goldstein, Melvyn C.
  1974. "Tibetan Speaking Agro-Pastoralists of Limi: A Cultural
  Ecological Overview of High Altitude Adaptation in Northwest Himalaya." *Objets et mondes, la Revue du Musée
  de l'Homme* 14, no. 4: 259-68.

Goodenough, Ward
> 1970. *Description and Comparison in Cultural Anthropology.* Chicago, Aldine.

Goody, Jack, ed.
> 1958. *The Developmental Cycle in Domestic Groups.* Cambridge Papers in Social Anthropology, no. 1. Cambridge, At the University Press.

Gordon, E. C.
> 1876. "The Watershed of Central Asia, East and West." *Journal of the Royal Geographical Society* 46: 381-96.

Gordon, Sir Thomas Edward
> 1876. *The Roof of the World: Being a Narrative of a Journey Over the High Plateau of Tibet to the Russian Frontier and the Oxus Sources on Pamir.* Edinburgh, Edmonston and Douglass.

Grahn, Douglas and Jack Kratchman
> 1963. "Variation in Neonatal Death Rate and Birth Rate in the United States and Possible Relations to Environmental Radiation, Geology and Altitude." *American Journal of Human Genetics* 15: 329-52.

Grierson, G. A.
> 1921. *Linguistic Survey of India: Specimens of Languages of the Eranian Family* 10: 457-65. Delhi, etc., Motilal Banarsidass.

Grousset, Rene
> 1970. *The Empire of the Steppes: A History of Central Asia.* New Brunswick, N. J., Rutgers University Press.

Gulick, John
> 1976. *The Middle East: An Anthropological Perspective.* Pacific Palisades, California, Goodyear.

Hanna, Joel M.
> 1974. "Coca Leaf Use in Southern Peru: Some Biosocial Aspects." *American Anthropologist* 76: 281-96.

Hardesty, Donald L.
> 1977. *Ecological Anthropology.* New York, John Wiley & Sons.

Hawley, Amos H.
> 1968. "Human Ecology." In *International Encyclopaedia of the Social Sciences* 4: 328-37. Edited by David Sills. New York, Macmillan and the Free Press.

Hayward, G. W.
> 1870. "Journey from Leh to Yarkand and Kashgar, and Exploration of the Sources of the Yarkand River." *Journal of the Royal Geographical Society* 40: 33-166.

Hedin, Sven
 1938. *The Silk Road*. Translated from Swedish by F. H. Lyon. New York, Dutton.
 1943-1945. *History of the Expedition in Asia, 1927-1935*. 4 vols. Göteborg, Elanders Boktriyckeri Aktiebolag.

Heer, D. M.
 1964. "Fertility Differences between Indian and Spanish Speaking Parts of Andean Countries." *Population Studies* 18: 71-84.

Helm, June
 1962. "The Ecological Approach in Anthropology." *American Journal of Sociology* 67: 630-39.

Hoff, Charles J.
 1968. "Reproduction and Viability in a Highland Peruvian Indian Population." In *High Altitude Adaptation in a Peruvian Community*. Edited by Paul T. Baker et al. The Pennsylvania State University Occasional Papers in Anthropology, no. 1. University Park, Pennsylvania State University Press.

Holt, P. M., A. S. Lambton, and B. Lewis, eds.
 1970. *The Cambridge History of Islam*, vols. 1, 2. Cambridge, At the University Press.

Humlum, J.
 1959. *La Géographie de l'Afghanistan: Etude d'un pays aride*. Copenhagen, Cyldendal.

Irons, W.
 1969. *The Yomut Turkmen: A Study of Kinship in a Pastoral Society*. Ann Arbor, University of Michigan Microfilms.
 1974. "Nomadism as a Political Adaptation: The Case of the Yomut Turkmen." *American Ethnologist* 1: 635-58.
 1975. *The Yomut Turkmen: A Study of Social Organization Among Central Asian Turkic-Speaking Population*. Anthropological Papers, no. 58. Ann Arbor, University of Michigan Museum of Anthropology.

Irons W. and N. Dyson-Hudson
 1972. *Perspectives on Nomadism*. Leiden, E. J. Brill.

James, William H.
 1966. "The Effects of High Altitude on Fertility in Andean Countries." *Population Studies* 20: 97-101.

Jochelson, W.
 1928. *Peoples of Asiatic Russia*. New York, American Museum of Natural History.

Johnson, Douglas L.
 1969. *The Nature of Nomadism: A Comparative Study of Pastoral*

Migrations in Southwestern Asia and North Africa. Chicago, University of Chicago Press.

Keyes, C. F. and A. B. Hudson
1961. "Some Critical Factors Involved in the Analysis of Cross-Cousin Marriage." Paper delivered at the annual meeting of American Anthropological Association, Philadelphia, November 1961.

Keyes, C. F.
1972. "Millennialism, Theravada Buddhism, and Thai Society." Presented at a symposium on religion and social change in Southeast Asia. Annual meeting of Association for Asian Studies. Also in *Journal of Asian Studies* (forthcoming).

1976. *Ethnic Adaptation and Identity: The Karens on the Thai Frontier with Burma.* Philadelphia, Institute for the Study of Human Issues.

Khan, M. Anwar
1963. *England, Russia and Central Asia: A Study in Diplomacy 1857-1878.* Peshawar, University Book Agency.

Kirby, D. R. S., K. G. McWhiter, M. S. Teitelbaum, and C. D. Darlington
1967. "A Possible Immunological Influence on Sex Ratio." *Lancet* (July 15), pp. 139-40.

Kormondy, Edward J.
1969. *Concepts of Ecology.* Englewood Cliffs, N. J., Prentice-Hall.

Krader, L.
1955. "Ecology of Central Asian Pastoralism." *Southwestern Journal of Anthropology* 2, no. 5: 301-26.

1957. "Culture and Environment in Interior Asia." In *Studies in Human Ecology.* Social Sciences Monograph, no. 3. Washington, Pan American Union.

1963. *Social Organization of the Mongol-Turkic Pastoral Nomads.* Indiana University Uralic and Altaic Series, vol. 20. The Hague, Mouton.

1968. "Pastoralism." *International Encyclopaedia of the Social Sciences* 11: 453-61.

1971. *Peoples of Central Asia.* Edited by J. R. Krueger. Indiana University Uralic and Altaic Series, vol. 26: 3rd ed. Bloomington, Indiana University Press.

Kuropatkin, A. N.
1882. *Kashgaria.* Calcutta, Thacker, Spink.

Kushkaki, B.

    1923. *Rahnuma-i-Qataghan Wa Badakhshan.* [Guide to Qataghan and Badakhshan]. Kabul, Ministry of Defense Press. (In Persian.)

Latham, Ronald, trans.

    1958. *The Travels of Marco Polo.* Harmondsworth, Penguin Books.

Lattimore, Owen

    1950. *Pivot of Asia: Sinkiang and the Inner Asian Frontiers of China and Russia.* Boston, Little, Brown.

    1951. *Inner Asian Frontiers of China.* Research series, no. 21. New York, Capital Publishing and American Geographical Society.

    1962a. *Nomads and Commissars.* New York, Oxford University Press.

    1962b. *Studies in Frontier History: Collected Papers 1928-1958.* London, Oxford University Press.

Lattimore, Owen and Eleanor Lattimore

    1968. *Silks, Spices and Empire.* New York, Dell.

Leach, E. R.

    1954. *Political Systems of Highland Burma.* Boston, Beacon Press.

Lehman, F. K.

    1967. "Burma: Kayah Society as a Function of the Shan-Burma-Karen Context." In *Contemporary Changes in Traditional Societies.* Edited by J. H. Steward. Urbana, University of Illinois Press.

Lewis, I. M.

    1961. *A Pastoral Democracy.* London, Oxford University Press.

    1965. "Problems in the Comparative Study of Unilineal Descent." In *The Relevance of Models for Social Anthropology.* Edited by Michael Banton. A. S. A. Monographs, no. 1. London, Tavistock.

Luknitsky, P. N.

    1954. *Soviet Tajikistan.* Moscow, Foreign Language Publishing House.

Mazess, R. B.

    1966. "Neonatal Mortality and Altitude in Peru." *American Journal of Physical Anthropology* 23: 209-14.

McClung, Jean

    1969. *Effects of High Altitude on Human Birth.* Cambridge, Harvard University Press.

McNaughton, S. J. and L. L. Wolf
  1973. *General Ecology.* New York, Holt, Rinehart & Winston.
Menges, Karl H.
  1968. *The Turkic Languages and Peoples: An Introduction to Turkic Studies.* Wiesbaden, Otto Harrassowitz.
Michaud, Sabrina and Roland Michaud
  1972. "Winter Caravan to the Roof of the World." *National Geographic* 141, no. 4: 435-65.
Minorsky, V.
  1929. "Wakhan." *The Encyclopedia of Islam* 4: 1103. London, Luzac.
Mirsky, Jeannette, ed.
  1964. *The Great Chinese Travelers.* Chicago, The University of Chicago Press.
Moncloa, F., J. Donayre, L. Sobrevilla and R. Guerra-Garcia
  1965. "Endocrine Studies at High Altitude." *Journal of Clinical Endocrinology and Metabolism* 25: 1640-42.
Monge, C. M.
  1948. *Acclimatization in the Andes: Historical Confirmation of "Climatic Aggression" in the Development of Andean Man.* Baltimore, Johns Hopkins Press.
Monge, C. M. and C. C. Monge
  1966. *High Altitude Diseases: Mechanism and Management.* Springfield, Ill. Charles Thomas.
Montgomerie, T. G.
  1866. "On the Geographical Position of Yarkand, and Some Other Places in Central Asia." *Journal of the Royal Geographical Society* 36: 157-72.
  1871. "Report of the Mirza's Exploration from Caubul to Kashgar." *Journal of the Royal Geographical Society* 41: 132-93.
Morgan, E. Delmar
  1869. "Progress of Russian Exploration in Turkistan." *Proceedings of the Royal Geographical Society* 14: 229-34.
  1887. "Russian Geographical Work in 1886." *Proceedings of the Royal Geographical Society* 9: 423-37.
  1893. "On the Pevtsof Expedition and M. Bogdanovitch Surveys." *Geographical Journal* 2: 55-63.
Murchison, Sir Roderick Impey
  1866. "President's Address to the Royal Geographical Society Delivered at the Anniversary Meeting on the 28th May 1866." *Journal of the Royal Geographical Society* 36: cxvii-cxcvii.

Napier, G. C.
    1874. *Collection of Journals and Reports.* London, George E.
        Eyre and William Spottiswoode.
    1876. *Memorandum on the Condition and External Relations
        of the Turkomen Tribes of Merve.* London .
Nelson, Cynthia, ed.
    1973. *The Desert and the Sown: Nomads in the Wider Society.*
        Institute of International Studies, Research Series, no. 21.
        Berkeley, University of California Press.
Netting, Robert M.
    1971. *The Ecological Approach in Cultural Study.* A McCaleb
        Module in Anthropology, no. 6. Menlo Park, Calif., Cunnings
        Publishing Co.
    1974. "Agrarian Ecology." *Annual Review of Anthropology*
        3: 21-56.
The New Encyclopaedia Britannica
    1974. "Pamir Mountain Area." *The New Encyclopaedia Britannica*
        13: 938-40. 15th ed.
Newsom, B. D. and D. J. Kimeldorf
    1960. "Species Differences in Altitude Tolerance Following X-
        Irradiation." *American Journal of Physiology* 198: 762-
        64.
Odum, E. P.
    1959. *Fundamentals of Ecology.* Philadelphia, Saunders.
Olufsen, Ole
    1969. *Through the Unknown Pamirs: The Second Danish Pamir
        Expedition 1898-99.* 1904. New York, Greenwood Press.
Paine, Robert
    1972. "The Herd Management of Lapp Reindeer Pastoralists."
        In *Perspectives on Nomadism.* Edited by William Irons
        and N. Dyson-Hudson. Leiden, E. J. Brill.
Parsons, T.
    1951. *The Social System.* Glencoe, Ill., Free Press.
    1960. *Structure and Process in Modern Societies.* Glencoe, Ill.,
        Free Press.
Quick, Horace F.
    1974. *Population Ecology.* Indianapolis, Ind., Pegasus.
Rahman, Fazlur
    1968. *Islam.* Garden City, N. Y., Doubleday.
Rappaport, R. A.
    1968. *Pigs for Ancestors.* New Haven, Conn., Yale University
        Press.

Razvi, M.
> 1971. *The Frontiers of Pakistan: A Study of Frontier Problems in Pakistan's Foreign Policy.* Karachi and Dacca, National Publishing House.

Riasanovsky, Valentin A.
> 1965. *Customary Law of the Nomadic Tribes of Siberia.* Bloomington, Indiana University Press.

Rodenbough, T. F.
> 1885. *Afghanistan and the Anglo-Russian Dispute.* New York and London, G. P. Putnam's Sons.

Rowton, M.
> 1974. "Enclosed Nomadism." *Journal of the Economic and Social History of the Orient* 17: 1-30.

Sahlins, Marshall D.
> 1968. *Tribesmen.* Englewood Cliffs, N. J., Prentice Hall.

Schneider, David M.
> 1965. "Some Muddles in the Model: Or, How the System Really Works." In *The Relevance of Models for Social Anthropology.* Edited by Michael Banton. A. S. A. Monographs, no. 1. London, Tavistock.

Schram, Louis
> 1954. *The Monguours of the Kansu-Tibetan Frontier.* Philadelphia, American Philosophical Society.

Schultz, Arnold
> 1969. "A Study of an Ecosystem: The Arctic Tundra." In *The Ecosystem Concept in Natural Resource Management.* Edited by M. Van Dyna. New York, Academic Press.

Schuyler, Eugene
> 1876. *Turkistan: Notes of a Journey in Russian Turkistan, Khokand, Bukhara, and Kuldja.* New York, Scribner, Armstrong.

Shahrani, M. Nazif
> 1978. "The Retention of Pastoralism Among the Kirghiz of the Afghan Pamirs." In *Himalayan Anthropology: The Indo-Tibetan Interface,* pp. 233-50. Edited by J. F. Fisher. The Hague, Mouton.

Shaw, Robert B.
> 1870. "A Visit to Yarkand and Kashgar." *Proceedings of the Royal Geographical Society* 14: 124-37.
> 1871. *Visit to High Tartary, Yarkand, and Kashgar (Formerly Chinese Turkistan) and Return Journey over the Korakoram Pass.* London, John Murray.

Shor, Jean and Franc Shor
  1950. "We Took the Highroad in Afghanistan." *National Geographic* 98, no. 5: 673-706.

Shor, Jean
  1955. *After You, Marco Polo.* New York, McGraw-Hill.

Skrine, Francis H. and Edward D. Ross
  1899. *The Heart of Asia: A History of Russian Turkistan and the Central Asian Khanates from the Earliest Times.* London, Methuen.

Spooner, B.
  1973. *The Cultural Ecology of Pastoral Nomads.* An Addison-Wesley Module in Anthropology, no. 45. Reading, Mass., Addison-Wesley.

Spular, B.
  1970. "Central Asia from the Sixteenth Century to the Russian Conquest." In *Cambridge History of Islam* 1: 468-673. Edited by P. M. Holt, A. S. Lambton, and B. Lewis. Cambridge: At the University Press.

Stein, Sir Aurel
  1912. *Ruins of Desert Cathay: Personal Narrative of Explorations in Central Asia and Westernmost China.* 2 vols. London, Macmillan & Co.
  1916. "A Third Journey of Exploration in Central Asia 1913-1916." *Geographical Journal* 48: 98-130, 193-229.
  1919. "The Desert Crossing of Hsuan-tsang." *Geographical Journal* 54, no. 5: 265-77.
  1921. *Serindia: Detailed Report of Exploration in Central Asia and Westernmost China.* 3 vols. Oxford, Clarendon Press.
  1922. "A Chinese Expedition across the Pamirs and Hindukush, A.D. 747." *Geographical Journal* 59: 112-31.
  1925. "Innermost Asia: Its Geography as a Factor in History." *Geographical Journal* 65, no. 5: 377-403 and 65, no. 6: 473-501.
  1928. *Innermost Asia: Detailed Report of Explorations in Central Asia, Kan-su and Eastern Iran.* 3 vols. Oxford, Clarendon Press.
  1964. *On Ancient Central-Asian Tracks.* Chicago and London, University of Chicago Press.

Steward, J.
  1955. *Theory of Culture Change.* Urbana, University of Illinois Press.
  1968. "Cultural Ecology." In *International Encyclopedia of the*

Social Sciences 4: 337-44. New York, Macmillan and the Free Press.

Stycos, Mayone
  1963. "Culture and Differential Fertility in Peru." *Population Studies* 13: 257-70.

Sykes, Percy M.
  1933. *A History of Exploration from the Earliest Times to the Present Day.* London, Routledge.
  1940. *A History of Afghanistan.* 2 vols. London, Macmillan & Co.

Tapper, Nancy
  1973. "The Advent of Pastun Maldars in Northwestern Afghanistan." *Bulletin of the School of Oriental and African Studies* 36: 54-79.

Tel Jana Adabeyat Institute
  1958. *Manac. Kirghizistan CCP Elemde Academycenen,* vols. 1-3. Frunz, Kerghizistanmambase. (In Kirghiz.)

Tominaga, Toshiro and E. W. Page
  1966. "Accommodation of the Human Placenta to Hypoxia." *American Journal of Obstetrics and Gynecology* 97: 679-91.

Trotter, Capt. Henry
  1878. "On the Geographical Results of the Mission to Kashghar, Under Sir T. Douglas Forsyth in 1873-74. *Journal of the Royal Geographical Society* 48: 173-234.

Turner, F. J.
  1961. *Frontier and Sections: Selected Essays.* Englewood Cliffs, N. J., Prentice-Hall.
  1962. *The Frontier in American History.* New York, Holt, Rinehart & Winston.

Vambery, Arminius
  1874. *Central Asia and the Anglo-Russian Frontier Question: A Series of Political Papers.* Translated by F. E. Bunnett. London, Smith, Elder.

Van Dyne, George M., ed.
  1969. *The Ecosystem Concept in Natural Resource Management.* New York, Academic Press.

Van Liere, E. J. and J. C. Stickney
  1963. *Hypoxia.* Chicago, University of Chicago Press.

Vayda, Andrew P., ed.
  1969. *Environment and Cultural Behavior: Ecological Studies in Cultural Anthropology.* Garden City, N. Y., Natural History Press.

Vayda, A. P. and R. Rappaport
   1968. "Ecology, Cultural and Noncultural." In *Introduction to Cultural Anthropology*. Edited by J. Clifton. Boston, Houghton Mifflin.
Vayda, A. P. and B. McCay
   1975. "New Directions in Ecology and Ecological Anthropology." *Annual Review of Anthropology* 4: 293-306.
Veniukof, M.
   1866. "The Pamir and the Sources of the Amu-Daria." Translated by J. Mitchell. *Journal of the Royal Geographical Society* 36: 248-65.
Wallace, Anthony F. C.
   1956. "Revitalization Movements." *American Anthropologist* 58: 264-81.
Weihe, W. H.
   1962. *The Physiological Effects of High Altitude*. New York, Pergamon.
Wheeler, Geoffrey
   1964. *The Modern History of Soviet Central Asia*. New York, Praeger.
   1966. *The Peoples of Soviet Central Asia*. London, Bodley Head.
Wilson, Godfrey and Monica Godfrey
   1945. *The Analysis of Social Change, Based on Observations in Central Africa*. Cambridge, At the University Press.
Wolf, Eric R.
   1966. *Peasants*. Englewood Cliffs, N. J., Prentice Hall.
Wood, John
   1841. *A Personal Narrative of a Journey to the Source of the River Oxus, by the Route of the Indus, Kabul, and Badakhshan*. London, John Murray.
   1872. *A Journey to the Source of the River Oxus*. New edition with an essay on the Geography of the Valley of the Oxus by Colonel Henry Yule. London, John Murray.
Younghusband, Francis
   1896. *The Heart of a Continent: A Narrative of Travels in Manchuria, Across the Gobi Desert, through the Himalayas, the Pamirs and Chitral, 1884-1894*. 2nd ed. London, John Murray.

Index

Printed in the United States
22085LVS00004B/46-204